Bureaucrats, Planters, and Workers

Bureaucrats, Planters, and Workers

The Making of the Tobacco Monopoly in Bourbon Mexico

by Susan Deans-Smith

 UNIVERSITY OF TEXAS PRESS, AUSTIN

For Georgina, Jack, and William

First Edition, 1992

Requests for permission to reproduce material from this work should be sent to Permissions, University of Texas Press, Box 7819, Austin, Texas 78713-7819.

∞ The paper used in this publication meets the minimum requirements of American National Standard for Information Sciences—Permanence of Paper for Printed Library Materials, ANSI Z39.48-1984.

Publication of this work has been made possible in part by a grant from the Program for Cultural Cooperation between Spain's Ministry of Culture and United States Universities.

Library of Congress Cataloging-in-Publication Data
Deans-Smith, Susan, 1953–
    Bureaucrats, planters, and workers : the making of the tobacco monopoly in Bourbon Mexico / by Susan Deans-Smith. — 1st ed.
        p.   cm.
    Based on the author's thesis (Ph.D.—University of Cambridge, 1984)
    Includes bibliographical references and index.
    ISBN: 978-0-292-72372-6
    1. Tobacco industry—Mexico—History—18th century.   2. Government monopolies—Mexico—History—18th century.   3. Tobacco workers—Mexico—History—18th century.   I. Title.
    HD9144.M42D43   1992
    338.1'7371'097209033—dc20   91-29116
                                                                CIP

Chapters 5, 6, and 7 are partially based on material which appeared in a different version in the essay "State Enterprise in Bourbon Mexico: Profits, Policies, and Politics of the Tobacco Monopoly, 1765–1821," *Journal of Policy History*, vol. 2, no. 1, 1990. Reprinted by permission of The Pennsylvania State University Press.

Contents

MAPS

FIGURES

TABLES

Acknowledgments

MANY DEBTS OF GRATITUDE are incurred during the course of a prolonged period of research. I would like to thank first and foremost David A. Brading, who directed the dissertation on which this book is based, for the intellectual guidance, inspiration, and support he has given me over the past few years. A number of colleagues have given generously of their time and talents and have provided incisive comments and critiques on various versions of this work. In particular, I would like to thank Woodrow Borah, Richard Graham, Brian Hamnett, John Lynch, Alan Knight, Richard J. Salvucci, Stanley Stein, and Eric Van Young. John W. Smith also provided a perceptive critique of the manuscript and made a number of valuable suggestions as to needed revisions.

My research time in the Archivo General de Indias was made considerably easier and much more stimulating thanks to the suggestions and company of Antonio Acosta, Salvador Victoria Hernández, Enriqueta Vila Vilar, Javier Ortiz de la Tabla, José Jesús Hernández Palomo, and, above all, Montserrat Fernández. Equally, my time in the Archivo General de México was made more efficient and enjoyable thanks to the unfailing generosity of Cayetano Reyes, Arturo Soberón, and Roberto Beristáin. I would also like to thank Enrique Florescano, Clara García-Ayluardo, Bernardo García Martínez, and Taka Sudo for the help they have extended to me on many occasions. José González Sierra and Adriana Naveda Chávez-Hita made my research time in Jalapa personally pleasant and professionally challenging. Enrique Kruze provided valuable suggestions and guided me through the notarial records of Orizaba and the colonial history of Veracruz. In the United States I would like to thank Pat Carroll for sharing his enthusiasm and knowledge of the history of Veracruz with me and Lorne McWatters with whom I shared a stimulating correspondence on the finer points of the history of the Mexican tobacco monopoly. I would also like to say a special thanks to my graduate students at the University of Texas at Austin who have provided and continue to provide a first-rate intellectual forum for the exchange of ideas.

This work would have been impossible without the generous and gracious help extended by the archival staff and directors of the Archivo General de Indias in Seville, the Archivo General de la Nación in Mexico City, the Archivo Notarial de Orizaba located at the Universidad Veracruzana in Jalapa, the Baker Business Library at Harvard University, the Benson Latin American collection at the University of Texas at Austin, the Biblioteca Nacional in Madrid, and the British Library.

A number of institutions and foundations have supported my research in various ways over the past few years. I would like to thank the Department of Education and Science, England, which provided me with a three-year state studentship and made it possible for me to begin my dissertation research in Spain and Mexico; the History Department at the University of Cambridge, which provided me with several research and travel grants; the Fellows of St. Edmund's College, University of Cambridge, who elected me to a residential research fellowship at a crucial time. I would also like to thank the University Research Institute and the Department of History at the University of Texas at Austin for financial support which enabled me to take research trips to England, Spain, and Mexico. The Institute of Latin American Studies at the University of Texas at Austin provided me with generous grants from the Andrew W. Mellon Foundation. Thanks also to the director of the Center of Latin American Studies at the time, Alex Zaragoza, and to the Department of History at the University of California at Berkeley, which provided me with the opportunity, as a visiting professor, to spend a thoroughly enjoyable and stimulating semester in Berkeley during the course of which I rewrote two of the chapters in this book. I owe a special thanks to the National Endowment for the Humanities, which granted me a Junior Research Fellowship, grant number FA-27678-88.

I would like to thank Jenny White and Barbara Spielman at the University of Texas Press for their patient disentangling of my convoluted prose. Special thanks to Theresa May, executive editor at the University of Texas Press, whose help to me during a difficult period over the past two years extended above and beyond the call of duty.

Finally, I would like to thank my parents Georgina and William

Deans. Without their unfailing support, my work on this book would never have begun. Above all, I thank for his unending patience, unremitting criticism, and enduring love, my friend, colleague, and husband John Williamson Smith, without whom this book would never have been finished.

Introduction

IN 1799, María Dominga Medina, an impoverished widow with five children, presented herself at the treasury office of the tobacco monopoly in Mexico City with one-quarter of lottery ticket no. 1580, the winning ticket of lottery 352 for the sum of 3,000 pesos. One of her sons had found the ticket in the street, and she wanted to claim her prize. The *fiscal* (crown attorney) saw things differently and decided that Medina should receive 300 pesos and was to be found a position in the royal tobacco manufactory in Mexico City.[1] Putting aside the temptation to speculate on the widow's private thoughts about the *fiscal*'s decision, his solution to her situation highlights two issues: the eighteenth-century state's increasing role in the lives of ordinary people and its direct management of economic enterprises, in this case, the tobacco trade. A state enterprise by 1765, the tobacco monopoly of colonial Mexico is the subject of this book. The central period covered in this work spans over half a century from 1740 until 1810.

By the 1790s the tobacco monopoly was one of the largest organized industries in colonial Mexico (along with silver mining and textiles) and employed almost 20,000 individuals. In fiscal terms, tobacco revenues were second only to the silver tithe as the most valuable source of government income and accounted for almost one-fifth of total state revenues at the peak of production. The reorganization of the tobacco trade under Bourbon management resulted in the restriction of tobacco production to a relatively small area in southeastern Mexico in the *villas* of Orizaba and Córdoba, two small towns, in the modern-day state of Veracruz. Supply of tobacco leaf was regulated through a series of contracts which determined who produced tobacco, the quantities to be produced, and the purchase price. The tobacco supplied to the monopoly was manufactured into cigarettes and cigars in six state-managed tobacco manufactories, the largest located in Mexico City, the political and commercial capital of the viceroyalty of New Spain. Monopoly goods were sold in government-licensed stores which were distributed throughout Mexico. Private trading and manufacture in tobacco goods became a punishable offense. Compliance with monopoly regulations was enforced by a military corps employed by the monopoly administration, although contraband trade of tobacco was never eliminated.

The tobacco monopoly has become over the past decades something of an *éminence grise* in the historiography of eighteenth-century Mexico, cited more than studied. Scholars routinely refer to the tobacco monopoly as an example of fiscal reform implemented by the Spanish colonial state to generate new revenues and as an example of Spanish statecraft which created hostility and resentment.[2] The few studies of the tobacco monopoly which we have tend to fall into two categories: the first is dominated by general institutional overviews of the monopoly; the second is made up of studies which focus on a particular aspect of the monopoly, often devoid of a wider context.[3] Together they produce a picture of a state enterprise which was monolithic, rigid, and oppressive and which provoked hostile, teeth-grinding responses from the populace. The methodology employed in this study has sought to provide as comprehensive a history of the monopoly as possible and one which examines its development from imperial and local perspectives. As a result, we provide a somewhat different assessment of the effects and development of the monopoly, one which identifies as much continuity as change after the monopoly was established, and a popular response characterized by accommodation as well as by defiance and resistance.

Apart from filling in a historiographical lacuna, however, why is the study of a state tobacco monopoly useful? There are two reasons. The first is that such a study enables us to examine the economic management and rationale of a state enterprise which manufactured cigars and cigarettes and, at the same time, provides a lens through which to look at the political economy of late-eighteenth-century Mexico. The second is that it also provides us with a case study of state and society in eighteenth-century Mexico and one which enables us to take a sharper, closer look at popular as well as elite responses to state reform.

The monopolization of the tobacco trade by the colonial state formed part of Spain's attempts to "recolonize" its American colonies, part of a wider strategy through which to advance the power of the eighteenth-century state—absolutism and colonialism in tandem. The advance of such power demanded increased revenues which in turn demanded new strategies to achieve such increases. The outcome was similar to the actions taken by other eighteenth century states which "scurried from expedient to expedient, seeking to squeeze more out of established sources of revenue, to invent and enforce new forms of taxation, to beg, borrow, and steal if necessary."[4] The Spanish economist Gerónimo de Uztáriz may have missed the mark somewhat when he described the monopoly as an "easy and gentle tax," but his economic logic was sound: it offered low price elasticity of demand. That is, consumption was not affected very much by a tax on tobacco, and it was a tax with enormous potential for raising revenue. The potential was more than realized and, once the monopoly was established in Mexico, revenues increased dramatically and with relatively little opposition. The major problems faced by monopoly bureaucrats, that is, constraints on supply, affected all large commercial enterprises in colonial Mexico, particularly the two most important industries in addition to tobacco, silver mining and textiles. In the long run, production could only grow at increasing cost. Growth did not come from any significant productivity change but from increasing the resources available to the industry. Limits were reached after 1790 precisely because of bottlenecks in supplies of raw materials, typical of the nature of economic growth in Mexico which made the colony vulnerable to scarcities.

Over the past two decades our knowledge of the Bourbon reforms in Spain and Spanish America has increased dramatically. Studies of Bourbon Spain and the growth of absolutism agree that the transition from a compromise and consensus state to an absolutist one was incomplete. At the same time, studies of the Bourbon reform measures in colonial Mexico provide varying interpretations of the outcome of individual reform measures. These range from successful increases in fiscal revenues and a "revolution in government" in the upper ranks of the imperial bureaucracy, to the abysmal failures of local government and a gradual slide from authority in the 1760s, to compromise or outright failure of reform measures by the beginning of the nineteenth century.[5] The monopoly, if nothing else, is a study in the limitations of the colonial state and one which reminds us that, even at its most intrusive, the Spanish colonial state was far from being a Leviathan force in peoples' lives. The establishment of the tobacco monopoly shows a tempered absolutism in action from the very beginning of its introduction. Its establishment occurred not through an abrupt show of absolutist strength but by co-optation of vested interests and a protracted introduction of its operations, which, if we look at its record on contraband, was incomplete. Its establishment alienated people, there is no question about that, and the newly found military strength of the colonial state was used when necessary to enforce its restrictions. But incorporation in the monopoly's operations created new vested interests which included Mexican merchants, tobacco planters, and manufactory workers who developed and shared a mutual interest with the colonial state in the monopoly's survival. The tobacco monopoly's implementation was not the result of a "revolution in government" per se, but rather the product of a reshaping of the private tobacco industry and a redirection of existing networks of power and interests. Its subsequent development depended upon negotiation and renegotiation between the colonial state and the planters and workers who sought to improve their position within the monopoly's structure, not its abolition.

State policy and power was obviously critical in shaping the structure of the tobacco monopoly but also partially responsible for its failure in the long term as a business enterprise. Until the heavy hand of Bourbon fiscalism, guided by financial desperation, prevented adjustments in the monopoly's organization to changing conditions, the monopoly bureaucracy proved quite adept at the identification of problems and attempts to solve them and also proved to be more efficient and perceptive as entrepreneurial managers than has previously been acknowledged. At the same time, group interests (both elite and popular) affected the monopoly's development and the efficacy of the state's policies to a greater degree than previously assumed. An emphasis upon political stability and short-term profits resulted in a basically conservative policy toward the tobacco manufactory workers and the planters. As a result, productivity gains were sacrificed to maintain a status quo in the workplace, and the goal on the part of the Bourbon state to displace merchants from the production of tobacco was never successfully completed. The problems experienced by the monopoly at the beginning of the nineteenth century did not originate from any simmering entrenched opposition but because of its own success, success which prevented any innovative reforms to improve its performance and productivity.

This, then, is a study of a state enterprise, but it is also a study of state and society. The monopoly as a subject of analysis is greater than the sum of its parts and incorporates many of the most important themes of eighteenth-century Mexican social and economic history, from economic growth and the supply of credit and capital to labor markets, popular protest, gender roles, and late colonial political culture. This work looks at the actions and ambitions of the government and the people most affected by the monopoly, the tobacco planters of Veracruz and the urban tobacco workers.

In recent years, a renewed interest in the relationship between state and society has emerged among historians in general, and historians of Latin America in particular, who have called for a closer examination of conflict and interaction between the state and various sectors of society. Scholars of colonial Mexico, however, vary in the importance they attach to the role of the state from those who see it as "a major force in the lives of the early Latin Americans, but . . . not altogether an independent force" to those who suggest we take "the state back out."[6] The contradiction in these assessments is not hard to reconcile if one avoids a reificationist or reductionist approach to the state and looks at what has been termed the "differentiated instances of state structures and actions" whereby "states are not likely to be equally capable of intervening in different areas of socioeconomic life."[7] A study of the monopoly reminds us that eighteenth-century Spanish absolutism was about more than raising revenues and armies, however crucial those needs were, and that it combined what has been termed "welfare" as well as "warfare" objectives which resulted in increasing attempts to expand the role of the state in peoples' lives. These were policies influenced by Spain's selective response to the influence of Enlightenment thought.[8] Growth in state power in colonial Mexico was experienced by people in the form of increased taxes, more efficient tax collection, regulation of industry, maintenance of public order, and attempts to control social behavior. Such growth in state power affected a wide variety of interests which often stimulated popular action in the form of riots, protests, and evasion of tax payments. At the same time, although the "state" as such was irrelevant for most people on a daily basis, it had an indirect impact on most peoples' lives, however tenuous, and a very direct effect upon those affected by the establishment of the tobacco monopoly. A study of the social groups involved in the monopoly's operations provides us, in some measure, with an exceptional example of the interaction between state and society. For all intents and purposes, both planters and tobacco manufactory workers were employed by the colonial state. Therefore, their contact with state authority was much more intense and sustained than possibly any other social group in colonial society and very different from the experience of rural inhabitants who rarely came into contact with the colonial state.[9] The point here is not to make dubious generalizations about popular responses to state reform based on the experience of the tobacco workers and planters. However, because we are dealing with groups whose lives were very much affected and in some ways changed by the colonial state, their actions can tell us something about the political culture of late colonial Mexico and, especially in the case of the tobacco workers, about popular response to the erratic, ambiguous advance of Spanish absolutism, what Stanley Stein has referred to as the "grass roots" response to Bourbon state-making.[10]

Careful examination of the tobacco monopoly provides us with the additional and somewhat rare opportunity to examine a social group little studied by historians of colonial Mexico, the urban working poor, and offers a unique insight into their responses to changes in their working lives and in their social and cultural experience of colonialism. It also allows us to examine what can be loosely termed as the Mexican variant of time and work discipline in the eighteenth century. In so doing, this study challenges recent interpretations of the colonial state and urban labor in eighteenth-century Mexico in general, and of the lives of the tobacco workers specifically. The few histories of urban labor and the colonial state in the eighteenth century tend to be characterized by reification of the colonial state's power or by naïve reflections on its paternalism.[11] Analyses of urban labor, especially of the tobacco workers, also tend to be dominated by uncritical assumptions of the strength and oppressive nature of the colonial state.[12] What we argue is that the actions of the manufactory workers suggest that, although they found themselves confronted by a state which was not afraid to lower their wages and to impose stricter work discipline, they were far from passive in the face of new demands on their time and lives. At the same time, however, the workers were not transformed into a homogeneous proletariat either.

This work is based on extensive examination of the voluminous monopoly records located in Mexico and Spain, and general colonial treasury and administrative reports. Although one must always be cautious about the inherent bureaucratic bias in such documentation, it must be pointed out that the monopoly records contain a veritable mine of documentation written from diverse perspectives, including a variety of letters and petitions from the manufactory workers and tobacco planters to the monopoly managers. Considerable quantitative data have been gathered from numerous sources and presented in aggregate and serial form to illustrate the relative magnitude of revenue production, volume of manufactures, prices, wages, and composition of the labor force. Regional documentation from Veracruz, primarily the notarial and parish records of Orizaba, were consulted and provide additional information on local economic conditions, on the social structure of the tobacco planters, and on agrarian conditions. Spanish terms specific to the tobacco trade and the Bourbon fiscal and administrative offices are retained but they are explained in the text and also in a glossary.

The chronological parameters of this study, 1740–1810, are somewhat unfashionable as far as recent colonial Mexican historiography is concerned. The reason for using the conventional periodization is not because it is the most valuable in understanding historical change and continuity in Mexican history, but because, in the case of the monopoly, 1810 constitutes a legitimate point of rupture. The Mexican insurgency of 1810 effectively destroyed the monopoly, and in the subsequent years, for the first time in almost fifty years, the monopoly was unable to finance itself, as virtually all revenues produced were used for the support of royalist forces. Leasing of monopoly rights to private entrepreneurs increasingly characterized monopoly organization in the 1830s and 1840s, while tobacco cultivation was permitted again throughout Mexico, and manufacture of tobacco products returned to the private sector.

This book is divided into three parts. Most of the narrative sections of the individual chapters cover the period 1740 to 1810, although Chapter 8 provides a brief narrative of the monopoly's fate between 1810 and 1856 when it was finally abolished.

In Part I, Chapter 1 describes the structure of the private tobacco trade in Mexico, the vested interests involved, and provides the political background to the monopoly's establishment. Opposition to the monopoly's establishment was, for the most part, dealt with by co-optation and inclusion into the monopoly's operations. The most significant and sustained opposition to the monopoly manifested itself in a contraband tobacco trade.

Chapter 2 analyzes the structure of the bureaucratic agency created to manage the monopoly, its problems, and the changes it experienced as it shifted from being an autonomous government fiscal agency to one increasingly subjected to the central fiscal administration of colonial Mexico. The composition of the monopoly bureaucracy and its links with private interests are examined and assessed in light of recent revisionist interpretations which challenge conventional views of the Bourbon bureaucrats as more efficient, impartial servants of the state than their Hapsburg predecessors. There is evidence of corruption within the monopoly bureaucracy, but, for the most part, the bureaucrats behaved as career professionals and identified their interests with those of the colonial state.

The second half of Chapter 2 analyzes the trends in revenue production, costs, and profits between 1765 and 1810, and the functions of tobacco revenues. Analysis of monopoly accounts, designed originally to provide revenues exclusively for use of the Spanish Crown in Spain, demonstrates that revenues were used for a variety of purposes which incorporated metropolitan, intercolonial, and domestic needs. Such a diversity of uses of monopoly revenues challenges traditional claims that such monies were shipped en masse each year to Spain.

Part II analyzes the organization of the supply of raw materials—tobacco and paper—and the politics associated with their production. Domestic policies, Spanish colonialism, and planter pressure influenced the regularity of supplies and the costs of tobacco for the monopoly. In Chapter 3 we see how, from the beginning of the monopoly's operations, contract conditions and prices for leaf tobacco proved to be a point of conflict between the colonial state and the planters. The monopoly tried to repress planter protest but such action was soon replaced by co-optation of the wealthy merchant-planters who finally succeeded in raising the purchase price for their tobacco. The supply of paper was beyond the control of the monopoly bureaucrats and was organized in accordance with Spain's mercantilist policies, which sought markets for its manufactured goods. Dependence upon imports of paper from Spain eventually proved to be an expensive weakness for the monopoly's operations and a contradictory consequence of Spanish colonialism. The conditions of supplies of tobacco and paper resulted in strategies which allowed merchants and private capital to continue to play an important role in the monopoly's operations.

Chapter 4 provides a description of the structure and organization of tobacco production and an analysis of the supply of rural labor, credit, and capital. The chapter examines what influenced the planters' responses to monopoly conditions, what determined their bargaining capabilities, and why the monopoly's attempts to displace merchant financing of tobacco production failed, leaving it with little choice but to agree to conditions demanded by wealthier planters. The discussion of the planters of Orizaba and Córdoba stresses the differentiation among them in terms of wealth and power. Included in the discussion is an assessment of the entrepreneurial behavior of the tobacco planters and the impact of monopoly production upon the structure of wealth and power in the *villas*. The supply of capital by the colonial state to finance the commercial production of tobacco may have created a new class of producers, but the financial role of the state in the long term did not undermine the merchant-planter elite's power. Rather, it contributed to its consolidation.

Part III examines the structure and rationale of the tobacco manufactories, the work regime established by the monopoly administrators, and the responses of the workers. Issues of supply and demand for tobacco products are examined in Chapter 5 as are responses to production crises. The description and analysis of the manufactories and their economic performance over the long term are used to consider on a wider level the nature of the late colonial economy and the characteristics of preindustrial enterprises. While the state manufactories did not, indeed could not, provide a basis for industrialization, they were not lacking in a rationale. The problems in production after the 1790s were as much a result of conservative fiscal policy as of structural imperfections in the colonial economy. The result was an increasing inability to meet demand, scarcities in the supply of cigars and cigarettes, and an increase in contraband.

Chapters 6 and 7 look at the conditions of labor and provide a profile of the manufactory workers. By the early 1780s, 90 percent of monopoly revenues was derived from sales of cigars and cigarettes on the domestic market (there were no exports of Mexican tobacco). Such an emphasis on manufactured tobacco products created an interdependent relationship between the manufactory workers and the colonial state. The largest tobacco manufactory located in Mexico City employed, at its peak, almost nine thousand workers, both men and women—an extraordinary size for a single manufactory anywhere in the world in the eighteenth century. The work regime of the manufactories and the changes implemented are discussed (alas, much more Thanatos and a lot less Eros in these manufactories, contrary to the popular image of Mérimée's *Carmen!*). Although monopolization enabled the bureaucratic managers to shift from work and wage conditions consonant with premonopoly arrangements to those which reflected and aspired to more rational "industrial" organization, the result was the emergence of a work regime which retained artisanal characteristics and traditions within a system of capitalist manufacture. The inability of the manufactory administrators to impose an effective form of work discipline on the workers raises questions about the paradoxes of labor and its supply in late colonial cities and towns and the working lives of the urban poor.

Chapter 7 provides a more detailed assessment of worker resistance, what angered the workers and why, and what strategies they used to achieve their goals. The analytical sections account for why the workers, given the conditions and situations which they encountered, did not present more of a political problem. In the process, theoretical issues concerning labor resistance, the problems of work discipline, and working class formation are discussed. Existing studies of the manufactories and their workers underestimate the resiliency and corporate strength achieved over the years by the workers through their mutual aid society, the Concordia. In part as a result of the conditions created by the state, the manufactory workers were able to define and defend their own interests and over the years acquired some influence over the content, pace, and structure of their workplace.

Finally, in Chapter 8, by way of a postscript, the development of the tobacco monopoly between 1810 and 1856 is assessed briefly. The political and economic problems of postindependence Mexico may have increased the problems experienced by the monopoly's new administrators and contributed to its abysmal fiscal performance, but it did not create them—structural problems beset the tobacco monopoly before the insurgency of 1810. A final section examines the costs and consequences of the tobacco monopoly for colonial Mexico.

A study of the tobacco monopoly of Bourbon Mexico shows that its development between 1740 and 1810 was shaped as much by local colonial imperatives and ambitions and the attempt by both workers and planters to protect their interests as best they could, as by the political and economic desiderata of the Spanish Crown. Paradoxically, the monopoly's success proved to be the cause of its problems. The objectives sought by the monopoly managers were not always achieved, as in the case of the merchant-planters, and some of the long-term consequences of the reorganization of the tobacco trade were unintended, as illustrated by the new-found ability of the workers to challenge their regal employer.

"THE WAY TO MAKE MONEY IS TO GET, IF YOU CAN,
A MONOPOLY FOR YOURSELF. HENCE WE FIND STATES
ALSO EMPLOYING THIS METHOD WHEN THEY ARE SHORT
OF MONEY: THEY SECURE THEMSELVES A MONOPOLY."

—Aristotle, *The Politics* ["Some Practical Considerations,
Especially on the Creation of Monopoly," Book I, p. xi]

PART I

1. Monopoly, Tobacco, and Colonial Society

WHEN CHARLES III ascended to the Spanish throne in 1759, he became a member of a very exclusive club of absolutist monarchs which included Frederick II of Prussia (1740–1786), Catherine II of Russia (1762–1796), and Joseph II of Austria (1780–1790). All of these monarchs harbored similar ambitions to a greater or lesser degree, and all of them experienced failure as well as success in the pursuit of absolutism. European monarchs' preoccupation with the consolidation of the state and centralized power became a necessity if a balance of power was to be maintained in a period of international rivalry. Military and economic strength, bureaucratic efficiency, and social stability were basic requirements for the state's survival and its growth. But so was the health of the individual: "the welfare state was closely connected with the warfare state: rulers were conscious that a large population, prosperous, . . . healthy and well organized, was better able to withstand the strains of wars. But the *Polizeistaat* [well-ordered state] also embraced such obviously peacetime concepts as urban planning, street lighting, the establishment of hospitals, workhouses and schemes of public employment."[1] If the emphasis was upon reform, however, it was reform from above, and with the idea of functional improvement rather than fundamental change in social and economic structures. Most monarchs did not wish to alter significantly the existing social order but to make it function more effectively in the interests of the state. Even so, absolutist monarchs found themselves waging two wars: one, internal to their own countries, against tradition and entrenched interests, distance, and inertia; the other against external aggressors.

Spain's pursuit of absolutism incorporated many of the strategies and problems described so far. The Spanish absolutist state was not constructed overnight but slowly, its completion hampered by traditional state servants and hostile private interests. The beginnings of its construction began with the accession of Philip V, Duke of Anjou, grandson of Louis XIV, and the first Bourbon to sit on the Spanish throne. It was not a peaceful transfer of power, and Philip's accession was confirmed only after the conclusion of a bloody conflict, the War of Succession (1702–1713). The victory signaled a change in ruling dynasties from the Hapsburgs, who had ruled Spain and its sprawling empire for almost two centuries, to the Bourbons. What Philip V inherited, however, was not the glittering, glorious, powerful empire of the sixteenth century, but a weak, shabby, and ailing edifice. The late decades of the seventeenth century under the fateful rule of Charles II (1664–1700) were disastrous for Spain, characterized not by imperial expansion and increasing wealth but by the reverse—military defeat at the hands of Europe's expanding powers, and famine and plague at home. The War of Succession changed "the political face" of Spain, both domestically and imperially, as its new monarch watched its European territories disappear.[2] Under the terms of the Treaty of Utrecht (1713), Philip was confirmed as ruler of Spain and the Indies, but the rest of the Spanish European possessions were partitioned off. The Austrian Emperor Charles received the Netherlands, Sicily went to the King of Savoy, and England acquired Gibraltar and Menorca. The following year, at the peace negotiations of Rastatt, France agreed to hand over to the Empire all Spain's Italian possessions, including Naples, Sardinia, and Milan.

Under the direct, guiding hand of Philip V, attempts were made to strengthen the state apparatus by centralizing power in the monarch's hands. To do that, the Hapsburg method of conciliar government was replaced, although never completely, by ministerial government. Instead of a horizontal structure of committees dominated by a conservative Spanish aristocracy, a vertical structure was introduced, at the top of which were the ministries, the Secretariats of State, Exchequer, Justice, War, Navy, and the Indies. Beneath these were the intendants in charge of economic reform and renovation at the regional level, and at the base lay a professional corps of salaried bureaucrats. The remaining power which challenged Bourbon authority was the Church. It too was subjected to attacks, not against doctrine, but against ecclesiastical jurisdiction, properties, and wealth, as the Crown adopted a regalist position to assert its power over that of the papacy.[3]

An efficient centralized administration may have provided the vehicle for Bourbon absolutism, but its construction required vast sums of money. Spain's loss of international power was exacerbated by deteriorating economic conditions of the late 1680s. Since Spain had few industries, the majority of its exports were agricultural products, and much of its American silver was used to pay for imports of manufactured goods from the rest of Europe. In effect, Spain acted as a conduit for commerce between its colonies and the rest of Europe. Spain's political and economic problems proved fertile ground for Spanish *arbitristas,* theorists who sought to provide enlightened solutions to them. Here we see the flourishing of some of the greatest minds of eighteenth century Spain—Benito Gerónimo Feijóo y Montenegro, Baltasar Melchor Gaspar María de Jovellanos, José del Campillo y Cossío, and Pedro Rodríguez de Campomanes.[4] A major theoretical influence upon policy formation was the comprehensive treatise on political economy by Gerónimo de Ustáriz, *Theórica y práctica de comercio y de marina* (*The Theory and Practice of Commerce and Maritime Affairs*). An ardent admirer of Colbert and the French version of absolutism, Ustáriz stressed the fundamental importance of foreign trade, the promotion of domestic industry, fiscal reform, and the intelligent management of overseas colonies.

If external enemies contributed to the build-up of the military and the navy by the burgeoning new state, so too did problems of empire. Spain faced a difficult problem with its American possessions. It had managed to maintain control over its overseas American dominions, but through inertia rather than through active government. As with its domestic political dealings, the Spanish Crown's incessant need for revenues in the sixteenth and seventeenth centuries resulted in policies based on expediency. Political bargains were struck with local elites, and bureaucratic offices were sold to raise the badly needed revenues. Spain governed its American possessions through negotiation and compromise: "The imperial state embraced both the metropolitan government and the administration in the colonies, but until about 1750 it was a consensus state, not an absolutist state . . . . the colonial bureaucracy came to adopt a mediating role between crown and subjects which may be called a colonial consensus."[5] The result of that consensus was the creation of semiautonomous oligarchies, formally subject to Spain's rule, but practically able to attend to their own interests rather than those of the Crown.

The early Bourbon monarchs made important strides in reform, but it was Charles III, renowned as much for his love of wolf hunting as statecraft, who brought Spain as close as it could get to an absolutist state. Charles' first setback, however, came quickly and it was a military one. After a late entry into the Seven Years War (1756–1763), Spain experienced a crushing defeat when Havana, "the Pearl of the Antilles," was captured by England in 1762. The following year, it was returned to Spain in exchange for Florida under the terms of the Treaty of Paris. The loss of Havana was a shocking demonstration of Spain's inability to protect its overseas dominions and resulted in a marked acceleration in the political, economic, and fiscal reforms upon which the Bourbons embarked to build up their lagging military forces. Ministers of Charles III turned to the reforms outlined by José del Campillo y Cossío in his *Nuevo sistema de gobierno económico para la América* (1743), published in 1762 as the second part of Bernardo Ward's *Proyecto económico*. It was Campillo who suggested that both Spain and America required reforms to stimulate economic development. Taxes should be structured to stimulate domestic as well as foreign trade, and to encourage the poor to produce and to become consumers. Campillo viewed good government as one which enabled its people to improve themselves and, in consequence, the state. He advocated direct state intervention in the economy to encourage industry, improve agriculture and transportation, and introduce new technologies. Campillo also saw nothing wrong with encouraging industries in the American colonies which did not compete with those of Spain. Finally, Campillo advised that a general investigation and assessment of Spain and its imperial possessions was necessary to determine what improvements needed to be made, and where.[6]

As the largest and richest of all of Spain's American possessions, Mexico became a particular target for the centralizing ambitions of the Bourbon state. During the period 1765–1771, José de Gálvez, appointed as visitor-general, traveled to Mexico to assess the colony's current condition and to prepare the ground for reform.[7] In the decades which followed his inspection, Mexico, like Spain's other colonial possessions, was subjected to a bewildering variety of political, administrative, and economic reforms, many of which were less than successful, and which have been subjected to the scrutiny of social and economic historians over the last few decades.[8] Mexico's inhabitants in the late eighteenth century witnessed reforms which affected both church and state, and all classes of society. The Jesuits were expelled in 1767, and thereafter the Church was subject to attacks on its autonomy. Administrative reforms displaced creoles (Spaniards born in America) from high-ranking positions and replaced them with peninsulars (Spaniards from Spain) newly arrived from Spain. Intendants, the epitome of the "interventionist ambitions of the Bourbon state," were appointed to act as regional governors to improve the administration of local government.[9] The silver-mining industry became the favored child of the Bourbons, supported by state subsidies and exemptions from taxes designed to provide incentives to would-be entrepreneurs. After centuries of a trade monopoly between Veracruz and Cádiz, the *comercio libre* (free trade) decree opened up new ports in Spain which could legally trade with Spanish America. The system of tax farming was replaced by direct revenue collection, carried out by a colonial bureaucracy. By 1790, residents of Mexico paid eighty-four separate taxes.[10] Royal monopolies were established for a range of goods—salt, cockfights, ice, mercury, playing cards, gunpowder, and tobacco. Commercial reform, reorganization of the tax structure, expansion in mining, and general economic activity, all underwritten by demographic growth, resulted in the revenue increases which the Bourbons so desperately sought. Public revenues in colonial Mexico increased from approximately six million pesos in 1765 to twenty million pesos by the early 1800s.[11] The contribution made to public revenues by the sale of tobacco products proved to be substantial, second only to the silver tithe, which ranked first, and it is to the rationale behind the establishment of the tobacco monopoly to which we now turn.

Tobacco has traditionally occupied a favored position in state taxation systems because of its popularity and high levels of consumption. The most expansive discussion of the advantages of a tobacco monopoly appeared in Gerónimo de Uztáriz' treatise on the Spanish economy. *Theórica y práctica de comercio:* "it is the most flourishing revenue of the Crown . . . and yet it is shared by millions of people. And though on this account it be but a trifle to each individual, it is a very great sum which is raised up on the whole: besides that it is in some measure a voluntary tax, as it does not fall upon any of the supports of life."[12] At the time of Uztáriz' recommendations, the tobacco trade in Spain was already monopolized and administered directly by royal bureaucrats. Established in 1636 under the Hapsburgs and initially rented out on a contract basis, the monopoly was gradually taken over by fiscal officers. Between 1717 and 1783, state monopolies were established throughout Spain's American possessions. The organization and administration of the tobacco monopolies were virtually the same throughout the empire, although the degree of state regulation varied.[13] In the case of Mexico and the Philippines, the state eventually took over all aspects of the domestic tobacco trade, from the purchase of leaf to the production of cigars and cigarettes manufactured in state-managed manufactories and marketed by government-licensed stores throughout the colonies. In Cuba and Venezuela, the monopoly managed the production of the exquisite varieties of raw leaf tobacco which grew in these colonies for export to Spain for processing in its domestic

manufactories as cigars, cigarettes, and snuff. Two varieties of tobacco grew in Venezuela which enjoyed popularity in Spain and
Northern Europe: the Berinas (*cura seca*) commanded high prices,
especially in Holland, the Germanys, Scandinavia, and the Ottoman
Empire, while *cura negra* was particularly popular in Spain itself.

Although Spanish American colonies, in addition to Cuba and
Venezuela, were free to ship tobacco to Spain for reshipment to
other European countries, discriminatory tariffs precluded their participation on any significant level. Cuban and Venezuelan tobacco
may have been of superior quality to that produced in the English
colonies, for example, but it was much more expensive and catered
to a small luxury European market. France, as Spain's temporary
ally, purchased the bulk of its tobacco not from Spain, but from its
enemy, England, because of more acceptable prices. French purchases from the Atlantic coast absorbed almost one-quarter of the
total crop from English America. An increase in the price of Spanish
American tobacco further restricted Spain's share of the French market. Several years later, in 1778, new international tariffs served to
restrict even further Spain's share of the world tobacco market. Pitt's
Tobacco Act, for example, placed a duty of 1s 3d per pound on British
and American plantation tobacco; the duty imposed on Spanish and
Portuguese supplies amounted to almost three times as much: 3s 6d
per pound.[14] Consequently, with an increasingly protectionist international market, Spain sought to control and restrict exports to
those tobaccos for which there was a demand, while control and
taxation of domestic colonial markets for tobacco acquired a new
importance for the Spanish state.

In the context of Spanish and foreign protectionist policies, the
only opportunity for tobacco exports from colonies other than Cuba
and Venezuela was at the intercolonial level. Mexico exported very
small quantities of snuff to Peru and Chile, but since the Spanish
American colonies all produced their own tobacco, there was no
room for a significant intercolonial tobacco trade to develop. For the
majority of colonies, then, monopoly policy developed within the
existing structure of the colonial tobacco trade and its domestic
markets. Whatever the consequences of monopoly, an abrupt abolition of an export trade was not one of them. Production of tobacco as
a cash crop for export was a postindependence development for the
majority of the Spanish-American colonies.

Advocation of a tobacco monopoly in Mexico began as early as
1642 when the Hapsburg bishop-viceroy Juan de Palafox recommended such a reform to his successor, the Conde de Salvatierra, in
order to raise funds for the maintenance of *la armada de barlovento*

(Windward Island fleet).[15] Nothing came of the proposal, and little attention was paid to the tobacco trade until the early 1740s. Two merchants, Francisco Sánchez de Tagle and Juan de Rodezno, submitted two separate proposals which requested that the Crown monopolize the tobacco trade but lease its management to them.[16] The *fiscal* advised that the projects be rejected on the grounds that the manufacture of cigars and cigarettes provided a source of income for many of the colony's poor, especially women, both in urban and rural areas. To deprive them of such an occupation was unjust, and "such is the situation that the monopoly suggested would in reality monopolize the work and labor of these artisans which is expressly condemned by the law, since it enriches one and impoverishes many."[17]

One year after the rejection of Rodezno's proposal in 1747, the Spanish Crown began to look more seriously at the possibility of monopolizing the tobacco trade in Mexico to increase state revenues. The imperative came from changes in Spain, changes particularly in the decade between 1740–1750. The War of Jenkins' Ear (1739–1748) was in progress, as Spain fought off British imperialist aspirations in Spanish America. With the Marqués de Ensenada appointed as secretary of finance, war, marine, and the Indies, secretary of state, and superintendent of revenues, policy initiatives focused upon the Indies trade and the Crown's "direct participation in it as a profit-maker."[18] Part of that direct participation may have included the monopolization of Mexico's tobacco trade. As a preliminary step toward the monopoly's establishment, a survey of the value of the domestic tobacco trade in Mexico was carried out in 1748. The estimated value of the tobacco trade was a staggering 12,348,000 pesos (cigars and cigarettes only—snuff was not included).[19] The possibility that the value of the trade was overestimated must be taken into consideration, but we could find no independent estimates to challenge or corroborate this figure. The survey of 1748 demonstrated where the most important concentrations of tobacco consumption were located: almost half of the estimated value was earned in Mexico City and its environs, some 5,840,000 pesos.[20] Mining towns and urban areas in the northern and northwestern areas of the viceroyalty made up the second-most important locations of tobacco consumption.

Although the results of the survey of the tobacco trade demonstrated the existence of a thriving and lucrative trade, no further action was taken. Curiously, the final decision appeared to be based on the relative worth of the snuff trade and not on the basis of the market for cigarettes and cigars. Given the reportedly low consumption of snuff, the Crown decided the establishment of a monopoly was not worthwhile.[21]

The reasons for the halting progress toward the monopolization of the tobacco trade are not completely clear. The defeat of the British and the peace which ensued may have had something to do with it, but so may the opposition of the viceroy of Mexico, the Conde de Revillagigedo the Elder, to the monopoly's establishment. He argued it was too controversial and likely to provoke protest from planters and tobacconists. An opposing view, and one which eventually prevailed, echoed Uztáriz' appreciation of the fiscal advantages of a tobacco monopoly to the Crown. A tobacco tax was not compulsory. No one was obliged to purchase tobacco products: "All decide whether to contribute to the profit of the monopoly by whether they purchase tobacco or not, as it is neither a basic commodity nor one of necessity . . . No one is obliged to make this contribution, nor is anyone bothered by orders, threats, or pressures . . ."[22] As far as economic philosophy was concerned, there was another reason—the only reason—which justified monopoly, and that was in response to a national crisis which demanded emergency revenues.[23] Justified or not, it was not consumption which was controversial, but production. By denying the opportunity to Mexico's rural population to grow tobacco, particularly the indigenous communities, the colonial state effectively removed the means by which many Indians managed to pay their tribute to the Crown. We shall return to this point later.

Within three years of Charles III's accession to the throne in 1759, the viceroy, the Marqués de Cruillas, received orders to establish a tobacco monopoly in Mexico from Julián de Arriaga, the minister of the Indies and the navy in 1761.[24] Response to such orders was hesitant, however, and a full commitment to monopolize the tobacco trade and industry in Mexico was clearly lacking. Halfway measures were implemented: tobacco and tobacco products were not to be monopolized immediately, but snuff from Havana was to be imported and sold in a few selected shops in Mexico City on the Crown's behalf. The initial point of this exercise was to undermine the trade of private snuff merchants by selling the commodity below market prices, driving them out of business and leaving the Crown as the sole distributor of snuff. Other than these arrangements, little was done by way of establishing a fully functioning monopoly, and it took a war and military defeat to galvanize the Crown into action. The temporary but humiliating loss of Havana to Great Britain in 1762 forced Spain to push ahead with fiscal and economic reforms designed to finance the renovation and expansion of its military and imperial defenses. Plans were drafted by a secret defense committee for the creation of colonial armies in 1764. In November of the same year, Juan de Villalba y Angulo arrived in New Spain as inspector-general of the army to implement the reform program. The royal order and *instrucción* of 1764, which he carried, expressed the need for new taxes to finance the raising of regular and militia units in the colonies.[25] The monopoly came into being because of imperial crisis and war, and it would eventually be destroyed by imperial crisis. Before we examine the early problems encountered in the establishment of the monopoly, an overview of the structure of the private tobacco trade of Mexico may be helpful.

Tobacco is often characterized as a "democratic" crop or the "small man's" crop because it requires little capital to produce and because the manufactured product demands nothing more than the raw leaf, a flat surface, and deft fingers. The organization of the tobacco trade in Mexico reflected these attributes: cultivation of the leaf was widely dispersed throughout the viceroyalty, and the manufacture and sale of cigars and cigarettes were carried out predominantly by small shopkeepers, artisans, families, and individual men and women. An additional characteristic of tobacco in Mexico was the important cultural role it played for many of the indigenous communities who used it in rites and ceremonies.[26]

In the years prior to the establishment of the monopoly, the most important zones of tobacco production were Guadalajara and along the western coastal regions, but particularly in the modern-day state of Veracruz, around the *villas* (towns) of Orizaba, Córdoba, and Jalapa. In general, merchants and planters engaged in business to sell tobacco to general store owners and tobacco store proprietors. The commercial structure of the trade differed somewhat according to the region. In Guadalajara, for example, the Bishop of Guadalajara reported that tobacco was the only crop in which the rich merchants were not interested and was grown predominantly by poorer farmers and Indian peasants, particularly in Compostela and Tepic.[27] In Orizaba, however, wealthier planters worked with merchants to whom they assigned consignments of tobacco to be sold in such cities as Guadalajara, Puebla, and the capital. Some of the *casas de comercio* (merchant houses) of Mexico provided the interior provinces with supplies of cigarettes. Merchant investment in the tobacco trade was not extensive, however, and there is no evidence that anyone built any fortunes based on the crop. In 1765 there were an estimated one hundred individuals who engaged in the wholesale tobacco trade.[28] Among the merchants listed was Antonio Bassoco, the nephew of the Marquis of Castañiza. Bassoco eventually became the Count of Bassoco after amassing one of the greatest fortunes of colonial Mexico. Tobacco, however, was but a fraction of his multiple interests in commerce, mining, and commercial agriculture.[29]

There existed a small export trade of snuff from Mexico to Chile and Peru, since the Mexican product was popular and reputedly of better quality, but tobacco leaf, cigars, and cigarettes were all for domestic consumption.[30] The survey of the tobacco trade carried out on the orders of Revillagigedo the Elder showed that very little *tabaco de polvo* (a finely powdered tobacco, much more delicate than the more thickly shredded *rapé*) was consumed in Mexico. In 1748, there were an estimated six snuff mills in Mexico City, but, as one merchant explained, commerce in *tabaco de polvo* was of very little importance in Mexico, and even the poorest merchant did not trade in it as a single commodity.[31] The most popular and widespread habit was the smoking of *puros* (cigars) and *cigarros* or *papelillos* (cigarettes), which provided the strongest market.[32]

Manufacture of cigars and cigarettes occurred in both rural and urban areas, a distribution which the monopoly reorganized, restricting manufacture to selected towns and cities. The inventor of cigarette manufacture in Mexico was, allegedly, one Antonio Charro, who, at the beginning of the eighteenth century, made cigarettes and sold them at the entrance of the Teatro de Comedias in Mexico City.[33] In so doing, he provided an example which many men and women followed thereafter. General descriptions emphasize the multitude of *cigarrerías* (tobacco stores and workshops) in Mexico City which sold cigars and cigarettes: "in each street there were between one and four, and it was rare for a street not to have one . . . they were open until 9 or 10 at night . . . Each cigarrería had its own sign on the front of the door, and on the cigarette packets was stamped the same insignia, for example, a hand, a trumpet, a mermaid, a pair of doves; there were cigarreros renowned and well-to-do."[34]

Tobacco workshops and stores ranged in size from small enterprises which employed wage workers to one-man or one-woman street stands in the viceroyalty's cities and towns, where "one hears the noise, incitements, and other insolences which the freedom and opportunities of their work encourage."[35] Descriptions of tobacco workshops are rare, and the ones which have survived convey the impression of relatively small, simple establishments: "with little capital required to maintain one, as a counter of four wooden boards and a frame which serves as a shelf, a display sign on the door, and six wooden trays would be adequate to equip any of these *oficinas* (workshops) . . ."[36] Proprietorship and labor relations varied from artisanal to protoindustrial. Women, in particular, made cigarettes on a putting-out basis for *cigarreros*, for owners of *pulperías* (general grocery stores) and for anyone who paid them a pittance for their trouble.[37] At the marginal end of the industry were the peddlers, often itinerants, who rolled a few cigars or cigarettes and sold them on street corners in the towns and cities through which they traveled.

Reports based on surveys of Mexico's *cigarrerías*, carried out between 1770 and 1773 by monopoly bureaucrats, confirm several characteristics of the structure of the private tobacco trade implicit in general descriptions. The industry was unusual in that it employed large numbers of women. Of the 146 *cigarrerías* in Mexico City surveyed by Riva Agüero in 1773, approximately one-half were owned by women. The total labor force employed in these shops amounted to 691, 30 percent of which was female. In an assessment of the *cigarrerías* of Guadalajara, out of 115 shops, only 8 belonged to men,[38] and in Valladolid half of the labor employed in the tobacco industry was estimated to be female.[39] The size of the businesses was relatively small in terms of the numbers of workers employed. Estimates of workers per workshop varied, but not by much: in Mexico City the largest establishment employed 31 workers, all of whom were women. The average number of workers per *cigarrería* was much lower, between 4 and 8.[40] In Puebla, the figure varied between 1 and 5 workers per *cigarrería*, and in Valladolid, between 1 and 12.[41] In workshops with a large labor contingent, as in the example cited earlier with 31 workers, presumably nonfamily wage labor was hired, but as most of the workshops were small family concerns, family labor was probably adequate. An evaluation of the licensed *cigarrerías* and *purerías* still in operation in Mexico City in 1770 noted they employed more than 2,000 people, with approximately 6 per shop, "the majority being family members who practice this trade."[42] In Guadalajara, the *factor* reported that, of all of the existing *cigarrerías*, only one employed hired labor, while the rest depended upon family members.[43] A monopoly survey also revealed that seventeen owners were widows or daughters of previous owners, confirming yet again the family interest in the trade, and generational continuity in the profession.[44]

Finally, although we have no information about rates of return on investments or levels and value of inventory, the general impression is that returns were moderate, although within a wide range of income. Of the daily profits reported by the *cigarrerías*, most did not exceed 1 peso daily, while the majority made between 2 reales and 7 reales daily.[45] The "exceptional few" earned daily incomes of between 4 to 20 pesos.[46] *Cigarreros'* appraisals of the capital value of

their businesses varied between 11 pesos and 120 pesos.⁴⁷ A related
characteristic of tobacco shop ownership was that the business comprised one of several economic interests and was a supplemental
rather than a dominant economic enterprise.⁴⁸

There really are no reliable figures on the numbers of individuals
employed in the tobacco trade prior to its monopolization in New
Spain. Estimates of the number of private shops ranged from 543 to
3,000 *cigarrerías*.⁴⁹ In a retrospective assessment of the monopoly's
establishment, however, the *director general* cited the highest number found of 3,275 *cigarrerías* throughout the viceroyalty, employing
an estimated total of 13,100 workers.⁵⁰

What the evidence suggests is that, prior to the Bourbon reorganization of Mexico's tobacco trade, the trade was dominated neither
by a powerful planter elite, nor by a mercantile elite but rather by
numerous small artisans concentrated in cities and towns, and by
planters and peasants scattered throughout the country, with few
links to powerful networks or entrenched interests. No powerful
merchant lobby existed which could challenge the monopolization
of the tobacco trade, and the region where tobacco was on the rise as
a major commercial crop in Veracruz was not hindered by the monopoly but was incorporated into its operations. What is significant
about the introduction of the monopoly is that, in the early years
between 1765 and 1770, major resistance came not from private interests but from within the Bourbon bureaucracy—a reflection of the
Bourbon state's own internal conflict between reform and tradition.

The intrigues and conflicts which evolved during the establishment
of the monopoly reflected the complicated process of reform, one
which, although carried out under the guise of enlightened absolutism, proved to be guided by co-optation and compromise, as well as
by bureaucratic fractiousness and antagonism. Between 1764 and
1778, several issues dominated the establishment of the monopoly:
who should manage the monopoly; how was it to be financed; and
what should its operations consist of: the sale of leaf tobacco only or
monopoly control over the manufacture of cigars and cigarettes as
well. The basic administrative framework of the state tobacco monopoly was established by 1768, but it was not until 1778, ten years
later, that the monopoly's structure resembled the instructions
which José de Gálvez took with him to Mexico in his capacity as
visitor-general.

Technically, such issues should never have arisen. Royal mandates
clearly stated the royal preference for direct administration and the
creation of royal tobacco manufactories. But the skeleton bureau-

cracy which was in place by late 1764 attempted to modify such decisions. Such action was not unusual and obeyed the longstanding axiom of colonial rule, "obedezco pero no cumplo" ("I obey but do not comply"). The disagreements reflect the difficulties encountered by reform-minded ministers as they attempted to erect an absolutist state in the face of tradition and conservative bureaucrats.

A royal order of 13 August 1764 finally decreed the establishment of the tobacco monopoly in Mexico although it did not become public knowledge until 14 December 1764.[51] The *instrucción* which accompanied the royal order to establish the monopoly outlined procedures to be followed and made clear the purpose of the monopoly: to produce revenues to help finance the cost of Spain's defenses. The outbreak of war between Spain and England delayed the original plan to sell snuff by the Crown, but supplies from Havana finally arrived in October of 1764. Juan José de Echeveste, a merchant from Mexico, was commissioned to manage snuff sales in Mexico City, with the sale prices pegged at between 25 percent and 33 percent below current prices. Echeveste put up his own bond and conducted the business at his own risk, without salary.[52]

The monopoly's structure was modeled after its counterpart in Spain. To help with the initial planning and organization, a director and *contador* (accountant) were recruited from officials experienced in management of the tobacco monopoly in Spain. Francisco Anselmo de Armona received the appointment of visitor-general and took Jacinto de Espinosa, *administrador* (manager) of the tobacco monopoly in Spain for the past thirty-six years, with him to organize and act as the first *director general* of the monopoly.[53] Armona died before reaching Mexico and was replaced by José de Gálvez. Espinosa assumed control of the monopoly in March 1765, guided by an administrative and judicial *junta de tabaco* (tobacco committee) composed of the viceroy as president and *juez conservador* (judge protector) of the monopoly, the *decano* (senior criminal judge of the *audiencia*, the high court), the *alcalde del crimen* (junior judge of the lower court) of the *audiencia*, and the *director general* of the monopoly. The *junta*'s role was to devise a strategy to establish the monopoly as quickly as possible but with minimum provocation of Mexico's populace.[54]

From 1 March 1765, the monopoly *tercenas* (warehouses) began to receive quantities of raw tobacco leaf. The first orders of the *dirección general* (directorate-general) and the visitor-general authorized governors, *alcaldes mayores* (magistrates), and other justices of New Spain to publicly declare the intentions behind the monopoly and to order all residents within their jurisdictions, especially merchants and traders, to surrender all existing stocks of leaf tobacco, snuff, cigars, and cigarettes to the Crown. An exception was made, temporarily, for the interior provinces and the bishoprics of Durango and Guadalajara. For the period of one calendar year the merchants in those regions were permitted to continue as the major suppliers of tobacco, but with tobacco purchased from the monopoly warehouses, until the monopoly itself could guarantee supplies. The reason behind the exemption was to reduce the risk of inadequate supplies of tobacco to the population in a lucrative region dominated by mining and ranching and with high per capita consumption.[55] Tariffs for monopoly tobacco and its products were itemized, fixed, and displayed on the outside of the royal warehouses for consumers to see—a practice which would be extended to the government-licensed tobacco stores—the *estanquillos*. The *director general* Espinosa reported the response of the public to be positive in general because of the "moderate level of the prices." Within the first year of monopoly operations, some 600,000 pounds of tobacco were sold to the public and to the *cigarreros* for 6 reales per pound.[56]

The "legal" tobacco-growing areas designated by the monopoly comprised several jurisdictions within the province of Veracruz: Orizaba, Córdoba, Teusitlán, and Jalapa, as specified in the royal orders of 30 July 1764. The only other region in Mexico where tobacco could be produced legally was in Yucatán. To avoid problems of supply and transport to the far south, separate contracts, modeled on those for the *villas*, were arranged with planters in Mérida and Campeche to produce small amounts for local consumption. The Yucatán case will not be discussed in detail in this work.[57] The consequences of such an order were clear: with the exception of a small region in southeastern Mexico, the production of tobacco as a commercial crop was prohibited to peasants and *hacendados* (rural estate and hacienda owners) alike throughout Mexico. The exceptions were those planters known to have a major stake in commercial tobacco production in Veracruz, who were incorporated into the monopoly's operations and became, in one sense, beneficiaries of state management of the tobacco trade.

In May of 1765, Espinosa traveled with Sebastián Calvo, a member of the *junta de tabaco*, to Veracruz to familiarize himself with the jurisdictions chosen to supply tobacco to the monopoly.[58] Arrangements were made for the establishment of *factorías* (administrative districts) in Orizaba and Córdoba. *Factores* and accountants were appointed, and Espinosa ordered the acquisition of warehouses, cellars, offices, and designated areas where garrisons should be erected for use by the monopoly's *resguardo* or guard unit. *Alcaldes mayores* in the selected jurisdictions of Veracruz received orders to make sure that local planters elect representatives to travel to Mexico City and negotiate with the *dirección general* the conditions under which production for the state would be organized and a set of "fair" prices for the purchase of their tobacco.

As the months passed, Espinosa expressed great concern over what he termed a lack of "experienced personnel," the result of which was an imperfect cadre of officials who neglected their duties and made efficient management of the monopoly impossible.[59] Despite royal orders to the contrary, Espinosa supported lease of the monopoly to the private sector in the five bishoprics of Valladolid, Guadalajara, Oaxaca, Durango, and Yucatán, while he believed that Mexico City and its general administration should be managed directly by the state. From Espinosa's perspective, private lease provided a bridge to eventual full state management, which would prevent popular unrest and which would solve a critical capital shortage faced by the colonial state. With the exception of Sebastián Calvo, the remaining members of the *junta de tabaco* agreed with Espinosa, and a decision was taken to lease out the monopoly. Espinosa's ability to maintain support for his position depended largely on his friendship with the viceroy Cruillas. Initially persuaded by the benefits of direct state management, Cruillas was finally convinced by Espinosa's argument that slow communications and inadequately trained personnel made direct administration too risky. A *bando* (proclamation) of 16 June 1765 invited bids for the contracts of monopoly lease for which a profit of 150 percent was offered as an incentive. No bids materialized, possibly because the risks were perceived to be too great. The monopoly already had a bad reputation because payment had not been made to merchants for stock which they had surrendered, and the April orders which prohibited production and trade in tobacco by private individuals had not been systematically enforced.[60] At this state in the monopoly's organization, the colonial state effectively took over direct control, partly because the private sector was unwilling to take the risk in its management.

By the time the Francophile José de Gálvez arrived as visitor-general in late August 1765, the monopoly was indeed in a parlous state. Not only was it bankrupt, but also the only evidence of its operation was confined to Mexico City and its vicinity. Virtually from Gálvez' setting foot on Mexican soil, he and Espinosa could find no common ground. The miserable state of the monopoly shaped Gálvez' opinion of Espinosa as not only an ineffective director but also a disobedient one. The supply of tobacco leaf for the monopoly's operations and for the tobacco farmers and planters of Mexico produced additional antagonisms between Espinosa and Gálvez, not because they disagreed over who was to produce the tobacco and where, but over the sale price of tobacco. The purchase prices agreed upon between Espinosa and the tobacco planters' representatives from the *villas* of Orizaba and Córdoba were eventually overturned by Gálvez for two reasons. Gálvez argued that the contract prices agreed to by Espinosa were excessive and prejudicial to the king.[61] More seriously, the favorable prices, in Gálvez' mind, proved that Espinosa favored the planters over the interests of the king. The problems of prices and contracts are the subject of Chapter 3.

A separate set of instructions accompanying the visitor-general was provided by the Marqués de Esquilache, *director general* of the tobacco revenues of all Spanish dominions. Gálvez was ordered to look upon the monopoly as the main objective of his commission, "as it will be one of the most grateful services which you can render to the king."[62] The powers granted to him in his capacity as visitor-general, with additional powers of intendant, authorized him to intervene directly in all decisions made by the *junta de tabaco*.

Gálvez' first priority was to reestablish confidence in the monopoly and to acquire capital to finance its secure establishment. The visitor-general immediately raised 100,000 pesos from the private sector, comprised largely of donations from Spanish merchants to cover payments for tobacco stock.[63] Their representative, Domingo de Lardizábal, offered on their behalf to supply "all the necessary capital to purchase delivered stocks of tobacco throughout New Spain without interest or any reward," to pay for tobacco stocks delivered by merchants in Mexico, and to provide capital for the purchase of the first tobacco crop produced under contract conditions.[64] Gálvez also received further assurances that, if necessary, he could depend on the use of the complete proceeds of the commerce of the fleet for the purpose of consolidating the monopoly's financial basis.[65] Gálvez acquired more capital and, on 10 September 1765, the *junta de tabaco* agreed to place the monopoly under direct state management throughout all of Mexico. An enthusiastic visitor-general reported to Arriaga: "In the short time of the month of September, I have seen the tobacco monopoly successfully established and accepted with praise throughout the kingdom because its inhabitants have understood the clement intentions of the king and the considerable benefits which will accrue to them when this renta flourishes in that it will exempt them from other contributions which could have been more onerous and grievous."[66]

Not one to rest on his laurels, Gálvez began to build his own *clientela* (body of supporters) upon which he could rely. Changes in monopoly appointments occurred during September 1765, all designed to provide Gálvez with a loyal base from which to oppose Espinosa's and Cruillas' obstructionist tactics. The most significant appointment was the promotion of the *contador general* Antonio del Frago to the newly created position of co-*director general*. In a blatant attempt to curb Espinosa, Gálvez reported to Esquilache that another *director general* was necessary to "restrain Espinosa who has assumed a despotic and absolute control of the monopoly."[67] Mathias de Armona, a known supporter of Gálvez, replaced Frago as the *contador general*. Confident in his progress, Gálvez predicted that by 1767 the monopoly would yield at least one million pesos in profit, but to achieve such ends "I shall need exclusive and absolute control of it, as intendant of the army and of the royal treasury."[68]

Gálvez' confident statements to Arriaga proved to be premature. Both Espinosa and the viceroy Cruillas were determined to challenge the visitor-general's authority and to shape the monopoly in a direction which Espinosa, in particular, deemed less controversial. One policy which Espinosa rejected vehemently was the decision to monopolize the manufacture of cigars, cigarettes, and snuff. We will return to this later.

In October of 1765, Gálvez left Mexico City to open the *feria de Jalapa* (trade fair) in Veracruz and to consult with merchants on a number of issues, including additional loans for the monopoly. The discussions also tackled the subjects of expeditions to northern Mexico—Durango, Sonora, Sinaloa, and Nueva Vizcaya—to repress Indian attacks, expeditions which merchants could also help to finance in the king's service. In return, all possible aid would be given to stimulate commerce. The process of "consultation" initiated by Gálvez with the merchants resembled the bureaucratic practice in Cuba designed to gain approval from the Cuban elite for commercial and administrative reform and certainly shows him in a less confrontational light than he is usually portrayed, negotiating by choice, while reserving repressive tactics for necessity.[69]

During his absence between October 1765 and January 1766, Espinosa, with the aid of Cruillas, persuaded many of the *flotistas* (import merchants) of Mexico City to rescind their offers of additional loans to Gálvez to finance the monopoly in order to remove the possibility of direct state administration of the monopoly. Largely as a result of Cruillas' persuasion, the offers of capital were withdrawn.[70] Despite corporate retreat, several merchants offered financial support to Gálvez. Pedro de Cossío offered whatever financial help his merchant house could provide.[71] At the same time, Domingo de Lardizábal corresponded with Gálvez to offer individual help. He was aware of the decision of his colleagues not to uphold their offers, although he wrote to the visitor-general that he was not sure who had influenced them.[72] Gálvez remained convinced that the merchants were subjected to unfounded rumors that the Crown would not pay back the loans and that "what is certain is that from the time of my departure for Jalapa the viceroy worked effectively to discredit my conduct and my word by whatever means possible and thus tried to negotiate the retraction of the offers made by the *flotistas* but was not completely successful . . . and this despite authorization and agreement from the *junta de tabaco*, including the viceroy, to raise loans for the necessary amounts, using as security the branches of government revenues for repayment of the loans."[73]

At least two different sets of loans and donations were raised as a result of Gálvez' negotiations on behalf of the monopoly and as part of a wider campaign to engage the merchants' participation in reorganization of the tobacco trade. The first amounted to 585,507 pesos and came from six individual merchants and on behalf of the members of the *cinco gremios mayores de Madrid* and the *compañía de gremios de paños de Madrid*.[74] A second set of donations which amounted to 1,200,000 pesos came from five individuals: Manuel Marco, Juan José de Echeveste, Domingo de Lardizábal, Fernando Bustillo, and Pedro Antonio Cossío.[75] Echeveste, Lardizábal, and Cossío, as supporters of Gálvez, would all reap their rewards. All received military honors and bureaucratic appointments in the Bourbon administration of colonial Mexico.[76] Echeveste, previously removed from his position as the *tesorero* (treasurer) of the monopoly by Espinosa, was reinstated by Gálvez to that post and later became director of the gunpowder monopoly; Lardizábal received the appointment of *tesorero* of the *alcabalas* (excise) in 1767.[77]

By far the most controversial act of the monopoly was the establishment of the state tobacco manufactories and the elimination of private manufacture of tobacco products, cigars, and cigarettes. Gálvez demonstrated his fidelity to royal orders to establish state manufactories when he ordered purchases of paper to be made at the *feria de Jalapa* in November of 1765 "in order that as many cigarettes as possible can be manufactured in the factories already established and [the Crown] can reap the profits . . ."[78] On Gálvez' orders experimental manufactories were set up in Puebla, Veracruz, Jalapa, Oaxaca, and Guadalajara. The visitor-general argued that the benefits of manufacture of tobacco products were simply too great to be ignored. Most of all, the manufactories provided the sine qua non of an absolutist state built on warfare and welfare objectives: profit for the king and provision of employment for the urban poor, "especially the many poor women who earn their living making cigarettes."[79]

The policy of state production of tobacco angered Espinosa who vehemently criticized Gálvez' decision to establish state manufactories.[80] The *director general* cited recent riots in Puebla as evidence of public opposition to the abolition of private manufacture, which, he argued, were merely a prelude to widespread protest against the monopoly in general. Reports from Puebla reported the appearance of graffiti which went beyond the traditional battle cry of disgruntled vassals of "Death to bad government, long live the king," and which read, more ominously, "Death to the king of Spain and long live the English," and "Death to Spain." Attempts to burn the monopoly offices were also reported. Cruillas informed Arriaga that practically any outburst in the city of Puebla could be attributed to the decision to abolish private manufacture of cigars and cigarettes.[81] Convinced of the causal links between popular disturbances and the state manufactories, Espinosa ordered an immediate return to private production and the suspension of monopoly manufacture in Veracruz, Guadalajara, and Jalapa. The viceroy supported Espinosa, convinced that hundreds of people would be adversely affected by such a reorganization of the tobacco industry and that the state should control only the production and sale of tobacco leaf.

Espinosa's reluctance to move too quickly and thereby alienate any support for the monopoly was reinforced by reports from local government officials and *cabildo* members (town councillors). The Mexico City *cabildo* was particularly angered at the actions of the *dirección general*. A spokesman pointed out that great resentment had been caused by the plan to abolish private manufacture. Since one of the central duties of the Mexico City *cabildo* was to look after the public interest and peace, current problems could have been avoided, and still could be, if *cabildo* members were included in the affairs of the monopoly. The spokesman's final comment revealed the real point of contention—a belief that jurisdictional protocol had been violated because the *cabildo*'s opinion on the establishment of the monopoly had not been requested.[82] Petitions were also received by the *cabildos* and *alcaldes mayores* of Durango, Zacatecas, and San Luis de la Paz, which outlined the "general repugnance" with which residents received news of the prohibition against the private manufacture of cigars and cigarettes.

Gálvez dismissed reports of public opposition as nothing more than excuses for local political elites to preserve a local tobacco trade from which they benefited indirectly or illegally. As an example, he cited the Bishop of Oaxaca who sold contraband tobacco under the protection of ecclesiastical immunity and also supplied playing cards (also a royal monopoly) to the villages and towns of the province.[83]

The initial enthusiasm for state manufacture originated in the healthy "profits" which the experimental manufactories yielded.[84] Further increases depended upon suppression of competition from the private tobacco stores and the capture of existing markets. Gálvez persisted with the argument that the policy of state manufacture of tobacco products must prevail, especially since monopoly revenues only began to increase significantly after the order of 17 March 1766, which prohibited private trade (with the exception of professional *cigarreros*), was implemented. By the end of 1766, the monopoly showed a profit of 239,098 pesos, after debts incurred in its establishment had been paid off. Frustrated nevertheless, Gálvez wrote the viceroy: "Many are the millions which the Crown has lost throughout the years in which the tobacco of Spanish America has been a product of free commerce. . . . such has been the negligence of those who govern these dominions so far from the Crown that they have not considered such important affairs or they have described difficulties which never existed."[85]

Wearied by the opposition of Espinosa and Cruillas, Gálvez perceived his major problem to be "how to tolerate with resignation and without the least bitterness the fact that an unfaithful viceroy . . . and a foolish and perverse director can destroy a work so great which they themselves could not accomplish." Indeed, Cruillas' behavior and politicking among the merchant community merely served to confirm Gálvez' views of the "ruinous government of the viceroys."[86] New appointments in 1766 altered the balance of power within the monopoly administration. Juan Antonio de Velarde was appointed as the *fiscal* and sat on the *junta de tabaco*. The viceroy Cruillas was replaced by the Marqués de Croix, a military man, who appeared to be less partial to Espinosa, and more inclined to follow Gálvez' orders.[87]

With the removal of the viceroy Cruillas, Espinosa lost his foremost ally against Gálvez. Supported by royal orders to establish the manufactories and by evidence that manufacture produced a higher profit than the sale of leaf, the *junta de tabaco* quietly acquiesced to Gálvez' policy for state manufacture. An order of 13 March 1766 announced that tobacco products could be legally produced only in the state manufactories. Elimination of the *cigarrerías* was to proceed "slowly, little by little . . . and to attract to the manufactory the best cigarette rollers to manufacture all the supplies required by the Real

Hacienda."[88] With the temporary exception of "professional" *cigarreros*, all other merchants and traders were prohibited from dealing in tobacco products of any type.[89]

Promulgation of the order to monopolize manufacture of cigars and cigarettes did not mean Gálvez had won his battle. The appointment of the *fiscal* Velarde resulted in a reassessment of state manufacture as a desirable policy. The *fiscal* received a full report of Gálvez' plans, a collection of complaints received from various *cabildos*, and reports of demonstrations against the monopoly. In a meeting of the *junta de tabaco*, the *fiscal* agreed with Gálvez that state control of the production of tobacco products would increase revenues, but he also argued that the Crown did not desire such revenues at the expense of "notable vexation and resentment" by the public and so cautioned against state manufacture.[90]

Due to a variety of opinions within the *dirección general*, ranging from outright opposition to ambivalence, state manufacture was stalled until a workable policy of elimination of the *cigarrerías* could be developed and implemented. The Crown's reasoning prior to 1763 as to why a tobacco monopoly should not be established was not lost on the *fiscal*. In spite of the reasons used to justify the implementation of the tobacco monopoly, they did not alter the social and economic reality of colonial Mexico. Velarde pointed out that Mexico City in particular would be affected, given the "vast" numbers of men and women employed in the tobacco industry, and since "there are many men who have sons and whose circumstances do not permit them to train as tailors or shoemakers."[91] The apprehension and fear of popular unrest were not unfounded. The summer of 1766 saw the mobilization of the silvermine workers of Real del Monte, and violent protests erupted against the expulsion of the Jesuits in 1767.[92]

Determined to avoid further delay, criticism, and dilution of powers, Gálvez sought full control over monopoly policy and the support of the viceroy. When Croix arrived in July of 1766, he dissolved the original *junta de tabaco* and replaced it with one having severely reduced powers. The Crown regarded the *junta* as the primary cause of the costly delays experienced by the monopoly (both financial and in terms of public confidence) and ordered it removed from any deliberations which concerned economic or administrative decisions.

After consultations with Gálvez and the *directores generales*, Croix issued a decree on 4 June 1767 which prohibited production and sale of tobacco by all merchants with the exception of professional *cigarreros*. These received licenses from the monopoly to continue with their trade on condition they purchased their leaf tobacco from monopoly stores.[93] No further licenses were to be issued, on the assumption that the *cigarreros* would, over the years, fade away, unable to compete with monopoly sales of tobacco products. Although the order failed to convince all the members of the *dirección general* of the advantages of state manufacture, it prepared the way for the control of and gradual elimination of the private *cigarreros* while, at the same time, allowing consolidation of the monopoly's administrative machinery.

The official ordinances of the royal tobacco monopoly of New Spain were published and approved by the viceroy and the Crown on 22 October 1768. The ordinances outlined the bureaucratic framework of the monopoly and defined the specific duties of all monopoly bureaucrats and employees.[94] Designed to prevent a repetition of the administrative chaos of the first three years, they remained virtually unchanged until independence from Spain. The *resguardo*, the police arm of the monopoly, created to eliminate contraband production and trade in tobacco commerce, was established throughout the viceroyalty. Two years later, in 1770, the royal tobacco manufactory in Mexico City opened its doors and began operations. During the next decade five other state tobacco manufactories were established, in Guadalajara, Puebla, Oaxaca, Orizaba, and Querétaro, as were the *estanquillos*, the royal tobacco shops. The structural foundations of the tobacco monopoly had been laid, foundations which experienced few modifications during the next fifty years of Bourbon management.

The founding years of the tobacco monopoly were fraught with conflict, particularly between Gálvez, on the one hand, and the *director general* Espinosa and viceroy Cruillas, on the other. The conflict between Gálvez and Cruillas in particular is well known, and there is no purpose in recounting the details here, but there are a few points to be made about the controversies surrounding the establishment of the monopoly.

Some scholars have suggested that bureaucratic conflict over government policy is not generated by personal idiosyncrasy or administrative factionalism, but is, instead, the outcome of "cleavages among interest groups in the elite. In the Spanish polity of the eighteenth century . . . bureaucrats and merchants coalesced into two principal factions."[95] The factions, themselves, may be described as "traditionalist," those who favored the status quo and local vested interests, and "reformist," those whose loyalties were directed "to the nation, rather than to microregions of familial roots."[96] The model is suggestive but problematic, especially if we consider the lobbying carried out by both Gálvez and Cruillas among the merchants to support or obstruct the financing of the monopoly.[97]

By 1764, after receiving news of the intended commercial and financial reforms being discussed by the Junta de Ministros, a special interministerial commission, the Consulado de Cádiz was clearly on the defensive, although it was unable to influence the outcome of the decisions. The significance of the legislation was that "the Consulado of Cádiz suffered a major blow," a blow which may have had repercussions elsewhere in the American colonies as they tried to regain their power.[98] In Mexico, the representatives of the Consulado de Cádiz and the Consulado de México had already witnessed attempts of the Crown to enforce greater control over the cochineal trade, located primarily in Oaxaca, and to tax production more efficiently.[99] The merchants may have anticipated further reform of the cochineal trade which would reduce their profits.[100] It is surely more than a coincidence that the representative of the Consulado de Cádiz, who petitioned for exemptions of cochineal from a new tax, was Domingo Ignacio Lardizábal, who also loaned money to Gálvez to finance the monopoly.[101] Such merchants as Cossío and Lardizábal grasped the opportunity to ally themselves with the new "regime" represented by José de Gálvez by supporting some of his projects and gaining his political favor—simple, shrewd *realpolitik*. They saw monetary support for the monopoly as a way to influence the direction of further reforms which affected their individual and collective interests more seriously. Any "alliance," however, was temporary and expedient.

Economic interests and alliances aside, a further consideration is that the question of power and who was to exercise it provided a singular problem between Gálvez and Cruillas. A consequence of the political changes demanded by absolutism generated conflicting views about government. The difference lay between those officials trained in the art of consensus politics and conciliar decision making, the "traditionalists," epitomized by such men as Cruillas, and the "reformists," like Gálvez, who acted in the interests of the colonial state and who wanted obedience not discussions.[102] Neither Cruillas nor Espinosa appreciated Gálvez' attempts to monopolize power and challenge their authority, and Cruillas interpreted Gálvez' actions as "a dangerous infringement by one corporate unit on another which could not go unchallenged."[103] While such terms as traditionalist and reformist may be useful indicators of political preferences and opinions, they need to be used with caution. There is no question that Gálvez was determined to implement controversial reforms which affected all levels of society. At the same time, the process by which the tobacco trade was reorganized suggests that the practice of consultation and co-optation as a political strategy was far from dead, even for Gálvez.

Tobacco monopolies are often portrayed as symbols of colonial oppression. Jacob Price reminds us, however, that such characterizations are not always valid given the indifference which the majority of inhabitants in France exhibited toward the monopoly established there.[104] There is no doubt that the Mexican monopoly engendered its own share of hostility and opposition which continued throughout the entire period of Bourbon management. Popular reaction over the years, however, demonstrated adjustment and acceptance as well as hostility and alienation. What we propose to do in the rest of this chapter is to examine, first, why there was not a stronger political opposition to the monopoly, and, second, when opposition occurred, who was behind it, and what form did it take?

Bureaucratic assessments of public reaction to the monopoly were for the most part sanguine. Espinosa reported that, although the monopoly "took away their trade [they] did not complain."[105] Díaz de la Vega also reported that "no *vecino* (property-owning permanent resident) had been bothered nor was authority necessary to enforce the changeover."[106] It is indeed the case that public response did not generate the sustained violence experienced by monopoly bureaucrats in New Granada or the Philippines, where riots, arson, and physical attacks were common. It is equally evident that the monopoly engendered criticism and hostility and that people were prepared to make their grievances known through petitions, complaints, and resistance.

We have already seen that no major challenge came from merchants because there existed no significant mercantile vested interests in the tobacco trade, and because the most important interests were incorporated into the monopoly's operations. There were protests, but for the most part, vested interests in tobacco were diverse, preventing a united front in the face of reform. It was the process of the reorganization of the tobacco trade which provided the key to its success, a reorganization which permitted readjustment and generated its own new vested interests in the monopoly. Gálvez' recruitment of merchants to monopoly positions, for example, was a shrewd move to stifle opposition. They acquired an interest in the survival of the new state enterprise, not to mention the opportunity to shape the local monopoly administration to their own needs. There were periodic rumblings from merchants throughout the late eighteenth and early nineteenth centuries, but nothing as articulated or organized as the Free Tobacco Movement which developed in Cuba in response to the presence of the monopoly. As we shall argue, the fiscal role of the monopoly and its stability as government collateral to secure private loans over the years deterred the formation of a mercantile movement for a deregulated tobacco trade.

There was no consensus about the anticipated effects of the monopoly upon the Mexican population. Sporadic demonstrations and public disturbances occurred during the first few years of the monopoly's establishment, but given the series of reforms to which the inhabitants of Mexico were subjected in the late 1760s, especially the expulsion of the Jesuits in 1767, it is difficult to isolate the monopoly as the most controversial of them all. Even "evidence" of a popular groundswell against the tobacco manufactories suggested that it was not always as "popular" as bureaucrats like Espinosa wished to believe. The *factor* of Puebla reported one incident to Gálvez which exemplified how opponents of manufacture uncritically accepted reports of protest against the royal manufactories. In the barrio of San Francisco in the city of Puebla in December 1765, a popular disturbance was blamed on the establishment of a state tobacco manufactory. The *factor* argued that the real cause was the misbehavior of soldiers who provoked a local crowd with their abusive actions toward a group of Indian women selling tortillas. The scuffle which ensued had nothing whatsoever to do with the establishment of experimental manufactories.[107] An investigation of a street demonstration in Oaxaca "initiated" by women to protest the establishment of the manufactory revealed that it was instigated by two members of the *cabildo* of Oaxaca.[108]

On a regional level, the establishment of the monopoly and its manufactories was welcomed by some and opposed by others who anticipated adverse effects upon the local economy. We will give two examples. The Bishops of Guadalajara and Oaxaca reported the ill effects of monopolization (or rather the exclusion of their regions from its operations). No tobacco effectively meant no tribute since the local indigenous communities depended heavily on it as a cash crop. Both of the bishops predicted the end result would be migration away from the area and economic desolation.[109] Some employers feared competition from the manufactories for labor, while those employers in towns without a manufactory anticipated an improved labor market as a result of the prohibition of private manufacture of cigars and cigarettes. To pacify fears of increased labor shortages, an order of 22 July 1778 declared that those people able to work in the manufacture of cottons and woolens should not be permitted to work in the manufactory of Guadalajara. After the manufactory opened in Guadalajara, the *director general* reported that jobs could not be provided for all previous owners and workers immediately, but that they had found temporary work for them in the cotton manufactories. Attempts to balance the labor needs of the tobacco manufactories and those of other local industries were, for the most part, unsuccessful. The presence of the manufactories, particularly the one in Querétaro, may have exacerbated the labor shortages experienced by textile owners, and affected the level of local wages.[110]

How many *hacendados, rancheros,* and peasants were affected by the monopoly's regulation of commercial production of tobacco is impossible to estimate. Alexander von Humboldt, critical of the monopoly, argued that its operations resulted in the destruction of previously thriving villages, such as Autlán, Ezatlán, Ahuzcatlán, Tepic, and Santixpac, all in the Intendency of Guadalajara. All were renowned for the abundance and excellent quality of tobacco which they produced, but, after monopoly regulation, "these formerly happy and flourishing countries have been decreasing in population since the plantations were transferred to the eastern slope of the cordillera."[111] Farmers from Guadalajara provide one of the few examples of sustained petition and protest, but with the objective of being incorporated into the monopoly's operations, not of lobbying for its abolition. They petitioned the Crown and the *dirección general* for permission to produce tobacco for the monopoly on the basis of comparative advantage. With the support of several monopoly bureaucrats, the planters argued that it would simply be cheaper to establish two production zones; one which supplied the southern, southeastern, and central regions from Veracruz, balanced by one in Guadalajara which would provide supplies to the far northern provinces, and the northwestern and north-central regions of consumption. Their petitions were ignored, although, as we shall see later, cost estimates were drawn up to test the proposition that savings would accrue to the monopoly if a second production zone was established.

The reports and letters of the monopoly bureaucrats and, indeed, the visitor-general's own reflections contain very little discussion about the potentially deleterious effects of the monopoly upon local agricultural economies. There appeared some rather cavalier assumptions that peasants and farmers could adjust to the changes and grow other crops. The implication was that resources would not necessarily be misallocated because of monopoly regulation, but would be redirected. Such logic is more explicit in the Bourbon management of the Philippine tobacco monopoly where bureaucrats justified the beneficial effects of such a monopoly by arguing that the local peasantry and small farmers, no longer able to grow tobacco, would be forced to produce badly needed food crops or to provide labor for the production of export crops, such as sugar.[112] Whether such redirection occurred in rural areas in colonial Mexico remains at the level of speculation, even if Humboldt would have us believe it did not occur.

The strongest case of collective opposition was organized by the *cigarreros* and *pureros*, the cigarette and cigar makers and sellers of Mexico City, but it was short-lived.

The *cigarreros* advised the *dirección general* of their opposition, not to the monopoly of trade in leaf, but to the policy of public manufacture of tobacco products. They expressed their fears about the ruin and misery which awaited their families and argued that the state manufactories were "against the will of God, and of serious harm to the King's vassals." The real victims of the policy were the *cigarreras* (female cigarette makers), who "throughout the kingdom have been deprived of this honest occupation, and suffer from hunger, deprivation, and misery, exposed to the greatest dangers." They requested simply that the king permit them to engage in the private production of cigars and cigarettes.[113] The petition was in vain. Yet the establishment of state manufactories failed ultimately to produce any major uprisings.

During the orchestrated closure of private tobacco stores and workshops over a ten-year period, as the silent compulsion of competition from the monopoly began to affect the *cigarreros'* profits adversely, more and more of them requested a position in one of the manufactories or an appointment as an *estanquero*, manager of a government tobacco store. The protests of the *cigarreros* died down as they became absorbed into the monopoly's operations. During the first few years of the monopoly's operation, the *cigarreros* received permission to continue with their own small businesses but were required to purchase their raw leaf from monopoly warehouses. As with the tobacco planters of Veracruz, the colonial state offered alternative employment with the monopoly, phased out the workshops slowly, permitting time to adjust to the changes, and, in the early years of state management of the manufactories, offered equal and possibly better working conditions compared with those of the private workshops.

The *estanquillos*, the state tobacco shops, were scheduled to open for business on 1 January 1775. Apparently 110 of them did open in Mexico City, allegedly without incident.[114] The basic plan called for the establishment of 80 *estanquillos* in the most commercially lucrative areas of Mexico City. Allocation of monopoly licenses to administer such shops was determined by the individual circumstances of each *cigarrero* who was surveyed by monopoly officials.[115] Those owners with large families received first priority in the distribution of licenses to administer an *estanquillo;* positions in the manufactories were offered to the wives and children of the proprietors. Widows, single women, and elderly shop owners also received priority in the distribution of licenses. Those *cigarreros* who were not granted a license received an offer of employment in the manufactories in positions according to their abilities, some as *proprietarios* (lifetime positions).[116] The option to work in one of the manufactories alleviated some fears of unemployment, particularly among the professional *cigarreros.*

The reorganization of the tobacco trade by the Bourbon bureaucracy permitted it to capitalize upon the large numbers of women employed in the private trade and to argue that eventually only women were to be employed in the manufactories, carrying out what was deemed to be "appropriate work" for women.[117] Rolling cigars and cigarettes was not, in comparison, appropriate labor for men, who "ought to be in the fields and the mines."[118]

Co-optation framed within a paternalist context, and reorganization of channels of authority from private employers to a public one, characterized the experience of those incorporated into the monopoly's operations: the tobacco planters of Veracruz and the *cigarrerías* of the towns and cities of Mexico. In the process, there appeared to be more of a continuity with old practices and less confrontation with the populace of Mexico than has previously been thought.

For those who were not incorporated into the monopoly's operations, their responses may be characterized as quietly subversive, often encouraged by a state which either looked the other way in the face of violations of monopoly restrictions or found its actions undermined by its own contradictory policies. This is not to say that repressive tactics were not used when necessary, actions which reminded the skeptics that the Bourbon absolutist state was something more than a fantasy of Charles III.

The most widespread and sustained opposition to monopoly regulation was manifested for many reasons and in many ways through contraband. Every nook and cranny provided potential shelter for contraband commerce—ships in port in Veracruz, private houses, general stores, convents, and even schools. Management of contraband proved to be less than effective for two reasons. The first was simply the scale of the task: too vast a terrain for too few *resguardo* soldiers.[119] The second, as we shall see, was that Bourbon objectives simultaneously supported and obstructed the *resguardo*'s actions.

The result was a de facto tolerance of contraband trade in tobacco, a situation not dissimilar from contemporary marijuana and coca production in the United States and Latin America.

Local practices by *alcaldes mayores*, priests, and *hacendados* undermined rather than reinforced the *resguardo's* efforts. The *directores generales* complained to Gálvez in 1778 that there still existed a great deal of negligence by the *alcaldes mayores* and their deputies in the prosecution of *contrabandistas* in and around Indian villages. The *alcaldes mayores* responded that they permitted illegal sales of tobacco to enable the Indians to fulfill their tribute obligations.[120] In response to a riot by Indian tobacco *contrabandistas* near the city of Guadalajara, the governor of the Colotlan military province, don Pedro Antonio Trelles Villa de Moros, suggested that the incident in question was the result of indiscrete behavior by monopoly officials in destroying illegal cultivation of tobacco. There was a real danger of losing "provinces preserved until now through the expenditure of much prudence and treasure." Local Indian parishioners of nearby Nayarit had responded with "general fermentation" to recent attempts to force payment of obligatory tithes. Trelles therefore asked, if the ecclesiastical tithe had been suppressed, what sense did it make to provoke a rebellion for the sake of a few tobacco plants?[121]

As usual, distance took its toll on bureaucratic efficiency. Enforcement of monopoly regulations in the frontier provinces of Mexico proved to be all but impossible. Bureaucrats complained about the logistical problems of enforcing the monopoly in areas outside effective state control and where tobacco played a major role in the local economies. In the far north, in New Mexico, Coahuila, and Texas, tobacco was extensively cultivated and was crucial as an item of barter in the frontier economy.[122] In 1782 the viceroy received reports from the provinces of Sonora and Sinaloa which described the futility of trying to implement monopoly regulations in a region where a variety of tobacco (*macuchi*) grew wild, and where the Indian tribes were accustomed to unrestricted access to tobacco.[123] Any concerted effort to establish the monopoly and destroy local production created the very strong risk of "a general uprising."[124] Frontier areas, the western and eastern coastal strips, and the indigenous south, including Yucatán and Chiapas, all remained on the margins of monopoly regulation and became notorious for contraband production. Distance and lack of adequate manpower precluded any serious, sustained attempt to enforce monopoly restrictions. Such energies and resources were reserved for the central, densely populated provinces, cities and their hinterlands, and mining towns.

Another suspect source of contraband were the muleteers who

contracted with the monopoly to transport tobacco and tobacco products between administrations. In 1798 José Esteban, an Indian tributary from Santa Ana Chautemplan in Tlaxcala, received a prison sentence of one and a half years for theft of tobacco during his trip from Córdoba to Mexico City.[125]

Organized contraband was carried out by both *gente decente* (respectable people) and bandit gangs. In 1791, three Indians from the town of Tlacotalpan, Tomás de Santiago, Pablo de la Cruz, and Eugenio Florés discovered a box which contained at first sight cartons of bars of soap, some of which, on closer inspection, had been hollowed out and filled with cigars and cigarettes. They loaded the illicit cargo, ready to take it to the local monopoly administrator, when several *gachupines* appeared and ordered them to leave the contraband alone.[126] The Indians replied that they were going to turn the cargo in, at which point one of the *gachupines* threatened to shoot them if they did not leave the tobacco alone. At the same time, one of the *gachupines'* servants took out a machete and wounded Tomás de Santiago. The Indians finally left without the contraband but informed the administrator of what had happened. The illicit cargo was finally discovered and impounded and, after a rather elaborate and complicated pursuit by the *resguardo,* 860 packets of cigars, 5,900 packets of cigarettes, and 31 pounds of snuff were discovered and confiscated. At least one of the *gachupines* and the machete-wielding servant were arrested and imprisoned.[127]

Reports of organized bandits who specialized in contraband tobacco abounded. One band in the sierra of Ceutla (in the modern-day state of Guerrero) survived by growing tobacco and selling it illegally to local villagers. They were reported to have had sixteen members, seven of whom were wanted for capital crimes which ranged from rape to murder; the remainder acted as servants and laborers in the illicit tobacco fields.[128]

Compounding the problems of monopoly enforcement were the "gray" areas of contraband. The use of tobacco as an ingredient in the manufacture of other "substances," for example, provoked allegations of unfair discrimination and presented the problematic of "fine-line" contraband. One example concerned the practices of Indian residents in the city of Puebla who purchased tobacco scraps to make *pisiete,* a concoction sold to the city's artisans but particularly popular with the bakery workers.[129] Mixed with lime and chewed, it produced juices which acted as a stimulant. The Indians believed it protected them from the harmful effects of inhaling excessive dust from the flour used in the baking process. After the *protomedicato* (the Board of King's Physicians) ruled that the substance was not harmful to health in 1804, the price of tobacco scraps was increased on the orders of the viceroy.[130] But by 1807 the Indian women of Puebla, who had always supported themselves through the sale of *pisiete*, complained to the viceroy that the local *estanquillos* no longer sold the tobacco scraps because they believed the women used them to manufacture coarse cigarettes, and so deprived the women of their livelihood.[131]

Individual acts of contraband born out of economic desperation and ignorance are illustrated by the following examples. Two women charged with illegal possession of cigars and cigarettes testified that they had purchased the leaf from a man from Córdoba whom they did not know, to make into cigars and cigarettes to sell to "very well-known persons" to earn money to support their families. Promptly told to gain a living some other way, the women were cautioned and warned that, if they were caught again, the punishment would be much more severe.[132] In the barrio of San Antonio of Córdoba, Teodora García was apprehended with two *manojos* (bundles) of tobacco. She testified that a man, a stranger, had left them with her temporarily, saying he would return to collect them but never did. García was ordered to pay the mandatory fine but, due to her indigence, was arrested. After a stint of five days in jail, García was released with the customary warning that, if she committed a similar crime and was caught, her treatment would not be so lenient.[133] Finally, on the road from Orizaba to Puebla, María Antonia Silva, her husband, a weaver, and their daughter were stopped and searched by the *resguardo*. They found eight ounces of tobacco which the family confessed they had purchased for 1 1/2 reales from a widowed tobacco grower in Orizaba. All the valued possessions of the family, including one silver peso, two handkerchiefs, six chickens, together valued at 6 pesos 3 1/2 reales, were confiscated. The usual costs were covered but at the expense of depriving the family of their belongings.[134]

These examples (and the cases are endless) provided evidence for the concern harbored by many government bureaucrats that punishments were meted out which did not fit the crime. Bureaucratic criticisms were made of the unfair and oppressive actions by the *resguardo*: "it is assumed that the rigor of the punishments for contraband only results in a true oppression of the vassals and the ruin of families . . . [the *resguardo*] ought to judge and use discretion in cases where small amounts of tobacco are found."[135] For the "petty" cases, the only punishment administered ought to be the appropriation of the tobacco, which should then be delivered to the local monopoly administration. In the case of the death of a contraband dealer killed by a *resguardo* guard, the intendant Manuel de Flon observed that the smuggler's death was completely unnecessary and called for the promulgation of new rules and orders to "remedy a cruel and arbitrary system which currently shapes the *resguardo*."[136] Although the degree of change engendered is unknown, a new order was implemented in 1803, designed to avoid excessive, unfair, or abusive behavior by the *resguardo* toward the colonial populace. Any individual or family found to possess contraband tobacco which did not exceed 200 pesos in value was not to be charged but simply deprived of the tobacco and given a severe warning. Those people found with tobacco worth in excess of 200 pesos were to be charged and punished as usual.[137]

The establishment of the tobacco monopoly legally prohibited the cultivation, manufacture, and sale of tobacco, cigars, and cigarettes to all but a small minority of the colonial population. It was without doubt an institution which provoked controversy, fear, and hatred, particularly among Indian communities and small farmers who scratched out a subsistence living by selling tobacco. It generated resentment among local bureaucrats who argued that the monopoly removed the only source of commerce through which Indians could pay their tribute, and among merchants who feared that what little local trade existed in their areas would be wiped out if local farmers could not produce tobacco. But if we ask what the establishment of the tobacco monopoly meant to the majority of the colonial population of Mexico, the answer is that there was a diversity of responses, a diversity which suggests that the population in general, and the workers and planters in particular, found different strategies and ways of adjusting to monopoly regulation. In between two idealized reactions of acceptance and rejection existed a range of responses— negotiation, adjustment, and resistance—all of which helped to reconcile Mexico's population to as much as alienate it from the regulation of the tobacco trade and the heavy, albeit erratic, hand of the colonial state. As such, during the late colonial period, the monopoly as a single political issue never amounted to very much. In combination with local grievances at the elite or popular levels, however, it could be used to channel and crystallize grievances against the Bourbon state and Spanish rule.

The monopoly's establishment was characterized as much by co-optation and moderation as it was by repression, a process which illustrates that even the most zealous of Bourbon reformers, José de Gálvez, was prepared to remain flexible in his political tactics. There was more than one Hapsburg ghost in the Bourbon governmental machine. The monopoly's appearance as a radical reform is somewhat deceptive. As we shall see later on, the monopoly provoked changes, but ones which were not always intended by the Bourbon state. The confrontational act of centralizing and controlling the manufacture of cigars and cigarettes was mitigated for most urban and some rural workers by their employment in the royal manufactories or as managers of *estanquillos*. Same job, different boss. In a similar manner, the tobacco planters of Veracruz were incorporated into the monopoly's operations and became participants in its growth. This is not to argue that monopoly policy and practice and its effects were always benign. There was violence and repression, as poor peasants caught in contraband production of tobacco would find out to their cost. But what about the fiscal results; did the monopoly fulfill expectations? We now turn to the nature of the monopoly bureaucracy, its administration of this state enterprise, and fiscal performance.

2. Monopoly Bureaucrats and Monopoly Finances: An Overview, 1765–1810

IN THE COURSE of two centuries of imperial rule, Spain's bureaucracy became a vehicle through which the interests of the state and local society were balanced. The problem by the beginning of the eighteenth century was that the balance tilted too far toward vested interests at the expense of the Crown. It was under Bourbon rule that attempts were made to produce "administrative sovereignty" to redress the balance of power in favor of the Crown. A particular problem in the American colonies was the dominance in government offices of creole bureaucrats who developed local ties and interests through marriage, kinship, and business partnerships, an example of the "traditionalist" type discussed in Chapter 1. To remedy the situation, reform-minded ministers sought to replace the "native sons" with impartial, professional peninsular officials. The bureaucrats recruited to manage and staff the offices of the tobacco monopoly formed part of this wider imperial project to establish a professional cadre of loyal, disinterested state servants.[1]

To better understand the administrative context within which monopoly policy was formed and implemented, we need to look at the organizational structure of the monopoly and at its bureaucratic managers and employees. We shall argue that the majority of the monopoly bureaucrats faced considerable problems, low wages and low morale. But they acted, for the most part, as a bureaucracy whose interests coincided with those of the colonial state. They may not have remained completely isolated from local society or immune to corruption but they were accountable for their actions. Whatever inefficiencies existed, they obliged the Crown by raising revenues.

The administrative foundations of the tobacco monopoly in Mexico were laid out in the *ordenanzas* or ordinances of the royal tobacco monopoly.[2] Designed to produce a uniform and responsible bureaucratic managerial structure, they contained specific instructions for the duties of all bureaucrats, from the *director general* to the *oficiales* (clerks), *estanquilleros*, and *resguardo* guards. Special emphasis was placed upon strict reporting and accounting procedures.[3]

The highest authority of the monopoly in Mexico lay with the viceroy acting in his capacity as *superintendente subdelegado de la Real Hacienda* (superintendent of the exchequer). All policy matters, disputes, and decisions were conveyed to the Real Hacienda in Spain where the general superintendency of the monopoly was located. The *dirección general*, originally headed by two directors to prevent concentration of too much power, was presided over by a single director after 1790. The real "beneficiary" of the single directorship was the ambitious Silvestre Díaz de la Vega, who occupied the post of *director general* for fifteen years between 1795 and 1810. Table 1 lists the *directores generales* and *contadores generales* of the monopoly between 1766 and 1821. Major policy decisions were made by the *dirección general* in consultation with the *fiscal de Real Hacienda*, with final approval from the viceroy. The responsibility for the distribution of duties within the *contaduría* (accounts) and *tesorería* (treasury) and their implementation lay with the *director general*.

The *contaduría* section dealt with all monopoly accounts, the compilation, auditing, and explanation of which occurred twice yearly, formulated as statements of the revenues, costs, and profits of the monopoly. The *contador general* (chief accountant) examined and certified the monthly reports of consumption, value, and costs incurred by monopoly administrations. Regional and branch managers and accountants kept records of all transactions. These were, in turn, submitted to the *contador general* for verification. Unlike most fiscal departments, which were required to submit their accounts to the Tribunal de Cuentas (court of audit) for auditing and verification, monopoly accounts were audited internally by the monopoly's own *contaduría* until the 1790s.

The monopoly *tesorero* (treasurer) was responsible for all revenues produced in the capital and the provinces. All monopoly receipts were deposited in the central monopoly treasury in Mexico City where they awaited transfer to Veracruz, and, from there, shipment to Havana and Spain. *Tercenistas* (monopoly wholesalers) and the *estanquilleros* of Mexico City delivered their takings on a weekly basis to the treasury; the administrations did so on a monthly basis which provided a quick turnover of capital for monopoly operations.

To facilitate centralization, standardization, and control of the tobacco trade, Mexico was divided into several *factorías* (administra-

Table 1.   Directores Generales *and* Contadores Generales
of the Tobacco Monopoly, 1765–1822

Directores Generales	Years	Contadores Generales	Years
Jacinto Díaz de Espinosa	1766–1777	Mathías de Armona	1766
with Antonio del Frago	1766–1767		
with Felipe de Hierro	1775	Felipe de Hierro	1767–1775
Felipe de Hierro with José			
de la Riva Agüero	1778–1792	Silvestre Díaz de la Vega	1779–1794
Felipe de Hierro	1793–1794	Francisco Maniau y	
		Ortega	1795–1806
Silvestre Díaz de la Vega	1795–1810	Joaquín Maniau	
		Torquemada	1807 (interim
			1808–1814
Pedro Simón Mendinueta	1811	Francisco José Bernal de	
		Quirós	1814–1818
Pedro María Monterde	1812–1813	Juan Antonio Unzueta	1819–1821
Joaquín Maniau			
Torquemada	1814–1818	Phelipe Santiago Sanz	1822
Francisco José Bernal			
de Quirós with			
Carlos López	1819–1821		
Carlos López	1822–?		

Source: AGI, Mexico 2255, Títulos de empleados; BN (Mexico) Caja Fuerte, Calendario manual y guía forasteros en México, for the years 1766–1770, 1772–1775, 1778–1779, 1782–1785, 1787–1788, 1793–1799, 1800–1801, 1803–1822.

tive and marketing districts) each managed by a *factor* (monopoly manager-cum-agent) and an administrator, with a bureaucratic staff to administer local monopoly affairs. Each housed royal monopoly *tercenas* (warehouses). By 1767, the *factoría* system extended throughout Mexico. Ten *factorías* were established in Córdoba, Durango, Guadalajara, Mérida de Yucatán, Oaxaca, Orizaba, Puebla, Rosario, Valladolid, and Veracruz, in addition to the general administration of Mexico. Four smaller independent administrations were located in Coahuila, Mazapil, Monterrey, and Santander (see map 1).[4] Contained within each administration were smaller subunits, *fielatos* (branches), generally located in small towns and villages, managed by *fieles* (branch managers). Finally, the smallest link in the chain of monopoly operations was the *estanquillo*, the government tobacco shop. Together, the structure provided links between the national and local levels of operation and the vehicles for information

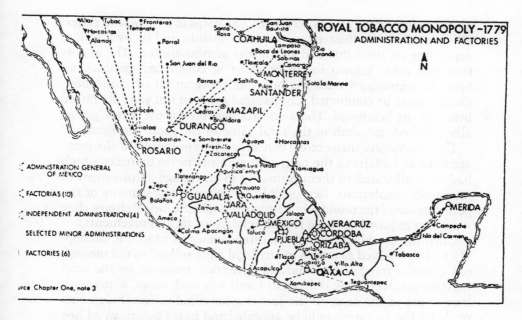

Map 1. The Tobacco Monopoly of Mexico, 1779

gathering, for accountability of employees, and for the marketing of tobacco products. The formal chain of authority ran from the *estanqueros* to the *fieles,* who, in turn, were accountable to the administrators, and these to the *factores.* All were directly subordinate and accountable to the *dirección general.* Such organization resulted in an intricate network of monopoly operations throughout the colony. Administrative authority and control, however, was far from uniform.

The transportation and distribution of tobacco products and money receipts were carried out by muleteers who received *guías* (licenses) which indicated the amount being shipped and its destination. The muleteers, rather like the planters, negotiated contracts with the monopoly to transport tobacco products to regions throughout Mexico.[5]

The military branch of the monopoly and its basic protection against contraband activity was the *resguardo.* Initially *resguardo* units were confined to the general administration of Mexico and Mexico City. As a result of decisions taken in September and October of 1765, orders were distributed for units to be established in all of the monopoly administrations. The corps of a *resguardo* generally consisted of a lieutenant, corporals, guards, and its own scribe, depending on the value and size of the administration. The guards traversed areas known to be locations of contraband production. Specific regulations outlined how the prosecution of *contrabandistas* was to be conducted. Confiscated goods or leaf were appraised before being destroyed. The guard responsible for the arrest generally received one-sixth of the total value of the goods confiscated.[6]

The *visitadores* (inspectors) concerned themselves with the management and affairs of the particular administrative districts which had been allocated to them primarily to encourage enforcement of monopoly regulations. Responsible for periodic assessments of the performance of the monopoly within their specific jurisdictions, they were also required to make recommendations for improvements.

Until the establishment of the intendancies in 1786, the monopoly *factores* served as judges in any legal suits related to the monopoly. Cases of fraud and contraband were tried, however, by the local magistrates, who were obliged to remit any such cases, along with transcripts of the case, to the *factores* for adjudication. Judgments made by the *factores* could be appealed and heard before an ad hoc *junta de tabaco*, the members of which comprised three *oidores* (judges) from the *audiencia*.[7] Monopoly employees and guards benefited from certain judicial exemptions. Any crimes committed by guards were reported to their commander who, in turn, reported the misdemeanor to the local *factor*. A royal order of 10 February 1790, however, declared that guards who committed crimes not related in any way to their duties were to be turned over to the civil legal authorities.[8]

The organization of the monopoly possessed something of the air of a modern corporation, not just with regard to the royal bureaucrats, but the tobacco planters and workers as well. Its structure provided rules for individual employee behavior. It bestowed upon its employees a quasi-*fuero* or corporate status which perhaps contributed to a sense of duty and loyalty to its functions. The monopoly motivated some of its employees to wax eloquent about its success. Joaquín Maniau Torquemada, a monopoly accountant, described the royal enterprise with some pride as "a true house of commerce and industry."[9] The organization of the monopoly described above changed little during the decades of Bourbon management. Changes did occur, however, in the identity of individuals and government institutions participating in monopoly policy formation at the highest levels. Before looking at the reasons for change and the consequences, we shall look more closely at these bureaucrats, their recruitment, working conditions, salaries and promotion, and performance.

We cannot say what percentage of the monopoly bureaucracy was composed of peninsular Spaniards, newly arrived from Spain, but we do know that they predominated in the highest ranking positions of *directores generales* and *contadores generales* and maintained this predominance until 1821. Recruitment of these bureaucrats was based on merit and competence. As the backgrounds of the appointees to the position of *director general* illustrate, this was defined as experience with either the tobacco trade or the tobacco monopoly. Hierro was recruited from the Spanish tobacco monopoly offices in Madrid. Espinosa, Frago, and Díaz de la Vega were all recruited from the tobacco monopoly and manufactory offices in Seville.[10] A clearly defined pattern of promotion existed between the post of *contador general* and *director general*. The positions shown on table 1 demonstrate that every *director general* (with the exception of Mendinueta and Monterde) occupied the position of *contador general* prior to promotion to *director general*.

Not much is known about the recruitment of the lower bureaucrats. The monopoly's *hojas de servicio* (service records), however, provide insight into the career patterns at the lower levels of the monopoly bureaucracy.[11] Service records were found for the administrations of Córdoba, Guadalajara, Mazapil, Mérida de Yucatán, Monterrey, Oaxaca, Orizaba, Puebla, Santander, Valladolid, and Veracruz. They cover the careers of the *factores, contadores*, administrators, inspectors, clerks, and *resguardo* guards for the years 1765 to 1799. What they suggest is the existence of a cadre of career bureaucrats who served the government in one capacity or another for their entire working lives, who gained experience in different offices, and who looked forward to the day when they would be promoted.

Transfers occurred among different government departments.[12] The accountant of the administration of Mérida de Yucatán served as administrator for Campeche for fifteen years before his transfer. The *oficial de libros* (bookkeeper) of the administration of Monterrey worked in the Querétaro tobacco manufactory for twelve years prior to his promotion.[13] Miguel Puchet, the Mexico City manufactory administrator, already possessed considerable experience of monopoly operations prior to his appointment as administrator. During eighteen years of service, beginning in 1768, he worked as *fiel de la tercena* (tobacco warehouse manager), and *oficial pagador* (cashier) in Puebla, and was promoted to administrator of the Puebla manufactory, where he served for five years before moving to the same position in the Mexico City manufactory.[14]

The service records also reflect the practice of transferring soldiers from the army or militia to the monopoly *resguardo* corps. In the case of a guard from Valladolid, his personnel records indicated twenty-seven years of employment by the monopoly, although seventeen of those were spent serving in the Regimiento de la Infantería de Asturias, not in the monopoly *resguardo*.[15] Positions in the monopoly bureaucracy were also used as rewards for loyal service to the government. The monopoly administrator of Guadalajara received his appointment after serving thirty-five years as captain in one of the royal regiments.[16]

Longevity of service stands out as a characteristic of monopoly employees in both high and low ranking positions. Hierro acquired a total of twenty-three years' experience; Díaz de la Vega, thirty-two years; Maniau y Ortega, eleven years; and Bernál de Quirós, eight years. For the lower ranks, the fiscal bureaucrats served, on average, a total of eighteen years.[17] Such service is especially notable among the *factores*. Of the seven listed, four had served the monopoly for thirty years and more, two for twenty-two and twenty-seven years. In the administration of Orizaba three of the highest ranking bureaucrats had all served together for at least forty years; all entered between 1765 and 1768 and, according to the service records, were still active in 1808. These were Buenaventura Mutis, the administrator of the manufactory, Gracían de Landagaray, *contador*, and Bernardo María de Mendiola, the *factor* of Orizaba.[18] The stability and longevity of bureaucratic service is consistent with the findings of Linda Arnold who argued that the viceregal bureaucracy of Mexico City experienced limited turnover, rarely more than 10 percent a year.[19]

How successful was the colonial state in isolating its bureaucratic managers from local society? It is difficult to say, since we have limited evidence, but the following observations may be made. First, we know that the majority of bureaucrats listed in the *hojas de servicio* were married (63 percent out of a total of 306) but we do not know whether they were married to local women despite government prohibitions against this.[20] Second, the co-optive strategy of recruiting merchants and tobacco shop owners already resident in Mexico automatically brought the potential of local influence into monopoly offices. Juan José de Echeveste and Francisco del Real, both peninsular merchants resident in Mexico City, received appointments to treasurer and inspector-general respectively. Juan de la Cuesta was appointed as the administrator-general of the general administration of Mexico after only five years in monopoly service, after a "life-time" in commerce.[21] As late as 1796, merchants were still being appointed to monopoly positions, evidently not through the normal promotion ladders. Joaquín Angulo Norrigaray, "a merchant by profession," received the appointment as *factor* of Guadalajara.[22] Third, the cadre of high-ranking monopoly bureaucrats may have been recruited on the basis of their knowledge and experience, but all of the peninsulars appointed to the position of *director general* and *contador general* already had links or developed links to the mercantile elite of Mexico City and Veracruz and possessed influential political contacts in both Spain and Mexico. After he left Seville, Francisco Maniau y Ortega settled in Jalapa, engaged in commerce, and became quite wealthy before his appointment to *contador general*. His son, Joaquín Maniau Torquemada, was the first creole to occupy the position of *director general*, after working as *oficial mayor* (chief clerk) and then *contador general* in Mexico City. Another son, Francisco Maniau Torquemada, a member of the Consulado de México, later became the Mexico City agent for the Consulado de Veracruz in 1799. Maniau's other two sons also occupied prominent positions in Mexico. José Nicolás, a priest, belonged to the Mexico City cathedral chapter. Ildefonso pursued careers in both business and government: he was appointed as a *contador mayor* (senior accountant) of the Tribunal de Cuentas and became head of the *contaduría* in late 1824.[23] José de la Riva Agüero was also the scion of an influential family and well-connected. One of his brothers sat on the Council of the Indies and another served as *contador general* of Indian tributes. Antonio del Frago was recruited in 1765, perhaps with the influence of his father-in-law, Rodrigo Antonio de Neyra, one of the wealthiest merchants in Mexico at the time, who died with an alleged fortune of over two million pesos.[24] Although we can identify the potential for corruption and influence peddling through the links between bureaucrats and the local society, particularly with the Mexico City elite, there is no compelling evidence that such family connections compromised their professional performance. Indeed, as one scholar has argued in the case of the Bourbon bureaucracy in Buenos Aires, "there is some suggestion that some bureaucrats with close family links to the local oligarchy were especially careful to conduct themselves in a more disinterested manner."[25]

The monopoly bureaucrats also appear to have been less vulnerable to co-optation by vested interests in Mexico because it is likely they were exempt from the payment of a *fianza* (bond). The practice of demanding *fianzas* proved to be one requirement of government service with contradictory consequences. *Fianzas* were traditionally requested of high-ranking bureaucrats to guarantee honesty among those responsible for large amounts of money, such as treasurers or accountants. These officials invariably turned to local merchants, the individuals most likely to have access to capital, to act as their *fiadores* (bondsmen). The problem, as pointed out in a recent work on the *alcabalas* (excise) administration in Mexico, was that the ties which such *fianza* relationships created could be exploited by the *fiador* to the detriment of government service.[26] The monopoly bureaucrats, however, appear to have been exempted from the presentation of a *fianza*. Indicative of Gálvez' apprehensions about the abuse created by the *fiador* system are the modifications he ordered implemented for the management of the monopoly in Buenos Aires. Gálvez informed the intendant that tobacco monopoly bureaucrats were to be exempted from posting such a bond so that "these ministers have no reason to be grateful to the merchants of that city, who are the only ones who are able to afford a bond and who will perhaps exact payment or special treatment because of the money that they have put forth."[27] As we saw in Chapter 1, as the first treasurer of monopoly revenues, Echeveste was required to post an initial bond of 12,000 pesos. In this case, however, Echeveste used his own capital, not another individual's—perhaps one of the reasons why a prosperous tobacco merchant was appointed in the first place.[28] The absence of additional discussion about or information on *fianzas*, however, suggests that an exemption similar to the one in the viceroyalty of the Río de la Plata was applied to the Mexican monopoly bureaucrats. Although the *fieles* and administrators were responsible for any losses (of money and stocks) due to robberies, the monopoly advanced them money to cover such losses, to be repaid at a later date.[29] The only employees formally required to have *fiadores* were the *estanquilleros*. This no doubt created opportunities for illicit deals with monopoly products.

By 1788, the state tobacco monopoly of Mexico employed 17,256 individuals, approximately 5,000 of whom were employed as bureaucrats, ancillary employees, and *estanquilleros*.[30] Despite modest salaries for the majority of bureaucratic posts, monopoly service exercised considerable attraction. A position as a royal bureaucrat endowed one with status, a guaranteed income, and a lifetime position. Positions in the monopoly were sought after at any level, but particularly at the middle and higher levels. When the position for administrator of the general administration of Mexico became vacant, there were 34 applicants, a mix of bureaucrats and private citizens. Included were the Mexico City manufactory administrator, the intendant-elect of the Philippines, a silver miner, and a Cádiz merchant.[31] The monopoly administration worked well for the most part and probably better than conditions warranted. The voluminous documentation, read with the most critical eye, reveals the workings of a fiscal agency which gathered up information about its transactions in minute detail, reported problems, discussed them, and made resolutions. Perhaps the most outstanding example of bureaucratic management in action (admittedly motivated by an impending loss of revenues) is provided by the rapid responses to reports of consumer distaste for the *nuevas labores* (cigarettes and cigars made using new, experimental methods) of 1780. The experiments were modified within the year. The particular situation is discussed at length in Chapter 5. There were problems with the day-to-day administration of such a large enterprise, however, and, as the century wore on and the monopoly's operations expanded, the peso-pinching mentality of the Crown and the unhappy mix of a traditional and a reformist imperial bureaucracy began to take its toll. The penurious condition of the Crown resulted in constant demands for reductions in bureaucratic staff to save on costs of administration. Neither monopoly bureaucrats nor the members of the *resguardo* were exempt from such cutbacks. Indeed, the persistent demand to reduce costs (one of the few consistencies in Bourbon policy) led to the amalgamation of the tobacco, playing card, sales tax, and gunpowder *resguardo* corps into one. As the Bourbons repeatedly discovered in many areas, efficiency was expensive and required investments they were simply unwilling to make.

Salaries of the monopoly bureaucrats, as shown in table 2, spanned a wide range between the upper and lower bureaucracy. *Directores generales* were well-compensated with a yearly salary of 6,000 pesos. Bureaucrats in the provinces received salaries pegged lower than those of the general administration of Mexico. Indeed, there were slight regional variations in the salaries earned by officials employed in similar positions. Such discrepancies occurred primarily because of the value placed upon particular administrations or as a result of successful petitions from employees for salary increases. Between 1765 and 1799, *factores* received a basic salary of 2,000 pesos. Some *factores* received supplementary salaries for their management of other branches of royal revenues combined with that of tobacco. The *factor* of Guadalajara, for example, earned 4,000 pesos annually: 2,000 pesos for supervision of stamped paper sales, combined with his monopoly salary of 2,000 pesos.[32] Regional *contadores* earned 1,200 pesos; the *tesoreros* employed in the administrations of Guadalajara and Valladolid received annual salaries of 1,700 pesos. In-

Table 2.   Salaries of Monopoly Bureaucrats of the Dirección General and the General Administration of Mexico, 1768–1825 (in current pesos)

Position	1768	1775	1788	1799	1825
Dirección General					
Director			5,000	6,000	6,000
Tesorero		3,000	3,000	3,000	
Asesor			1,500	1,500	
Escribano			500	500	
Proveedor					1,600
Portero			600		
Contaduría General					
Contador and Director	6,000				
Contador	3,000	3,000	4,000	4,000	
Oficial Mayor	2,000	2,000	2,500	2,500	
Oficial Segundo	1,500	1,500	2,000	2,000	
Oficial Tercero		900	1,500	1,500	
Administración General del Arzobispado de México					
Administrador Principal	3,000	4,000	4,000	4,000	4,000
Administrador de Estanquillos		2,200	2,200	2,200	
Fiel Administrador		1,200	1,600	1,600	
Fiel de Peso		1,000	1,350	1,350	
Contador		1,500	1,500	1,500	
Visitador		1,000	1,000	1,000	
Interventor	600			500	
Tercenista	500	800	800		
Escribano			400		
Oficial de Libros	800	1,000	1,000		
Escribiente		500	600	600	

Source: Arnold, *Bureaucracy and Bureaucrats,* information from Table A.13, Salaries of Positions in the Renta de Tabaco, pp. 144–145; for 1788, BN (Madrid), Mss 10.361, Fonseca and Urrutia, *Libro de la Real Hacienda,* vol. 7, f. 67.

spectors were paid 1,000 pesos, *resguardo* lieutenants, 800 pesos, corporals, 600 pesos, and guards, 500 pesos annually. Lower level officials such as *tercenistas* (wholesalers) and *fieles* earned between 450 and 800 pesos.[33]

Irrespective of rank, salaries for the most part remained flat during the late eighteenth and early nineteenth centuries. The first increases noted were in 1812, but they were few and occurred at the highest-ranking levels of *director general* and *tesorero*. For the rest, the salaries changed little, as table 2 shows. This was the case for the Mexican colonial bureaucracy as a whole and for bureaucrats in other parts of the Spanish empire.[34] Consequently, like the rest of the colonial population, monopoly bureaucrats were subject to the effects of inflation and increasing hardship of the late eighteenth century. This did not provide solace to these bureaucrats, particularly the *oficiales* whose workload increased while their income decreased.

Monopoly bureaucrats were not passive in the face of their problems, particularly their immobile salaries, and resorted to a variety of strategies to rectify them, strategies which ranged from the diffident presentation of petitions to the more assertive act of fraud. In 1787 the twenty-eight *oficiales* of the *contaduría general* petitioned for an increase in salary due to the increasingly high cost of living in Mexico City and the difficulties of supporting a family. Although the *dirección general* recommended and approved the salary increases, the decision was overruled by the king due to the increasing debts of the Crown.[35] In what appeared to be a recognition of the worsening financial situation of some of the bureaucrats, a royal order which prohibited employees of revenue departments from participating in private trade or commerce exempted monopoly employees in those *fielatos* which did not yield more than 1,000 pesos in profits. However, those not situated in such administrations remained subject to the prohibitions.[36]

The extent of corruption among monopoly bureaucrats is unknown, but several cases of fraud and embezzlement of monopoly funds provide limited evidence of its occurrence. Francisco de Bustamente began his service as administrator of the district of Guanajuato in 1766. Forty years later, in 1805, he was suspended after certain "errors" were discovered in his accounts. With a fixed stipend of 1,600 pesos, various "commissions" had increased his receipts to over 6,000 pesos.[37] Don Angel Antelo, the administrator of the combined tobacco, gunpowder, and playing card monopolies of Real de los Alamos, Sonora, was the central character in a case which began in 1773 and dragged on until 1797. The case concerned 9,000 pesos of monopoly money which had been found missing and Antelo's violation of ecclesiastical immunity when he imprisoned a priest for contraband activities. Antelo was finally imprisoned and his possessions embargoed and sold to replace the embezzled 9,000 pesos.[38] In 1779, a *regidor* (town councillor) of Veracruz and the *factor* of the monopoly were charged with fraud and embezzlement of 18,000 pesos in cash and 5,000 pesos worth of cigars and cigarettes. The *factor* was placed under house arrest. Shortly afterwards, both the local *contador* and *fiel de almacenes* (tobacco warehouse manager) were suspended from their duties as accomplices.[39]

Even the highest colonial official in the land, the king's personal representative, the viceroy, was not immune. Viceroy Iturrigaray, along with his wife, was charged, among other things, with "selling" contracts to individuals to supply paper to the tobacco manufactories in return for commissions in 1806 and 1807. The purchase price agreed upon was 12 pesos per ream, but the stocks were bought up at 13 pesos per ream, the extra peso pocketed by the viceroy and his wife. The viceregal pair was ordered to repay the total amount received.[40]

What is striking about these cases is that they were perpetrated not by those low-ranking clerks who would have felt the pinch of inflation the hardest but by the middle-ranking bureaucrats who had the ambition to be wealthier than their bureaucratic salaries permitted and the opportunity and influence to carry out such acts. There is no evidence that the rank-and-file monopoly bureaucrats participated in graft and fraud. This may be because they had little or nothing to offer.[41]

Low salaries took their toll on bureaucratic efficiency, but "efficiency" as such was questionable even in the early stages of the monopoly's operation. In the explanatory notes to a general summary of accounts for the years 1765–1774, there was a comment which stated simply: "not being able to find [the money] in the coffers of the monopoly . . . more than half a million pesos is missing . . . we do not know how, nor where it has been spent."[42] Cold comfort, indeed, for historians of the royal fisc. As government use of monopoly revenues increased, the accounts became more diversified and complicated, all of which generated masses of paperwork. The collection, processing, and auditing of accounts fell behind. A report submitted by the *director general* in 1792 showed that out of a current batch of 337 monopoly accounts, only 123 were partially or fully audited; the remainder had not been touched.[43] By the beginning of the nineteenth century, the *contador general* protested, "Due to the insufficient salaries, very few of the clerks are competent or care for their work; those that do are ill from overwork, and there exists a serious backlog in the accounts."[44]

The *dirección general* submitted petitions to increase the number of bureaucrats and their salaries beginning in 1799 and was still submitting petitions in 1806 to no avail.[45] While the *dirección general* demanded more bureaucrats if competent management was to continue, Spain demanded less. Orders from Madrid in 1799 called for a reduction in personnel. Policies to reduce the number of bureaucrats, refusal to increase salaries, and the revocation of traditional exemptions enjoyed by the monopoly employees could not help but contribute to low levels of morale and standards of work.

The *resguardo* provides a case in point. In 1782 the total number employed in the *resguardo* corps for all of Mexico (including all ranks and substitutes) amounted to 300, a woefully inadequate number to carry out the ambitious aims of the *dirección general*.[46] Granted they were supposed to be aided in their duties by "vigilant" and loyal magistrates, but their task was doomed from the beginning by the expectation of so much from so little. Even in the most sensitive of regions, the tobacco producing *villas* of Córdoba and Orizaba, there was no significant increase over the years in the number of guards appointed to combat contraband production. In Orizaba, for example, the total number of guards actually decreased from 37 in 1782 to 32 in 1788. In Córdoba, there was a similar trend as the total number of guards declined from 38 in 1788 to 27 in 1805.[47]

Low wages, according to the inspector-general Francisco del Real, were disastrous for the maintenance of an effective guard, as "all find themselves indebted, poorly clothed, poorly fed, with their horses in an equally miserable condition."[48] It was not just low wages which undermined the *resguardo*'s efficiency. Overwork, uncooperative local officials, and contradictory support for their police actions all combined to produce a less than efficient and perhaps erratically violent *resguardo* force, which, as we saw in Chapter 1, aroused hostility in the general populace. Given the nature of their duties, opportunities for corruption were ample but, like other bureaucratic employees, guards were accountable for their actions. To disprove allegations of fraud on his part against the monopoly, the *dirección general* ordered one guard to describe his activities and itemize his expenditures in a daily journal while on an expedition in pursuit of smugglers.[49]

The monopoly bureaucrats perhaps were better at policing one another than they were the rest of the population. Monopoly employees brought to the attention of the *dirección general* "violations" in procedure. In so doing, they were actively engaged in upholding the established rules against nepotism and corruption and in protecting their rights, their jurisdiction, and their honor. Positions which came open, which technically were to be filled according to established rules of promotion, could be and were used as sinecures for private citizens whom the Crown wished to reward as an act of patronage. The inconsistency of appointment and promotion criteria did not go unnoticed, particularly when the expected route of seniority and merit was violated by the *dirección general*.

One of the most controversial cases, at least from the perspective of the *oficiales* in the central accounts section in Mexico City, concerned the appointment of Joaquín Maniau, the son of the *contador general* Francisco Maniau, to the position of *oficial mayor*. The *oficiales* pointed to Joaquín's lack of experience and the fact that the appointment violated promotional procedure (although according to bureaucratic transfer regulations, it did not), and argued that it presented too great a risk for impartial management of monopoly funds. If the *director general* became indisposed for some reason, temporary power passed to the *contador general* and the *oficial mayor*; in this case, it would result in the concentration of power in the hands of father and son.[50]

Perhaps the outrage experienced by the *oficiales* in the *contaduría* becomes clearer if we consider the glacial pace of upward promotion within their ranks. By 1815 the *contaduría* in Mexico City employed twenty-five clerks. Don Pedro Caravera, fifty-three years old, single, and undoubtedly very weary, would have risen to the position of *oficial mayor* had it not been for the promotion of Joaquín Maniau. Caravera began his career in the *contaduría* as *oficial 24* in 1777; it had taken him thirty-eight years to climb up the ladder to *oficial segundo*, only to be thwarted at the last minute. Don Antonio Urizar possessed virtually the same record. He entered as *oficial 24* in 1778 and thirty-seven years later, at the age of fifty-six, reached the rank of *oficial tercero*.[51] Any outside promotions not only served to slow down a bureaucrat's career but possibly eliminated forever, after a lifetime of service, the chance to reach the highest rank on the ladder and the salary which accompanied it.

Monopoly bureaucrats also proved to be their own best, if biased, critics. Although born out of factionalism, the rumbling of egos, and elbowing for promotion, the submission of "projects" to improve the monopoly's performance illustrates the competitiveness fostered within the bureaucracy. Don José Pelleramo drew attention to himself when he criticized the general ineptness of monopoly employees, the protection of such "ineptness," and incursions upon his "powers" as administrator-general. Pelleramo, in his quest to prove his point, submitted several calculations which "proved" the monopoly was far from reaching its potential. By 1783, according to his calculations, the monopoly had lost some nine million pesos.[52] The *contador general* viewed such "statistics" as nonsense, not without reason, and dismissed Pelleramo's allegations. After fifteen years of complaints, counter-complaints, and fractious involvement, José

Pelleramo was dismissed from his position as administrator-general of Mexico City. Pelleramo was not alone in his perspective that the monopoly was not as profitable as it should be. Carlos López, a candidate for the new directorship of the monopoly during the troubled times of the insurgency, based his recommendations for improvement and renovation of the monopoly on the premise that it was not that the monopoly had experienced a decline in its revenues, but that it had never reached its potential in the first place.[53]

Linda Arnold argues that the Mexican viceregal bureaucracy maintained a high morale and a strong esprit de corps.[54] While we would agree that there certainly is evidence of the existence of an esprit de corps, bureaucratic morale was subject to a good deal of wear and tear. At the very least, low salaries for the majority of monopoly bureaucrats and manipulation of a promotional process which combined rational and patrimonial procedures could only lead to low morale, and, if not alienation, then certainly frustration. The most taxing problem for the monopoly bureaucracy, however, came not so much from the individuals with all their hopes and disappointments, loyalties, and frailties, but from internal institutional conflict between the monopoly and the Tribunal de Cuentas which undermined the powers of the *dirección general.*

The major change in monopoly administration and management occurred in the critical area of policy formation and the composition of the administrative bodies responsible for such decisions. Originally, a significant characteristic of the monopoly was its autonomy vis-a-vis the Real Hacienda and Tribunal de Cuentas. Following the ministerial reorganization after Gálvez' death in 1787, the monopoly began to lose its autonomy in policy formation and implementation, becoming increasingly subordinated to the Tribunal de Cuentas; at the same time, monopoly administrators' and *factores'* regional authority was diluted by the intendancy system.[55]

Royal orders of 26 April, 1765, and 25 February, 1777, decreed that neither ministers of the Real Hacienda nor of the Tribunal de Cuentas were to intervene directly or indirectly with the affairs of the monopoly. The monopoly remained autonomous in policy formation and fiscal audit, although all policy decisions were ultimately to be approved by the *superintendencia general subdelegado de Real Hacienda y Dirección* in conjunction with the *contaduría general.* With the deaths of Gálvez in 1787 and Charles III in 1788, modification of some of the visitor-general's political creations began. The office of the *superintendente subdelegado* was reunited with the office of the viceroy, and the *junta superior de Real Hacienda* (chief finance committee) emerged as the central authority in exchequer and intendancy affairs, forming a committee which possessed the power to implement its decisions. In 1792, under the watchful eye of the viceroy Revillagigedo and at his suggestion, the Crown ordered the Tribunal de Cuentas to examine the accounts of the tobacco monopoly. Díaz de la Vega, as *director general*, complained that the Tribunal de Cuentas' objective was to convert its function of audit into that of executive authority over monopoly affairs. This central court of audit was notorious for its fiscal conservatism and its opposition to risky and expensive reforms. Díaz de la Vega's predecessor, Felipe de Hierro, had already attempted to circumvent the court's participation in the budgeting of tobacco revenues and departmental personnel matters. He had requested that the viceroy assume all responsibility for decisions related to internal management of the monopoly. After Hierro retired, Díaz de la Vega took up the fight to maintain departmental autonomy, only to experience the Council of the Indies' refusal to approve his request to preserve monopoly autonomy. The Tribunal de Cuentas' auditing and consultative functions were upheld, and in 1806 the Council of the Indies ordered that it should participate in all significant decisions which affected fiscal affairs, including those of the monopoly.[56]

The establishment of the intendancy system in Mexico served to weaken, rather than strengthen, lines of authority and jurisdiction. In December of 1786 the Ordenanzas de Intendentes were finally promulgated, designed to reform colonial administration at the central, provincial, and district levels.[57] Twelve intendancies were set up which matched to some degree the monopoly administrations. The intendants possessed broad powers. They served as the chief executive officers in provincial government, responsible for the implementation of all royal decrees and viceregal edicts; in fiscal affairs they acted as the chief provincial officers. Any complaints or suits which arose in a local branch of revenue or from its officers went to the intendants for adjudication. The *dirección general*, monopoly administrators, and *factores* found themselves enmeshed in a confused bureaucratic structure, as intendancy and monopoly objectives clashed and lines of authority became crossed as "the intendancy served as a true intermediary authority. For this reason the directors of the excise and the tobacco monopoly resented and attacked the powers of the intendants even more than the *audiencia*."[58]

Conflict over policies and decisions which affected the monopoly clearly exacerbated the antagonisms between the *directores generales*, the intendants, and the ministers of the Tribunal de Cuentas, given the new restrictions on the independence of the *directores generales.* From the early 1790s, attempts to reform and develop the monopoly to adjust to changing political and economic conditions by the *dirección general* were stifled, but not without a fight. Restraint, not risk, was encouraged by the Tribunal de Cuentas, a reflection of wider changes occurring in imperial administration, which favored "a policy of restraint in taxation . . . and to more civil behaviour towards colonists."[59] This provides a perfect example of the contradictions of Bourbon reform policy and the conflict it engendered. After the 1790s, the monopoly was caught between the modernity of the intendancy system and the conservatism of the Tribunal de Cuentas. This represented possibly the worst mix of Hapsburg and Bourbon agencies of political and fiscal management and reduced the *dirección general*'s powers.

Recent studies of the Bourbon reform of its imperial bureaucracy are mixed in their conclusions. On the one hand, some historians view the outcome as relatively successful. D. A. Brading describes the Bourbon achievement as a "revolution in government." Linda Arnold argues that the professionalization of the Mexican bureaucracy at the viceregal level not only served the interests of the Crown, but also successfully tied the interests of the viceregal bureaucrats to those of the Crown, such that "within the bureaucracy of empire the state became an end in itself."[60] Linda Salvucci, on the other hand, suggests that the reforms may have introduced "new men," but they retained the "old ways."[61] She argues that Gálvez' "new men" did not behave much differently than their discredited predecessors. Corruption and co-optation of various sorts continued to plague the bureaucracy, and the attempts of the Bourbons to create an autonomous, impartial state bureaucracy failed. In the case of the viceroyalty of the Río de la Plata, Susan Migden Socolow argues that the major stumbling block to the creation of a rational bureaucracy was the colonial state itself. At best, ambivalent, at worst, hostile to its own bureaucratic creation, the colonial state consequently undermined efficient administration.[62] The bureaucrats of the tobacco monopoly certainly cannot be described as representing a "revolution in government." They were not necessarily impartial or immune to corruption, but their actions and performance suggest that they carried out their responsibilities and developed a vested interest in the colonial state, which made them something more than new men behaving in old ways. The monopoly bureaucrats constituted a core of professional bureaucrats who viewed their own interests and careers as synonymous with those of the monopoly's operations and survival. The surprise is not that they fell short of the ideal of honest, efficient state servants but that they carried out their duties as well as they did, given the context of their actions. Migden Socolow's contention that the colonial state undermined its own bureaucratic agencies aptly characterizes the position of the Mexican tobacco monopoly and its bureaucratic managers. The level of revenues from the sale of tobacco products depended in some measure on the effectiveness of the monopoly bureaucracy as managers of the monopoly. We turn now to an examination of monopoly finances between 1765 and 1810.

Between 1765 and 1810 monopoly gross revenues increased from 1,417,846 pesos to 9,558,697 pesos (current pesos), an annual compound rate of growth of 4.4 percent; profits grew by 6.3 percent (239,097 pesos to 3,579,950 pesos), while costs of production grew by only 3.3 percent (1,178,748 pesos to 5,078,747 pesos).[63] If we measure the period 1778–1809, when all private trade and manufacture of tobacco goods had been eliminated, then the growth figures are less dramatic: the growth of total revenues remains respectable at 1.98 percent per year, costs exhibit a steady 2 percent growth, but profits grew more slowly at 1.21 percent per year. (See Appendix I for a listing of the specific figures.) Figures 1 and 2 show the proportionate changes experienced in the growth trends of monopoly revenues, costs, and profits; table 3 demonstrates the changes in revenues, costs, and profits in pesos quinquennially between 1765 and 1810.

Table 3. *Revenues, Costs, and Profits of the Royal Tobacco Monopoly, by Quinquennium, 1765–1810 (in current pesos)*

Quinquennium	Total Revenues	Total Costs	Profits
1765–70	8,269,070	5,007,999	3,261,070
1771–75	15,286,410	9,749,814	5,536,547
1776–80	24,403,853	12,870,319	11,533,535
1781–85	32,223,503	16,098,419	16,125,083
1786–90	30,554,396	14,627,269	15,927,127
1791–95	33,377,941	15,765,969	17,611,973
1796–1800	38,203,242	19,104,878	19,098,361
1801–05	39,770,617	20,074,224	19,696,392
1806–09*	37,153,764	22,135,279	15,018,544

*Four years only.
(Detail may not add up to total because of rounding)

As figure 1 shows, the sharpest and most accelerated period of growth between 1768 and 1785 incorporates the transition from a combination of private and public to public management and monopolization of the tobacco trade in Mexico. The period 1786–1810 shows a much slower, modest trend upwards, but with an acceleration between 1805 and 1810. This period witnessed a steady expansion in supply to match a demand stimulated by the expansion in commerce after the promulgation of the *comercio libre* decree in 1786. The period 1786–1789 shows a slight downturn, as demand was reduced following the effects of Mexico's horrendous famine of 1786. Despite its devastating aftermath, causing a short term reverse in the general trend, there was a quick recovery. The downturn between 1799 and 1804 occurred because of reduced supply due to shortages of paper between 1798 and 1802. External political problems were just as much to blame for the levels of manufactory production as were domestic constraints. Spain's war with Great Britain weakened the monopoly's operations and illustrated the vulnerability of the monopoly to breakdown because of its reliance on imports of paper from the Peninsula. British naval blockades between 1796 and 1802 virtually crippled paper shipments from Spanish paper manufactories to Mexico; output decreased, as did inventory stocks, which were drawn upon heavily to compensate for reduced production. The response, as we shall see in Chapter 3, was to stockpile paper. Renewed British blockades between 1804 and 1808 failed to be so disruptive to manufactory output, but profits suffered due to the continued stockpiling of paper supplies. Underlying the stable secular upward trend in revenues was Mexico's increasing prosperity and expansion in commerce, mining, and, above all, its demographic growth, which helped to raise total demand between 1765 and 1810.

Figure 2 shows the change in the relationship between profits and costs of production, and the expansion in the latter after 1796. Between 1799 and 1809, profits showed very little growth at 0.4 percent. Conversely, costs of production grew at an annual compound rate of 1.9 percent for the same period. By the mid-1790s, total costs were growing at a faster pace than total revenues. The sharp upturn in the costs curve after 1800 was largely due to bulk purchases of paper and increases in the purchase price of tobacco. Producing cigars and cigarettes, like many other products, particularly silver, was simply getting more expensive in the late colonial economy.

The growth rates of monopoly revenues are commensurate with general estimates of the rate of growth in government revenues calculated by scholars in recent years. Richard Garner, for example, es-

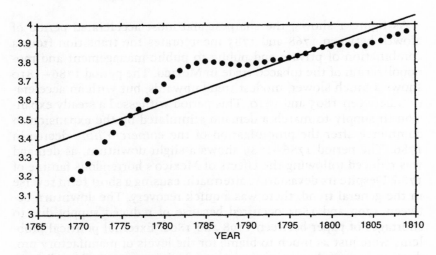

Figure 1. Total monopoly revenues, 1765–1810 (five-year moving average). *Source:* see Chapter 2, note 63.

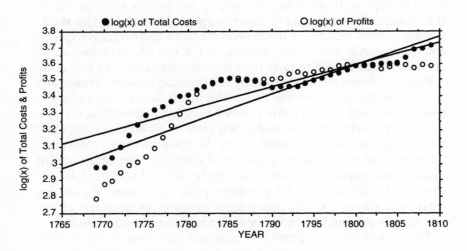

Figure 2. Total costs and profits of monopoly, 1765–1810 (five-year moving average). *Source:* see Chapter 2, note 63.

timates that revenues rose 2.2 percent between 1701 and 1755 and 3.1 percent between 1756 and 1809. He argues that "The acceleration in growth during the second half of the eighteenth century is related to the changing treasury operations in those late decades."[64] But where do monopoly revenues fit into the structure of government finances, and what role did they play in the growth of domestic and peninsular government revenues? Before looking at this question in greater detail, we will examine the regional distribution of monopoly revenues and the breakdown of monopoly costs of production.

In his *Ensayo político sobre el reino de la Nueva España*, Alexander von Humboldt calculated that the majority of the population of New Spain was concentrated in the five intendancies of Mexico, Guadalajara, Guanajuato, Puebla, and Valladolid, and that these provinces carried "the major part of the costs of the State."[65] As a consequence, it is not surprising to find that they provided the major share of monopoly revenues. Although the monopoly produced for all of the geographical territory of Mexico, including the far northern frontier zones of California, New Mexico, and Texas, the most lucrative markets developed within a very clearly defined central-northwest area. This area encompassed the central valley of Mexico, an area of diverse regional economies, from the rich agricultural heartland of the Bajío to the lucrative mining zones of the north. Table 4 shows quite clearly that, out of the fifteen administrative divisions, five accounted for the production of the majority of revenues. The administration-general of Mexico, Valladolid, Guadalajara, Puebla, and Durango together accounted for 87 percent of all revenues between 1776 and 1800.[66]

The breakdown of costs in table 5 illustrates the stable and changing components of monopoly costs. Fixed costs, made up of administration (salaries and rents), amounted to an average of between 23 and 25 percent, while variable costs, made up of raw materials (paper and tobacco), manufacture (predominantly labor), transport, *alcabalas*, and imports from Havana, accounted for the lion's share of between 75 and 77 percent. The majority of variable costs were accounted for, however, by raw materials and manufacture, between 61 and 75 percent of total variable costs. The dramatic change of the percentage share in the cost of paper supplies and purchases is self-evident. Up until the disastrously expensive war with Britain between 1796 and 1802, paper comprised some 2 percent of total monopoly expenditure; by 1800, it accounted for a staggering 25 percent (on an individual yearly basis), the result of bulk purchases of paper at high prices. Transport averaged 8 percent of costs, although hidden transportation costs in the shipments of paper from Spain, which

Table 4. Distribution of Profits According to Administration in Quinquennia, 1766–1800 (in current pesos)

Adminis-tration	1766–1770	%	1771–1775	%	1776–1780	%	1781–1785	%	1786–1790	%	1791–1795	%	1796–1800	%
Mexico	480,890	36	775,304	30	1,227,621	30	1,445,481	29	1,130,978	24	1,407,757	26	1,578,647	25
Valladolid	333,744	25	591,204	23	982,044	24	1,320,568	27	1,211,698	22	1,328,808	24	1,507,499	24
Guadalajara	240,702	18	425,448	17	747,935	19	856,698	17	1,035,415	22	1,219,766	22	1,413,786	22
Puebla	73,893	6	208,786	8	293,718	7	415,846	8	401,839	8	396,293	7	521,004	8
Durango	73,993	6	189,331	7	279,129	7	326,636	7	319,689	7	409,848	7	497,012	8
Rosario	—		79,685	3	140,814	4	171,140	3	172,638	4	199,619	4	217,821	3
Oaxaca	54,859	4	105,251	4	118,302	3	151,189	3	143,958	3	157,989	3	207,710	3
Veracruz	23,657	2	60,043	2	74,203	2	15,215	1	124,798	3	138,870	3	191,847	3
Monterrey	12,936	1	43,133	2	53,942	1	69,341	1	81,698	2	88,295	2	91,388	1
Santander	6,674	1	31,031	1	46,900	1	60,657	1	60,657	1	68,628	1	70,732	1
Coahuila	9,934	1	14,983	1	21,940	1	26,701	1	31,510	1	37,768	1	41,943	1
Merida	12,629	1	18,591	1	19,297	1	17,510	1	17,551	1	14,416	0.5	18,513	0.5
Mazapil	—		11,489	1	12,909	1	15,336	0.5	13,571	1	15,800	0.5	17,964	0.5
Orizaba & Córdoba operate at losses														

Source: Compiled from individual accounts of each administration, AGN, Tabaco 466, report of Díaz de la Vega, 23 August 1797, for years 1766–1795; AGN, Tabaco 151, 120, 160, 38, 28, 31, 21, 54, 509, for years 1796–1800.
[Totals may not add up to 100 because of rounding]

Table 5. Breakdown and Distribution of Total Costs of Tobacco Monopoly, 1776–1809 (in current pesos)

Quin-quennium	Administrative Salaries	Rentals	Transport	Cost of Leaf Tobacco	Cost of Paper & Shipping	Cigars & Rapé from Cuba	Alcabala	Costs of Labor & Manufacture
1776–1780	3,092,068 (23%)	344,677 (2%)	1,159,834 (9%)	3,004,704 (23%)	437,084 (3%)	94,268 (1%)	278,298 (2%)	4,910,266 (37%)
1781–1785	3,642,173 (23%)	280,440 (2%)	1,173,075 (7%)	4,068,392 (25%)	685,438 (4%)	81,078 (1%)	346,121 (2%)	5,821,685 (36%)
1786–1790	3,534,029 (24%)	271,419 (2%)	1,142,595 (8%)	3,725,021 (25%)	157,933 (1%)	83,901 (1%)	124,971 (1%)	5,587,231 (38%)
1791–1795	3,679,566 (23%)	335,743 (2%)	1,009,907 (6%)	4,847,022 (31%)	164,255 (1%)	71,736 (1%)	100,205 (1%)	5,557,518 (35%)
1796–1800	4,041,615 (21%)	353,511 (2%)	1,213,110 (6%)	4,329,227 (23%)	3,372,004 (18%)	66,170 (0.5%)	255,299 (1%)	5,473,924 (29%)
1801–1805	4,128,848 (21%)	371,277 (2%)	1,756,286 (9%)	5,067,709 (25%)	1,735,413 (9%)	88,529 (0.5%)	249,638 (1%)	6,625,507 (33%)
1806–1809*	3,713,405 (17%)	219,293 (1%)	1,236,617 (6%)	6,488,058 (29%)	4,096,492 (19%)	59,747 (0.5%)	173,085 (1%)	6,049,509 (27%)

Source: AGI, AGN, *Relaciones generales;* Tabla 1, Tabla que demuestra las ventas, los gastos y las utilidades sobre el tabaco, November 1843, R. C. Wyllie, "México. Noticia sobre su hacienda pública bajo el gobierno español y después de la Independencia." In *Documentos para el estudio de la industrialización en México, 1837–1845,* ed. G. B. Robinson, pp. 348–349.

*Four years only.

(Totals may not add up to 100 because of rounding)

are not itemized separately, mean that the percentage figure errs on the low side. The policies developed to accomplish cheap and regular supplies of raw materials and the problems inherent in these policies are considered in Chapter 3.

The ratio of variable to fixed costs was high and ranged between 4:1 and 10:1. With the exception of the construction of the first publicly financed tobacco manufactory, completed in 1807, buildings for manufactories, warehouses, administrative offices, and residences were all rented and never exceeded 2 percent of total costs.[67] The *estanquillos* belonged to, or were rented by, the licensees at no cost to the monopoly other than the commissions paid to the distributors; transport was acquired, like leaf tobacco, on a contract basis with muleteer teams, but with no investment in securing the monopoly's own transport. The state was not prepared to invest very much in the monopoly and it was with some accuracy that Lucas Alamán described the Bourbon tobacco monopoly as "a large industrial speculation."[68]

We return now to the question of monopoly revenues, their expenditure, and functions. Technically, the Mexican tobacco monopoly revenues formed part of the *masa remisible*, funds which were not to be used for government spending in Mexico but shipped directly to Spain. Scholars of the fiscal history of colonial Mexico have somewhat uncritically accepted contemporary descriptions that tobacco moneys were shipped en masse, but it is evident from an examination of monopoly accounts that this was not always the case.[69] The extant monopoly accounts show that Mexican monopoly revenues functioned in various ways, over and above production of hard cash for Spain, which incorporated metropolitan, domestic, and intercolonial needs. Such functions ranged from the subsidization of other American tobacco monopolies and participation in the credit market of colonial Mexico to debt servicing of the Real Hacienda of New Spain.

There is no question that Mexican tobacco revenues became a significant, reliable, and much needed source of government income. Between 1776 and 1809 monopoly revenues accounted for between 12 and 22 percent of total state revenues (in current pesos).[70] One of the more astute viceroys of Mexico, Revillagigedo the Younger, expressed his recognition of the monopoly's fiscal contribution: "Of all the articles monopolized, there are few in which private persons would not make more profit than does the king . . . This would not be true . . . in the tobacco revenue, for it would be very hard to substitute any other measures which would produce so much revenue."[71]

The tobacco trade in general proved to be a critical source of government income both in Spain and throughout its empire. Revenues earned from the tobacco monopoly in Spain accounted for an average of 28 percent of the peninsula's total public domestic revenues.[72] The tobacco monopolies of Spanish America collectively made significant contributions to Crown revenues, making their survival all the more important. It was the Mexican monopoly which played a pivotal role in the financing of an empire-wide tobacco monopoly. The statistics for trade between Spain and Spanish America for the years 1778–1796, the period of *comercio libre* (free trade), provide an insight into the contribution of Spain's American tobacco monopolies to royal revenues. Shipments of tobacco leaf imported into Cádiz on behalf of the Crown monopolies represented an estimated 13.6 percent (72,850,000 pesos) of the total value of imports for the period, the second-most valuable single source of revenue. The single-most valuable source was made up of imports of gold and silver on the Crown's behalf, which accounted for 14.5 percent of the total value of commodities imported into Cádiz between 1782 and 1796. Within this category of gold and silver imports, the Mexican tobacco monopoly played its role. Assuming that the silver from monopoly sales in Mexico is included in the gold and silver shipped on the Crown's account, then the *reported* value of silver from monopoly sales for the same period between 1782 and 1796 made up almost 22 percent of the total amount of gold and silver shipped.[73] It is unlikely that royal ministers possessed any accurate sense of the real contribution of tobacco to government income, but they recognized its strategic importance and tried to ensure that the American tobacco monopolies received adequate financing.

Annual subsidies or transfers of money were taken out of Mexican monopoly receipts and sent to Cuba, Louisiana, and, on occasion, Santo Domingo, for purchases of tobacco leaf for the Seville and Madrid manufactories. By the late 1790s about 3,500,000 pesos had been transferred to Cuba, and, between 1786 and 1795, 1,049,981 pesos were shipped to Louisiana. The Mexican monopoly effectively acted as a banking mechanism, the funds from which were used to help finance other tobacco monopolies and ensure supplies of tobacco leaf to the Spanish manufactories.

A general assessment of the disbursement of monopoly revenues earned between 1765 and 1795 shows that, out of a total of 69,207,799 pesos, 64 percent of that amount was reported as having been shipped directly to Spain; "loans" to the Real Hacienda and debt servicing accounted for 29 percent, the annual payments to Cuba and Louisiana for tobacco shipments to Seville accounted for 5.5 percent, while the remaining 0.5 percent was spent on materials for the con-

Table 6. *Amounts of Silver Reported Shipped to Spain in the First Four Months of Each Year (in current pesos)*

Year	Amount	% of Total Annual Profits
1786 (for 1785)	1,474,391	44.8
1787 (1786)	912,936	29.5
1788 (1787)	2,000,000	68.4
1789 (1788)	2,009,996	69.1
1790 (1789)	1,730,131	47.9
1791 (1790)	1,030,467	30.3
1792 (1791)	403,773	11.7
1793 (1792)	1,250,000	33.6
1794 (1793)	2,484,262	72.5

Source: Report of Maniau y Ortega, 30 April 1794, AGN, Tabaco 452.

struction of the Mexico City state tobacco manufactory.[74] All these proportions remain roughly the same for the late eighteenth and early nineteenth century, as shown in table 7, with the exception of 1802, when no revenues were shipped to Spain. War resulted in the revenues being spent in the colony itself.

On an annual basis, between 1786 and 1794, shipments of monopoly revenues in silver reported as sent to Spain within the first four months of each year ranged from a low of 11.7 percent of annual profits to a high of 72.5 percent, as shown in table 6. The range may be accounted for by variations in shipping, relative amounts retained in Mexico for the purposes described above, or simply by the possibility that some of the figures, such as the low of 11.7 percent, represent only a partial shipment for the year in question. Bourbon accounts do have something of an alchemic quality to them. As we have been cautioned recently, account totals and annual income were not the same.[75]

The breakdown of the expenditure and distribution of monopoly moneys for selected years (presented in table 7) reflects the varied uses of monopoly funds, and, at the same time, an increase in the amounts from monopoly revenues which remained in the colony.[76] The use of monopoly funds also indicates the monopoly's increasingly important banking function in an economy in which coin was always in short supply, and in which there existed no formal banking institutions.

The late eighteenth and early nineteenth century saw the expansion of the role of corporate and state bodies such as the Consulado

Table 7. Distribution of Monopoly Profits (in current pesos) (selected years)

Year	Remittances to Spain (Amounts reported)	%	Domestic Loans, Interest Repayments	%	Havana, Louisiana	%	Construction Costs of Royal Tobacco Manufactory	%	Total Profits
1793	2,679,498	78	492,000	14	73,166	2	171,426	5	3,416,090
1796	3,339,853	85	341,902	9	189,166	5	65,304	2	3,936,225
1797	1,569,410	42	2,118,454	56	75,666	2	10,292	0.2	3,773,822
1800	1,399,166	41	2,013,434	59	N/R	—	2,528	0.07	3,415,128
1801	2,550,000	70	975,459	27	113,500	3	2,556	0.06	3,641,515
1802	No remittances	—	4,051,702*	100	N/R	—	2,564	0.06	4,054,266

Source: AGI, Mexico 2295, AGI, Mexico 2293, AGI, Mexico 2290, AGI, Mexico 2286, AGI, Mexico 2281, AGI, Mexico 2292.

*The breakdown is as follows: loans to Cajas Generales, 67%; interest paid by royal treasury on loans from the Real Tribunal de Minería, 5%, and for the Tribunal de Consulado (includes payments in Querétaro), 4%; funds deposited in the Cajas Generales of Mexico City, 24%.

(Totals may not add up to 100 because of rounding)

de México, the City of Mexico, and the Real Hacienda into the credit market, a market in which one of the prime debtors was the colonial state. Attracted by the "apparent security," particularly of the Real Hacienda, lenders looked to the state's revenues, including the monopoly and *alcabalas*, as sources of such security.

Beginning in the 1780s royal officials began to acquire large loans on behalf of the Real Hacienda from institutions, particularly the merchant and mining guilds. The frequency and quantity of loans increased throughout the rest of the eighteenth century, as late colonial inflation and prolonged warfare combined to impose impossible demands on the royal fisc. By the end of the eighteenth century, "the royal treasury consistently outspent its income and was seriously in debt year after year to the colonial elite."[77] By 1794 the Spanish Crown claimed an internal debt in Mexico of 8,532,324 pesos; by 1810 it had risen to 31,000,000 pesos and, two years later, the official total was 35,489,020 pesos, although the Junta Superior de Real Hacienda claimed it was closer to 41,751,507 pesos.[78]

Loans from Mexican monopoly revenues began as early as 1779, when all monopoly receipts were deposited in the Mexico City treasury for the purpose of "urgent needs."[79] A royal decree of 8 July 1787 ordered that all profits of the Renta de Tabaco de Indias (tobacco monopolies in the Spanish American colonies) be used to pay off Crown debts.[80] In 1788 the *contador general* reported the total "loans" made to the treasury between 9 July 1779 and 24 December 1787 amounted to 18,009,167 pesos, of which 4,062,599 pesos had been repaid, leaving an outstanding debt of 13,946,568 pesos.[81] As of 1799 the total debt of the Real Hacienda of New Spain to the monopoly amounted to 7,235,650 pesos, "without counting one million pesos which by a viceregal order of 8 April was delivered to the ministers of the Cajas Generales for shipment to the Real Fuerte de Perote."[82]

The breakdowns of monopoly expenditure for 1783, 1793, and 1794 identify quite clearly the individuals and institutions to whom the monopoly paid interest (generally 5 percent) or made loan repayments on behalf of the Real Hacienda. In 1783 an itemized list of twenty-four creditors included the Marqués de Castañiza, several *cofradías* (confraternities), and the Junta Académica de las Tres Artes. Combined, the total loans amounted to 364,529 pesos in principal, while the interest payments totaled 14,870 pesos. All were short-term loans of approximately eight months to one year.[83] In the accounts of 1797–1799, the mining and merchant guilds of Mexico City figured prominently as creditors. With an interest rate set at 5 percent, the treasury of New Spain used the monopoly as a special mortgage for all repayments and redemptions of loans from the tribunals. For 1797 the monopoly was to be mortgaged for 15 million pesos. The disbursement of funds for the fiscal year of 1797 comprised 1,569,410 pesos for shipment to Spain (42 percent) and 1,988,948 pesos (including interest payments) for loans made to the Cajas Generales (56 percent).[84] In 1799 the mining guild received a payment of 66,860 pesos, interest on the principal of 2,610,057 pesos, and, in April of the same year, a *libranza* (promissory note) was also drawn against the monopoly in favor of the Consulado de México for 39,210 pesos. In 1815 the Consulado de México declared loans made against monopoly revenues to the value of 3,094,126 pesos, approximately 25 percent of its total loans of 12,464,911 pesos.[85] Despite the periodic diatribes against the monopoly by the Consulado de México, it may be that, as the government demanded more loans from the private sector, leading merchants and miners developed an interest in the maintenance of the monopoly as a source of secure government collateral, given its successful and consistent performance over the decades.

There is no doubt that, while monopoly funds were shipped to Spain as intended, they were also used for domestic purposes, primarily as a source of immediate capital funds for the needs of the general treasury, but particularly for collateral and debt servicing. In the long term, the use of monopoly revenues as collateral proved to be the first step toward the renting out of the monopoly and the sale of tobacco bonds. These formed the basis of financing the monopoly in post-independence Mexico and the relationship between the Mexican state and capitalists, who provided short-term credit and managed a growing internal debt in the context of a chaotic and deteriorating fiscal system. Relevant here is the example of Tomás Murphy, a Veracruz merchant, representative of a new breed of merchant that was ambitious to take advantage of the new opportunities offered by Bourbon commercial and economic reform and that, to further individual interests, sought alliances with the state by coming to its aid during times of crisis. In the late 1790s Murphy provided aid to the *dirección general* when it desperately required paper supplies and also formulated a plan in the 1820s for repayment of government debts to the planters of Orizaba and Córdoba.[86] When normal monopoly operations broke down between 1810 and 1821, Tomás Murphy was one of the merchants who was given commissions to distribute monopoly goods and negotiate for capital loans to finance its operations.

Despite inefficiencies, the monopoly bureaucrats adhered to their imperial mandate to raise revenues, but the growth curve of monopoly revenues, while impressive, is also deceptive. Although revenues continued to increase at the beginning of the nineteenth century, the costs of production gradually increased and slowed the growth in profits. To understand why that happened, we must take a closer look at the determinants of and constraints on the development of the monopoly as a state enterprise. We begin with an account of the methods devised to acquire supplies of paper and tobacco leaf for the Bourbon tobacco manufactories.

PART II

3. Tobacco and Paper: The Politics and Problems of Supply

ONCE COMMITMENT to the royal tobacco manufactories was made, the *dirección general* was faced with the need to supply the two fundamental raw materials required for cigar and cigarette manufacture: paper and tobacco. For most of the late eighteenth century, paper supplies were imported from the peninsula, a policy which worked well in peacetime, but collapsed during times of war. Since commercial production of tobacco was restricted to the areas around the *villas* of Córdoba and Orizaba, the *dirección general*'s attention was focused on the region of Veracruz in southeastern Mexico. Together, these supply policies reinforced the colonial character of the tobacco trade, although they were offset somewhat by the development of the state manufactories. In the supply of both tobacco and paper, merchants continued to play an important role in the monopoly's operations, particularly when supplies were threatened. This chapter looks at the methods employed to secure tobacco and paper supplies, the problems that were encountered, and how they were resolved.

It is perhaps worth beginning with an overview of the production trends of tobacco between 1765 and 1810. Figures 3 and 4 present a graphical sketch of tobacco production by value and volume between 1765 and 1810. The secular trend of aggregate production moved steadily upwards, with a marked increase in value and volume after 1804. The total harvests from the *villas* increased in value from 390,232 pesos in 1765 to 1,378,016 pesos in 1806, a fourfold increase. The volume of tobacco produced by the *villas* for the monopoly increased from 1,768,851 pounds in 1765 to a peak in 1806 of 5,295,330 pounds.

Originally, the tobacco growing areas included Teusitlán and Jalapa, but they were excluded in 1770 because the costs of the *resguardo* to contain contraband proved to be disproportionately high

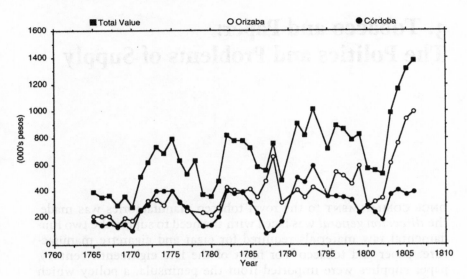

Figure 3. Annual value of tobacco harvests for Orizaba and Córdoba, 1765–1810 (in current pesos). *Source:* see Appendix III.

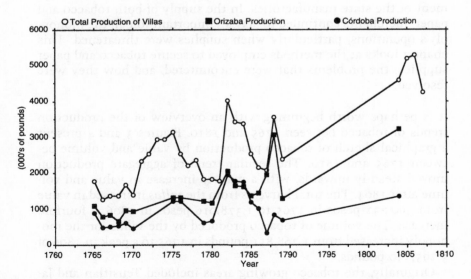

Figure 4. Annual volume of tobacco harvests, Orizaba and Córdoba, 1765–1805 (selected years, in current pesos). *Source:* see Appendix II.

compared to the yield in tobacco produced.[1] After 1770, the two main areas of tobacco production supplying the Bourbon monopoly were Orizaba, which incorporated Zongólica, and Córdoba, which incorporated Huatusco, all of which were located in an area easier to control as far as contraband was concerned (see map 2). The production zone remained unchanged until the emergency measures implemented following the Hidalgo rebellion of 1810 permitted tobacco cultivation in most of the intendancies. Combined, the *villas'* tobacco production accounted for an average of 90 percent of the total amount spent on leaf tobacco by the monopoly. The remaining 10 percent was made up by purchases from Yucatán, and, when necessary, emergency imports from Louisiana, Venezuela and Cuba.

During the period of Bourbon management, monopoly bureaucrats were quite successful at implementing a price policy in favor of the monopoly's costs. There was no increase in purchase price for almost forty years, as shown in figure 5. Such stability, however, occurred at the expense of peaceful relations between the monopoly and the planters, subjected the contract system to strain, and, on occasion, demanded alternative methods to acquire tobacco.

Purchase prices for tobacco were not the result of market forces but of periodic "negotiations" between the monopoly and the planters. As such, they became a contentious political question and tested the Bourbon state's ability to balance its interests against those of the planters. The functioning of a bilateral monopoly renders price analysis inappropriate, but one useful way of thinking about the organization of the supply of tobacco and monopoly-planter relations is provided by Al Hirschman's model, laid out in his work *Exit, Voice, and Loyalty*. Hirschman argued that there are two main types of activist reactions to discontent with organizations to which one belongs or does business: to *voice* one's complaints, while continuing as a member or customer in order to improve matters; or to *exit* from the organization.[2] At the same time, the organization or business may respond to voice and exit options in a number of ways, ranging from repression to co-optation. Hirschman claimed that a principal intent of his work on exit and voice "was to show that there is a wide range of economic processes for the efficient unfolding of which both individual, economic action (via exit) and participatory, political action (via voice) have important constructive roles to play."[3] Hirschman's model is suggestive at a number of levels. As we shall see, in the case of monopoly, what began as a policy of encouragement of "voice" by way of contract negotiations by planter representatives quickly turned into one of repression, retaliation, and reprisals. When that proved unsuc-

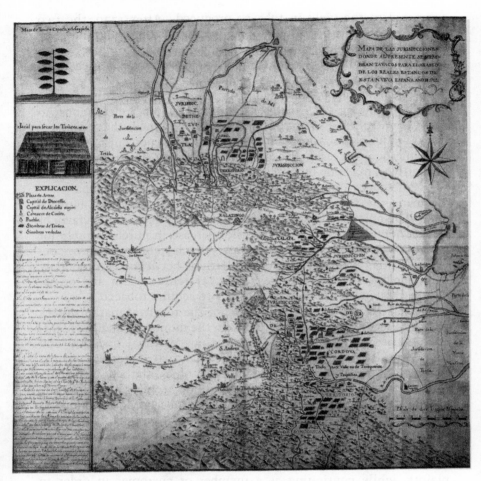

Map 2. Areas of Tobacco Production—Orizaba and Córdoba, 1769

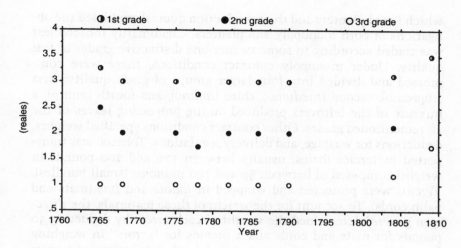

Figure 5. Tobacco prices, 1765–1810. Compiled from monopoly contracts, various *legajos*, AGN, AGI, ANO.

cessful, the monopoly attempted to co-opt the most vocal and influential planters through preferential treatment of an "articulate oligarchy." At the same time, measures were taken to restrict exit on the part of the planters, although this was less successful. In the planters' case, however, the preferred strategy was not exit but the exercise of enough influence and power through their "voice" to improve profits in an otherwise advantageous relationship. We shall begin with a brief description of the contract system and then examine its problems, and the consequences of these for supply of leaf tobacco between 1777 and 1810.

After the official announcement of the monopoly's establishment in 1764, viceroy Cruillas ordered the planters from Córdoba and Orizaba to elect representatives to travel to Mexico City and negotiate the first contract with the *dirección general*.[4] Terms for the initial contract were agreed upon by both parties and approved by the viceroy on February 21 1765. The terms of agreement embodied within the first contract of 1765 established the basic guidelines for regulation and production of tobacco and remained virtually unchanged for the duration of Bourbon management of the monopoly. Enumerated clauses and their attendant documents (licenses and registers which listed planters and their production quotas) stipulated the obligations of both monopoly and planters. Customarily tobacco leaf was traded according to some twenty-one distinctive grades of leaf quality. Under monopoly contract conditions, these were compressed and divided into four larger groups of grade quality: first (*supremo*), second (*mediano*), third (*infimo*), and fourth (*punta*), a mixture of the leftovers produced during processing leaves of the aforementioned grades. Other contract conditions specified weights, deductions for wastage, and delivery regulations. Tobacco was transported in *tercios* (bales, usually between 170 and 200 pounds in weight) composed of between 80 and 100 *manojos* (small bundles). *Tercios* were protected and wrapped in *jonote* and *lias* (mats and palm cords). To account for the weight of these materials, the *dirección general* determined the weight of each *tercio* by deducting 30 pounds for mats and cords and 2 pounds for "errors" in weighing from the gross weight of each *tercio*. A further deduction of 10 percent of the gross weight compensated for losses from drying and shrinkage while tobacco remained in storage. Once the net weight was determined for each *tercio*, the planter received the agreed price per pound according to its class. The *alcabala* (sales tax) and *diezmo* (tithe) also added to the list of deductions borne by the planters. The monopoly bore the cost of transport of leaf from the *villas* to Mexico City. Initially, planters received half of the total value of their crops on delivery and the other half eight to fifteen days after delivery of all harvests was completed. Gradually, the schedule of payments changed so that planters received the full value of their crops at the time of delivery and evaluation.

The monopoly determined the quantities of tobacco to be produced based on production needs. Planter representatives and specially appointed monopoly officials shared responsibility for the distribution of licenses to planters holding contracts which indicated the quantity of *matas* (plants) allocated to each individual. The quantity assigned reflected, at least in theory, a compromise between the total amount of leaf required by the monopoly, the total number of planters who wished to contract, and the productive capacity of each planter. Planters were permitted to plant an additional 10 percent of their total allocation to help compensate for losses through plant disease or adverse weather. If the harvest in any one year exceeded the projected yield required by the monopoly for a one-year supply, the successive year's allocation was reduced proportionately. The quota system embodied the regulatory function of monopoly policy, combined with penalties for violation of such quotas by the planters. Planters who exceeded the quantities indicated on their licenses (over and above high yields in excessively good growing years) were fined or received short prison terms. If a planter continually exceeded his quotas, he was summarily removed from the monopoly register and permanently prohibited from producing tobacco.

On delivery of each crop, every *tercio* was examined and assessed by two experts, one chosen by the monopoly and one by the planters' representatives. Disagreements over assessment of leaf were settled by a *tercero en discordia* (arbitrator) appointed by the *alcalde mayor*. Assessments of a tobacco crop often resulted in regradings, whereby a planter's first-grade leaf was deemed to be only second-grade by the assessors, or second-grade leaf third-grade, and so on. Such examination on the part of the monopoly signified an attempt to introduce "quality control" of the tobacco produced, although the process served to alienate planters rather than encourage them to improve their farming methods. Grade mixing was prohibited, as was the inclusion of shoots or suckers. Once again, violation of such rules resulted in exclusion from the general register of tobacco planters.[5]

From the planters' perspective, there were advantages to be gained from the monopoly's operations. Two central problems for any agricultural producer in colonial Mexico were eliminated, the uncertainty of markets and access to credit. Planters now had a guaranteed buyer, one who paid in cash and on time, who paid transport costs, and who advanced interest-free credit to help pay for production costs.[6] The monopoly's advancement of credit had a political and social, as well as an economic rationale: to favor the small farmer, to incorporate the Indian into the market economy, and to counter the dominance of wealthy *hacendados* and bypass local mercantile investments in commercial tobacco production.[7] To achieve such objectives, the monopoly needed to make credit available to small farmers and planters. The first *director general*, Jacinto de Espinosa, familiarized himself with the planters' situation prior to the establishment of the monopoly. He originated the policy of credit advances to planters in an attempt to reduce the growers' dependence upon local merchants and *hacendados* for such advances. "The tobacco farmers and rancheros who occupy and maintain themselves in the sowing and production of tobacco in Orizaba, Córdoba, and other places are poor . . . they request money from *hacendados* and merchants for their costs of production . . . as such it is crucial they be assured that the monopoly, on behalf of the Treasury, supply similar advances which merchants and traders made to them previously, in specie and not in kind."[8]

For the bureaucrats, then, tobacco production under monopoly management implicitly demanded a reorganization of its financing and the social relations upon which it was based. This was done by the provision of an alternative to local merchants' *avíos* (advances of money and goods) in the form of monopoly credit. A fundamental problem with this, however, was the securities demanded by the monopoly and the production capacities of individual planters. From the beginning, the monopoly found itself confronted by wealthy planters, particularly those that may be characterized as merchant-planters, who represented the local elites, and who had interests in both commerce and agriculture in Orizaba and Córdoba. In Hirschman's terms, they constituted an "articulate oligarchy," and it was from this "oligarchy" that the planters' representatives were recruited to negotiate with the *dirección general* over contract prices and conditions. At least nineteen separate contracts were negotiated between 1765 and 1812. These lasted for a specified number of years or "at the King's pleasure." Each new contract negotiation provided an opportunity for both parties to press for new advantages or adjust conditions to suit changing circumstances.

The very first contract negotiation between the planters and the monopoly ended in controversy and clearly influenced the planters' perceptions of monopoly policy and their distrust of the *dirección general*. At the center of the controversy was the purchase price for tobacco, the single most contentious issue between the planters and the *dirección general*.

The initial task was to establish a set of prices agreeable to both monopoly and planter. The method chosen by the planters to calculate their selling price for each grade of leaf was to take the highest average value of each of the three major categories of tobacco. This produced 3.25 reales per pound for the first grade, 2.5 reales per pound for the second, 1 real for the third, and 24 reales per *arroba* (25 pounds) for the fourth grade or *punta*.[9] Approved by Espinosa, who argued that the prices would provide a good incentive for efficient production, the planters' prices formed the basis for the first contract, which was settled on 30 January 1765 in Mexico City, and was to last for three years. Neither Sebastián Calvo nor the viceroy, however, agreed with Espinosa's approval. Calvo argued that the purchase prices would yield a profit "never seen or heard of in any business," and expressed contempt for the planters' behavior: "The obstinacy and tenacity of the deputies of Córdoba and Orizaba . . . is born of a false supposition because they are persuaded the king is obliged to pay the prices they command, as tobacco is a commodity necessary for the establishment of the monopoly."[10] According to calculations carried out by both Calvo and the viceroy, the average purchase prices should have been pegged lower at ranges between 2.1–3 reales per pound for first grade, 1.3–1.5 reales per pound for second grade, and 0.6–0.8 reales per pound for third grade.[11] The viceroy also pointed out that the planters gained considerable advantages from the contracts, since the monopoly treasury paid them in specie, and since they no longer paid agents' commissions or the costs of transporting their crops to Mexico City. Espinosa ignored both Calvo's and Croix's advice to reduce the prices specified in the first contract, only to be ignored himself by the visitor-general, José de Gálvez, who arbitrarily rescinded the prices of the first contract and imposed the lower prices of 3 reales, 2 reales, and 1 real per pound for the three grades. The planters' first experience of monopoly management and its price policy was one of indecision and a divided house, followed by arbitrary acts which ignored the planters' suggestions. This was not the most auspicious beginning to a business relationship.

Gálvez's decision to ignore the original purchase prices cost the planters a 4 percent loss on the value of their first harvest; the total payment was 588,747 pesos, 22,477 pesos less than the original prices would have produced. The planters' central concern, of course, was to regain the ground lost on prices due to Gálvez's policy. They declared that the 1765 prices did not permit them to earn an adequate profit, discouraged careful production, and that the stated purchase price did not take into consideration a 10 percent reduction for the weight of materials (mats and cords) used to package the tobacco. Planter representatives argued that, on average, tobacco farmers experienced one good year in twenty. Therefore, the base price needed to be pegged at a higher level to absorb losses during bad years. The monopoly's imperative, however, was to keep costs of raw materials low. Despite planters' protests, Gálvez convinced viceroy Croix that the right decision had been made. The planters were ordered to maintain "perpetual silence" on the matter.[12]

Despite their protests, the planters accepted the reduced prices. This suggests that, while they did not appreciate the arbitrary act of the visitor-general, privately they thought that the prices would still permit them to earn some profit, particularly with the costs absorbed by the monopoly and their newly acquired protected status as the Crown's planters. A new contract, which was to last for two years (1767–1769), was agreed upon on 15 September 1767. Prices were the same as those imposed by Gálvez. Planters were required to deliver their tobacco sixty days after bundling instead of the previous thirty days. This signified a potential additional loss for the planters, since another 30 days risked greater shrinkage while the tobacco lay in storage and required the payment of an extra month's rent for those planters who did not possess their own storage facilities.[13] Deductions for weight loss and wrapping materials remained the same.

Lack of coordination and exchange of information between the inspector-general Francisco del Real and the planters over production quotas and reassessments of their own gradations of the tobacco added to resentment against monopoly management and its arbitrariness.[14] In 1775, while planters prepared their lands for autumn sowing, they received notice of a general reduction of between 10,000 and 11,000 pounds, a 31 percent drop. All existing licenses were collected, and new licenses, reflecting the new reduced individual quotas, were reassigned. In the meantime, the planters had already paid out more than 50,000 pesos for seed and labor, and requested that the monopoly receive the excess tobacco which would have to be harvested anyway. The *fiscal* counseled the *directores generales* to accede to the planters' request, partly in order to secure the harvest without further delay. He very pointedly announced, however, that the cited sum of 50,000 pesos was the product of a "vivid imagination," and that the amount invested by the planters could not possibly have exceeded 14,000 pesos. Regardless of how much money was actually invested, this appears to have been the last time the *dirección general* arbitrarily changed production quotas.[15]

After only five years of the contract system, the *dirección general* reported shortages in tobacco supplies in 1771 and 1772. Imports were necessary from Caracas, and half a million pounds of leaf tobacco was shipped to Mexico early in 1771 to replenish stocks.[16] The shortages, however, occurred due to poor planning and bureaucratic infighting rather than any problems inherent with production.[17] Thereafter, the *dirección general* looked for ways to prevent future supply problems. Between 1775 and 1790 the *dirección general* combined several strategies to eliminate delay in tobacco production and to resist planter pressure to increase purchase prices, strategies which ranged from force to negotiation. Attempts were made to eradicate the corporate strength of the planters through the dissolution of the *cuerpo de cosecheros* (planters' association) and the elimination of collective contract negotiations. Other strategies were expedient, short-term, and expensive. Attempts at state intervention and the takeover of tobacco *ranchos* gave way to preferential treatment of cooperative planters.

The consistent delays in contract settlement, caused by predictable disagreements over purchase prices, threatened quality and quantity of tobacco supplies each time a contract was renegotiated. Abolition of the *cuerpo de cosecheros* and collective contract negotiations provided a solution to a recurrent and expensive problem, although one which proved to be ineffective in the long term. De facto planter representation continued and resurfaced due to the sheer expense and impracticality of individual contracts. In conjunction with the *dirección general's* announcement that the 1774 contract was to be terminated in 1778, a further announcement ordered the abolition of any form of "*cuerpo, comunidad, o gremio*" of tobacco planters. The term "*diputados*," signifying the planters' representatives, was removed from the contract clauses wherever it appeared and replaced by "*contratantes*." In place of the practice of election of representatives, planters were to contract on an individual basis from 1 October 1777.[18]

The abolition of planter representation produced mixed responses from the planters. The *cabildos* of Orizaba and Córdoba, the members of which were predominantly tobacco planters, opposed the ban on representation and collective contracts, but to no avail.[19] The *dirección general* remained unconvinced that dissatisfaction with monopoly prices was unanimous among tobacco planters and blamed planter protest on the wilful ambition and self-interest of the local elites.[20] The inspector-general, Francisco del Real, argued that the planter representatives and their constituency formed the real source of opposition, "generally the wealthiest, who earn the largest profits, which is sufficient incentive to oppose lower prices."[21]

By 1778 the individuals selected to represent planter interests were either local government officials (*regidores*) with commercial interests, high-ranking military, or wealthy planters. The cost of sending representatives to Mexico City for contract negotiations was high, varying between 300 and 3,000 pesos. The amounts were raised by a charge, generally between 4 and 6 reales, made on each *carga* of tobacco harvested. If the amount fell short of the costs incurred during the negotiations, the difference was made up by the representatives themselves. This shifted the balance in favor of the wealthier planters. Poorer planters remained unconvinced (or so they claimed) that the representatives merited such expenditure and were sceptical about whether their interests were actually defended in the process. As a result, the importance of credit advances again received attention. These were designed to aid the poorer planters, who were traditionally "financed and subjugated by the others [wealthier planters]; . . . who would probably be content with less profit . . . [In this way,] the ideas of the opulent planters will be banished."[22] The *fiscal* urged settlement of a policy which assured mutual gains for the treasury, the consumer, and the planter, but, at the same time, warned that no losses should be risked by the monopoly due to delays caused by the planters' recalcitrance.

The abolition of the planter representatives and the *dirección general's* insistence on individual contracts at reduced prices in 1777 provoked a quick response. Some planters threatened not to fill their tobacco quotas because they could not afford to at these prices. In retaliation and in a blatant attempt to penalize the protesting planters, the *dirección general* made two announcements. It made clear that any shortages in tobacco supplies would be met by imports from Louisiana, thereby bypassing recalcitrant planters who presumed to abuse their "privileged" position by forcing their demands on the monopoly by threatening to jeopardize supplies of tobacco.[23] Secondly, in a more radical move, the *dirección general* decided to produce its own tobacco directly. The inspector-general received orders to choose lands for state production within the *villas* and to inform local landowners and the *cabildos* that the monopoly took priority in rental of lands over other bidders, irrespective of their agricultural interests. Orders were dispatched on 18 March 1778 to the *cabildos* of the *villas*, to the regional *alcaldes mayores*, and to the colonels of the Regimiento de Granada and provincial militias that, if necessary, they were to give "aid" to the inspector-general in the establishment of the colonial state's own tobacco cultivation.[24]

The combined threat of forced sale of tobacco *ranchos* and the state's move to produce its own tobacco took its toll on the planters. By late March of 1778, the inspector-general reported that most planters from Orizaba finally had agreed to sign individual contracts according to prices and conditions set by the *dirección general*. The planters in Córdoba, however, continued to resist.[25] In addition to the use of the military to enforce monopoly policy if necessary, planters were informed that no further pleas, complaints, or petitions about prices would be considered. Any planter who failed to contract within a three-month period would be excluded from the tobacco register and prohibited from producing tobacco for the duration of the new contract. In response to the *dirección general's* action, the Cordoban planters complained that the bureaucrats intended "to dispossess us of our own *ranchos* . . . To achieve this, they [the *factores*] have notified us to present sworn statements within four days which describe our *ranchos* and equipment on hand . . . Not only are we in danger of our own ruin but so is the entire jurisdiction since tobacco is the main crop upon which the inhabitants depend. We cannot agree to hand over our *ranchos* (as the inspector-general wishes) if our final decision is not to produce tobacco, as we still need the land for the cultivation of maize, beans, and other crops for our subsistence."[26] Despite such protests, at the end of March 1778, Cordoban planters began to arrange their contracts on an individual basis for 1778 and 1779. In the meantime, the monopoly achieved a reduction in purchase prices for tobacco for the second time in fourteen years, at the same time that the monopoly increased the sale price of cigars, cigarettes, and leaf tobacco. First-, second-, and third-grade tobacco were to be purchased by the monopoly in ranges between 2 5/8 and 2.5 reales, 1 5/8 and 2 reales, and 1 real, respectively, and 20 to 22 reales an *arroba* of *punta*. The planters' agreement to contract in the face of reduced prices, however, came too late to forestall direct monopoly production and tobacco imports. These only served to increase antagonistic relations.

Planter and direct monopoly production coexisted between 1778 and 1780. The inspector-general formed an optimistic assessment of the achievements of the new policies and argued that most of the planters from both *villas* viewed individual contracts favorably. He expressed reluctance to return to the old system of negotiation through representatives. At the same time, Real suggested that if the planters continued to accept the "fair" prices of the individual contracts, a new general contract ought to be renegotiated, on the understanding that the monopoly retained the option to produce tobacco directly if it so chose.

Although the monopoly took over *ranchos* in both *villas* between 1778 and 1780, Córdoba bore the brunt of direct monopoly production. *Ranchos* were purchased or rented in the departments of Palotar, Tetela, and Totutla. Those *ranchos* transferred by planters were appraised and, if the inspector-general decided upon a purchase, then a regular sale of property went into effect. At least fifteen *ranchos* were purchased by the monopoly at a total cost of 29,797 pesos and eventually resold to their owners for 29,192 pesos.[27] The *factor* of Orizaba and the inspector-general drew up plans for management and production on the *ranchos*, which included appointment of administrators and *mayordomos* (overseers, stewards), and the hire of local Indian labor for fieldwork. The *mayordomos* in charge of daily work compiled accounts of all payments made for labor at the end of each week, which were then passed on to the administrators. The latter managed between four and five *ranchos* each, kept accounts of all expenditures made and the production of each *rancho*, and submitted monthly accounts to the inspector-general.[28] By February of 1779 the *dirección general* had supervised the takeover of eighteen tobacco *ranchos*.[29] The distribution of to-

Table 8.   Volume and Value of Tobacco Production, 1779 and 1780

	Net Pounds		Peso Value	
	1779	1780	1779	1780
Monopoly	507,045	479,027	125,361	99,686
Córdoba	610,056	671,200	136,002	144,326
Orizaba	1,222,731	1,166,411	240,085	213,734

Source: AGN, Tabaco 352, director general Hierro to Mayorga, 18 May 1780.

bacco production between the planters and the monopoly for 1779 and 1780 is shown in table 8.

The years 1778 to 1780 were particularly bad ones for the planters, not simply because of direct production by the monopoly, but because of drought, plant disease, and the losses which the planters argued monopoly prices did not permit them to cover. Harvests delivered to the monopoly in Orizaba declined in number from 121 in 1778 to 72 in 1779 and 60 in 1780, an all-time low since the beginning of the contract system.[30] Córdoba suffered the most in 1779. Due to an excessively long dry spell, much of the tobacco dried out prematurely in the fields. Almost one-fifth of the crop was lost, and the tobacco harvested, although of superior quality, was inadequate to cover costs of production. The monopoly also suffered losses. One-half of the monopoly's tobacco crop was lost as smallpox ravaged the local Indian population and reduced the labor force.[31] The inspector-general estimated that those Indians who survived owed the monopoly more than 5,000 pesos received as advance wages, with a loss of 1,000 pesos owed by the victims of the epidemic.[32]

The director general remained pessimistic about the future of the contract system, even though most planters had returned to their ranchos and fields: "The tobacco harvests are the solid rock upon which is built the finest jewel which the Real Hacienda possesses . . . the issue of tobacco production is the only one which . . . this dirección general has been unable to resolve . . . since the beginning of the monopoly this has caused, and will continue to cause, a great deal of work and debate."[33] The viceroy, however, judged the monopoly's strategy of direct production successful: "The harvests of the Crown were an opportune method . . . to contain the tobacco planters' pride, unjustly unhappy with the profits with which the monopoly provides them . . . never satisfied with the high prices paid for their harvests, the most expensive known in both Americas . . ."[34]

Francisco del Real, the inspector-general, supported the production of tobacco by the monopoly on a long-term basis, but the project was finally rejected by the *dirección general*. The viceroy ordered all direct monopoly production to stop, and, beginning in 1781, planters repurchased their *ranchos*, generally for the price at which they had sold them to the monopoly. Purchases were not outright and payments were made to the monopoly over a three-year period, between 1782 and 1784, until the price was paid in full.[35]

In addition to the recurring price question, Bourbon politics and allegations of bureaucratic corruption impinged upon the planters' world, created new antagonisms, and influenced the planters' responses to contract conditions. In particular, however, between 1779 and 1786 the activities of two royal officials aggravated the planters in distinct ways. The first case, at the local level, concerned the public duties and private practices of the inspector-general Francisco del Real. The second case, at a higher level, incorporated the planters indirectly into the increasingly strained relations between José de Gálvez and his ambitious protégé, the talented but erratic Pedro de Cossío. Both cases were linked by the temporary removal of the inspector-general from his duties and his replacement by Cossío for the purpose of a quick negotiation and settlement of new contracts with the planters.

The controversy which surrounded Francisco del Real focused on allegations of corruption and abusive practices by the inspector-general. Real, a peninsular Spaniard from Jerez and personal friend of José de Gálvez, was active in the tobacco trade prior to the monopoly's establishment. The circumstances of Real's appointment as inspector-general are not clear but he held the position until 1789 despite his local ties and controversial behavior. By the 1770s he occupied the position of *regidor* on the Orizaba *cabildo*. He married María Ignacia Díaz de Zevallos (his second marriage), the creole daughter of Ana de Leiva and Juan Díaz de Zevallos. The Díaz de Zevallos family was one of the most powerful in Córdoba and possessed considerable investments in both sugar and tobacco. Not surprisingly, Real's public duties and decisions were looked upon with considerable suspicion by both the *dirección general* and by aggrieved planters, aware of his local ties, political power, and personal interests.

As inspector-general of tobacco and commander of the *resguardo*, Real's primary responsibilities were to ensure that planters conformed to their contract obligations and to supervise general management of tobacco production within the *villas*. In short, the position of inspector-general was a powerful one which, from the planters' perspective, was consistently abused by Real. He never supported the planters' price demands and incurred their collective wrath by vigorous regradation of their crops and by his support for direct production of tobacco by the monopoly. Described as men "haunted by an implacable hatred of this individual [Real]," the planters sought every opportunity to discredit the inspector-general and have him removed.[36]

Real's difficulties with the settlement of new contracts, combined with the constant accusations and attacks against him, persuaded the viceroy to remove him temporarily and replace him with Cossío while the charges against him were investigated. Complaints against Real varied from maltreatment of Indian workers to embezzlement of monopoly funds. The parish priest of Córdoba complained to the Bishop of Puebla that the inspector-general purchased planters' equipment and *ranchos* well below a fair price and, as a result, many planters were reduced to begging on the streets."[37] Another priest, Manuel Pérez Maldonado, from the village of Izhuatlan, complained to the viceroy that Real, in the name of the "powerful shadow" of the king, abused and mistreated the Indian workers by whipping them while they worked on the monopoly's tobacco *ranchos*. In addition, Real refused to pay a fair rent for their lands, some of which he had forcefully appropriated on which to grow the monopoly's tobacco crops.[38] The real scandal, however, involved Real's alleged defrauding of the monopoly of some 70,000 pesos, most of which came from mismanagement of monopoly *ranchos*. One example of Real's methods involved purchases of beans for the workers on monopoly *ranchos*. The purchase price was set at 3 *granos* per *carga*, but accusers claimed Real charged the monopoly 13 *granos* and pocketed the remaining 10 *granos*. Other general charges concerned Real's "abuse" of his authority and patronage of several planters to whom he gave favorable quotas and assessments of their yearly crops.[39] There was no question that Real had his own interests in Orizaba and Córdoba. Real claimed that when he accepted the appointment of inspector-general, his existing capital amounted to 44,000 pesos. Ten years later, in 1778, he stated his assets as his annual salary of 4,000 pesos and his debts as 18,000 pesos, acquired when he used his own funds to cover local monopoly costs when official funds were delayed. At the time of his death, however, his will listed a sugar hacienda worth approximately 40,000 pesos (acquired through his marriage), a work hacienda, and one *rancho*; he rented two other haciendas from the Conde del Valle and Pedro de Goitia.[40]

Francisco del Real eventually was exonerated of all charges and reinstated, but it is not clear whether the *dirección general* believed in his innocence, could not prove any of the allegations, or simply looked the other way. Given the alternative (Pedro de Cossío, who turned out to be no alternative at all) Real had, in fact, performed his duties well and appeared to support policies favorable to the Crown, even if it alienated many of the wealthier planters.

Real also had his supporters, not least of which was José de Gálvez. Closer to home, however, Antonio Hernández Navarro, an administrator of monopoly *ranchos*, summed up the beliefs of the inspector-general's supporters by laying the blame squarely on the vested interests of the planters: "It is certain the commission which Real exercises is naturally odious to everyone. He deals continually with people who are concerned with nothing except their own interests which results . . . in malice and lies. Most people engaged in tobacco production are uncultured, uncivil, and possess neither scruples nor integrity . . . One cannot find among them an individual possessed of the judgment, intelligence, committment, and energy to be found in Real."[41]

Displeased with the decision to reinstate Real after the removal of Cossío, many planters moved to rescind their contracts. The *dirección general* assured them that Real would not cause any problems. Appeals could be made to the *director general* if they were dissatisfied with any of the inspector's actions.

Pedro de Cossío's case emerged out of very different circumstances. As we saw in chapter 1, Cossío, a Montañes merchant and resident of Veracruz, gained Gálvez's favor through the provision of loan capital to set up the monopoly in Mexico. The result was a political friendship which culminated in Cossío's appointment to the experimental office of *superintendente subdelegado de real hacienda*.[42] In conjunction with the suspension of Real from his duties, the planters from both *villas* wrote to the viceroy stating that they were willing to contract in accordance with the prices and conditions of the last general contract for a period to be specified by the king. In response, Cossío received orders to travel to the *villas* and organize new general contracts. Not long after his arrival, two new general contracts were approved by the planter communities of both *villas*. In one sense, these represented a small triumph for the planters. Purchase prices were altered from those imposed in 1779 by the inspector-general to those stipulated in the last general contract of 1773, that is, 3 reales, 2 reales, and 1 real for first-, second-, and third-grade tobaccos, respectively, and 22 reales per *arroba* for *punta*. The speedy resolution of contract negotiations should have pleased the viceroy, but it did not. Never far from controversy, Cossío's role in placating the planters only aroused suspicions of

pandering to local vested interests and of favoring the regional interests of Veracruz at the expense of those of the Crown. Audacious but
politically clumsy in his negotiations with the planters, Cossío encouraged them to demand the inclusion of a new clause into the general contracts. The controversial clause stipulated that, for the duration of the contracts, the inspector-general would not participate in
the distribution or receipt of tobacco quotas.[43]

A royal order of 1 March 1782 approved the new contracts negotiated by Cossío but with the provision that Francisco del Real be reinstated in his position as inspector-general and that Cossío be re-
called immediately. José de Gálvez concluded that Cossío sought to
ingratiate himself with the planters for private profit and prestige
and that "a despicable alliance between Cossío and the insolent
Montañes planters" was the result.[44] One study of Cossío suggests
that the eventual objective behind such machinations was Cossío's
desire for permanent appointment as the new inspector-general.
Powerful as the position was, Cossío undoubtedly had higher ambitions.[45] After three tumultuous and controversial years in office between 1779 and 1782, Cossío was dismissed in the wake of "the 'in-
finite clamour from all classes of persons about the despotism,
hardness, and bad treatment' of his term of government."[46]

Whatever Cossío's faults, his negotiations with the planters were
successful, and the *dirección general* approved the "new" purchase
prices. The change in purchase prices persuaded many planters to
overcome their objections to the reinstatement of Real. The conditions agreed upon also incorporated the introduction of overlapping
contracts: one to run from 1781 until 1786, the other from 1785 until 1790. The overlap of contracts may have reduced delay somewhat
but certainly did not reduce the protests and demands for increased
prices by the planters, as the events of 1786 were to demonstrate.

During new contract negotiations in January 1786, the temporarily reinstituted planter representatives complained to the *dirección
general* that Orizaba and Córdoba had been reduced to "ruin" largely
due to the inadequacy of monopoly prices and adverse weather conditions. The negotiations broke down almost immediately when the
representatives began making demands for another price increase;
they were ordered to withdraw immediately. The *fiscal* ordered the
directores generales to devise a method which would bring an end
to the planters' persistent complaints over prices. As far as the
inspector-general was concerned, the monopoly had two options.
One option was to redesignate the zone of tobacco production, possibly in the jurisdiction of Jalapa, around the area of Coatepec.[47] The

other option was for the monopoly to revert once again to its own production.

By early July 1786, none of the planters from either jurisdiction came forward to sign a contract. Just as any chance of negotiation of a new general contract crumbled, several wealthy planters, critics of monopoly prices, stated their willingness to sign a contract based on existing prices on condition they be allowed to plant as much tobacco as they requested. Antonio Montes Argüelles, one of the most prominent planters of Orizaba, offered to plant between twelve million and thirteen million *matas*. To gauge the magnitude of this, up until 1786 the largest single individual allocation amounted to six and a half million (which, coincidentally, went to Montes Argüelles), but average allocations ranged between 50,000 and 300,000 *matas*. In addition, Montes Argüelles requested a credit advance of 60,000 pesos to be paid in two separate installments. His reasons, at least those he gave to the inspector-general, involved nothing more than his desire to contribute to the progress of the royal patrimony and to avoid the total ruin of his "patria, which is inevitable if tobacco is not produced, since all other commerce depends upon it."[48] Montes Argüelles offered 100,000 pesos as security against the advance. Other planters made similar offers; Pablo and Rafael García, father and son, applied for a quota of six million plants, while Benito Rocha, a *regidor* from Zongólica, requested a quota of two million plants. Faced with a choice between increasing prices and agreeing to the conditions of influential and wealthy planters, the *dirección general* chose the latter in the hope of stifling further delay and future protests. As a result, in 1786 over half of the total tobacco crop in Orizaba was produced by two families, the Garcías and Montes Argüelles. Shortly thereafter, many other planters came forward to sign a contract. The method used to "persuade" them was not approved by either the *factor* of Orizaba or the inspector-general. When the *factor* refused to pay out the advances because the securities of Montes Argüelles and the Garcías were questionable, the *dirección general* ordered him to withdraw from the settlements and placed Real in charge of finalizing details of the new contract. The inspector-general also disapproved of the large allocations but carried out his orders. Real used the situation, however, to promote his own policies. His first preference was to persuade the *dirección general* to return to direct production by the monopoly. Failing that, the inspector-general favored the removal of tobacco production from the *villas* altogether. He argued that it was only fair to grant licenses to a large number of poor *rancheros* and farmers whose livelihoods depended upon tobacco production, although his defense of the "small man" had something of a hollow ring to it. Real continued to blame self-interest of the wealthy planters, who intimidated the smaller farmers, *rancheros*, and peasants. Real's assessment was supported by the opinions of *rancheros* who were critical of the wealthier planters. José Martínez Malcueto, a creole from Córdoba, complained to the inspector-general of the serious damage caused by the "unjustified capriciousness of the *principales* (wealthy planters) who persuade the planters not to contract."[49] Like many other planters in his position, tired of delays and tedious discussions, he had contracted with the monopoly for the next five years. The criticisms made against the wealthy planters only encouraged the *dirección general* to forbid planter representation once again.

The planters' *cuerpo* had something of the quality of a corporate hydra whose "heads" kept reappearing despite repeated prohibitions against it. Taking advantage of the arrival of a new viceroy, the *directores generales* argued that "the nomination of representatives . . . by the planters is prejudicial to them and to the monopoly; to the former because they are charged high costs to support the deputies, whose authority is engaged to ensure benefits to the powerful planters, which leaves the poor *pegujaleros* dependent upon them; to the latter because the four or five representatives, who are generally wealthy and in league with others of their class, find it difficult to agree upon prices . . . as they are only concerned with their own profit, without any consideration for the interests of the monopoly."[50] Subsequently, a new order was issued which prohibited any further election of planter representatives. The problem remained, however, of how to settle contracts swiftly and efficiently. Without spokesmen, individual contracting and negotiation was a cumbersome, unwieldy, and slow process. Not surprisingly, informal representation continued apace simply because it was easier, as did continued formal prohibitions against such representation.

One of the most devastating agricultural crises experienced in Mexico occurred in 1786, and undoubtedly contributed to the *dirección general*'s decision to accede to the demands of planters such as Montes Argüelles. The effects of the crisis were not uniform throughout the kingdom, and the *villas* exemplified the unevenness of the damage. Orizaba was not severely affected, but 1786 and 1787 were bad years for Córdoba, and it is not surprising that the planters became more vocal in their demand for increases in prices. In 1786 they produced just over one million pounds of tobacco worth 228,770 pesos; the following year, they harvested 337,790 pounds, worth 83,582 pesos. The planters' account of their misery was confirmed by the *alcalde mayor*, who pleaded with the monopoly for relief and monetary aid for the planters. He described a scene of abandoned *ranchos* and deserted, overgrown fields. The *villa* of Córdoba presented a pitiful image of derelict, empty houses.[51] The following year, the *cabildo* informed the viceroy of a drastic depopulation of the *villa* from an estimated 24,000 to 12,000 inhabitants.[52] The *dirección general* remained unimpressed and unmoved by the planters' voices and demands. Some planters chose a drastic form of "exit"—migration to other areas—or shifted to another crop.

The paradox of the 1786 decision to approve large tobacco quotas lay in the willingness of the colonial state to co-opt its critics by granting them special favors, in this case large tobacco quotas in excess of a million *matas*, that is, to rely, when all else failed, on the very planters they sought to curb and control. In Hirschman's terms, "by giving the complainant preferential treatment the delinquent organization seeks to still his voice and to buy him off: in this manner, it may once again avoid having to improve the general quality of its performance."[53] Over the next two decades opportunism was only reinforced by the monopoly, which began to use planters' past performance during attempted boycotts as a way to reward or penalize them—anything but an increase in prices. If, like Antonio Montes Argüelles, they agreed to contract at existing prices, they received preferential quotas.

Underlying the negotiations and modifications in contract conditions which occurred between 1778 and 1790 were imports of tobacco from Louisiana. It is unlikely that such imports indicated any carefully thought out, deliberate "grand" strategy to coerce the planters into producing tobacco at prices which they believed to be too low, even though it may have been used as such. Rather, imports represented the Crown's attempts to improve colonial finances and make colonies pay for themselves. It is likely that, with or without the unfavorable reactions of the planters which delayed production, tobacco from Louisiana would have been imported anyway. Mexico provided a proximal market for a product which Louisiana could sell and thereby help to finance itself. Between 1778 and 1788, 5,664,912 pounds of tobacco, valued at 834,677 pesos, was imported into Mexico from Louisiana, with the bulk of imports occurring between 1784 and 1788.[54] Interest in Louisiana tobacco was based on its excellent quality, making it suitable for mixing with the tobacco from the *villas*, and because it could, therefore, provide a supplement to *villa* production, reducing the risk of inadequate supplies for the monopoly.[55]

Shipments from Louisiana proved to be problematic, largely be-

cause of the packing and processing practices of the Louisiana planters. By 1784 the *dirección general* began to fear that supplies from
Louisiana exceeded what was needed. In addition, Mexican consumers, especially women, preferred the milder taste of the Mexican tobaccos as compared to the stronger, more aromatic varieties from
Louisiana. On the advice of the *fiscal* Posada, and after consultation
with the *directores generales*, the viceroy notified the governor of
Louisiana that no further imports of tobacco from Louisiana were to
be permitted after 1789.[56] Thereafter, Louisiana tobacco was exported to Spain to supply a new snuff factory in Seville. Subsidies for
Louisiana's tobacco trade, however, continued to be paid from the
coffers of the Mexican monopoly.

In the late 1780s two changes in bureaucratic appointments provided the monopoly with its most directed and talented management. These appointments, at the same time, illustrated the limitations of the monopoly's power. The first was the replacement of a
co-directorship by a single *director general*, Silvestre Díaz de la
Vega. The second saw the arrival of a new viceroy, Revillagigedo the
Younger, one of the most zealous of the Bourbon viceroys. Both held
strong views as to the direction the development of Mexico's economy should take and so possessed a sense of the "wider" picture
within which the monopoly operated. Díaz de la Vega wrote a
lengthy treatise which addressed the problems of Mexico's economy
and agriculture, and made recommendations for improvements. Employment, in both industry and in agriculture, was of particular importance to Díaz de la Vega: "the man without an occupation is a
dead man for the State; those who work are like living plants which
not only produce but also propagate . . . wherein lies the true increase of the population and prosperity of the State."[57] The link between Díaz de la Vega's professed ideals and practice was manifested
in his support of monopoly policy enabling small planters and subsistence peasantry, the *pegujaleros*, to produce tobacco for the monopoly, despite protests from the *resguardo* inspectors and wealthier
rancheros. In this, his views reflected those generally held by Bourbon ministers, who upheld the ideal of small proprietary farmers and
condemned monopoly of landownership.[58] Partly because of these
views, Díaz de la Vega antagonized the planters in much the same
way as Francisco del Real and became their new focus of hostility. In
1810, in the final years of Díaz de la Vega's service to the monopoly,
two spokesmen for the planters candidly described him as "a bad
servant of the king and an enemy of all his best vassals."[59]

Despite Díaz de la Vega's ideals, he made no serious attempts to alter agricultural practices or land distribution within the *villas*. He was, however, determined to have first-hand experience of the contract system and tobacco production and to meet with the planters. He travelled to the *villas* in August 1797, the first visit of a *director general* since the reconnaissance journey of Calvo and Espinosa 30 years earlier. Díaz de la Vega, with the aid of the *factores* and the inspectors in attendance, personally settled the individual production quotas. It was during his trip that, much to his horror, such practices as sale of licenses and bribery of monopoly officials to increase quotas became apparent. The going rate for increases in production quotas was 100 pesos per additional 100,000 plants, providing a major source of contraband. Such violations of production quotas further distorted the distribution of production among planters. Collusion between *resguardo* officials and planters to benefit from contraband trade was believed to be prevalent, although no documented cases came to light. The problem for Díaz de la Vega, of course, was how to eradicate such practices, and there is no evidence that he ever did.[60]

Reacting to problems with the planters in previous decades, Revillagigedo took the opportunity to make the monopoly's position clear. He issued a decree in February of 1790 which itemized new conditions by which the planters must abide. Should the monopoly need to reduce its production levels, any reduction was to be shared in proportion among the planters under contract. Production in excess of the amount indicated on the planters' licenses was to be destroyed and the planter treated as a defrauder of the monopoly. Plant disease or adverse weather conditions were unacceptable reasons to press for a price increase or to withdraw from an existing contract. Warnings were also issued to the *factores* of the *villas* that they were to report any planters who attempted to intimidate or persuade other growers not to contract or to otherwise disobey monopoly conditions and officials. Finally, the 1786 contract prices were to prevail, although a new system of grading was introduced which distinguished between whole and damaged tobacco leaves (*enteros* and *rotos*).[61] The decree was circulated to the *factores* and *subdelegados* of the *villas* and to the intendant of Veracruz. The message was tempered with the additional announcement that those planters who came forward in 1786 to contract would be given preference in the quota allocations for tobacco production in 1790.[62]

At least one decade in the monopoly's history—that of the 1790s—proved to be free of conflict, or at least conflict which delayed tobacco production. New contracts were signed in 1790, 1791,

Table 9.   Inventories of Tobacco Leaf,
1790–1796 (in tercios*)

1790	35,078
1791	40,176
1792	42,855
1793	49,111
1794	55,193
1795	52,034
1796	48,865

Source: AGN, Renta de Tabaco 6, report of contador
general, Existencias de tabaco . . . , 27 May 1796.
*One tercio contained, on average, 170 pounds.

1794, and 1796, each one to last for five years, which "guaranteed" supplies until 1799 and 1801. Despite the energetic direction of Díaz de la Vega and Revillagigedo, it is more likely that the peace of the 1790s was partly the result of the previous twenty years of negotiations and struggles and the gradual co-optation of the merchant-planters. A source of antagonism was eliminated, at least in the short term, when the position of inspector-general was not renewed after Real's death in 1789. The post was divided between the factores of the villas, and the lieutenants of their respective resguardos.[63] The 1790s also witnessed benign weather, excellent growing conditions, and abundant harvests. Projected production in Córdoba for 1792 was 9,700 tercios, but 12,072 tercios were delivered. In 1793 the deliveries totalled 10,600 tercios, when only 7,000 tercios were expected.[64] The levels of leaf inventory increased between 1790 and 1796, as shown in table 9. Good inventory stocks, the monopoly's first line of defense against shortages, worked reasonably well until the first decade of the 1800s, a point to which we shall return in chapter 5.

Paradoxically, plentiful harvests raised their own set of problems. These simmered in the late 1790s and created increasing protest in the early 1800s, not so much by the wealthy planters but by the poorer to middle farmers and rancheros. Given the virtually fixed prices of tobacco for the last fifteen years, combined with inflation and increasing costs of production, profits were falling, and the hard years were difficult for many planters to withstand. Rafael García, a deputy inspector of the Orizaba resguardo, argued that the abundance of the tobacco harvests was not simply due to excellent growing conditions but also to the role of the pegujaleros (subsistence peasants) who deliberately produced excess or illegal amounts of leaf and then sold them to the wealthier planters. The latter mixed the poor quality leaf with their own and sold it to the monopoly under the guise of an abundant crop. The *factor* of Córdoba requested that all *pegujaleros* be prohibited from production for the rest of the year and their allocations distributed among the planters. He agreed with García that any progress in the management of tobacco production depended upon the elimination of the *pegujaleros*. To do so would help swell the rural labor force and probably increase the quality of tobacco. Both the *factor* of Orizaba and the *director general* rejected suggestions to eliminate the *pegujaleros* from tobacco production and argued that "since its establishment, the monopoly has been particularly anxious to deal carefully and fairly with the *pegujaleros*, who rely on tobacco for their survival."[65] The *factor* of Orizaba candidly put forth a more pragmatic reason: "Above all else they are the reserve body upon which the monopoly counts against the threats of the tobacco growers."[66] The *director general* was aware that exclusion of the *pegujaleros* from tobacco contracts might have reduced contraband and increased tobacco quality, but it would only serve to concentrate power into the hands of a few planters, leaving over four hundred *pegujaleros* with their families to "a future of misery and wretchedness."[67] The concentration of power into the hands of a minority of planters, however, was already a fact and had not been achieved without a little help from the monopoly.

As a compromise measure, in May 1794 all planters received orders to the effect that those who did not rent or own a tobacco *rancho* and equipment and who had no fixed residency were to be excluded from the tobacco registers. Exempt from this tightening of the regulations were those subjects who owned small *ranchitos*, who possessed no other source of income, and who were skilled workers—a rather broad spectrum.[68]

In all its sometimes Byzantine operations, the monopoly, apart from monetary loans, made no other investments in the *villas* to improve the techniques of production or provide general curing facilities, both of which would help to improve the quality of the tobacco. It was the lack of adequate facilities for the curing and processing of tobacco which drove many of the smaller planters to seek financing from and become indebted to wealthier farmers. There were discussions about the possibility of building monopoly curing sheds which smaller planters could use, but the problem was never seriously addressed by the *dirección general*. Unlike their Por-

tuguese counterparts in Brazil who attempted to improve production techniques, the Bourbons concentrated more on profit and immediate returns and sacrificed development along the way.[69]

The prosperity of the 1790s did not continue, nor did the new rulings of the *director general* and the viceroy prove to be effective. The
first few years of the nineteenth century witnessed new strains and
tensions between the planters and the monopoly, influenced by both
local and international developments. One immediate effect was a
renewed focus on purchase prices and the more disturbing question
of whether the *villas* could continue to supply the quantities of tobacco demanded by the tobacco manufactories.

When the news of peace between Spain and Great Britain arrived
in 1802, the *dirección general* ordered increases in the output of tobacco products in order to increase supply and restock a depleted inventory of leaf, cigars, and cigarettes. Due to shortages of paper supplies, caused by embargoes of Spanish shipping by the British, the
monopoly began to sell increasing quantities of tobacco leaf to compensate for and supplement the reduced number of cigarettes manufactured. In the process, the existing tobacco inventories had been
heavily drawn upon. But for many of the planters, the abundant
yields of the 1790s were eclipsed by three years of disastrous harvests between 1800 and 1803. In 1799 the value of the tobacco crop
in Orizaba amounted to 590,224 pesos, the highest of the decade,
and the second highest since the establishment of the monopoly.
The following year the total crop value declined by over half to
275,402 pesos, the lowest value in almost twenty years. The years
1801 and 1802 were not much better.

Reports flooded in from Orizaba, in the same way that they had
from Córdoba twenty years before, with descriptions of economic
crisis and chaos.[70] The *subdelegados* of the *villas* received orders to
appoint a spokesman to testify on the planters' situation.[71] The elected spokesman, José María Ortuño, outlined the major grievances of
the planters and the reasons why they believed tobacco production
was fundamentally unprofitable. Ortuño's argument is summed up
in the following extract from his report:

> There is no doubt that the monopoly is almost in ruins . . . at-
> tempts to refute this are made by painting a fantasy of flourish-
> ing towns in which prosperity and abundance abound. New
> manufactories are described . . . a thriving commerce with rapid
> and lucrative turnovers, and all because of the presence of the
> tobacco monopoly . . . This is an illusion . . . the money which

the planters receive is distributed in daily wages and tools, which increases commerce . . . It is despicable to argue that, because others are rich, then so are the planters; no one can believe that the opulence and population increase of these *villas* can be equated with the wealth of the planters. These, far from gaining, lose all that which is advanced to them by the monopoly. Wages paid to workers may encourage trade, but at the expense of the growers . . . 300,000 pesos lost to the planters will enrich the merchants . . . there is no circulation . . . only a violent extraction of money . . . and how much more violent is the commerce for the desecration and extinction of that blood which gives life to the planters . . . today we cannot prepare the fields or cure our tobacco without advance credit . . . those who grow maize and wheat and who sold at 2 reales, today sell at 6, 8, or even 10 reales, but tobacco has been sold at the lowest prices when everything else has increased threefold.[72]

Further complaints focused on the high cost of labor and its unreliability, once more singling out the *pegujaleros* as part of the general problem. There were also complaints about the concentration of wealth and tobacco profits in the hands of the local merchants, so that "the entire profits [of the tobacco trade] are concentrated among twenty-five or thirty merchants, and even that [number] can be reduced to two or three."[73] Ortuño concluded, somewhat dramatically, "The king does not wish to have beggar slaves who, shaking the chains of their misery, breathe only painful laments . . . what help can come from the poor possessed of a melancholic wretchedness and consumed by hunger and scarcity?"[74]

Even the *factores* of the *villas*, Mendiola and Robles, agreed that costs of production had increased, daily wages by at least one-third, and food and animal prices by one-half. Such increases justified a raise in the purchase price of tobacco, but agreement between the planters and the monopoly over the magnitude of a raise proved elusive.[75] Table 10 indicates the prices suggested by the planters and the *factor* of Orizaba. After lengthy consideration by the *contador general* of a multitude of reports, which detailed estimated costs using a combination of prices, the only decision reached was a negative one: the planters' suggestions were unacceptably high. Increases in credit supplements advanced, however, were authorized. Once more, the planters responded that they would not negotiate new contracts without the increases they had stipulated.[76]

In the face of the planters' demands, the *director general* counseled the viceroy to revert to direct production, as the monopoly had

Table 10. *Price Proposals of Planters and Monopoly, 1804*

	1st Grade	2nd Grade	3rd Grade	Punta
Existing prices*	3	2	1	25
Planters' proposals	3.25	2.5	1	24
Factor's proposals	3.125	2.125	1.125	28

Source: AGN, Tabaco 350, Mendiola, García to *director general*, 25 January 1804.
*Prices in *reales*.

done some twenty years before. He had already ordered inspectors to compile estimates of the quantity of tobacco which planters with unexpired contracts and *ranchos* available to the monopoly could produce.[77] There was opposition to such a recommendation, which appeared to many officials as no solution at all. The tobacco inspector for Córdoba, Marcos José de Hería, strongly advised against state production, especially in light of the increase in costs of production and shortages of labor which planters, particularly those in Córdoba, faced.[78] Hería found support for his argument from the illustrious ministers of the Real Tribunal de Cuentas, much to the annoyance of Silvestre Díaz de la Vega. The Tribunal's ministers argued that the losses suffered by the monopoly in its first attempt at direct production should persuade the *director general* that to repeat this strategy was folly. The most measured solution was to agree to the prices suggested by the planters and implement increases in monopoly credit. Increased supplements and prices, combined with increased quantities, ought to provide enough incentive to planters to contract.[79]

The *dirección general* disagreed and elected to employ a carrot and stick approach to its problems. It was decided to implement direct production but, at the same time, to increase the purchase price for tobacco, although at levels below those demanded by the planters, and to reward planters who came forward to contract as they had in 1786. The tobacco produced during the year 1803–1804 would be purchased at 3.125 reales for first grade, 2.125 reales for second grade, 1.1875 reales for third grade, and 32 reales for an *arroba* of *punta*.[80]

The monopoly took over *ranchos* in both *villas*, eleven in Orizaba and twelve in Córdoba, between 1804 and 1808. It produced on its own account 28 percent of the projected harvest for the 1804–1805 growing year.[81] The *contador general* calculated that, by not agreeing to the prices demanded by the planters, savings of 55,580 pesos were secured. What he failed or simply chose not to consider was that the cost of purchase and rental of *ranchos* amounted to some 103,105 pesos.[82] In other words, the policy caused financial losses, just as it had in 1778.

With direct production established once again, but in combination with a slight price increase, many planters agreed to settle two new contracts, one to run from 1806 until 1809, and the other from 1807 until 1812.[83] A jubilant viceroy reported to the *director general* in May 1806 that those planters who previously were unwilling to contract "have now done so . . . the arbitrary and despotic nature of the planters has been curbed."[84] Not for long. Three years later, in 1809, after exactly the same confrontation and, once again, viceregal approval of direct production in the face of planter resistance, prices were increased once more to exceed those based on the original contract of 1765: for first grade, 3.5 reales, for third grade, 1.666 reales, and 44 reales for an *arroba* of *punta*.[85]

The volume of tobacco harvested between 1804 and 1807 was the highest ever produced. The price and credit increases had the desired effect. In Orizaba, the number of planters receiving credit advances increased from 44 in 1786 to a high of 176 by 1809, as shown in figure 6. Despite inflation and increasing costs of production, the ex-

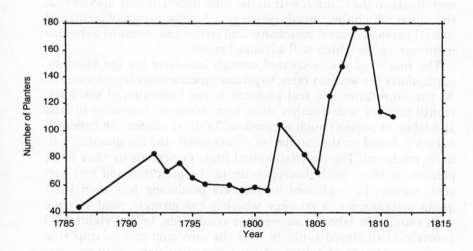

Figure 6. Number of planters in receipt of monopoly credit, Orizaba, 1778–1810. Compiled from various *legajos* for the individual years, ANO.

pansion in volume and prices provided a new speculative opportunity for profit. The *factores* of Orizaba and Córdoba noted the
entry of people who had never produced tobacco before the adjustments in prices in 1804.[86] Although there was an increase noted in
the number of planters across the board, the most significant expansion occurred among those planters who received at least one million *matas*. The average number of planters who received credit to
produce in excess of one million *matas* between 1786 and 1802 was
2; between 1802 and 1811 the number increased dramatically to an
average of 18 planters. The benefits of expansion were not evenly
distributed, and for some planters the increases came too late.
Ramon Gené, a peninsular, had grown tobacco for twenty years. Between 1801 and 1804 he had lost more than 8,000 pesos and could no
longer continue to produce the crop.[87]

It is worth noting here that the increase in prices and production
levels coincided with the implementation of the hated *consolidación de vales reales* of 1804.[88] Quite what role the *consolidación*
played in planters' decisions, however, is unclear. The calling in of
clerical loans and mortgages, which caused such consternation
throughout the kingdom, was not discussed in monopoly correspondence. However there is no evidence that planters were exempted in
any way. The supply of rural credit by the colonial state over the
years may have reduced the level of indebtedness of planters and
merchants to the Church within the *villa* region. It may also be that
the threat which the *consolidación* posed to the supply of credit and
capital persuaded local merchants and farmers to invest in a government enterprise which still advanced credit.

The increased prices created enough incentive for the planters,
particularly the wealthy ones, to produce increasingly large amounts.
At the same time, the real problem at the beginning of the nineteenth century was whether there were adequate resources of land
and labor to support such expansion. Table 11 shows the expected
harvests, based on the number of plants sown, and the quantities finally produced. The shortfall varied from 11 percent in 1802 to 44
percent in 1807. Such discrepancies in the projected and real harvests cannot be explained by planters producing less than their
quota assignments, a strategy which some growers used to cope
with unreliable labor. Poor weather conditions, falling yields, and
contraband all played a role. In 1808 the *dirección general* imported
1,592,219 pounds of tobacco from Cuba, Louisiana, Caracas, and
Guatemala to supplement *villa* production.[89] With the idea of attracting new growers, the *dirección general* agreed to a further price
increase in 1809. However, it is possible that the problem was no

Table 11. *Quantities of Tercios of Tobacco Expected and Received*

Year	Number of tercios *Expected*	Number of tercios *Received*
1801	20,000	15,068
1802	30,000	26,796
1803	35,204	25,200
1804	37,758	26,494
1805	40,820	30,556
1806	40,820	31,149
1807	45,000	25,047

Source: AGN, Tabaco 498, *contador general* to *director general*, 6 May 1808.

longer the combativeness of the planters, but that monopoly requirements based on an upward demand curve could no longer be met adequately with tobacco production restricted to the *villa* region. As we shall argue in Chapter 5, even if the planters could continue to expand output, there was increasing evidence that the manufactories' output had reached its limit within the existing structure of organization. Lack of modification of manufacturing would impose a ceiling on the level of production that would only encourage contraband and dissatisfaction among the planters. Sustained discussion of the problem was prevented by the Mexican insurgency. When Morelos and his rebel troops marched into the province of Veracruz, part of their military strategy to destroy the Crown's resources was to burn the tobacco fields, leaving behind ravaged and destroyed fields.[90]

The settlement of contracts between the tobacco planters of Veracruz and the monopoly provided supplies of tobacco leaf for the colonial state's tobacco manufactories between 1770 and 1810, although the arrangements were increasingly subject to breakdown after the 1790s. What began as an attempt to displace the merchants from tobacco production and to repress their "voice" soon was transformed into a relationship of compromise and co-optation, with a much more successful outcome. In the process, a small group of merchant-planters wielded some influence in contract negotiations and limited the actions of the monopoly. Even if planters' complaints were legitimate, their continued production of tobacco suggests that it was still the most profitable crop relative to the alternatives and the existing markets. The real problems which both planters and monopoly faced at the beginning of the nineteenth century were whether the expanded demands after 1804 exceeded the production capabilities of the *villas* and whether the time had come to modify the organization of tobacco production in colonial Mexico.

Unlike tobacco, which was produced domestically, paper was imported from Spain. Shortages were not uncommon but did not threaten production until the 1790s, when war with Great Britain and embargoes interrupted shipments from Spain to Mexico. Domestic production of paper was never an option, a consequence of the colonial economic relationship which distorted development in both Spain and Mexico, compromising monopoly profits. The alternative in times of crisis was to rely on merchants to acquire paper supplies. One scholar has observed that the establishment of the state tobacco manufactories tested the capacity of the Spanish paper industry to adequately supply the paper required for production. Actually, the test lay rather with the ability of monopoly bureaucrats to find alternatives when Spanish colonialism became its own worst enemy and Spain's incessant wars prevented imports of paper.[91]

A product central to the monopoly's operations, paper was used not just for rolling cigarettes, but also for packaging the products. In the first few years of the monopoly's operations, paper was purchased from Mexican import merchants and imported from Genoa. In 1775 a contract was made with the merchant house of Nicholas Henrile of Genoa, renowned for the quality of its paper, to provide 24,000 reams of high quality paper for the state manufactories on an annual basis.[92] The quality proved to be inadequate and, in 1778, the contract was terminated.[93] During the same period, the *dirección general* experimented with substitutes for paper wrappers for cigarettes. One option was maize leaf, and a group of women tobacco workers from Guatemala experienced in using maize as the outer wrapper for cigarettes were brought to Mexico City. After a series of comparative exercises, the *dirección general* concluded that the use of maize wrappers was more expensive than the existing method using paper.[94]

The final solution was a logical one, at least from the perspective of the Bourbons—import paper from Spain. What better way to help Spain's economy than by stimulating the paper industry through large and sustained demand from the tobacco manufactories of Mexico. A monopoly official was despatched to Spain to select paper from local manufactories. The assumption was that the interest expressed by the Crown in paper supplies for the tobacco manufactories in Mexico would stimulate interest on the part of local entrepreneurs to invest in paper mills, and that this would "deprive the foreigner of the profit from this commerce."[95] In the process, the perennial difficulty of acquiring an adequate amount of the right quality of paper would be eliminated.[96] Once achieved, the state manufactories would gain access to reasonably priced, high quality paper, local industry in Spain would be stimulated, and the need to import paper from outside of Spain, particularly from Genoa, would be eliminated.

In the early 1780s samples from paper mills in Catalonia, Aragon, and Valencia were judged to be inadequate as cigarette wrappers and required improvements before any firm contracts could be signed on behalf of the tobacco monopoly in Mexico. The improvements proved satisfactory and the intendants of Catalonia and Valencia received orders to produce as much paper as possible for the state manufactories, a minimum of 108,000 reams annually. By the late 1780s the Compañía de Navieros de Málaga, through their agent Juan Murphy, signed contracts to ship paper from Spain to Mexico.[97]

Although paper shortages occurred in the 1770s and early 1780s due to the American War of Independence, supplies were not seriously disrupted. In fact, the late 1770s was very much a period of adjustment and response by the monopoly to stable production levels, as competition from the private shops disappeared. If anything, inventory levels were judged to be too high and reductions in production occurred in an effort to balance supply and demand. The 1790s witnessed quite the reverse. After the outbreak of war in 1797, paper shipments stopped. As supplies dwindled, the *dirección general* commissioned resident merchants to buy up stores of paper from merchants in Veracruz and Mexico City for the manufactories. On the orders of viceroy Branciforte, José de la Torre bought up supplies in the port of Veracruz. Antonio Bassoco on behalf of the Consulado de México, the merchants' guild, was ordered to do the same with stores of paper in Mexico City. While a few upright citizens agreed to sell for the price at which they had originally bought the paper, others were not so accommodating. The result was an escalation in paper prices. Between 1776 and 1779, the price of paper ranged between 3 and 5 pesos. Between 1797 and 1799 prices shifted to a new level and ranged anywhere between 10 and 26 pesos per ream in Mexico City.[98] The opportunities for quick and opportunistic profits prodded the *dirección general* to warn merchants who purchased paper on its behalf that they were not to reveal the identity of the real buyer. Sellers automatically increased the price once they realized the purchaser was the monopoly. As a result, specula-

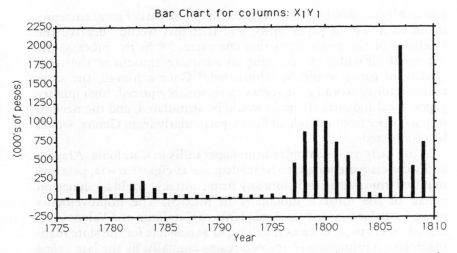

Figure 7. Annual purchases of paper, 1775–1810 (in current pesos). Compiled from the *relaciones generales* for individual years and various *legajos* in Tabaco and Renta de Tabaco, AGN, and Audiencia de México, AGI.

tion with paper stocks resulted in what the viceroy termed "great profits to the [paper] trade, of almost three million pesos," at the expense of the monopoly.[99] Figure 7 shows the shift in the trend of paper purchases as the monopoly began to stockpile. The *dirección general* found itself suddenly incorporated into larger global processes, both political and economic, which its managers could not control.

The *dirección general* argued that the purchases had to be made to avoid riots by the manufactory workers at the prospect of massive layoffs or even closure of the manufactories; it was, after all, not just in the interest of the workers, but of the state, and of the safety and security of the public, to ensure that the 11,000 families who depended upon manufactory work be able to continue with their daily labors. As such, merchants had a civic duty to help the Crown.[100] The decision made by the Junta Superior de Real Hacienda in August of 1797 authorized purchases of paper from merchants of Mexico City, leaving the others to buy and sell on a free market, after they had declared under oath the amount of their existing stocks of paper.[101]

One way of acquiring emergency stocks was to grant special favors to favored vassals, the *agraciados*, in return for services rendered to the king. Tomás Murphy was one such favored merchant, as we argued in Chapter 2. He may also have been the beneficiary of the influence of Francisco Maniau Torquemada, the son of the *contador general*, and the Mexico City agent for the Consulado de Veracruz. In partnership with Tomás Murphy, they offered supplies of paper to the monopoly in 1798 and 1799.[102] As part of his favored status, Murphy acquired the right to trade with Jamaica, as well as with Hamburg, Lisbon, Copenhagen, and Cuba. Murphy also bought up supplies from Havana at prices considerably less than those in either Spain or Mexico. In 1800 the market price in Veracruz was 17 pesos; the purchases pending from the intendant of Havana were priced at 9.5 pesos. Murphy accumulated various commissions and contracts from the government. In 1806, for example, on behalf of the commercial houses of Gordon, Murphy y Reid, and Irving y Cía of London, Murphy arranged the transport of mercury, paper, and effects of the Real Hacienda to Veracruz.[103] José Gutiérrez y Cubas, a Veracruz merchant, also benefited from the situation and in 1800 contracted with the monopoly to supply paper. He was permitted to travel to Jamaica to purchase stocks of paper found in the possession of Spanish prisoners, on the condition that he sell it to the Real Hacienda for half its current sale price in Veracruz.[104] Three years later, Gutiérrez y Cubas, in partnership with the merchant house of Llano y Regato, contracted to ship paper from Spain and Genoa.[105] Merchant commissions signified the beginning of an increasingly important role played by merchants in monopoly affairs and, by extension, their increasingly important relationship to the colonial state.

The measures taken to acquire paper proved successful but expensive. By 1800 the manufactories consumed some 144,000 reams of paper annually, an increase from the 1780s and 1790s when the estimated consumption was between 108,000 and 120,000 reams. Maniau Torquemada calculated that as of May 1800, the total quantity of paper purchased from merchants amounted to 181,953 reams, worth 2,942,436 pesos, with an average purchase price of 16 pesos per ream.[106]

For a very brief period, the *dirección general* considered the possibility of establishing its own paper mill. An investigation was carried out to see whether, in fact, any mills existed in Mexico which could be adapted to the monopoly's needs, but nothing came of such discussions.[107] The outbreak of peace in 1802 served to forestall any further discussion of domestic paper production or the problem of supply. During the years of war with Great Britain, the purchase price from merchants in Mexico increased to 18 pesos. 1806 accounts for the Mexico City manufactory listed two prices for single reams of paper, 5 pesos and 12 pesos. By 1809 paper prices declined somewhat, with a ream selling at between 9 1/2 and 10 pesos in Mexico and 5 to 6 1/2 pesos in Veracruz.[108] While monopoly bureaucrats could, as we have seen, manipulate tobacco prices and co-opt planters, their ability to adjust the conditions of paper supply was much more restricted. Indeed, without the cumbersome weight of Spanish colonialism, the logical step to deal with problems with paper would have been to set up paper mills in Mexico and incorporate them into an already vertically integrated industry. As we argued earlier, the thought crossed the *dirección general*'s mind but given the emphasis on the stimulation of Spanish manufactures, it proved not to be a realistic option.

There were additional social and political considerations which supported Spain's protection of its paper industry and the prohibition against establishing one in Mexico. Interruptions in shipments of paper due to the war with England created problems and the threat of unemployment not only for the thousands of tobacco workers in Mexico, but also for their counterparts in Spain. Representatives of the paper makers in Catalonia, Aragon and Valencia petitioned the Crown for help to alleviate distress. Don Antonio Fontanelles, a paper maker in Barcelona, expressed the problems which afflicted the eight paper manufactories while 300,000 reams languished in local warehouses waiting to be shipped out from Cádiz. Lack of payment due to delays in shipping and lack of further demand resulted in the families who depended on work in the paper factories being "submerged in an abyss of miseries."[109] The representatives of the paper workers in Valencia and Aragon had already requested increases in the number of reams to be produced by the local manufactories, as they believed that, with the coming of peace, the tobacco manufactories in New Spain "would flourish."[110] In 1819, similar letters and petitions expressed the distress of paper workers: "The large number of families who depend on work in the paper manufactories of Catalonia will be reduced to starvation and misery if they cannot work." Just as they had done prior to the war, the workers requested that new contracts be made to supply paper to the tobacco manufactories in Mexico and Puebla.[111]

An alternative to the establishment of paper mills in Mexico in response to paper shortages would have been to reduce the risk of increasing costs by eliminating manufactures and concentrating on the sale of leaf. A private entrepreneur probably would have opted for one of these. From the Spanish state's perspective, however, the imperative to establish paper mills in Mexico simply did not exist. At the time, there was undoubtedly unbounded, if unfounded, confidence that Spain would emerge victorious from its military engagements. Paper production and supply to Mexico were perceived as nothing more than temporary casualties of war. Once imperial communications were reestablished, the colonial symbiosis between paper manufacture and cigarette production would be restored. The *dirección general* eventually tried to steer monopoly policy in the direction of abolishing the manufactories, but to no avail. In the meantime, the supply of a critical raw material remained expensive and subject to shortages. The temporary solution, and the one chosen, was to stockpile. Although both tobacco and paper underwent the greatest increases in cost outlays, from an average of 30 percent of total costs between 1765 and 1795 to 41 percent between 1796 and 1809, paper costs proportionately accounted for the most significant increases, from approximately 2 percent to 25 percent of total costs. There were political consequences as well as fiscal ones, as decisions made in Spain eventually reached the streets of Mexico City and influenced the lives of the tobacco workers. These consequences are discussed in greater detail in chapters 6 and 7.

The monopoly bureaucrats developed methods through which tobacco and paper supplies were produced for the state manufactories, the first by way of a contract system with the planters of Veracruz, the second by imports from Spanish mills. Both tended to reinforce the colonial character of Mexico with its emphasis upon a cash crop in a restricted area and the prohibition against the development of domestic paper mills. Supplies acquired were adequate to support the state enterprise in tobacco but were subject to increasing costs and expedients, and to tensions and breakdown, particularly in the case of paper after 1796. The tobacco planters proved themselves able to protest unacceptable contract conditions and to retain their "voice," despite attempts on the part of the monopoly to stifle it through retaliation and penalties for challenging contract conditions. The *dirección general* found itself confronted by the ambitions of a local elite which sought to use the opportunities for profit and power offered by the monopoly. We turn next to a closer consideration of the organization of tobacco production and an examination of the tobacco planters. Who were the planters, particularly the "articulate oligarchy," and what effect did the monopoly have upon the society and economy of Orizaba and Córdoba?

4. Merchants, *Rancheros*, and Peasants: The Tobacco Planters of Orizaba and Córdoba

A SINGULAR CHARACTERISTIC of agricultural production in eighteenth century Mexico was that it gradually became subordinated to Mexican merchants and the Church, who were the only ones able to supply capital and credit in a specie-scarce economy. There was no formal banking system; the Church and kinship networks filled the vacuum. The government was not in the habit of lending, and, as we saw in Chapter 2, was much more likely to borrow than to lend. Tobacco production proved to be one of the exceptions, as the colonial state attempted to stimulate its expansion by providing capital in the form of interest-free credit.

The original intention of the *dirección general* was to replace the role played by merchants in the tobacco trade, partly to try to avoid the type of confrontation which it eventually experienced throughout its dealings with them, and partly to encourage increased production and economic growth. Monopoly financing of tobacco planters provides an interesting comparison with Bourbon attempts to stimulate the silver mining industry. Both initiatives incorporated measures designed to reduce the economic role of powerful merchants. Unlike the successful outcome in the case of mining, where silver miners and small provincial merchants found financial independence, the monopoly failed, in the long run, to eliminate merchants and large landowners from tobacco production and the dependence of smaller planters and peasants upon them.[1]

Within the tobacco producing region, Orizaba emerged as the dominant tobacco producer and experienced considerable growth during the late eighteenth century, although such growth was increasingly dependent upon a single crop. The long-term impact of the monopoly operations upon the local elite of Orizaba was to strengthen and consolidate its power, not to undermine it. This was a result of the monopoly's expedient agreements with the merchant-planters in order to guarantee supplies of leaf tobacco to its manufactories. In this chapter, we will look at the structure of tobacco production, land, labor, and financing. Although our main focus will be on Orizaba, we will also look more closely at the planters of Orizaba and Córdoba and examine the effects of an expanding tobacco economy upon them.

Positioned at the base of the volcano Citlatépetl, Orizaba is situated in a fertile valley, with a temperate climate and well irrigated by rivers in the very rich agricultural area of central Veracruz. Orizaba, along with closely neighboring Córdoba to the east, Jalapa to the north, and the port of Veracruz to the northeast, became the most important commercial, agricultural, and administrative centers of colonial Veracruz. Orizaba lay 45 leagues from Mexico City, 31 leagues from the port, 26 leagues from Jalapa, and 4 leagues from Córdoba. The trip from Orizaba to the capital could be made in three to four days.[2] Orizaba's location at 4,000 feet above sea level made it considerably more comfortable to live in than either Córdoba or Veracruz. Proximity to the coast allowed ready access to international markets, and the royal highways connected Central Veracruz with the markets of interior Mexico.

If the economic growth of the region of Veracruz is judged on the value and fluctuations in its *alcabalas* (excise), admittedly a risky assessment, it was one of the most dynamic for the period 1778–1809. It was the only administration in the southeastern regions which demonstrated such growth, an expansion confirmed by the movement of tithes.[3] Orizaba, Córdoba, and Jalapa (the capital of the modern-day state of Veracruz) accounted for almost 84 percent of total *alcabalas* collected in Veracruz (excluding the port itself, which was administered directly by the directorate of Aduanas in Mexico City). Of the three towns, Orizaba not only demonstrated the greatest rate of growth, but was also the only one which experienced sustained growth during the period under consideration, compared, for example, with the fluctuations experienced by Córdoba.[4] Such growth was founded on the expansion in tobacco production in the late eighteenth century and the injections of government and private capital which financed its production.

The important role and dominance of tobacco as a commercial crop, particularly in the case of Orizaba, is reflected in the increasing contribution of *alcabalas* levied on tobacco to the total *alcabalas* collected annually. In the 1780s tobacco sales in Orizaba accounted for approximately 34 percent to 44 percent of total *alcabalas,* increasing to 50 percent by the 1790s, and exhibiting a massive jump to 75 percent in 1806. Córdoba retained a narrower range of between

25 to 48 percent between 1780 and 1806, with an average of 40 percent.[5] Overall, between 1765 and 1806, 15,350,945 pesos was paid out to planters in Orizaba and 11,194,749 pesos to Cordoban planters (see figure 3a and Appendix II). By the 1790s, although Orizaba boasted a variety of artisans such as tailors, carpenters, servants, shoemakers and weavers, the most important industry was the tobacco manufactory, which employed 182 men. The second-most important occupation, local commerce, employed 140 *tratantes*, or commercial dealers, while the third-most important occupation, tailoring, employed 76 individuals.[6] Both agriculture and industry, then, became increasingly dominated by tobacco, and, to a large degree, tobacco's fate determined that of Orizaba, a relationship which contemporaries acknowledged.[7]

By the early 1760s, apart from tobacco, livestock, and food staples such as maize, barley, wheat, and vegetables, the only other major cash crop produced was sugar, the dominant producer of which was Córdoba. In 1779 José de Quiroga described the Von Thünen-like structure of land use in and around Córdoba: "All of the area which is not mountainous is occupied by the *rancherías* of the planters from both *villas*, with the difference that those lands within a radius of two leagues of Córdoba are owned by the inhabitants of Córdoba and occupied not solely by the production of tobacco, but also of sugar, maize, and vegetables; in the surrounding area outside of this circle are planters from both *villas* and also the Indians who have contracted with the monopoly."[8]

Toward the end of the eighteenth century, increasing specialization in sugar production occurred to the exclusion of secondary production such as maize and beans, unlike the previous century. Such foodstuffs were purchased from Indian producers and nearby *rancheros*. Many of the contracts for the rental of *cabildo* lands specified which crops were to be grown, to ensure supplies of maize and other food crops, so that sugar *hacendados* could concentrate only on sugar. In this way, the local *cabildo* (with many of the sugar *hacendados* as majority members) acted in a regulatory manner to ensure the production and supply of staples to the sugar haciendas, without having to produce it themselves. There were, nevertheless, frequent complaints by sugar *hacendados* against the intervention of the state in favor of local tobacco farmers, often, allegedly, at the expense of sugar.

The sugar *hacendados* were a tight group which exercised power at all levels. Following the establishment of the monopoly, some of them became financiers of, or rented out lands to, tobacco planters, while a few of the most important sugar *hacendados* and members of the founding families of Córdoba invested in tobacco production. Most notable among these was José Leyva who, together with his wife, Doña Catalina Esparragosa, founded one of the powerful land-owning families which dominated Córdoba in the eighteenth century.[9] For the most part, however, the major sugar-planter families did not engage in tobacco production. In 1770, only seven out of twenty-five sugar haciendas engaged in tobacco production, and the tobacco farming areas remained distinct from those where sugar was grown.[10] The concentration on sugar in Córdoba increased after 1796 when the production of *aguardiente* (cane distilled liquor) was authorized, opening up a new domestic market, and following the Haitian slave uprising which disrupted Caribbean sugar production for the European markets.

The presence of two important cash crops in Córdoba may account for the more modest growth in tobacco production, as sugar provided an alternative for local agricultural entrepreneurs and reduced the capital available to invest in tobacco. The increase in the number of sugar haciendas, from fifteen in 1793 to twenty-three in 1808, suggests that improved market conditions of the late 1790s may have persuaded some of the wealthier Cordoban planters to concentrate their investments in sugar haciendas. The attraction was not confined to Córdoba, however. By the beginning of the nineteenth century there was increasing financial involvement in Cordoban sugar by Orizabeño merchants who controlled part of the local sugar production but who also had tobacco interests. When the sugar hacienda Las Palmillas (La Concepción) was sold in 1809, bids were put in by the Orizabeño merchant and tobacco planter Don Manuel Rocha, who offered 71,500 pesos. He was outbid by a Veracruz merchant, Don Pedro Gómez Rodríguez, who bid 73,000 pesos. Since the value placed on the hacienda was 58,732 pesos, the high bidding suggests the lucrative nature of the property and sugar production.[11] The more modest expansion in tobacco production in Córdoba can also be attributed to periodic epidemics, population decline, and destructive weather conditions, which were more severe over the long term in Córdoba than in neighboring Orizaba.

The population of the *villas* was relatively small. In the early 1750s the parish of Orizaba housed some 13,424 souls (all racial categories).[12] By the 1790s the town of Orizaba had a population of 7,074 excluding its Indian residents. Within its jurisdiction (defined as including Ingenio, Tomatlan, and Maltrata) the population increased to 9,119 souls, but this is still an incomplete number since Indians were not included in the population count.[13] The *factor* and *subdelegado* provided by far the highest population estimate for the parish of Orizaba of between twenty and thirty thousand by the early 1800s. Such an estimate, however, was based on personal impressions and probably errs on the high side. [14] The population of the parish of Córdoba in 1754 was 19,992 (including all racial categories). [15] By way of comparison, in the 1790s the largest city in the kingdom, Mexico City, had an estimated population of 112,926, followed by Puebla, with 52,717 inhabitants, and, in third place, the mining town of Guanajuato, with 32,098 inhabitants. [16]

Indians comprised between 45 and 47 percent of the *villas'* population, a lower proportion than for the Intendency of Veracruz as a whole, which amounted to 74 percent. [17] As with the rest of the indigenous population of Mexico, the local native population reached a nadir by the early seventeenth century but slowly recuperated by the end of the same century. Although Indian communities were afflicted by epidemics which affected the region in 1774, 1779, 1786, 1788–1789, and 1813, the number of Indian tributaries in Orizaba and Córdoba continued to increase throughout the eighteenth century. By 1802 there were an estimated 7,532 Indian tributaries in Orizaba and 2,354 in Córdoba. [18]

As we shall see later, by the beginning of the nineteenth century the labor market of the tobacco producing regions favored the seller, not the buyer. Given the dynamic nature of the region, referred to earlier, and the expanding role of tobacco, the increasing demand for labor may have outstripped the pace of population growth. This accounts in part for the high costs of labor experienced by the planters and suggests that their demands for increased prices for their tobacco had a legitimate basis. Patterns of land ownership provide another explanation for an unreliable labor supply, and we now turn to look at the structure of land tenure and tobacco production.

The pattern of land tenure in the *villas* was one of the most important factors which affected the structure and organization of tobacco production. The tendency, exhibited elsewhere in Mexico, of appropriation of village lands and swelling numbers of a rural proletariat was not to manifest itself in Córdoba and Orizaba until the mid-nineteenth century. Access to small plots of land did not prevent peasants from working on the *ranchos* or haciendas of wealthier planters, but the relatively widespread distribution of *ranchos* and Indian villages with their own lands limited the supply of labor. The general picture which emerges of the range of property ownership resembles that found in Oaxaca and southern Mexico, as opposed to the property relations characteristic of the Central Valley or the North, as described by William Taylor: "A large number of small ranches and farms account for most of the land controlled by Spaniards. Spanish landowners, many of whom were creoles, were numerous and not particularly wealthy."[19]

The haciendas within the *villas* were not large compared with other regions. The size of most properties in Córdoba and Orizaba by the early nineteenth century was between 634 and 2,115 acres. By the 1830s the hacienda Encinal in Orizaba was situated on 1,587 acres, San Diego on 3,173 acres, and Tequila, by far the largest, on approximately 8,665 acres.[20] The *ranchos* measured anywhere between 50 and 1,481 acres, the largest ones clearly overlapping with the size of a small hacienda.[21] In 1791 property listings for Orizaba included forty-two tobacco *ranchos,* four haciendas, one *trapiche* (sugar mill) and two *molinos* (mills).[22] In 1794 Córdoba had an estimated eighty-two tobacco *ranchos.*[23] Assessments of the value of the tobacco *ranchos* varied between 300 and 10,000 pesos.[24]

Land tenure and conditions of tenancy among the tobacco planters varied from ownership of haciendas and *ranchos* to the more common lease and rental of plots of land. The most extensive properties were owned by absentee aristocratic landowners, the Conde del Valle de Orizaba, the Marqués del Valle de la Colina, and the Marqués de Sierra Nevada. Like many other absentee owners, they became rentiers and leased out their properties. Francisco Rengel, a tobacco planter, for example, rented the hacienda of Encinal from the Conde del Valle.[25] All of the rentiers retained representatives in Orizaba to manage their affairs, including tobacco production for the monopoly.[26] Resident owners of local haciendas, such as Buenavista, Monteblanco, Potrero, and Toxpa, who specialized in sugar and livestock, also rented out lands to tenants who were primarily tobacco planters. José Bringas, owner of the hacienda of Tecamaluca, combined livestock ranching, tobacco production, and rental of lands to tenant farmers. Eleven *rancherías* belonged to the hacienda, six of which were rented to tobacco farmers.[27]

Many of the wealthy planters, including the merchant-planters, owned several small to medium size *ranchos* rather than large haciendas. The property and wealth of *rancheros* who produced tobacco varied widely. They could be independent landowners, tenants of larger landowners, subsistence farmers surviving on three or four acres, or anywhere on a continuum between the two extremes.[28]

Planters could also rent lands from the *cabildos* of the *villas* or from the surrounding Indian villages. The *factores* of both Orizaba and Córdoba repeatedly mentioned in their reports to the *dirección general* that the majority of lands on which tobacco was grown belonged to the *cabildos.*[29] It was common for planters to rent from the Indian villages which surrounded the *villas*. The accounts of the Indian *cabildo* of Orizaba for 1798 and 1802–1804 demonstrate the vitality of these land rental agreements. In 1802, for example, the *cabildo* received a total of 2,049 pesos in rent from Spaniards farming on its lands. They were owed 385 pesos in outstanding rental payments and 40 pesos from the Indians of Ixhuatláncillo for permission to collect firewood.[30] The Indians of Ixhuatlán, in the jurisdiction of Córdoba, rented out lands in Tetela to several tobacco planters in 1778 and, several years later, to the monopoly, when it produced tobacco directly.[31]

One of the reasons the *dirección general* selected the *villas* as the main region of tobacco production was because of the high quality of the leaf produced there and the reputation it enjoyed throughout Mexico. The notarial records indicate the presence and functioning of tobacco *ranchos* as early as 1728. Orizaba leaf was sold throughout Mexico and found strong markets in Mexico City, Puebla, Guadalajara, and the *tierra adentro* (the internal provinces).[32] By the 1730s and 1740s almost 400,000 pounds of tobacco were produced in Orizaba, valued at 100,000 pesos annually. The southeast and northeast of Orizaba, where soils were generally good, and which produced tobacco with a thin leaf, emerged as the primary producers of the crop.[33] Between 1765 and 1804, Orizaba's tobacco production increased three times, from 1,082,063 pounds to an estimated 3,216,910 pounds in volume. Tobacco production in Córdoba was more modest: from 879,714 pounds in 1765 to a peak of 1,967,070 pounds in 1782 (see figures 3a and 3b, and Appendix II). But how well distributed were the tobacco allocations?

Before we go any further, we need to be clear about who planted tobacco and under what conditions. As we have already seen in chapter 3, the planters were a mixture of peasants, the *pegujaleros*, *rancheros*, and merchant-planters. Tobacco as a cash crop has a particularly high unit value. The plant can be produced on small plots of arable land relative to other cash crops, such as wheat and other grains, and requires little capital investment in tools, which makes it attractive to both prosperous and poor farmers. As a result, many poor peasants, the *pegujaleros*, and farmers applied for a license from the monopoly to produce tobacco, even if they were ineligible for monopoly credit or were not financed by other planters.[34] It was these *pegujaleros* who eventually caused problems for the middle planters, who would have preferred the peasants to work for them, not compete against them. There was another type of *pegujalero*, small subsistence farmers, often from Indian villages, who received credit from the wealthy planters in the form of *avíos,* advances of money, tools, and commodities, to produce part or all of the latter's tobacco allocations.[35] In addition to these planters, more prosperous *rancheros* and farmers received monopoly credit. At the top of the social and economic pyramid of growers were the wealthy merchant-planters who formed a "tobaccocracy," and who also received monopoly credit.

For most planters, despite their protests about prices and contract conditions, tobacco remained the most profitable alternative. The same names of planters appear year after year on the contracts and credit registers. As tobacco production increased over the decades, those planters who could expand their individual quotas did so. Florentino Avila, for example, began with 80,000 plants; by 1810, some twenty-five years later, his production quota amounted to 3 million *matas.*[36] The quantity of plants cultivated by individual planters varied from the *pegujaleros* who usually produced between 5,000 and 10,000 *matas* (between one and two acres) to those *rancheros* who ranged from 50,000 to 500,000 *matas* (ten to one hundred acres). Most of the planters who received credit advances were the small to middle farmers, some of whom were content to plant a small crop of about 100,000 to 150,000 *matas.* Others were ambitious to expand but would not risk doing so under existing prices and conditions.

The distribution of the annual quotas of tobacco demonstrates the tendency toward a concentration of production in the hands of a few, the merchant-planters. In 1778 26 percent of the planters in Orizaba acquired 72 percent of the total volume allocated, leaving 74 percent of the planters with 28 percent of the volume. By 1807 17 percent of the planters received 62 percent of the total amount of tobacco to be sown, leaving 83 percent of the planters with 38 percent of the total volume.[37] In Córdoba, in 1779, 47 percent of the tobacco quotas distributed went to 11 percent of the planters.[38] By 1790 8 percent of the planters received 49 percent of the total tobacco quotas. The concentration of production into a few hands was increased by the kinship networks which pervaded Orizaba and Córdoba, as fathers, mothers, brothers, sons-in-law, nephews, and grandmothers all received individual tobacco allocations. One such example is provided by the peninsular Francisco del Puy y Ochoa. By 1810 his tobacco quota amounted to four million plants; combined with his stepsons' quotas, the amount totalled some eleven million plants.[39]

What effect did the expansion in the volume of tobacco production have on land ownership and the land market in the long term, and what strategies did the planters use to expand their output? In the case of the planter Florentino Avila, discussed earlier, the expansion of his tobacco crop demanded an increase in land to plant the crop, from sixteen to six hundred acres.[40] Production was carried out on *ranchos* and haciendas, but the particular structure of land tenure and the labor supply contributed to the retention of *avío* arrangements with smaller producers, particularly the *pegujaleros*. The crop itself also affected planters' strategies, as there are limited returns to scale in the cultivation of tobacco. The wealthy planters, especially the merchant-planters, expanded their production in the long term, not by monopolization of land, as occurred in other regions, but by expanding their relationship with smaller planters and the peasantry and by concentrating more on the processing and curing of the crop. The land market did not stand still, however, and, although we cannot trace the pace of land acquisition, concentration, and turnover of properties, there is evidence which points to increasing demand for and pressure on the lands of the *villas*.

Throughout the late colonial period, as agriculture became more profitable, often combined with population increase, marginal lands were brought under cultivation for food staples while the best land was reserved for the most profitable crops. Landowners expanded their landholdings at the expense of nearby Indian village lands and eliminated traditional "rights" such as access to firewood, water, and pasture privileges, and began to charge money for these "services." Such changes often resulted in court cases and provoked indigenous rebellions and uprisings.[41] In the case of the *villas*, there were few reports of Indian rebellions among the villagers as a result of land disputes and attempted expropriations, but in Orizaba there was an abundance of land litigation which concerned Indian communities. As early as 1724 Spaniards and Indians were arguing over the lands of Guayabal, as were the Marquesa de Sierra Nevada and the Conde del Valle de Orizaba. The Condes, in turn, seemed to be in perpetual conflict with the *cabildo* of Orizaba. Several of the cases were found in favor of the Indian litigants. All concerned alleged illegal use of lands or claim to proprietorship. In 1808 Don Lorenzo de Guardamuro, owner of the sugar hacienda Nuestra Señora de la Concepción, Tuxpango, accused the Indians of Naranjal of deliberately and "despotically" trying to despoil him of part of the lands of his hacienda by moving several wooden crosses which served as boundary markers.[42]

The rise in rents in Orizaba suggests increasing demand for land over the decades, plausibly connected to the increase in the volume of tobacco production and the growth of Orizaba in general, although the data are too contradictory and exiguous to be conclusive.

Increasing rents may have been due to inflation, although the situation more resembled that of Yucatán where increased levels of production and investment, not inflation, accounted for the major share of the growth in estate values in the late eighteenth century.[43] In 1767 the planters' representatives reported that rent for approximately twenty acres averaged 20 pesos (1 peso per acre).[44] In 1781, the *factor* of Orizaba, Mendiola, reported that the "average" rent for twenty acres was between 25 and 50 pesos (1.25–2.25 pesos per acre).[45] By 1803, the *factor* of Orizaba, not given to hyperbole, observed that the increases in rent experienced by the *arrendatarios* (planters who leased out land) in Orizaba were almost "insupportable," although he neglected to provide any figures.[46]

The suggestion of an upward trend in rents in these fragmentary figures is confirmed by upward shifts in rents paid to Indian communities. In 1731 Antonio de Castro rented a *rancho* located in fine tobacco-producing lands from the Indians of the *villa* of Orizaba for 300 pesos annually on a six-year contract. Several decades later, in 1778, Pedro Cubas rented it for 700 pesos. In 1785 litigation occurred over the rent charged by the *cabildo de naturales* of Orizaba for the same *rancho*: 1,800 pesos for a nine-year contract, effectively more than doubling the rent over an eight-year period. The rent was deemed to be "excessive."[47] Antonio Bolaños rented some land in Cuichapa from the *cabildo* of Orizaba for five years at 250 pesos annually, beginning in 1785. In 1807 Mariano Barragán took over the five-year rental contract, by which time the annual rental payment was set at 880 pesos.[48] A final example of rent increases concerns the Indians of the village of Naranjal, close to Orizaba. Between 1790 and 1798 their lands became part of a bidding war. In 1790 Juan de Segura rented lands in Cuichapa for five years at 300 pesos annually. When it was time for the contract to be renewed, Pedro María Fernández, a tobacco planter from Orizaba, offered 350 pesos annually for seven years, to begin in 1799. He increased his bid to 450 pesos in 1798 when José de Limón, a tobacco planter of some wealth, made a bid of 380 pesos. Not to be outdone, the *regidor* of Orizaba, Julián de Romanos, offered 400 pesos. Finally, Limón outbid everyone and acquired the rental property for a seven-year term at 570 pesos. Surveyors of the property claimed that, although the soil had little substance, a fair yearly rental sum was between 500 and 600 pesos.[49]

A different indicator of pressure on land and its excessive use in tobacco production was a gradual decline in yields per acre. While total production for the *villas*, especially Orizaba, increased steadily in absolute terms, falling yields in some areas were reported due to the steady impoverishment of the soil through failure of the planters to leave land fallow and allow it to recuperate. The tobacco plant it-self is notorious for its debilitating effects on soil, and fields needed to be left fallow every few years. Repeated production on the same tract of land led to soil erosion, depletion of plant food, and the risk of soil toxicity.[50] The *factor* of Orizaba recognized the existence of diminishing returns as early as 1778 and described its effects quite accurately when he observed that planters who made poor profits did so because "they found themselves paying more to produce the same amount of tobacco."[51] José de Quiroga criticized the seeming ignorance of the planters in their farming practices. He described areas of Sumidero, a popular area in Orizaba for producing tobacco, as "almost sterile" and observed that "the farmers of the area are completely unaware of the art of improving worn-out land . . . the insistence and need to produce tobacco on any land whether good or bad . . . is the reason why one can see the variety of fortunes which result . . . There is nothing more typical than to see in such a small area, side by side, the results of fertile and infertile lands."[52] Qui-roga's assessments were accurate, not only in the differing fortunes of tobacco planters, but also with regard to increasing infertility of some areas of production, as harvests of the late eighteenth and early nineteenth centuries began to exhibit signs of declining yields per acre. In the 1780s the planters tried to incorporate a new clause into their contracts with the monopoly which requested that landowners rent out the uncultivated areas of their property for a "fair price" for new tobacco production. Their reason was that much of the land on which they grew tobacco no longer produced normal yields.[53] For Orizaba in 1780 the estimated yield per acre was 428 pounds; in 1805 it had declined to 314 pounds, suggesting a progressive de-cline.[54] As shown in table 14 the variation of *tercios* produced from 100,000 plants in the 1780s ranged from 30 to 42; by 1805 the in-spector Rafael García estimated that the range had shifted down-ward to between 26 and 35 *tercios*.[55] For the monopoly officials fur-ther evidence of poor yields was provided by the production trends for 1801–1807, when the monopoly suffered from severe shortfalls in the tobacco harvests, as we discussed in chapter 3.[56] Plant disease, excessively bad weather conditions, and the planters' strategies all affected the quantity produced, but it is likely that falling yields contributed to the general problem of harvest shortfalls.

Repeated production of a tobacco crop on the same tract of land must have resulted in lower yields and poorer quality leaf, which re-sulted in higher costs of production to produce the same amount of tobacco. It was those planters who could afford to fertilize, to allow their land to lay fallow, or to acquire new lands who would profit most. The protected status under which the planters sheltered and a guaranteed market did little to encourage improvements and experimentation with new farming methods. At best, tobacco planters aimed to produce crops with a high proportion of first-class leaves, but there is little evidence that they developed anything remotely approaching what one scholar has called a "tobacco mentality," a way of life in which individuals evaluated themselves and others according to the quality of their tobacco leaf, and in which their lives were paced by the stages of tobacco cultivation.[57] One reason must surely be the protected status of the wealthier planters under the monopoly, but also the methods used to acquire labor and the shortages in the labor supply faced by the planters.

Tobacco is a labor-intensive crop and requires attention all year round, despite a relatively short growing season.[58] As we have argued, its production does not lend itself to economies of scale, and the acreage which one fieldhand could cultivate efficiently was relatively small.[59] This undoubtedly provided part of the prosperous planters' rationale to continue to finance Indian producers in the surrounding villages by means of the *avío*, although that was not necessarily a guarantee of high-quality tobacco. Once the Indian producers turned over the tobacco to their *aviadores*, the latter still required workers to process the tobacco. A constant complaint of planters was the high cost of labor and its unreliability, a complaint common among *hacendados* and farmers throughout Mexico. The preponderance of small properties and land-holding Indian villages had important ramifications for the organization of tobacco production and the labor supply for the tobacco fields. Unlike the changes which occurred in the labor supply in regions such as Guadalajara, where demographic growth was rapid in the late eighteenth century and created a labor surplus, labor remained scarce in the *villas* throughout the late eighteenth and early nineteenth centuries. The intensification of commercial agriculture increased competition for labor, but the methods used to acquire it reinforced the coexistence of wage labor and more coercive mechanisms such as debt peonage and the *repartimiento de labor* (labor draft).

The supply of labor in Orizaba and Córdoba was a problem even before the *villas* were incorporated into the monopoly's operations and continued to present problems for both bureaucrats and planters into the early nineteenth century. Planters reported such problems to the *dirección general* and described their primary method of mobilizing labor through the *enganche* method: "we distribute money to them [the Indians] in advance on the condition that they repay us with their labor . . . Many workers have a lot of money distributed among them."[60]

Field labor, for the most part, was provided by the local Indian population.[61] Indian *pegujaleros* who cultivated small tobacco plots left them in the care of their wives and children while they went off to earn cash wages on the tobacco *ranchos* owned by prosperous Spanish and mestizo farmers. Their numbers, however, were inadequate to satisfy local demand. As the inspector-general Francisco del Real described the situation, "On average an Indian's crop does not exceed 10,000 plants, generally more like 4,000 or 5,000, which does not demand his personal attention for more than one or two days per week; the remaining days are spent earning a daily wage in the nearby *rancherías* of Tlasoloapa, Tenejapa, and Naranjal where workers are invariably scarce for the production of tobacco."[62]

Rafael García, the *resguardo* inspector for Orizaba, reported that the *operarios* (workers) were not subject to any coercion on the *ranchos* "as they are free workers (*gente libre*), and, after they finish their daily work, they sleep at other *ranchos* or in the nearby settlements where they have relatives."[63] Planters, rich and poor, and monopoly administrators were obliged to traverse the region surrounding the *villas* in search of Indian labor. Even offers of high daily wages, at least from the planters' perspective, failed to attract adequate labor, especially in the 1790s and early 1800s.

If access to and control of Indian labor was critical for field labor, a problem which some planters solved through *avío* arrangements, acquisition of *tabaqueros* (skilled tobacco workers) proved to be a constant concern to all planters because the final quality of the tobacco harvest was only as good as its workers. Workers were required to sort, string, store, and bale the tobacco to ready it for delivery to the monopoly warehouses. *Hacendados* and *rancheros*, including the merchant-planters who owned *ranchos*, employed *mayordomos* (stewards) to oversee production of their crops and general administration of their *ranchos*. They also employed *sirvientes*, *operarios*, and *labradores* (resident workers and day workers). Prosperous *rancheros* such as Gerónimo Baltierra, a creole planter who owned a ranch in Tecama, had eight *sirvientes* on his property.[64] Don José Vivanco, the owner of the hacienda Encinal, settled on the property his Spanish *mayordomo* with his family, six *sirvientes*, three *operarios*, and two Spanish *labradores* (farmers).[65] Doña Bernarda Rendon owned three *ranchos* in Sumidero. On these three properties lived a total of 52 *operarios* (resident wage workers) with their families and three muleteers.[66] On the *rancho* which Marcos González rented from the Marqués del Valle de la Colina lived two *vaqueros* (cowboys), twelve *operarios,* and three farmers.[67] It is likely that share-cropping was practiced, an ideal arrangement given the circumstances, but we have no evidence of its use.

Labor constituted the largest proportion of the costs of production of a tobacco crop, as Antonio de Sobrevilla, the inspector-general's lieutenant, observed:

> Labor is without doubt the greatest outlay [of a planter], not just for the *jornales,* but also for the money which remains owing due to workers who run away or die, because generally a worker becomes indebted . . . the Indian *tlaquehuales* work for between 3 and 5 reales, which is given to each one before they begin their tasks, but there is not a farmer who is not owed outstanding money . . . they do not stay in the fields for the time specified, which adds to the costs because men have to be hired to travel to the villages and bring them back.[68]

The total cost estimated for the production of 100,000 plants (which needed approximately 20 acres and 10 men) was 1,102 pesos of which 841 pesos or 76 percent was invested in labor.[69] Other estimates were slightly lower and ranged from 53 to 55 percent of total costs.[70]

The distinction between unskilled and skilled *tabaqueros* is reflected in the wage differentials paid to workers according to their tasks. The rates paid by the monopoly to their day workers in 1781 are shown in table 12. The high wages for the sorters is notable, especially since the average wage for rural workers was between 2 and 3 reales.[71] Creoles and mestizos dominated the ranks of the skilled tobacco workers. Mulattos and free blacks were often employed as skilled packers and balers of tobacco.

The inspector-general reported that rural wages increased between 1779 and 1786. Monthly salaries of *sirvientes,* for example, increased by 25 percent and, with the increased prices of the food provided them, the overall increase amounted to 33 percent.[72] The real problem, in the inspector-general's opinion, however, was the unresponsiveness of Indian workers and poor management by their bosses, who failed to send them out on time to begin sowing and weeding in the tobacco fields and created unnecessary delays. Planters resorted to paying for three work crews to acquire one, thus tripling the normal cost. By the 1800s planters offered a daily wage of 4 reales and food, almost double the average rate for rural workers in colonial Mexico.

Rural workers were subjected to coercive practices, especially

Table 12. Occupation and Wages in Tobacco Cultivation, 1781

Occupation	Daily Wage/Quota
Sowing of tobacco seeds	2.5 reales/1,000 seeds
Transplanting of seeds	2.5–3 reales plus food ration; Indian *tlaquehuales* received 2.5 reales
Clearing and weeding of land	3 reales daily
Topping and suckering	3 reales daily
Cutting	3 reales daily
Stringing of leaves	4 reales/100 sartas
Hanging of leaves	7 reales/300 sartas or 3 reales daily
Taking down of leaves	5 reales/1,000 sartas
Sorters	5 reales daily
Balers	2.75 reales daily

Source: AGN, Renta de Tabaco 44, inspector-general to *contador general*, 1 May 1781.

debt peonage, but the levels of debt owed by the Indian workers to their bosses indicate that they used the high and persistent demand for labor to their advantage. In so doing, the case of the indigenous peasantry incorporated into the commercial production of tobacco provides us with further evidence of how the rural poor could impose limitations on elite exploitation. Recent reassessments of debt relations in commercial agriculture suggest that debt peonage encompasses a variety of relationships and degrees of coercion. At one extreme is the model of an oppressed peasantry virtually enslaved by their debts to their masters in "debt bondage"; at the other extreme are those relations in which the debts function as "perks," with minimal coercion and voluntary indebtedness. The debt relations formed between peasants and planters are closer to the paradigm of debts as "perks," suggesting a balance in favor of labor.[73] Several examples follow. When the *dirección general* stopped direct monopoly production in 1781, the *factor* of Orizaba reported to the viceroy that Indian villages within the jurisdictions of the *villas* San Juan de los Llanos and Jalapa owed the monopoly 10,179 pesos. Over the next several years the monopoly tried to recoup the debts by making the Indians pay in silver or work off the debts in the tobacco fields of the planters who had contracts with the monopoly.[74] Planters were owed large sums of money from their workers and *aviados*. José Limón, a prominent planter, had acted as *aviador* of the Indians of Naranjal for seventeen years. In 1799, he distributed 4,000 pesos among them, not because such an amount represented the costs of production of his crop, but because that was the amount requested by his *aviados*. As a result, Limón was owed a considerable amount of money in debts which the Indians had accumulated over the years. He appeared somewhat resigned to the fact that the only way to regain his money was to continue to advance credit on the assumption that the debts would eventually be paid off. By 1807 María Pardiñas estimated the debts of her Indian *aviados* to be a staggering 15,500 pesos.[75] Such relations were not unique to tobacco. On the hacienda San Antonio de Azizintla, which produced maize, barley, and wheat, the owner, Don Antonio de Bringas, was owed 503 pesos in debts from his workers; he, however, owed his *mayordomos* and workers 4,295 pesos (an average of 31 pesos each).[76]

There is little evidence of debt peonage as "bondage" being practiced by the planters, which is not surprising given that very few planters possessed the facilities or capital to retain workers on their property. That was not necessarily true of the strategies used by the administrators of the monopoly's *ranchos*. In 1787 the planters' representatives wrote to the inspector-general with complaints of continued and serious shortages of labor. They pointed out that when the monopoly produced tobacco directly they used "stocks, chains, and shackles" to maintain the necessary labor, and that without resorting to such tactics it was virtually impossible to ensure a stable labor supply.[77] The extent of this practice is not known, but, in any event, it failed to protect the monopoly from outstanding debts with the Indians.

There was no question, however, that the expanding tobacco economy tested the local rural labor supply to its limit, so much so that the colonial state was required to intervene. Labor scarcities clearly preoccupied the *directores generales*, since there existed "an indispensable necessity for workers to work in the tobacco fields which belong to the monopoly and to the planters because the inhabitants of the two contracted jurisdictions, although numerous, are inadequate to provide sufficient labor for the production of this crop in the vast quantities which are required for the monopoly's needs."[78] The state's strategy was to coerce Indian workers through the revival of the traditional labor draft, the *repartimiento de indios*.[79]

In the 1780s, when the monopoly produced tobacco directly, the problem of the labor supply became quickly obvious. Orders from the *dirección general* permitted Indian work crews to be drafted from the villages in the jurisdiction of Jalapa, an indication that workers needed to be brought in from greater distances to supplement local supplies. The inspector-general disbursed money to the local *alcaldes mayores* for distribution among the governors of the Indian villages. Bosses of the Indian work crews received 1 peso for every 10 pesos paid out in wages to workers. Locally known as the *súchil*, it was a bonus payment to encourage adequate recruitment of labor.[80]

The Indians were not particularly passive in the face of such demands for draft labor. Twelve villages within the jurisdiction of Jalapa requested exemption from such work based on hardship caused by traveling such long distances. Changes of climate between their homes and that of Córdoba had caused many of the villagers to fall ill with fevers on their return, some fatally. The villagers of Jilotepec complained that since 1771 they had supplied lime and crews for road construction, new barracks, and other buildings and now were required also to grow tobacco, for which they did not have a sufficient surplus of workers. There were barely enough workers in the village to produce their subsistence food crops. On the grounds of necessity and for fear of creating a precedent for such exemptions, the *dirección general* denied all such requests. The conflict did not stop there. Many of the workers simply refused to stay and fled with apparent impunity into the surrounding sierra, resulting in further losses for the monopoly and planters.[81]

Once again, in 1804 the *factor* of Córdoba appealed to the *subdelegado* of San Juan de los Llanos to send workers to labor on the monopoly and private tobacco *ranchos*. Córdoba lacked an estimated 250 workers. Requests were directed to justices in the intendancy of Puebla. Early warning by the inspectors and *factores* of the *villas* that labor shortages would seriously hinder the provision of the necessary supplies of tobacco proved to be accurate. Increasing competition for labor between tobacco planters, sugar planters, and also other state projects (construction of the royal highways between Veracruz and Mexico City via the *villas*), and the establishment of militias in the region placed considerable strain on the existing labor supply. Wages paid to workers on the royal highways were high and ranged between 4.5 and 6 reales. Captain José Manuel de Zevallos complained of the impossibility of maintaining a prepared, fully manned militia if the exemption from militia duties customarily enjoyed by skilled *tabaqueros* continued to be enforced.[82] Hence, in addition to the tobacco monopoly, there were two other state concerns in the same area competing for the same labor. After several pleas from the *factores* for "effective" aid, the viceroy issued an order designed to ameliorate the situation, although it fell far short of the steps required by local monopoly officials. *Subdele-*

gados were subsequently ordered to search out "vagabond Indians" of no fixed residence or occupation and employ them in the tobacco fields. In addition, assessments were made of all labor available from the Indian villages. This labor was then divided between the *villas,* for work in the tobacco fields, and road construction. Officials in charge of highway labor were forbidden to hire anyone who was not absolutely necessary. Exemptions from militia service remained in force. Orizaba, judged not to have such a serious problem with labor, found some of its Indian villages assigned to Córdoba and the royal highway.[83]

According to the planters, the quality and quantity of labor remained insufficient. They questioned the real benefits of monopoly policy in securing labor, especially at the beginning of the nineteenth century. In 1804 the inspector of tobacco for Córdoba, Marcos José de Hería, argued that, "even with the order which sanctions work crews from nearby villages, this is only useful for weeding of the fields . . . They are useless for topping, cutting, stringing . . . sorting and wrapping bales, tasks which demand skilled workers. These are so scarce that planters do not have even one-quarter of those they require for the tasks in the fields and the curing of tobacco."[84]

The problem of labor for the tobacco planters poses an interesting paradox. On the one hand, planters complained unceasingly of labor shortages; on the other hand, the volume of tobacco production increased considerably over the decades. Even if we assume a steady population increase, the expansion in tobacco production strained local labor resources, but it is also evident that, if the wage offered was high enough, labor responded. Herein lies the problem for many of the middle planters, who, knowing the price for their tobacco, could more or less predict their income from their harvests and estimate what could be spent on labor. To expand, they needed more workers, but more workers meant a greater expenditure on labor and fewer profits. It is not surprising, then, that, by the early 1800s, planters, particularly the smaller ones, were pleading for new exemptions to help reduce the costs of tobacco production, and pressuring the *dirección general* to exclude *pegujaleros* from the tobacco registers so they could be hired as workers. But how many *pegujaleros* were there, and what would have been the outcome of their elimination from the tobacco registers? By 1789 *pegujaleros* who were not financed by anyone but had acquired a license to produce tobacco and then sold their crop to wealthier planters numbered 209 and had acquired 12 percent of the tobacco allocations; in the same year, the *pegujaleros* financed by merchant-planters num-

bered 578 and accounted for 35 percent of the total crop.[85] To eliminate the *pegujaleros* from the tobacco registers would have created a
considerable number of rural workers, but it would also have undermined the production strategy of the wealthy planters and threatened
stable supplies of tobacco to the monopoly warehouses. The *dirección general* was not willing to take the risk, which explains its reluctance to restrict the *pegujaleros'* participation in tobacco cultivation.

Planters found themselves caught up in the rapidly expanding
commercial production of tobacco and needed to develop strategies
to mobilize local labor resources, which did not mobilize easily. For
some planters, unreliable and expensive labor resulted in a cautious
response to increased demands for tobacco by the monopoly. In combination with demands for labor for other agricultural interests and
economic activities in general, intensification of tobacco production
in the *villas* undoubtedly placed a severe strain on the rural labor
supply. The continuation of the tried and trusted *avío* system remained a rational option for those wealthy planters who could afford
to finance smaller planters. We will now consider the structure and
function of *avío* arrangements in the wider context of the financing
and supply of credit in tobacco production and in its profitability.

As we have argued, prior to the establishment of the monopoly, merchants produced tobacco by means of the distribution of *avíos*, a
common business practice in colonial Mexico. Tobacco planters
generally received *avíos* in both kind and specie from local merchants, *rancheros*, or other tobacco planters. One of the *directores
generales*, Antonio del Frago, provides us with a description of how
the *avío* system worked: "The principal planters and merchants acting as *aviadores* supply to the poor the amounts necessary for their
crops . . . partly in money and partly in goods and foodstuffs from
their shops on the condition that they deliver all their harvests [to
them] . . . a small number of individuals, particularly those in the
villas of Córdoba and Orizaba, enjoy all the profits, and not the
people in general."[86] The recipients of such advances included Indians from the nearby villages and Spanish or mestizo *rancheros*.
The majority of those financed were the controversial *pegujaleros*,
most of whom were Indian villagers, but a variety of people drawn
from different agrarian classes received *avíos*. The *avío* distributed
could be in commodities or cash, or a combination of both. Only one
example of a contract between an *aviador* and one of his *aviados*
was found. The contract conditions agreed to by the two parties
were laid out as follows:

"I declare, don Antono Chávez, that I agree to this arrangement with don Manuel Feo according to the following conditions:
  1. I am obliged to deliver to him [Feo] all the tobacco which I can harvest on my ranch in 1773 . . . he will assess it so that I can make payment of the quantity which I owe him . . . if it does not cover the *avío* (financing), he has the right to all my equipment and goods which belong to me and my *rancho* . . . Don Manuel, for this, and in return, is obliged to give me every 15 or 20 days those staples such as salt, chiles, butter, milk, soap, and [illegible] the work clothes for the boys (also the clothing necessary for my wife) until the tobacco is harvested on my ranch . . . "[87]

Chávez's *aviador*, in turn, received financing from Don Manuel Rodríguez, a *cajero* (apprentice merchant) of Orizaba, a partnership which began at least as early as 1768.[88]

Aviados usually managed their tobacco crops to the cutting and stringing stages, after which the tobacco was "sold" *enversa* (strung) to their *aviadores* who determined its price (below the prices fixed by the monopoly) and deducted any advances made. Like silver, tobacco had two prices—the one set by the *aviador*, and the official price paid by the monopoly.[89]

Aviados produced tobacco on their own lands or on their *aviador*'s lands, and sometimes on both. Pedro Juárez, for example, a tributary Indian from the village of Tequila, owned plots of maize and tobacco in Zongólica. He received *avíos* from Antonio Montes Argüelles, who had financed him for "a long time as a protector," and, even though the lands in Zongólica were better suited for tobacco cultivation, he was obliged to travel to Tequila to sow tobacco for Argüelles.[90]

The advantage of the *avío* arrangement lies in the spreading of risk, certainly not in the elimination of it. Because the small farmers, particularly the *pegujaleros,* needed the advances due to their poverty, they became dependent on the small elite group of merchant-planters and wealthy *rancheros.* Farmers and *rancheros* from both *villas* informed the viceroy that tobacco production had become "a monopoly of a few individuals who make lucrative arrangements with the poor growers who are forced out of sheer necessity to comply, as what little wealth they have is tied up in a miserable *rancho,* and their equipment is useless for anything else other than tobacco production. They are forced to tolerate whatever conditions are imposed upon them, as they have no other means of supporting their families . . . they prefer a lost future in order to survive the present."[91] If they had a bad harvest they could find themselves in the situation of being unable to deliver a sufficient quantity of tobacco to cover any advances already received. This applied to the management of monopoly advances also. At the same time, many of the *pegujaleros* probably had nothing to lose and saved some of their best tobacco for contraband deals where they could receive a better price than from their *aviadores*. This provides an interesting case of the subsidization of the black market in tobacco, originating in government credit, trickling through the hands of the merchant-planters into those of the *pegujaleros*.

The number of *aviados* financed by tobacco planters varied widely. Antonio Montes Argüelles, one of the wealthiest planters, had 38 non-Indian *aviados* in fifteen different places. He also acted as the *aviador* of 358 Indians in the sierra of Tequila and distributed money to the pueblos of Capoluca, Tonalisco, Naranjal, Tuspanguillo, Tlasololapa, and Tequila.[92] The Indian villagers of Tequila, Naranjal, and Coetzala, categorized as *Indios pegujaleros*, were financed by several of the larger planters. In Zongólica, of 29 planters, 23 financed the production of their crops by advancing credit to the majority of the Indian population of the village, approximately 483 Indian planters.[93] *Aviados* generally produced between 5,000 and 10,000 plants each. Less wealthy but prosperous *rancheros* funded anywhere between 1 and 50 *aviados*. Melchor Ramos, for example, funded 4 *aviados* in Tenajapa, 7 in Coetzala, and 5 in Naranjal. In the village of Tenajapa, Antonio Albelda had a total quota of 190,000 *matas*, of which he produced 100,000 plants directly on his own *rancho* and divided the remaining 90,000 among 9 *pegujaleros*, with 10,000 each.[94]

Table 13 illustrates the distribution of *avíos* to tobacco planters and the relative share of quotas produced by planters in receipt of *avíos* in Orizaba over a twenty-year period. What it suggests is that the monopoly credit supplements may have encouraged and enabled more farmers and *rancheros* to engage in tobacco production, as their share in production increased from 32 to 51 percent. As tobacco production expanded, so did the percentage of planters in receipt of *avíos*, increasing from 63 to 67 percent, as well as their relative share of total production, which increased from 28 to 35 percent. Certainly by 1789, the majority of tobacco growers were in receipt of *avíos*. What the figures in table 13 also suggest is that the *aviadores*, predominantly the merchant-planters, gradually reduced direct production, possibly as a response to the supply and cost of land and labor. Instead, they concentrated on the processing (dry-

Table 13. *Percentage Distribution of Tobacco Production by* Aviadores, *Aviados, and Non-*Aviados, *1769, 1779, and 1789, Orizaba*

	1769		1779		1789	
	% Planters	% Crop	% Planters	% Crop	% Planters	% Crop
Planters without avíos	24	32	18	42	32	51
Aviadores + aviados	76	68	82	58	68	49
Aviados' production	63	28	74	26	67	35
Aviadores (direct production on ranchos)	13	40	8	32	1	14

Source: Calculated from contracts for 1769, 1779, and 1789. AGN, various *ramos.*

ing and curing) of tobacco and favored production of their tobacco quotas through a reinforcement of the *aviador* system, rather than a rejection of it. The increasing incorporation and intensification of the use of the surrounding Indian peasantry to produce tobacco through the *aviado* system continued into the nineteenth century and is illustrated by the case of a wealthy and prominent planter, Francisco Puy y Ochoa. In 1802, out of his quota of 3,799,038 plants, 1,675,679 plants, 44 percent, were distributed among his Indian *aviados* in the sierra of Tequila, the remainder to be produced on his own *ranchos*. In 1805, three years later, and with an increased quota of 5,500,000 plants, 96 percent was distributed among 482 Indian *aviados*, once more concentrated predominantly in Tequila.[95] Effectively, Puy y Ochoa had shifted from producing just over 2,000,000 plants to a mere 200,000 plants on his own *ranchos*. His *aviados* increased from 358 to 482, as did the quantity of tobacco distributed to each Indian, from 5,000 to 11,000 plants.

The *avío* system underwrote the development of a powerful merchant-planter cadre with which the *dirección general* had to contend and ultimately depend upon to produce the necessary supplies of tobacco. But why was this not undermined by the credit advances paid out by the monopoly?

The original idea behind advancement of interest-free credit to planters to supplement costs of production was to offer an alternative to the traditional financing by merchants through the distribution of *avíos*, to encourage more farmers to invest in tobacco production, and to discourage continued mercantile involvement in tobacco cultivation. One *director general* argued that, "If the merchants, who up until now have enjoyed most of the advantages from the sale of this crop to the king, removed themselves from its production, it would serve as a balance . . . for the body of the true farmers because they could increase the amount which they cultivate . . . it is only fair that the merchants content themselves with large profits which they will earn from the increase in population which they can anticipate and which, as a consequence, will result in greater consumption of goods."[96]

There were two reasons why merchant-planters were not removed from tobacco production or from their role as suppliers of rural credit and replaced by the monopoly. The first reason is related to who benefited from monopoly credit. The guarantees required by the monopoly excluded a large percentage of rural producers, as is demonstrated by the relatively few numbers of planters in receipt of monopoly credit advances. Second, and more speculatively, we would argue that the monopoly underfinanced planters, which resulted in a continued dependence upon local merchants and merchant-planters by farmers, peasants, and *rancheros*. This is not to say that monopoly credit advances did not have an impact. They may have enabled some smaller planters to expand their tobacco production in a way that would not have been possible otherwise and may have accelerated the transition from subsistence to commercial farming. They also provided capital support upon which tobacco production could expand, but the main beneficiaries of such expansion and credit allocations were the merchant-planters.

Planters were eligible for monopoly *suplementos* (credit advances) provided they possessed mortgageable property to at least the value of the amount loaned (and preferably half as much again) or could find a *fiador* to guarantee the loan. In some cases, both were required. Advances were allocated in accordance with the tobacco quota to be produced. Originally, in the 1770s and 1780s, such advances were graduated so that, for fieldwork, 200 pesos were paid for every 100,000 plants sown, and 50 pesos for 1,000 *sartas* (bunches) dried and cured. The advances increased to 500 pesos and 100 pesos respectively (effectively doubling) by the beginning of the nineteenth century. Credit advances were divided into four payments. Each "installment" was designated for fieldwork or the curing of tobacco. Benito Antonio Rocha's advance for his crop in 1794 amounted to 9,000 pesos. He collected two payments of 3,000 pesos each in November and December of 1794, and the remaining two, of 1,500 pesos each, in January and February of the following year.[97] By separating into installments the total amount advanced the *dirección general* ensured that funds were used for the reason intended. The monopoly also took great care to ensure that its advances were covered, deducting the total from the gross value of the harvest before the *diezmo* and *alcabala* were deducted. If a planter's crop failed to cover the amounts advanced (and this was not infrequent), the monopoly reserved the right to be paid first, before any other existing creditors, after sale of the unfortunate individual's property.[98]

If we also bear in mind that the estimated cost of production by the *factor* of Orizaba of cultivating 100,000 *matas* was just over 1,000 pesos, then monopoly credit supplements acted as just that, supplements, and did not necessarily cover the costs of production. This is illustrated in the following example. Don Miguel Fernández, a tobacco planter, was owed money by his partner, Manuel Antonio Calderón. Fernández received an advance from the monopoly of 4,300 pesos to cultivate 500,000 *matas* on his *rancho* but spent a total of 5,689 pesos, thus investing 1,389 pesos of his own capital. Calderón's crop was valued at 5,332 pesos, which left a debit of 1,032 pesos.[99] Small wonder that debt relations continued apace, and access to private credit remained important. It is likely, then, that whatever the aspirations of the Bourbon bureaucrats to support small farmers, their strategy to achieve it through allocation of rural credit fell short of the mark. The result was a continuation of debt and credit relationships which reinforced relations of dependency between the wealthy and poor planters, and which enabled the wealthier planters to pressure the *dirección general* for higher purchase prices.

Commercial transactions and the attendant debt and credit relationships were not confined to the territorial limits of the *villas,* and we can speculate that merchants from Veracruz had a hand in the financing of tobacco production. Commercial contacts between Orizabeño and Veracruz merchants occurred through normal business practices and marriage. Don Manuel de Ayos, resident merchant of the port, gave power of attorney to Don Juan Antonio de Cora, one of his business representatives, in Orizaba in 1757. Cora was a leading tobacco planter, and it is likely that, if he needed credit for tobacco production, *avíos,* or for any other business, Manuel de Ayos was prepared to help him.[100]

Partnerships in tobacco production were common, illustrating debt and credit networks among rich and poor, Indian and Spanish, farmer and merchant. They occurred at any stage of the production of the crop, during sowing, harvesting, and curing. They incorporated third and fourth parties and often ended in unpaid debts. In

1803, for example, Francisco Mexia sowed 50,000 plants in Chocaman. Until it came time to dry the leaves, he had spent 190 pesos. At this point he became partners with Ramón Baltierra, who offered to reimburse him for the amount and provide the necessary care and curing, with both of them sharing half of the losses or profits. The crop's value, after all deductions, amounted to 295 pesos. Total costs, however, came to 395 pesos, which meant that between them they lost 100 pesos, or 50 pesos each. Baltierra, however, violated his agreement and failed to pay Mexia the 50 pesos outstanding after taking his share of the losses.[101] Baltierra, in turn, owed 193 pesos to another partner, Antonio Joaquín Iznardo, in a partnership established in 1802 and renewed in 1803.[102] Several prominent merchant-planters owed considerable sums of money to the owner of the hacienda Tocuila. Don Benito Antonio Rocha and his wife, Doña María Pardiñas, owed a combined debt of 1,200 pesos, and Don Juan Bringas a debt of 1,000 pesos.[103]

Monopoly credit underfinanced the planters. This had important consequences for those who could benefit from the advances, especially when combined with the necessary guarantees. As we argued in Chapter 3, although the numbers in receipt of monopoly credit in Orizaba increased after 1804, they were relatively small. They ranged from 83 in 1792 to 176 in 1809. Moreover, the allocations of credit favored the wealthy planters after 1800. In 1792 three planters (4 percent) in receipt of monopoly credit planted one million *matas* and above; by 1809, the numbers in receipt of credit who planted in excess of one million *matas* had increased to 26 (15 percent). The poorest planters in receipt of monopoly credit, who planted between 10,000 and 59,999 plants, accounted for 22 percent of the total number receiving credit in 1792 and 19 percent in 1809 (although this still represented an increase in the actual numbers, from 18 to 33). The middle planters, those who produced between 60,000 and 500,000 plants, also experienced an increase in their numbers. In 1792 they constituted 73 percent (60); by 1809, they constituted 61 percent (107).

The production of tobacco passed through "a multitude of hands," and the organization resembles what Karl Kaerger described for cocoa production in nineteenth-century Ecuador, where owners provided capital and incentive to small planters who, in turn, hired day laborers and paid them with credit advanced by the plantation owners. The result was that no one knew exactly who owed what to whom.[104] The expansion of commercial agriculture subsidized by the colonial state opened up opportunities to small farmers and planters, but it did not radically change the existing structure of financing tobacco production and the social relations upon which it was based, which continued to depend on networks of dependence and debt relations. Monopoly credit represented another line of rural credit, albeit a valuable one, in the web of credit and debt arrangements which linked Indian villagers, *rancheros, hacendados,* and wealthy planters.[105] Such linkages were certainly not uncommon in late-eighteenth-century Mexico, or in many other places and times when new opportunities in commercial agriculture arose either because of new demand in domestic markets or the world market.[106]

An additional consideration here is that, in the specific case of the *villas,* government credit provided an alternative to the Church, the normal source of agricultural credit even for the wealthy planters. There still existed a hidden reliance upon Church credit, since many of the larger advances by the state to wealthy planters were based partly on securities which included haciendas which, in turn, had Church mortgages. For the most part, however, the Church's role in tobacco production, apart from collecting a healthy *diezmo,* was minimal.

Studies of commercial agriculture in colonial Mexico and elsewhere in Spanish America agree that an average annual net return on agricultural capital was about 5 percent, which was also equal to income derived from lending money at interest (the price of money), and which Van Young posits was "probably a good deal lower than the profits from large-scale commercial or mining enterprises."[107] What rate of profit could a planter expect to earn on his capital investment? Simply stated, we do not know. Considerable amounts were earned by planters, but we do not know what this income represented as a proportion of a mixed agricultural enterprise. The most we can do is look at the bare economic facts of costs of production and simple profit figures.[108]

Planters and bureaucrats were never able to agree upon the profit which an average crop of 100,000 plants would yield. Contrary to the inspector-general, his superior, Antonio de Sobrevilla insisted that no account could be considered typical due to the varieties of soil, climate, unpredictable effect of plant disease, labor supply, and so forth. Yields and the quality of tobacco varied not just between years but between planters in the same region and in the same year. Assessments of costs of production for 1767 and 1781 demonstrate a variety of calculations and give the capital invested in such production. The estimates listed in table 14 detail the "average" costs and profits from an allocation of 100,000 plants. The ranges are extreme, from losses to a considerably high profit of 34 percent, high enough to hold the attention of planters through the years of bad harvests.

Table 14.   Estimated Costs of Production and Profit, 1767 and 1781

Source	Year	Yield/100,000 Plants & Value	Costs of Production (pesos)	(reales/ pound)	Profit and % Estimate	
Deputies of the *Villas*	1767	42 *tercios* 1,384 pesos	1,207	1.1	167	14
Factor of Orizaba	1780	42 *tercios* 1,509 pesos	1,207	0.9	300	29
Inspector-General	1781	36 *tercios* 1,350 pesos	1,003	1.1	346	34
Inspector-General	1781	46 *tercios* 1,725 pesos	1,315	1.1	409	31
Alcalde Mayor of Orizaba	1781	30 *tercios* 832 pesos	849	1.1	Loss of 16 pesos	
Alcalde Mayor of Orizaba	1781	30 *tercios* 948 pesos	849	1.1	99	12
Resguardo Lieutenant Sobrevilla	1781	No estimate on grounds that there are too many variations in conditions of production to be able to generalize	1,012		No estimate	

Source: AGN, Renta de Tabaco 44, planter representatives of the *villas* to viceroy, 26 May 1767; Report of *resguardo* lieutenant Sobrevilla, 25 April 1781; inspector-general to *contador general*, 1 May 1781; José Antonio de Arsú y Arcaya, *alcalde mayor* of Orizaba to viceroy, 9 April 1781. (Totals may not add up due to rounding)

Between 1765 and 1806 the value of tobacco production in Orizaba increased almost fivefold, from 211,575 pesos to 998,131 pesos; Córdoba's increase was more modest, with an increase from 178,640 pesos in 1765 to 389,885 pesos in 1806 (see figures 3 and 4 and Appendix II). Most of the profits from tobacco production, however, were concentrated in the hands of the merchant-planters, as is illustrated by the distribution of individual payments received for harvests. In 1773, in Córdoba, the total value of the tobacco harvests amounted to 397,810 pesos, of which eight planters received 124,577 pesos; effectively, 7 percent of the planters received 31 percent of the total value of the crop, while 93 percent of the planters received 69 percent of the total value. In Orizaba, in 1779, 43 percent of the total value of the crop was paid out to 8 percent of the planters (four in number), leaving 92 percent of the planters (fifty-one) with 57 percent of the total value. One planter, Antonio Montes Argüelles, received a considerable 61,942 pesos, profits which made up 26 percent of the total value of the tobacco harvests (240,149 pesos). The majority of the planters received payments within a range of 1,570 pesos to 3,118 pesos, but payments were as low as 22 pesos.[109] In 1792 the payments for harvests in Orizaba suggest that the wide range in profits continued. Manuel José Hernández received a paltry 10 pesos from his crop valued at 360 pesos, after monopoly credit, *diezmo,* and *alcabalas* were deducted; Felipe Torres received 331 pesos for his crop valued at 3,531 pesos, while Doña Bernarda Rendón received 21,416 pesos from her harvest worth 36,000 pesos.[110]

Bankruptcy was not uncommon among the tobacco planters, even among those with diversified interests. Don Manuel Antonio Calderón turned his possessions over for assessment and repayment of debts, observing that "the low prices [of tobacco], the high prices of basic materials, and all that is necessary to pay the daily wages of the workers have risen to such exorbitant extremes." Combined with other "accidents," his debts increased until he had no choice but to declare bankruptcy. Calderón owed a total of 1,190 pesos, including 100 pesos to the Indians of San Martín Ocotitlán for rental of lands, and 950 pesos to a merchant in Veracruz. A *rancho* belonging to Calderón was deemed to be in a "poor condition and situation" and valued at 455 pesos.[111]

It was with considerable accuracy that the *factor* of Orizaba, Mendiola, explained the reasons for the varied fortunes of the planters: "Some, with the income from their harvests, invest and trade in other goods from which they reap an independent profit."[112] The tobacco planters were far from homogenous in their backgrounds and wealth. In chapter 3, we spoke of the actions of an "articulate oligarchy," those wealthy planters who belonged to the elite of the *villas*. We will conclude this chapter with an examination of this elite, their power, and wealth. How different were the circumstances of the merchant-planters compared with those of the other planters?

The composition of the tobacco planters as an economic group reflected the wider socioeconomic hierarchy prevalent in late colonial Mexico.[113] At the base was a predominantly Indian peasantry, the *pegujaleros*, in a broad-based middle were the mestizo and Spanish *rancheros* and farmers, and at the top, the wealthy Spanish merchant-planters, most of whom were peninsular Spaniards. This tripartite division is somewhat crude, and we offer it only as a general typology of the mix of agrarian classes who produced tobacco. Even within the separate ranks of planters, there was considerable differentiation and blurring at the edges of each group—sometimes a "prosperous" *pegujalero* was virtually indistinguishable from a poor *ranchero*. There are identifiable differences, however, which are best illustrated by examples of the makeup and economic situation of each class.

The majority of the *pegujaleros* were Indian villagers and mestizos who rarely produced more than 20,000 plants. Distinctions were made between those *pegujaleros* who functioned more like a rural proletariat and those subsistence farmers who were funded by the wealthier planters. Rafael García, inspector of the Orizaba *resguardo*, described the latter as *hombres de bien* (decent men), small farmers with their own *ranchelos*, who were experienced at tobacco growing and possessed no other means of survival. A few received monopoly credit, and the rest simply applied for a small quota of tobacco and then sold the harvest to other planters. The former, "less desirable," group consisted of migrant agricultural workers who had no fixed residence and moved between Orizaba and Córdoba according to their needs. They requested licenses to grow tobacco and then made a quick cash profit by selling the licenses to other planters, enabling them to produce more tobacco than their own quotas indicated.[114]

The *rancheros*, poor and prosperous, made up the majority of planters who received monopoly credit. Unlike the wealthier planters, they were much more likely to live on their *ranchos*, often as tenant farmers with a few hired workers, finance a few *aviados*, or both, to carry out their tobacco production. Their tobacco quotas fell in a range between 100,000 and 500,000 *matas*. They engaged in mixed livestock ranching, and grew maize and vegetables. This gave them something to fall back on if the tobacco harvest failed, but their major source of income was tobacco. The differences within the *ranchero* ranks are illustrated by the following examples. At the upper end was someone like Sebastián Rodríguez, a prosperous *ranchero*. In the 1791 *padrón* (census), he was listed as a peninsular and *administrador de justicia* for the village of San Miguel de Tomatlan. He farmed on his ranch in Pedregal, owned a small one-story house, and raised livestock in addition to growing tobacco. These, in addition to his tobacco-curing sheds, general storehouses, and farming equipment illustrate the scale of his ranching operation. Apart from producing tobacco on his *rancho* in Pedregal over the years, as early as 1786 Rodríguez also grew tobacco on lands in Tecama, Tetela, Tomatlan, and Tlapalan with a few *aviados*. By the 1790s he had reduced his tobacco production from 470,000 plants to an average of 150,000, and, by 1800, was down to 64,000 *matas*. He finally sold his *rancho* in Pedregal to Don Francisco del Puy y Ochoa for 2,000 pesos in 1805. His son, Don Sebastián José, took over the management of their tobacco production with a quota of 200,000 plants in 1807 and had doubled that amount to 400,000 by 1810. They used their own moderate wealth as a guarantee for monopoly credit, assessed by 1810 to be worth 4,500 pesos.[115] Manuel Callejas planted 100,000 *matas* in 1790 on his *rancho*. By 1804 he increased his quota to 200,000 *matas* and doubled that to 400,000 *matas* by 1810. He listed three houses and two *ranchos* worth 6,500 pesos as security for his loans from the monopoly. Vicente Martínez began planting tobacco in 1806 with a quota of 600,000 *matas*. He listed ownership of two *ranchos*, one valued at 6,500 pesos. He also owned three houses and considerable livestock, including horses, mules, and oxen. Together his property amounted to 10,250 pesos. José Beltrán typified the poorer type of *ranchero*. In 1790 he planted 40,000 *matas*; by 1809 his quota had increased to 50,000 *matas*. His security for monopoly credit was a small house and guarantees by his mother and brother.

The merchant-planters share many of the characteristics described above, but their tobacco production was on a much larger scale; invariably they cultivated in excess of one million *matas*. What really distinguished the merchant-planters from the other planters, however, was their membership in the ranks of the local elite and their wealth and power.

The participation of the local elite of Orizaba in tobacco production is illustrated by a variety of evidence. A listing of the members of the *junta de comercio* of Orizaba in 1777 shows them to be virtually all tobacco planters, as does a cross reference between contract registers of planters and the *padrón* of 1791; most of the peninsular and creole military officers also participated in tobacco production. In 1782 all members of the *cabildo* were registered tobacco growers.[116] Few of the wealthy planters described themselves as tobacco planters by occupation. Instead they identified themselves as merchants, small traders, or by their official positions as local government or military office holders, yet their names occur repeatedly on the extant tobacco registers, with the largest quotas of tobacco. The familiar pattern of a close interweave among families, vested interests, and political officeholding was certainly prevalent by the late 1780s. In 1791 the *juez subdelegado*, Patricio Fernández, the *alcaldes ordinarios*, Blas Antonio de Couto and Benito Rocha, the *regidor decano perpetuo*, Juan de Cora, and *regidores*, Julián Romanos, Iñigo y Vallejo, and José Anastasio Rendón, were all tobacco planters. Marcos González and José Joaquín Rengel del Castillo, who both held high-ranking military positions, respectively captain of and sublieutenant in the Regimiento Provincial de Córdoba, also contracted to produce tobacco. José Anastasio Rendón served as an *abogado* of the Real Audiencia of Mexico and also served as *regidor* for the years 1793–1794.[117] In 1800 only one member of the *cabildo* of Orizaba could not be found among the lists of names on the tobacco registers.[118] Peninsular Spaniards dominated the planter elite; only two, Fernández and Rendón, were creoles.[119] The influence of these planters was strengthened by the recruitment of the tobacco planters' representatives. Antonio and Manuel Montes Argüelles served in 1764, 1770, 1774, and 1778; Cora and González served as representatives in 1786.

The merchant-planters were in a position to take advantage of the tobacco economy through the use of their existing wealth, political positions, and networks to build up their interests in tobacco and to manipulate monopoly conditions to their advantage. Investment in a combination of commercial agriculture, tobacco, and livestock, particularly pack mules, urban property, and commerce, both local and extraregional, formed the basis of wealth and influence for the planter elite and reflected the diversification of their economic interests. The investment in urban property reflects a rational response to the wider demands for services in Orizaba, most notably temporary housing for merchants and travelers between Mexico City and the port of Veracruz and, eventually, cantonment towns, where large numbers of troops found themselves crammed into "urban centres where there were limited rental accommodations."[120] Such diversified investment was not an uncommon practice among wealthy families in colonial Mexico and provides us with yet another regional example of such a strategy.

Cathy Duke found a similar pattern for Córdoba with regard to the relationship between family, political office, and economic interests. Planters "worked as a group through the elite who themselves owned ranchos . . . As a social group . . . the rancheros utilized the family as the vehicle for securing and preserving their principal assets, the tobacco ranchos. They protected their wealth through marriage and consolidated it through an interlocking system of family ownership."[121] Their diversified interests and local political and social roles are illustrated in the following case studies.

Antonio Montes Argüelles of Orizaba best exemplifies a merchant-planter. In the 1760s he possessed the contracts for the collection of *alcabalas,* and the *abasto de carne,* the right to supply meat to the local population. His bulls for the local *abasto de carne* for both *villas* were valued at 18,000 pesos. A peninsular Spaniard, he served as *regidor* on the *cabildo* of Orizaba and also as a planter representative in the early 1770s. By 1786 he lived in a house worth 20,000 pesos in Orizaba and owned two *bóticas* (pharmacies) and a general store worth 30,000 pesos. Montes Argüelles' economic portfolio was completed by the ownership of several tobacco *ranchos* and income from his yearly tobacco harvests. His total estate was valued at 283,600 pesos, of which 144,812 pesos was tied up in debts which had to be repaid.[122] Antonio Montes Argüelles appeared to have the proverbial fingers in every pie. Married to Doña Bernarda de Rendón from Córdoba, Antonio represented the interests of Don Juan Bernardo de Segura Zevallos, a wealthy sugar planter from Córdoba.[123] He was also related to Don Manuel de Amez y Larriba, a merchant of Orizaba married to Luisa Montes Argüelles. Amez y Larriba owned a livestock *rancho* in San Antonio Tenecalco, in the jurisdiction of Talizcoyan, a *casa de comercio,* and distributed *repartos* (goods and money) to "all classes of people," including tobacco planters, but especially to cotton producers in Jalapa and Ojitlán, who "owed him a great deal."[124] Montes Argüelles' power and wealth was passed on to his sons, Antonio and Manuel. Antonio, after serving on the Orizaba *cabildo,* died fighting for the Royalist cause in 1812, while Manuel eventually was elected as deputy to the first General Congress of Mexico for the province of Veracruz, preserving the family's power and status in the region.[125]

Montes Argüelles was not alone in his standing and wealth. By the 1790s, a number of men and women formed the core of the planter elite. Francisco Florentino Avila, a creole, owned six houses, a general store, and two tobacco *ranchos*, with a combined total value of 56,000 pesos. Domingo Piñeiro owned four houses, three tobacco *ranchos*, and 150 mules, collectively valued at 51,268 pesos. A final example is provided by Anna María Pardiñas, the creole widow of a very prosperous planter. By 1807 she owned fourteen houses worth 60,623 pesos and *ranchos* and mules worth 7,010 pesos. The characteristics of the merchant-planters provided by these case studies may be identified in all those growers who planted in excess of one million *matas*. Of the thirty planters identified who planted over one million *matas* at least once, all had multiple economic interests, urban property, a shop, several *ranchos* or a hacienda, and influence with local government officials and military officers, either through family or business partnerships or through holding office themselves. In most cases their wealth and family position reinforced each other: they acted as each other's creditors and *fiadores*. Their interlocking relations were also consolidated through membership in a *cofradía* (brotherhood).

Shortly after the establishment of the monopoly, the planters formed a *cofradía*. On 18 April 1767 the *regidor* Juan Antonio de Cora and Julián de la Llave, on behalf of all of the tobacco planters, the *gremio de tabaqueros*, swore allegiance before their special saint and "patron of the tobacco fields, the Queen of the Angels, María Santíssima Señora de la Soledad." Their annual fiesta was celebrated on the third Sunday of September. Each planter contributed 1 real per *carga* of tobacco annually. Surplus amounts, after expenses of the *cofradía* and its annual celebration were paid, were placed in the hands of the planter representatives who, when there was a sufficient amount, invested them in property. Although no records of the planters' *cofradía* were found, the dominant role of the merchant-planters in this institution is confirmed through references to its *mayordomos*. Francisco Cueto held the position in 1796, while Francisco Puy y Ochoa occupied the position by 1805.[126] The point here is that, despite the complaints of the smaller growers against the merchant-planters and their increasing dominance of tobacco production, the structure of the local social and economic hierarchy and its power was reinforced and legitimated to a degree by institutions such as the *cofradía*. As such, the elimination of the planters' *cuerpo* and representation in contract negotiations made little difference to the underlying structure of power and influence.

Such patterns of power and wealth have been sketched out by Brading, Van Young, and Lindley, who argue that landowners were certainly not "an endogamous caste," but engaged in multiple activities as merchants, urban property owners, or professionals simultaneously.[127] Van Young found that by the 1750s the hegemony of landowners in local political affairs began to erode and was replaced by city merchants who could not be identified as landowners, although landowners continued to be represented in city government.[128] The situation is different in the case of Orizaba, where merchants who were also planters continued to dominate local political affairs before and after independence from Spain and formed a nascent agricultural bourgeoisie. Rather like the oligarchy described by Lindley in his study of Guadalajara on the eve of independence, the planter elite of the *villas* were not the "elegant millionaires of Mexico City" but a particular oligarchy "defined by the potential and limits of the region that nurtured it."[129] The context of the region may have been different, but the familiar basis of colonial power and wealth was there: a mixture of interests in agriculture and commerce, access to or participation in the affairs of local government, and social wealth and power firmly embedded in family networks, credit relations and inheritance. In the end, it was this wealth which provided the basis for the merchant-planters' "voice" which spoke out against monopoly prices and contract conditions, and also for their gradual domination of tobacco production, aided by monopoly credit.

The demands made by the monopoly for tobacco provided a stimulus for the expansion of tobacco production in Orizaba and Córdoba, especially when accompanied by state loans. The impact on the local society and economy, however, reinforced certain dependent relations. First it reinforced the relationship between the merchant-planters and the peasantry. Although the monopoly may have encouraged increased commercialization among the peasantry and smaller planters, the continuation of *avío* arrangements consolidated debt relations and the relative power of the planter elite. Second, there was an increased dependence on tobacco by all planters and on the monopoly as a bureaucratic enterprise. The tobacco economy reinforced the colonial structure and the existing social and economic hierarchy, whose interests, for the most part, coincided with those of the colonial state. The objective was to negotiate better terms, not to challenge the structure of the monopoly. As we saw in Chapter 3, such negotiations took place and, in the process, the early breathless enthusiasm to favor the small farmers evaporated as the traditional alliance between the colonial state and a regional elite, a creation of the colonial state in some measure, was maintained. The political and economic relationships which emerged between the state of Veracruz and the national government of Mexico City in the nineteenth century were shaped in part by the vested interests in tobacco, which flourished under the monopoly in the *villas,* and around which the planters united in those first chaotic and dismal years of the Mexican Republic.

PART III

5. Organization, Production, and Policies: The State Tobacco Manufactories, 1765–1810

AFTER THE ELIMINATION of private tobacco workshops and stores, the manufacture of tobacco products was restricted to a few towns and cities. Between 1765 and 1779 six tobacco manufactories were established in the viceroyalty of New Spain: in Guadalajara, Mexico City, Oaxaca, Orizaba, Puebla, and Querétaro. Several variables affected the development of the manufactories and their performance: worker-management relations, imperial fiscal policies, and war. The tobacco manufactories proved to be successful in the short term inasmuch as they achieved their objectives—to provide revenues for the Spanish state. The major obstacle to their development, however, was not poor or inefficient management, but the colonial state itself. Any early tilting at modernization and the exceptional move of encouraging industry in Mexico by the creation of the manufactories, managed by bureaucrats who sought ways to improve them, was strangled by a sclerotic imperial polity which favored the status quo, both political and economic. Any incentive for new developments or technological innovation was not only lost but actively discouraged. Like other branches of colonial industry, such as mining and textiles, expansion in manufactory production could not be sustained in the long term, since it depended upon an increase in factor supplies rather than any significant changes in productivity. We will begin with an examination of the rationale of the manufactories and the organization of manufactory production and distribution and then look at the long-term production trends and characteristics of the manufactories. Finally we shall consider the constraints on the manufactories' development and the problems experienced by monopoly management between 1780 and 1810. Because labor relations occupy such a central role, they are discussed separately in Chapters 6 and 7.

Two reasons combined to provide the rationale for the manufactories, profitability and provision of employment for Mexico's urban poor. With regard to profit, the bureaucrats adopted an opportunity-costs approach to determine which method used tobacco resources more profitably, sales of tobacco leaf or of manufactured products. As Jon Cohen has argued for the economic rationale of early mill production in England, their owners "implicitly or explicitly were compelled to do their sums; they had to estimate the expected return on various options open to them and select the one that brought the highest pay-off."[1] This is precisely what the monopoly bureaucrats, under Jóse de Gálvez's guidance, did. The trial manufactures showed that one month's sale of cigars and cigarettes yielded 6 percent more profit compared to the sale of an equivalent quantity of leaf used to make the cigars and cigarettes.[2] Manufactured products also suited the poor transport facilities in the viceroyalty; there was less wastage and less cost in the transport of manufactured goods than of tobacco leaf, which was delicate and dried out quickly, becoming too brittle to use.

Location of the manufactories in selected cities and towns provided surplus labor supplies, which worked to the advantage of the monopoly and ensured cheap labor. The rationale for monopoly manufacture also focused on the need to produce good quality products, free of the adulteration and shortchanging for which the *cigarrerías* had an infamous reputation. A cheaper but better-quality product would help to persuade consumers that the changes about to be wrought by the monopoly were to everyone's advantage. Centralized manufacture, with workers under the supervision of skilled cigar and cigarette makers, provided the most effective vehicle to achieve such objectives.

The *dirección general* may not have shared Gálvez's unbounded faith in the concept of state manufacture of tobacco products, but one fact about which they could not disagree was the thriving market which existed for tobacco products. Foreign travelers in Mexico and bureaucrats alike concurred on the prevailing penchant for tobacco. The *fiscal* Velarde noted with some contempt that a Mexican would forsake a tortilla for a cigarette. Joel Poinsett, during his travels to Mexico in the early nineteenth century, described how he was surprised "to see several young ladies, pretty and well dressed, smoking cigars. I knew that it was the custom of the ladies to smoke but supposed they would only do so in private . . . the Mexican gentlemen do not seem to dislike it and the tale of love is whispered and vows of fidelity are interchanged amidst volumes of smoke."[3]

Assessments of the 'market' by monopoly bureaucrats not only emphasized the widespread use of tobacco, but also that demand cut across class, age, gender, and occupation. Most consumption, however, was "by poor people and from the middle classes, who often only buy one or two packets."[4] Since supply conditions in preindustrial economies made price reduction difficult, increases in aggregate sales of manufactured goods were likely to be achieved either through an increase in consumers' incomes, the finding of new markets, or the capture of existing markets.[5] It was the latter strategy which shaped the organization and location of the manufactories, as the monopoly sought control of existing markets.

The monopolization of the tobacco trade reorganized the industry from one which produced for local economies to one which produced for what can loosely be described as a "national" market, rare in an economic context characterized more by fragmented, regional, self-sufficient markets.[6] Here we encounter the main reason for the massive size of the Mexico City manufactory's labor force, at its peak, almost nine thousand workers. The Mexico City manufactory supplied its own administration of the central Valley of Mexico and the administrative units of the north and northwest: Coahuila, Durango, Guadalajara, Monterrey, Rosario, and Valladolid. In addition the manufactory also supplied the highly lucrative mining centers of Guanajuato, San Luis Potosí, Sombrerete, and Zacatecas. The names of the two main *patios* (work areas) of the Mexico City manufactory described the markets for their products; the Patio del Reyno manufactured cigars and cigarettes for the northern and northwestern regions, while the Patio de México's products were for Mexico City and the Valley of Mexico. The Querétaro manufactory operated as an adjunct to the Mexico City manufactory and helped to supply the Guadalajara and Valladolid regions. The tobacco manufactory in Guadalajara supplied its immediate region, as did the manufactories of Puebla and Oaxaca. Veracruz, Córdoba, Jalapa, and part of Puebla were supplied by the Orizaba manufactory.[7] Querétaro, Puebla, and Guadalajara produced only cigarettes, not cigars, while Mexico City, Orizaba, and Oaxaca produced both. This pattern of manufactory production and individual specialization persisted for the next fifty years (see Map I).

The monopoly maintained the same range of tobacco products provided by the private trade but concentrated predominantly on cigars and cigarettes. In the beginning it followed a policy of competitive pricing, first, to drive out the remaining private *cigarreros* and, second, to gain support of the consumers by selling more cigarettes and cigars at the same price. The strategy was abandoned once the private trade was completely abolished.

The marketing and pricing strategy employed by the *dirección general* in the early years of the monopoly's operations provided six *cigarros* more for each class than had the *cigarreros*, so that the consumers, "far from disliking the *estancos*, will receive with approval the greater benefits which the Renta gives to them."[8] In the 1760s consumers received on average 48 *cigarros* per half real and 10.5 cigars per half real. Those consumers who wished to make their own cigarettes could also purchase from the *tercenas* a maximum of four *manojos*, bunches of tobacco of different grades.[9] Leaf tobacco could be purchased in quantities of one ounce, two ounces, four ounces, eight ounces, and one pound, for 1/2 real, 1 real, 2 reales, 4 reales, and 1 peso respectively. The main reason for sales of leaf tobacco was to permit consumers to "modify" cigarettes to their own individual taste by adding tobacco, but it only encouraged legal purchase of tobacco for illegal manufacture and trade. In Valladolid the *factor* reported that approximately one-third of leaf tobacco sold on a monthly basis went to impoverished women who used it to make cigars according to the style and taste of local consumers and sold their wares clandestinely for a small profit.[10]

Tabaco de polvo (snuff) was sold in three general grades—*exquisito, fino,* and *común*. Prices varied according to grade and quantity. In 1778 *exquisito* was the most expensive and sold for 2.5 reales for two ounces, 5 reales for four ounces, and up to 20 reales for 16 ounces. *Común*, the cheapest type of snuff, sold for 0.5 real for half an ounce, up to 8 reales for 16 ounces. In the middle was *fino*, which customers could purchase in quantities which ranged from 0.5 real for half an ounce to 16 reales for 16 ounces.[11]

The practice of selling loose cigarettes for *tlacos* (copper coins or shop tokens) to enable the very poor to purchase some products and of giving the *adelea* (loose cigarettes as change in a transaction) continued under monopoly management. Sales of *palos y granza* (cuttings and waste tobacco) also continued, based on the custom of the *cigarrerías*. Traditionally Indians bought waste tobacco to manufacture *pisiete* and for chewing.[12] One-half real purchased a pound of *palos* and half a *quartilla* of *granza*. The trade was estimated to be worth approximately 6,000 pesos a year. The *dirección general* argued that such sales would not interfere with the sale of cigarettes and cigars. Moreover, it was worth placing both types of tobacco in all of the *estanquillos* so as not to lose trade with the Indian consumers, [13] although as we saw in Chapter 1, official opinion on this matter changed in the early nineteenth century.

Monopoly goods were sold out of government-licensed tobacco shops, the *estanquillos*. Located primarily in the major cities and towns of Mexico, they were also found on haciendas and in *obrajes* (textile mills).[14] Continuity between the old tobacco trade and the monopoly enterprise is reflected in the *estanquillos'* locations, the same as under private ownership. In Mexico City approximately 50 percent of the royal *estanquillos* were in the same location they had occupied as private shops.[15] By 1788 Fonseca and Urrutia reported 2,258 *estanquillos* operating throughout the viceroyalty of Mexico. This is a number which errs on the low side if we consider that, while their report included the number of *estanquillos* in the capitals of each province and their outlying administrations, in the case of the general administration of Mexico, only numbers for Mexico City were given.[16] As the numbers of *estanquillos* declined throughout the late eighteenth century, distribution may have become increasingly more deficient and contributed to shortages of supplies. In 1775 there were 110 monopoly shops in Mexico City; by 1813 there were 66 government outlets.

Estanqueros were required to open their shops from 6 a.m. until 10 p.m. daily. Sales outside of these times were prohibited, and violation of such regulations resulted in the loss of the license. Those individuals who received licenses were required to post a bond as security against theft, fraud, or losses. They were required to display monopoly price lists in their shops to prevent fraudulent pricing. The responsibilities of the *estanqueros* included payment for lighting of the shops, any applicable rent, and costs of transport from the administration to their *estanquillo*.[17] Herein lies one of the economic advantages to the monopoly; apart from patronage and commissions on sales, no investment was made in the retail stores. They were financed by the *estanqueros* themselves, who covered many of the overhead costs of the distribution of monopoly goods.

Only family members could work in the licensed stores. Salaries were paid on a commission basis, generally between 4 and 9 percent of sales, although a minimum and maximum income was established, so that no *estanquero* earned less that 6 reales or more than 22 reales per day. Snuff was sold from six specially designated *estanquillos*, whose managers earned a 5 percent commission on its sale value. Attempts were made to correlate income earned under private ownership with projected income under monopoly management. Average annual incomes of *estanqueros* in Mexico City in 1781

ranged between 400 and 599 pesos.[18] By 1801 the range had widened
to between 361 and 854 pesos.[19] Twelve years later the range had expanded even further to between 276 and 1,200 pesos. Of the total
number of *estanqueros* (66), over half (34) earned annual incomes of
between 480 and 708 pesos. Of the remaining 32, 21 percent (13)
earned between 720 and 1,200 pesos, and 28 percent (19) earned between 276 and 468 pesos.[20] The management of an *estanquillo* did
not provide a luxurious living for the majority of store managers, but
it offered a comfortable life, especially when compared with the
earnings of the manufactory workers (or any other workers, for that
matter).

The *estanquillos* also provided some security and semblance of a
"decent" living for some of Mexico's working women. In 1775 half
of the 110 *estanquillos* which operated in Mexico City were managed by women. In 1801, of the 64 government stores in operation,
women managed 67 percent (43) of them. A similar pattern prevailed
in the provinces. Out of 115 *estanquillos* in the city of Guadalajara,
93 percent (107) were managed by women.[21] We also see longevity of
service, similar to that of the bureaucrats, and generational continuity in the management of *estanquillos*. In 1795, out of the 64 *estanquillos* in operation in Mexico City, over half (36) were managed by
individuals who had received licenses at the beginning of the monopoly or whose children had taken over the shops when their parents retired or died.[22]

With a concentrated production and marketing network, reliable
transport to ensure shipment of supplies throughout the viceroyalty
was critical. The conditions of supply of mule trains remain the
least well documented. As with paper and tobacco, the *dirección
general* contracted with muleteers for their services for a specified
number of years. The prices agreed upon do not reflect any cost advantages to the monopoly and were commensurate with general
prices of overland transport. In 1784 one *arroba* (25 pounds) of
leaf tobacco cost 3.5 reales, one *carga* (200 pounds) or two *cajones*
(crates) of cigars and cigarettes cost 4 pesos, and one *carga* of paper
cost 3 pesos 6 reales.[23] By 1800 the contracts to transport tobacco
from Córdoba to the general warehouses in Mexico City stipulated
rates of 3.5 reales per *arroba* of leaf tobacco and 4.5 reales per *arroba*
of cigarettes, the same prices which appeared in contracts signed for
the period 1779 to 1783.

Not only was transport expensive, it was slow and resulted in
wastage and losses of tobacco in transit. One estimate placed such
losses at between 3 and 4 percent of total cargo.[24] For paper to reach
Mexico City or Oaxaca from the port of Veracruz took almost one

month; the trip to Querétaro took longer, one and a half months. The lengthiest trip was to Guadalajara, which could take up to two months. Such time estimates did not take into consideration myriad accidents which could befall the mule trains. Several muleteers who left Veracruz on 8 October fell ill in Perote en route to Oaxaca (a route filled with detours due to floods). The teams finally arrived in Oaxaca on 5 December, twenty-seven days overdue.[25] During times of crisis, such as war, the *dirección general* found itself subject to arbitrary embargoes of mule trains due to colony-wide shortages. When arms and supplies were shipped to Veracruz for defense purposes, monopoly mule trains became a natural target. During the war between Great Britain and Spain in 1779, the king ordered a general requisition of all mule trains to transport flour and other staples to Veracruz and Havana. Such an order came at a time when a general scarcity of mules was reported, and resulted in mules being not only difficult to acquire, but also expensive.[26] Unreliable mule trains hindered the provision of regular supplies to the population as much as the growing inability of the manufactories to match demand did.

After 1780, when private production was abolished, cigars and cigarettes comprised between 90 and 95 percent of total annual sales. Sales of leaf tobacco accounted for between 4 and 9 percent, with the remaining 1 percent accounted for by sales of snuff and imported Cuban cigars. Figures 8 and 9 show the volume of cigars and cigarettes manufactured and sold in Mexico between 1773 and 1810. In 1780 Mexico City produced 63 percent of the total cigarette output and 64 percent of the cigar output; by 1790 its share in output had increased to 66 percent for cigarettes and 71 percent for cigars. For the same period Orizaba and Oaxaca respectively produced on average 21 percent and 7 percent of the cigar output.[27] Between 1780 and 1810 production of packets of cigarettes increased by 49 percent, from 87,224,461 to 130,532,955 packets. Cigar production increased by 79 percent, from 8,971,100 to 16,085,927 packets. For the same period sales of cigarette packets increased by 55 percent, from 78,466,734 to 121,377,189 packets; sales of cigars increased 151 percent from 6,654,836 to 16,712,433 packets. The peso value of cigar sales increased from 415,927 to 1,044,527 pesos; cigarette sales increased from 4,904,170 to 7,585,074 pesos.[28]

Even if we assume the effects of inflation, which reduce the real peso value from tobacco sales, there is no doubt that steady growth occurred in the volume of production of both cigars and cigarettes, although shortages in supplies were a problem by the beginning of the nineteenth century. During the decades of Bourbon management

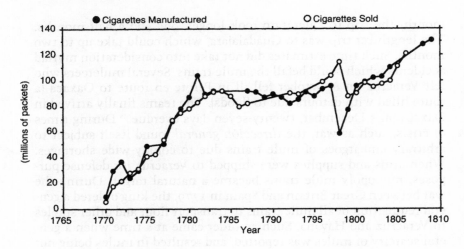

Figure 8. Packets of cigarettes manufactured and sold, 1765–1810.
Source: see Appendix III.

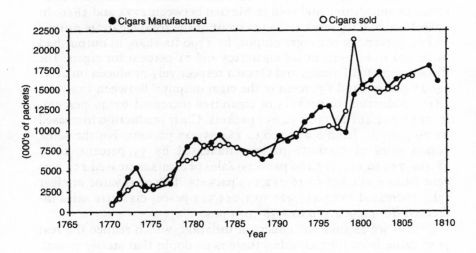

Figure 9. Packets of cigars manufactured and sold, 1765–1810.
Source: see Appendix III.

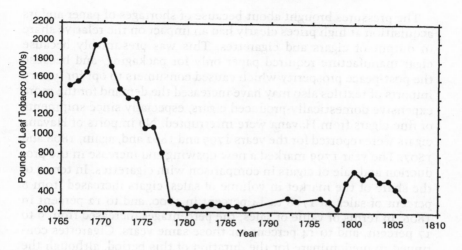

Figure 10. Consumption of leaf tobacco, 1765–1810. Compiled from the *relaciones generales* for selected years and various *legajos* in Tabaco and Renta de Tabaco, AGM, Audiencia de México, AGI, and Biblioteca Nacional, Mexico City.

and regulation, sale of leaf tobacco eventually became a small proportion of the total value of tobacco products sold and comprised, on average, between 6 and 11 percent of total value between 1780 and 1809, compared with 72 percent in 1770, prior to the abolition of the *cigarrerías*. As Figure 10 shows, however, there was an increase in leaf sales between 1798 and 1804, partly due to an increase in supplies to compensate for reduced cigarette production. After 1804 leaf sales began to decline, as inventory levels were readjusted and output of cigars and cigarettes increased once again. Overall, between 1780 and 1806, the volume of leaf sold increased by 42.5 percent from 242,190 to 345,157 pounds.

As a buffer against fluctuating supplies of manufactured products, the monopoly kept large inventories, usually a full year's stock of all goods. Since inventory levels are not always deliberate, we cannot assume that those of the monopoly represented only a buffer against inadequate supplies, as opposed to overproduction during the early years of the manufactories.[29] We cannot determine the percentage of stock which represented excess production, but the decline in inventory holdings between 1797 and 1801 suggests that stocks were drawn on to compensate for reduced output and were not replenished to the same degree as they had been in the previous decade.

The pressures brought about because of shortages of paper and its acquisition at high prices clearly had an impact on the relative share in output of cigars and cigarettes. This was presumably because cigar manufacture required paper only for packaging, and because the post-peace prosperity which caused consumers to opt for luxury imports of textiles also may have increased the demand for the more expensive domestically-produced cigars, especially since shipments of fine cigars from Havana were interrupted. No imports of Havana cigars were reported for the years 1799 and 1802 and, again, 1806 and 1807. The year 1799 marked a new upswing and increase in the production and sale of cigars in comparison with cigarettes. In terms of the share of the market in volume of sales, cigars increased from 8 percent of sales in 1778 to 14 percent in 1800, and to 12 percent in 1806. In terms of value of sales, the percentages increased from 9 to 17 percent, and to 14 percent for those same years. Cigarettes continued to predominate for the duration of this period, although the supply of cigars increased as the *dirección general* sought to adjust production levels and product to scarcities of paper. The ratio of cigars to cigarettes sold reflects the progressive changes in cigarette and cigar production:

1773–1776	1792–1799	1800–1806
1:50	1:40	1:26

Crude calculations of the average unit costs of a packet of cigars and cigarettes between 1778 and 1800 suggest that minor economies of scale occurred but were not sufficient to prevent an increase in costs of production in the long term. Indeed, the low level of fixed costs suggests that economies of scale were not the basis of the manufactories' production. The calculation of unit costs is made difficult by the variations in the amount of tobacco and paper used in manufacture, since this was not constant, nor was the price of paper after 1796. Table 15 indicates the variations in the amount of tobacco used per packet of cigarettes and cigars. Based on a calculation of the estimated average total cost per cigarette-packet-equivalent, the cost of producing a packet of cigarettes after 1780 fluctuated between 2.36 and 3.48 *granos* (12 *granos* equalled 1 real).[30] Given the sale price of a packet of cigars or cigarettes of 1/2 real (6 *granos*), each sale yielded between 3.64 and 2.52 *granos* per cigarette-packet-equivalent.

The costs of the manufactories and their greatest expenditure, labor (leaf and paper were categorized separately), are illustrated in table 16. The costs of the Mexico City manufactory declined after 1798 as a result of a reduction in its labor force, but the reduction

Table 15.   Changes in Volume of Tobacco per Packet of Cigars and Cigarettes, 1776–1806 (selected years)

Year	Ounces of Tobacco/ Packet of Cigarettes	Ounces of Tobacco/ Packet of Cigars
1776	0.6	0.9
1779	0.4	0.8
1780	0.4	0.7
1781	0.3	0.5
1782	0.5	0.6
1783	0.4	0.6
1806	0.5	0.7

Source: 1776, AGI, Mexico 2259, report of Hierro, de la Riva, 10 October 1776; 1779, AGN, Renta de Tabaco 71, report of accountant of Orizaba manufactory, Juan de Arias, 1779; 1780, 1781, 1782, BN (Mexico) Mss 1332, manufactory accounts, f.265–265v, f.267–267v, and f.283–284v, respectively; 1806, AGN, Tabaco 96, manufactory account, 11 February 1807.

was offset by increases in Querétaro's costs. Manufactory labor as a proportion of total costs, however, declined after 1795, as shown in table 5, from an average of 37 percent in the quinquennium 1776–1780 to 33 percent for the quinquennium 1801–1805. What this suggests is that the *dirección general* looked to its wage bill as a way to cut production costs and did so quite successfully by slashing piecework rates between 1779 and 1795. It was able to do so because of the surplus supply of labor in the manufactory towns and an increasingly female workforce after 1790. We will consider the issue of labor recruitment and control in greater detail in chapter 6.

What the manufactories' costs suggest about the monopoly as an enterprise is that it was characterized by capital-saving rather than labor-saving developments in its operations. Comparable with both the colonial mining and textile industries, growth was extensive rather than intensive, and the absence of any significant increase in productivity implied that, in the long run, the monopoly's costs would increase as it expanded output. Despite continued, if increasingly slower, growth, there were shortages in supply of tobacco products, largely the result of a conservative fiscal policy and the consequences of Spanish colonialism. One of the most serious problems, the supply of paper, under other circumstances could have been remedied by the establishment of domestic paper mills. As we saw in Chapter 3, this was not an option for the Bourbons. Even if we

Table 16. Costs of Manufactories, 1769–1805 (in current pesos)

Year	Mexico City	Guadalupe	Querétaro	Guadalajara	Puebla	Oaxaca	Orizaba
1769	29,212						
1772	488,377				12,768	38,376	63,328
1774	384,709				11,662	39,489	67,183
1775	741,904				17,467	39,624	48,419
1776	719,930				14,150	37,592	66,085
1793	704,272		115,457	86,986	105,686	43,185	40,610
1796	804,339				—	—	—
1797	772,413		166,226	83,354	105,416	43,454	45,706
1800	472,652	148,247			—	—	—
1801	446,468	150,676	295,676	102,137	145,827	53,126	65,497
1802	478,428	166,331	281,215	99,642	146,449	53,065	60,065
1803	444,864	156,241	319,212	100,848	141,412	59,028	59,190
1804	436,911	167,401	405,028	102,381	117,536	63,885	73,355
1805	510,280	127,982	503,766	102,145	119,425	52,379	67,608

Source: AGN, AGI, various legajos, Estados Generales for the specified years.

assume, for the moment, that paper supplies were not a problem, the concern with the political stability of the workers and a reluctance to finance more manufactories presented fertile conditions for innovations which would have increased productivity and eliminated the need to employ more workers. This did not occur and confirms general views about the entrepreneurial role of the state: "It is probably easier to exaggerate than to describe accurately the entrepreneurial importance of government activity. Official economic policy was marked by inconsistency, inefficiency, and expediency. The State, in its pursuit of political, religious, or financial ends did not hesitate to sacrifice economic interests to its large goals."[31] Public enterprises such as tobacco, like private ones such as mining and textiles, exhibited successful growth, but with limited potential, which could only result in scarcities of supply in the long run.

The trend in the sale of tobacco products suggests that demand for monopoly products was inelastic at relatively low price ranges. In other words, demand was not a problem. Consumers experienced several price changes between 1765 and 1810. The changes were not due to scarcity or inflation but to royal orders to increase the price of leaf tobacco. The successive increases made by the *dirección general*, by changing numbers of cigars and cigarettes per packet sold for 1/2 real, are shown in table 17. The reduction in the number of cigarettes per packet implemented during the course of the eighteenth century meant that, by the beginning of the nineteenth century, consumers actually paid almost half as much again for a packet of cigarettes (depending on the class), since they received less than half of the initial number of cigarettes for their 1/2 real.

Despite the price increases for tobacco products, per capita expenditure on tobacco between 1793 and 1806 indicates that demand continued to expand slowly. In 1793 sales totalled 6,684,864 pesos, which amounted to approximately 1.3 pesos per capita (based on an estimated population of 5,200,000); by 1806 sales amounted to 9,116,393 pesos or 1.5 pesos per capita (for an estimated population of 6,100,000). Per capita purchases for 1793 and 1806 changed in volume as shown in table 18.

The increasing consumption of tobacco products raises some interesting questions in light of recent assessments of economic trends in colonial Mexico. Our understanding of the economy of late colonial Mexico has increased considerably over the last decade, and recent studies have generated as much heat as they have light on the matter. The eighteenth century was a prosperous one for Mexico.

Table 17. Price Changes in Monopoly Products, 1765–1800

Year	Packets of Cigarettes Class	Number/ Packet	Packets of Cigars Class	Number/ Packet	Leaf
1765	10s	42	6s	6	6–7.5 reales/pound
	11s	48	8s	8	
	12s	54	12s	12	
	13s	48	16s	16	
	14s	48			
1775	10s	42	No change		8 reales/pound
	11s	54			
	12s	60			
	13s	60			
	14s	60			
	23s	60			
1778	10s	36	5s	5	8 reales/pound
	11s	48	7s	7	
	12s	48	10s	10	
	13s	48	14s	14	
	14s	48			
1780	10s	33	No change		10 reales/pound
	11s	42			
	12s	42			
	13s	42			
	14s	42			
1800	10s	32	No change but one		No change
	11s	40	extra class added of 16s		
	12s 13s 14s } No change		16		

Source: AGN, Renta de Tabaco 1, Tarifa del precio a que se ha de vender el tabaco de Rama, polvo rapé, los puros y cigarros, Díaz de la Vega, 1 January 1775; Tarifa del precio . . . , Díaz de la Vega 1 January 1778; Fonseca y Urrutia, *Libro de la Real Hacienda*, vol. 7, f. 140, AGN, Renta de Tabaco 70, Tarifa del precio . . . 20 June 1780; AGN, Renta de Tabaco 37, Tarifa del precio . . . January, 1800.

Between 1742 and 1810 the population of colonial Mexico almost doubled, increasing from an estimated 3.6 million to 6.1 million. During the same period, silver output tripled. But if the last three-

Table 18. Per Capita Consumption of Tobacco Products in Mexico, 1793 and 1806

	1793	1806
Cigarettes	17 packets	19 packets
Cigars	2 packets	3 packets
Leaf	1 ounce	1 ounce
Snuff	0.05 ounces	0.03 ounces

quarters of the eighteenth century saw a period of general economic expansion, it was also one subjected to a sustained inflationary trend and scarcities.[32] In the years after 1780, livestock, food, and land prices all rose in Mexico, while the price of imported goods from Europe fell. Since wages in general did not rise, the real income of wage earners, rural and urban, declined, and the purchasing power of silver fell. A recent assessment of the late colonial economy, specifically of Central Mexico, emphasizes the impoverishment of the urban and rural poor and the "serious problems in the economy of Central Mexico in the late eighteenth century."[33] The series of seventeen indicators of economic activity used to document such impoverishment surprisingly did not include tobacco consumption. If it had, the trend in tobacco consumption would have diverged from the rest of the indicators and shown an opposite, upward trend. While the trend in consumption of a commodity which behaves differently from others is certainly not sufficient to disprove the authors' argument, an argument with which, for the most part, we agree, it raises an interesting question. Why did tobacco consumption continue to grow while other indicators of economic activity showed a decline in consumption? As has been recently pointed out, part of the problem here lies with the sources of the historical data. Contradictory trends in indicators of economic activity stem not so much from the particular methodology used to interpret the historical statistics, but from the figures themselves and the agencies which constructed them.[34] The tobacco monopoly revenues provide a case in point. We have two sets of figures for tobacco revenues, one compiled by the *dirección general*, the statistics upon which this study is based, and the other which could be constructed from the records of the *caja matríz* (central treasury) of Mexico City.[35] If they are compared, we see divergent trends, one upward, based on the accounts of the *dirección general*, and the other downward, although very erratic, based on the accounts of the *caja matríz*. We cannot in this particular work solve the problem of reconciling the different accounts for all government income, but the discrepancies between the amounts reported by the *caja matríz* and the *dirección general* of the tobacco monopoly suggest the continuing need for historians to exercise caution in the interpretation of revenue figures and the significance attributed to them.

To return to the question of why tobacco consumption remained stable perhaps we can shed light on this problem by comparing tobacco with another article of popular consumption, pulque, which experienced a decline in sales in the late eighteenth century. José Hernández Palomo's work on pulque suggests that, as sale prices rose, demand turned elastic, and the consumption of pulque declined after 1785. Increases in the sale price of tobacco products did not have the same result.[36] Why? The likely explanation for the divergent trends between pulque and tobacco consumption has to do with demand elasticity. Tobacco as a commodity is generally recognized for its inelasticity of demand, historically and in contemporary terms, and has few substitutes (coca in the Andes is an exception). Robert C. Nash has argued that the demand for tobacco in England in the eighteenth century was

> highly inelastic within a broad range of prices and incomes. This inelasticity is demonstrated by the speed with which the demand for its mild narcotic pleasures spread, once the commodity became known, and the fact that it quickly became an article of mass consumption even in poor countries where there was little or no demand for other imported luxuries. Correspondingly, although rapidly adopted as an everyday habit, consumption soon reached a point where popular craving was satisfied and in this saturated state further growth tended to be slow.[37]

Such a trend is consistent with the consumption of tobacco in colonial Mexico. Figures 5a and 5b show moderate but sustained growth between 1780 and 1810.

The decline of pulque consumption after 1785, in combination with other indices, has been interpreted as evidence of the growing impoverishment of Mexico's inhabitants, at least in central Mexico, during the last decades of the colonial period. The growth in tobacco consumption, however, suggests that we may be drawing the right conclusions for the wrong reasons.[38] Studies on consumption patterns indicate that we cannot assume that reduced consumption *necessarily* indicates reduced income. Changes in consumption do not reflect income movements accurately because consumption is affected by changes in relative prices.[39] The English tobacco trade of the eighteenth century and the decline in tobacco consumption provide a suggestive comparison and demonstrate the danger of drawing simplistic conclusions about downward trends. Jacob Price found a close inverse correlation between gin and tobacco consumption which suggested a shift from tobacco to gin between 1720 and 1760. Price argued that it was a purely statistical correlation with no corroborative evidence, but Robert Nash took the connection between two "luxury" products one step further and argued that the decline was explained not by gin consumption, but by a combination of factors: increases in smuggling of tobacco and the increasing popularity of snuff compared to tobacco.[40] The point is that whichever substitution was made, the observed "decline" resulted from shifts in expenditure rather than no expenditure at all. We cannot substantiate a similar argument for the Mexican case, that is, that there was a shift from pulque to tobacco, but the existence of contraband trade in both of these products and legal and illegal trade in other alcoholic beverages, require that we continue to increase our understanding of consumption patterns, prices, and income.[41]

Given the rationale of the manufactories and their eventual employment of over 13,000 workers, what exactly did the Bourbons create? A succinct characterization of the manufactories is not easy. Alejandra Moreno Toscano has observed that the major change introduced by the manufactories was the concentration of a large number of workers in one establishment. Such concentration "originating from the need to improve the productive process derived from a policy monopolistic in character imposed by the crown with fiscal objectives . . . from these beginnings . . . the first great manufacturing establishment resulted in the least 'industrial' of the establishments of the 19th century."[42] Such a description, however, does not tell us very much. Indeed, it is much easier to say what the manufactories were not than to say what they were. The idea of an expanded workshop oversimplifies their structure, while protofactory suggests control over time and materials which was not present. The literature on the origins and characteristics of the early factory system suggests that the tobacco manufactories possessed elements of a modern factory: concentration of large numbers of workers in a single establishment, wage labor, and supervision of workers. There was a categoric distinction between the workplace and residence, and ownership of materials and capital was firmly in the hands of the state, not the producer.[43] Nevertheless, monopoly control of the production process remained imperfect. Throughout Bourbon management of the manufactories (and beyond), the element of "putting out," whereby cigarette workers received paper to prepare at home for the following day's work, continued as part of the production process of the manufactories. Manufactory supervisors were only partially able to control the use of a primary material, which continued to impose an artisanal quality on production within the manufactories. Although a division of labor occurred in the manufactories, the majority of the workforce was composed of cigar and cigarette rollers, all manual workers. If we define the term factory by its function to increase productivity and decrease costs, then the tobacco manufactories' performance falls short of the mark.[44]

Like many "big" enterprises of the late seventeenth and eighteenth centuries, the tobacco manufactories remained a hybrid form of production, comparable to what Joan Scott has described for the glassworkers of Carmaux, a combination of artisanal production within a framework of capitalist manufacture.[45] Without the support received from the colonial state and the legitimacy to establish manufactories in the first place, there was really no reason for their existence.[46] In spite of considerable differences concerning rationale, level of capital investment, scale, and relations of production, the tobacco manufactories fit into the same economic spectrum as the *obrajes* (textile mills) of colonial Mexico. In the case of the *obrajes*, relative labor costs provided few incentives for innovation.[47] While the same may be said for the manufactories, one of the most important obstacles to innovation was the colonial state which, despite its desperate need for revenues, chose social stability and safe monopoly profits over further development of the manufactories.

The manufactories demonstrate characteristics typical of late colonial industries in general. They were able to grow to a certain point but then began to exhaust further possibilities. The very institutions and arrangements which enabled them to grow became burdensome and obstructed innovation and development. How and why this happened is the issue to which we now turn.

Problems beset the manufactories almost from the day they opened, but it was during the 1790s that they were subjected to the greatest scrutiny, and the most significant attempts to improve manufactory discipline and output occurred. Spain's interminable wars adversely affected the manufactories' operations. The royal order to increase the sale price of tobacco leaf to boost revenues for Spain's military expenses stimulated a series of discussions and attempted reforms in the manufacture of tobacco products. Such reforms resulted in extreme consumer dissatisfaction, protracted and sometimes vituperative conflict between members of the *dirección general*, and an ad hoc approach toward solutions of problems, favoring no-risk policies designed to preserve the revenues from tobacco and the political acquiescence of the tobacco workers. Approval of reform measures was often the result of coincidental needs, rather than an informed, judicious assessment of their importance. The consequence in the long term was to sacrifice any major innovation in manufactory organization, which eventually resulted in a bottleneck for the supply of tobacco products. Many of the weaknesses which the 1790s exposed were not remedied. Paper remained at the center of the manufactories' problems; control over supplies and supervision of its use by workers remained unresolved problems when the new Mexican republic reluctantly took charge of the monopoly.

Spain's involvement in the War of American Independence and its subsequent campaigns against the British in America between 1779 and 1783 accelerated demands for defense moneys. The Mexican monopoly received two royal orders in 1778 and 1780 to increase the sale price of leaf tobacco from 6 reales to 8 reales per pound. The consequence of this was a series of discussions which raised the question of the profitability of the manufactories and whether or not they should be abolished. It is worth a digression here to demonstrate the calculations and logic used by monopoly bureaucrats to argue the relative advantages or disadvantages of state manufacture.

The calculations used in the manufactory accounts reflect an ongoing evaluation of the opportunity cost of maintaining the state manufactories, an assessment of the relative advantage of sales of manufactured products compared to those of tobacco leaf. When the monarch ordered an increase in the sale of leaf, the relative advantage of manufacture over sale of tobacco leaf declined. The substitution of the notional value of tobacco leaf for its actual cost price to the manufactories (an average of 2 reales per pound), becomes clear in the comparison between total costs reported for cigar and cigarette production in the Mexico City manufactory and total costs of the monopoly's entire operations. From 1778 until 1794 the former exceeds the latter, clearly an impossibility.[48] In a report compiled by the *contador general* in 1795 on the profitability of the Mexico City manufactory, he concluded that, between 1769 and 1794, the manufactory's profits had declined from 50 to 27 percent, with an average profit of 31 percent.[49] The "profits" reported by the *contador general* are arrived at by dividing the profit figure by the value of raw leaf invested in manufacture at its retail, not cost, price. For the year 1787, for example, the monopoly accountant's calculations may be reconstructed as follows:

Total cost of production reported = 3,516,568 pesos (total monopoly costs = 3,036,654 pesos)
Total value of production = 4,274,368 pesos
Profit = 757,799, or 30%

The figures used in the calculation are based on the value of tobacco invested, 2,015,269 lbs. at 10 reales per pound (sale price) = 2,519,086 pesos; the profit = 757,799 pesos, hence:

$$\frac{757,799}{2,519,086} = 30\%$$

Note that a simple profit calculation of $\dfrac{\text{profit}}{\text{total sales of product}}$ produces the following calculation:

Total cost of production = 1,501,299 pesos (2,015,269 lbs. at 2 reales, the average cost of leaf to the monopoly)
Total value of production = 4,274,368 pesos

$$\dfrac{2,773,069}{4,274,368}$$

Profit = 65%

If we recalculate the costs of the manufactory production using the cost price of leaf, the trend in manufactory profits, not surprisingly, is reversed and increases from 51 percent in 1769 to 65 percent in 1794, but decreases again to 51 percent by 1806.[50]

This, then, was the method by which the *directores generales* measured the utility of the manufactories. It also explains why the *director general* Felipe de Hierro felt compelled to suggest that the manufactories be abolished in the very year, 1778, that private manufacture was eliminated and that, for the first time, all six manufactories were in operation. It was also the year that the monarch ordered an increase in the price of leaf tobacco, and so the question of opportunity costs came up immediately. Members of the *dirección general*, most notably the *contador general* Díaz de la Vega, disagreed with Hierro's plan to eliminate the state manufactories, since it would "destroy with one blow the happy progress of the Renta which was owed principally to the establishment of the manufactories and would result in grave damages to the royal interests, to the multitude of poor workers, and to good order, especially if the old *cigarrerías* were reestablished, full of iniquity, dissolution and much fraud."[51] The *director general* received a warning not to bring up the subject of abolition of the state manufactories again.[52] Instead the manufactories' workforce was to be expanded as much as possible to ensure adequate supplies of tobacco products to match demand throughout the kingdom.

Hierro nevertheless embarked on a strategy to implement savings to offset the differential caused by the increase in the sale of leaf tobacco. The *director general* instigated the notorious *nuevas labores de cigarros* (experimental methods of tobacco manufacture) in an attempt to reduce costs by the reduction of the number of cigarettes per packet and the quantities of paper and tobacco used to make them.[53] Figure 5b shows a jump in production between 1780 and 1781 of 16 percent, compared with an average of 10 to 12 percent for the previous three years. Very quickly, however, reports began to flood in warning of decreases in consumption of the new cigars and cigarettes in Mexico City because of consumers' dissatisfaction with their poor quality. Part of the problem was the reduced amount of tobacco. Manufactory accounts indicate that the experimental manufactures used on average between 0.3 and 0.4 ounces per packet of cigarettes, compared with an original 0.6 ounces, and between 0.5 and 0.6 ounces per pack of cigars, compared with an original 0.8 ounces in 1776. Over the next few decades, amounts of paper and tobacco fluctuated but never reached the same levels as during the early 1770s. Additionally, the use of the *palmeta* or flat stick to smooth the cigarettes to give them "an attractive appearance, smoothness, and uniformity" was eliminated because it slowed workers down.[54] The *contador general* Silvestre Díaz de la Vega, contrary to Hierro's views, argued for the reintroduction of the *palmeta*, noting that when consumers purchased packets of cigarettes, they checked them to see if they were all of similar quality; if they were not, they simply refused to buy them. Díaz de la Vega believed that consumer dissatisfaction was so great that, if nothing was done to improve the products, people would become so exasperated they would either stop smoking or seek out contraband cigarettes.[55]

In response to Díaz de la Vega's request for a full report on the state of demand following the introduction of the *nuevas labores*, the administrator-general of the archbishopric of Mexico submitted 87 certified reports (one of several batches) from administrators, branch managers, and *estanqueros*, who all agreed on the poor quality of the cigarettes. Reports of declining sales and complaints of the poor quality of cigarettes continued to appear on the desk of the *dirección general*. Consumers complained that the products were impossible to smoke because they were too brittle, went out at every puff, or flared up in one's face after being lit, that different classes were barely distinguishable from one another, and often two or three cigarettes in a packet were lacking.[56] The effects on consumption were already beginning to show. In some areas, people had stopped buying manufactory cigarettes, although some reports suggested that poor quality was not the only reason that people were buying fewer cigarettes. The manager of Tetecala reported reductions which began as early as 1778. Whereas consumers had smoked a packet of cigarettes a day, now a packet lasted them for three days. Some simply stopped smoking altogether.[57] Francisco de Aragón reported that, in Ixmiquilpan, increased prices of basic commodities generally affected the amount of tobacco purchased. The inhabitants of his jurisdiction were mainly Indians and "poor people who used to buy five dozen, now they buy four dozen and some simply do not buy at all."[58] The high price of maize, in particular, affected consumption. In Santa María Amealco, the local *estanquillo* used to make between 60 and 65 pesos a month; now its intake was down to 40 pesos a month. Many local consumers who customarily spent 4 reales per week (for eight packets) now only spent 1 1/2 to 2 reales (for three to four packets).[59] In short, they halved their consumption in order to purchase maize.

In 1782 the *contador general* wrote to José de Gálvez, now Minister of the Indies, suggesting that many of the problems stemmed from a lack of standardization in the manufacture of cigarettes and that cigars and cigarettes were made with too little tobacco. In 1781 1,403,237 pounds should have been used, but with the new system of less tobacco per *tarea* (piece-work quota), only 1,311,780 pounds were used, another reduction of 6.5 percent. Díaz de la Vega, as usual, could not resist a final comment on how the implementation of the *director general*'s system instead of his own was resulting in losses instead of gains for the monopoly.[60] In the years which followed, various options were explored to reduce costs but maintain an acceptable product at the same time.

Several experiments with machines were conducted in the manufactories. The experiments performed with a drum-driven shredder in 1785 proved controversial and ultimately unsuccessful. Introduced by a Mexico City merchant, Alonso González, the shredder was designed to shred tobacco evenly and quickly. As a result, the tobacco used by the rollers would be a finer, better texture, better cut, and with less wastage than the current system permitted (one pound of leaf tobacco yielded on average twelve ounces of shredded tobacco).

Several observers were appointed to report to the viceroy as to the machine's utility. They included the *fiscal*, the *director general*, the inspector-general of tobacco for the general administration of Mexico, the director of the *nuevas labores*, the administrator-general of the monopoly for the archbishopric of Mexico, and José de Alzate, the foremost scientist of his time, for his "knowledge of machines."[61] Out of four experiments conducted, the fourth yielded the most favorable results, and demonstrated that the shredder would save the monopoly 96,017 pesos, and possibly as much as 200,000 pesos, a year.[62] However, the *director general* and *contador general* based their judgment on the negative results of the first three tests.[63]

The final judgment rendered was that the invention was neither useful nor profitable. Far from saving money, it would increase costs; with the level of wages in the manufactory, the machine would actually cost more to maintain on an annual basis. Why the *director general* and *contador general* were opposed to the machines is unclear. The failure of the machine to perform uniformly was explained by worker sabotage, or so it was alleged, carried out on the manufactory administrator's orders. It may be that they feared an outburst from the workers if news circulated that fewer workers were necessary, or perhaps they harbored a genuine suspicion of the machine's capabilities.[64]

In 1786 the Mexico City manufactory administrator reported on the large numbers of cigars and cigarettes being manufactured illegally in "convents, schools, and private houses, and purchased by individuals who, through necessity, have stopped buying from the *estancos.*"[65] The consumers' "necessity" came from increased prices and declining quality. The manufactory administrator argued that manufactory products were not to blame; the culprits were the Mexico City *estanquilleros* who damaged the manufactory's products by recutting cigarettes and reducing the numbers in each packet.[66] An investigation carried out by a crown assessor, Don Eusebio Sardinero, provided another explanation. The assessor, after a not particularly thorough survey of three *estanquillos*, found the cigars and cigarettes to be well made but commented that the real problem lay in the capriciousness of consumers' tastes, fickle at best. Nevertheless, Sardinero recommended to the *dirección general* that it would be better to retain the traditional thickness and weight of the product.[67]

The 1790s proved to be a critical period for the manufactories, and the decade began with a bolt from the blue. In January 1792 a royal order proclaimed the king's desire to abolish the tobacco monopoly, since he was "convinced of the dislike of his vassals for the monopoly." At the same time, however, he also wished to know the best and most effective method by which to eliminate the enterprise without affecting the existing substantial revenues which it provided. With memories of the massive Tupac Amaru rebellion in Peru and the Comunero uprising in New Granada (both of which occurred in 1781) still painfully fresh, reports of public disturbances against the tobacco monopolies in the Philippines and Venezuela in the early 1790s caused consternation among royal ministers. Despite such fears, nothing came of the suggestion to abolish the Crown's tobacco monopolies, primarily because no suitable fiscal alternative could be found.[68]

The context of the monopoly's development over the next few years was shaped by the interaction of a number of influences, but particularly by a heightened sensitivity to political and social disorder. First, there was a need to improve the quality of manufactory cigarettes and cigars. Second, the search to reduce costs and improve the efficiency of the use of raw materials, particularly paper, continued. While the appointment in 1792 of a new, enthusiastic, and ambitious manufactory administrator, Miguel Puchet, provided the person to carry out the necessary reforms, he received only moderate support from the Crown. Third, monopoly autonomy in policy formation had gradually been reduced since the late 1780s, leaving it vulnerable to the conservative influence of the Tribunal de Cuentas. Fourth, the pressure from Madrid to improve the level of monopoly revenues increased. In 1794, as a consequence of an order designed to improve control over the use of cigarette paper by workers, the Mexico City manufactory tobacco workers rioted and attempted to strike. It was only after this protest that the manufactory administrator's push to reduce the number of workers in the Mexico City manufactory and to tighten up manufactory regulations received royal support.[69] Two years later Spain was at war with England. The consequences of the war years were twofold for the monopoly; they interrupted supplies of paper to the manufactories, making its efficient use even more imperative, and they increased the need for revenues with which to finance the war effort. Plagued by conflict both within and outside of the empire, the *dirección general* and the colonial state found themselves confronted by two opposing imperatives. To increase revenues from the monopoly required a rationalization and reorganization of the manufactories; to do so risked agitation from the tobacco workers and threatened social peace.

The concern of the colonial state and the manufactory administrator over the size of the Mexico City manufactory workforce was mutual but for different reasons. The former feared social unrest in its colonies; the latter concluded that the workforce was unnecessarily large, which resulted in inefficient work and poor products. Several steps were taken, which will be discussed in more detail in Chapter 6. One of those steps, however, was the issue of a royal order which placed a limit on the number of workers that could be employed in a single manufactory. The major target of this order, of course, was Mexico City. The decision to reorganize the Mexico City manufactory workforce raised a much more important question, however, and that was whether or not the manufactories should be abolished altogether, and, if not, what was to be done about them.

As we have argued, the initial call for abolition of the manufactories by the *director general* Hierro was based on his argument that manufactory profits were beginning to decline, especially in comparison with the heady figures of 50 percent of the early days. Ten years later, however, in 1790, Díaz de la Vega, an opponent of Hierro's original plan, began seriously to question the profitability of the manufactories, precisely because the profits continued to decline in the 1790s. The difference between the 1780s and the 1790s was significant. Not only had the most serious worker protest experienced by the monopoly occurred, but the supply of paper to the manufactories was jeopardized by British embargoes of Spanish shipping after 1796. The central issue, then, was again a consideration of opportunity costs—was it more profitable to sell only leaf and to return manufacture to private entrepreneurs? Díaz de la Vega advocated a modified version of Hierro's original plan to abolish the manufactories, restore manufacturing to the private sector, and sell leaf only. The elimination should be accomplished slowly, and a small manufactory kept in operation in Mexico City.

The impetus to reform the manufactories or find alternatives to monopoly revenue took on new energy after the workers' riot of 1794. Between 1795 and 1805 numerous debates and hypothetical costs of modified monopoly arrangements appeared which demonstrated the pros and cons of a return to private manufacture. Cost estimates showed that, if the monopoly were to sell leaf only, in order to match existing revenues it would have to raise the price of leaf to 13 or 14 reales. An equally serious problem was raised by the *contador general* who observed that the monopoly was already suffering losses due to a lack of supplies of cigars and cigarettes to the northern provinces.[70] The *contador general* agreed with Díaz de la Vega that the monopoly should restrict its activities to the sale of leaf and regulate private tobacconists. Excessive costs of manufacturing, including the free 'smokes' which the manufactory workers indulged in while carrying out their daily toil (to the amount of 60,423 pesos a year) would be eliminated.[71] One or two small manufactories which employed women only should be kept open and used as a base to rebuild the state manufactories if sale of leaf did not produce adequate revenues.[72]

The decision about the manufactories' future did not lay solely in the hands of the *dirección general*, very much to the chagrin of the *director general*. Present during consultations and discussions, in addition to the members of the *dirección general*, were the *fiscales* (treasury and civil) and the ministers from the *exército y Real Hacienda* and Real Tribunal de Cuentas. Díaz de la Vega's resentment against what he perceived to be outside interference may explain in part the protracted nature of these discussions and his intransigence on some of the issues. Not surprisingly, the treasury ministers, influenced by the prospect of risking three million pesos' worth of revenue, disagreed with the recommendations of the *director general*. They discounted the 'losses' view of the manufactories, outlined the advantages of the manufacturing system which were the key to monopoly revenues, and argued that private enterprise would never be able to employ the same numbers employed by the monopoly. "We have had this system now for 20 years with more than 7,000 workers . . . who provide for their families with the wages earned in the manufactory; the public is accustomed to the use of the manufactory goods, having virtually forgotten the time of free trade; the Real Hacienda has a secure and steady revenue of more than 3 million pesos, all of which suggests that no changes should be made, and, if they are, they must be done slowly and cautiously."[73]

Such was the general consensus of the members of the Audiencia and ministers of the Real Tribunal de Cuentas de la Contaduría Mayor de México and the Real Exército (Army). Despite Díaz de la Vega's contention that the ministers of the Tribunal de Cuentas lacked an adequate knowledge of monopoly accounts and what the figures meant, it was the latter who correctly identified the opportunity cost method of evaluating the manufactories' profitability: "they always use the value of leaf tobacco as *if it would have been sold at the price established for this good*" (author's emphasis).[74] The ministers viewed the proposal to abolish the manufactories to be far too great a risk. The *dirección general* could not guarantee that the same volume of tobacco would be traded under competitive conditions, especially with the price of leaf pegged at 12 or 13 reales. Such a high price would prevent small tobacconists from making a decent living, or they would sell their products at such outrageous prices that consumption would drop, and contraband would still offer an attractive alternative. The *fiscal* reported the findings of the ministers of the Tribunal de Cuentas, who adamantly supported the continuation of the manufactories. "Neither due to anticipated losses, which are far from being realized in the manufactories, nor in search of greater profit, which is very uncertain and contingent upon many things, is there any reason to abolish the manufactories, despite the confidence of the monopoly ministers in their project."[75]

Here we see the differing priorities of two state agencies. The trea-

sury officials defended the existing organization of the manufactories, which produced significant revenues, and concluded that "the
Renta is flourishing, revenues have not declined considerably, no
changes ought to be made other than to improve control over contraband activities, and general abuses in the system such as excessive
costs and wastage in the manufacturing process."[76] The insights of
the treasury ministers were correct, but they adopted a somewhat
selective perspective on the problems which the manufactories
faced. It was the *dirección general* which realized the dilemma of an
industry which did not have complete control over one of its main
raw materials—paper—and which was restricted in how many
workers could be employed in a single manufactory. The fear was
whether the existing manufactories were capable of producing adequate supplies for the viceroyalty. In 1798 the *contador general*
warned of the need to increase output by one-third due to increasing
scarcities.[77]

The prevalent view of the *dirección general* was that no major increases in production by the existing manufactories were possible.
To do so would create more problems than it would solve.[78] In addition, a royal order of 8 January 1795, reissued in August 1800, placed
a limit on the number of workers who could be employed in a single
manufactory.[79] The limit was not specified by a particular number
but it is clear that the order was directed at the Mexico City manufactory workforce. In the meantime, a series of assessments was conducted of the relative capacity of each manufactory to expand (excluding the one in Mexico City). Only Querétaro was judged capable
of expansion, partially because of location, and partly because of
confidence in local labor supplies and the willingness of workers in
Mexico City to migrate there if necessary.[80] As we shall see in Chapter 6, Querétaro experienced the largest increase in the number of its
workers. This constituted a decentralization of the workforce away
from the administrative capital and out into the provinces between
1797 and 1798. Aside from this measure, however, without investing additional start-up capital to increase the number of manufactories, expansion in production was limited. As population grew
and, with it, demand, the monopoly would be increasingly unable to
supply the necessary quantities.

Although persuaded that abolition of the manufactories may be
necessary due to the "threat" which a large number of workers presented to the political stability of Mexico City, the viceroy remained
unconvinced that sales of only leaf tobacco would produce revenues
equal to or greater than those currently earned from the sale of
manufactured goods. He suggested that the most suitable solution

was to divide yearly production among the major administrative districts, in towns which possessed large or growing populations, and to establish new manufactories. Such a reform would remove the burden from the state of maintaining control over the unwieldy manufactory in Mexico City and solve the problem of the limit on the number of workers in a single manufactory.[81]

The more optimistic bureaucrats envisioned collaboration between private and public interests in that local merchants would be more than willing to provide suitable buildings for manufactures at "reasonable" rents, or that local *cabildos*, grateful for a new industry, would help to finance the establishment of local manufactories. The major savings to be gained by moving much of the production out of Mexico City and into the provinces, however, would come through transport and wages. The standard of living was cheaper in the countryside, so lower wages could be offered, which would reduce costs of manufacture. New manufactories would be closer to their local and regional markets, which would permit a quicker response to orders from local *estanquillos*. Consumers would have access to a fresher product rather than the inventory-stale products purchased in areas far distant from Mexico City.[82] Such arguments were countered by observations that there was no guarantee that adequate labor existed in the places targeted, and that necessary start-up costs would have to come out of monopoly revenues.

The newly constituted *junta superior de Real Hacienda*, set up to decide on reorganization of the manufacturing system, voted for seven new manufactories: one in the *villa* of Guadalupe, one league's distance from Mexico City, to absorb the manufactory's "excess workers", an additional manufactory in Guadalajara, two in Valladolid and San Luis Potosí, Aguascalientes, and one in Durango. The small manufactory of Guadalupe opened its doors in 1799. This simultaneously permitted a reduction in the number of workers of the Mexico City manufactory and their reallocation, reducing the possibility of social tension.[83] There was little significant practical advance thereafter in the establishment of the remaining new manufactories. In 1802 the manufactory administrator, Puchet, reported that the workers were already producing at maximum capacity and that, if output was to be increased, more workers were necessary.[84] Successive proposals reduced the number of new manufactories to four. The *contador general* suggested that, financially, the most sensible action entailed completion of the building of the state manufactory in Atlampa in Mexico City, since a half million pesos had already been spent on its foundations. Not to finish it constituted unnecessary financial waste on the monopoly's part.[85]

The *director general* continued to insist that the greatest problem faced by the monopoly was the inadequate provision of supplies to the various regions of Mexico.[86] Increases in production, especially after 1802, were needed, partly to restock monopoly inventory, but also in response to increased demand. Cigarette output declined in 1798 and 1799 because of paper shortages, and huge withdrawals from inventory stock left levels dangerously low. It was usual to keep almost a year's inventory (based on the previous year's sales) in stock, but by the late 1790s such inventories were depleted and had not been fully replenished. Table 19 shows the inventory holdings listed for the years 1792–1806, and indicates the changes in the levels of inventory between 1797 and 1801 of packets of cigars and cigarettes, pounds of leaf tobacco, and reams of paper. Inventories of leaf tobacco experienced a short-term glut between 1798 and 1802 as supplies piled up due to reduced production of cigarettes. Unfortunately, a series of poor harvests after 1802 left the monopoly with less than one year's inventory of leaf tobacco. In 1802 renewed supplies of paper and the need to build up inventory supplies resulted in increases in production quotas by the monopoly at a time that, as we saw in Chapter 3, was problematical for the tobacco planters.

The *director general* continued to receive reports which confirmed the problem of shortages in supply.[87] Monopoly officials in 1802 commented that confiscated tobacco should be used and not destroyed, as was the custom, because they feared that such action would provoke riots, especially among indigenous communities who complained about insufficient quantities of cigarettes available for purchase. It made more sense to allow local use of such tobacco at the normal prices.[88]

In August of 1804 the viceroy ordered plans to be prepared to establish the proposed new manufactories, but the plans were never implemented.[89] In the same year, the Crown ordered, as the *contador general* had suggested, completion of the unfinished building financed by monopoly capital, which would house the operations of the Mexico City manufactory. The first state-financed manufactory opened its doors to the workers on 20 May 1807, but it was by no means a solution to supply problems, nor did the investment made represent a Bourbon commitment to modernization and innovation. Rather, what it represented was a lack of fiscal alternatives. Moribund reasoning for a moribund state.

The insurgency of 1810 disrupted the manufacture of tobacco products in the Mexico City manufactory. Production continued for only eight years under the Bourbons and only four of these were uninterrupted by rebel incursions. There is ultimately an ironic sym-

Table 19. Inventory Stocks and Value, 1792–1806 (in current pesos)

Year	Value at Retail	Value at Cost	Packets of Cigars	Packets of Cigarettes	Leaf Tobacco (pounds)	Reams of Paper
1792	16,843,089	8,676,096	7,178,609	101,158,450	8,495,685	201,086
1793	17,829,097	8,721,536	8,226,068	97,328,654	9,764,513	182,783
1796	17,092,928	7,885,005	15,198,152	84,143,447	10,005,743	45,596
1797	15,811,603	7,541,109	15,042,247	75,800,143	9,422,387	9,889
1798	14,990,235	5,488,719	12,080,647	24,832,578	14,401,986	21,747
1799	14,501,112	5,076,734	5,225,306	13,075,035	11,472,792	67,503
1800	12,299,956	4,919,141	5,722,435	20,293,012	9,063,786	64,053
1802	8,163,858	3,687,686	8,302,850	27,965,338	4,250,344	88,347
1803	9,171,081	5,044,616	8,991,195	33,362,727	4,276,327	332,378
1804	8,712,965	4,905,718	10,137,633	43,052,758	3,683,116	216,173
1806			7,492,200	43,817,358		

Source: AGI, AGN, Estados Generales for the respective years.

metry between two architectural icons of Spanish state-building, the newly constructed Mexico City manufactory and its counterpart in Seville. If the magnificent establishment in Seville embodied the triumphant ascent of the Bourbon state, its counterpart in Mexico City symbolized the transience of that achievement.

The development of the manufactories in late colonial Mexico was restrained by conservative policies, both fiscal and political, which blocked the *dirección general*'s attempts to adjust the organization to changing conditions. The *dirección general* found itself pressured by Madrid to continually increase monopoly revenues, but, at the same time, was confronted by an intransigent, conservative state which eschewed any risk in reorganization of the manufactories. Paradoxically, the manufactories became victims, and not beneficiaries, of their fiscal success. Instead of developing strategies to improve them, the Spanish state settled for earning monopoly rent at the expense of innovations and new processes. The irony of such conservatism is that it undermined the actions of monopoly bureaucrats who exemplified the type of career bureaucracy which the Bourbons sought to create. These bureaucrats were capable of identifying problems and devising policies to solve them, but were constantly thwarted by an ailing state edifice. Any regime which inherited the monopoly manufactories inherited their intrinsic problems and their incapacity for sustained and increased production. No technical innovations were introduced, nor were any adjustments made to respond to the changing circumstances of paper supplies due to the effects of warfare. In short, what the monopoly manufactories faced is what Ravi Ramamurti has termed a "bureaucratic" mode of behavior, characterized by a limited capacity to respond to changes and a high exit barrier, typical of many state enterprises.[90] The limitations on the organization and productivity of the manufactories not only came from fiscal conservatism, but also from worker recalcitrance. The work regime established by the monopoly and the workers' response to that regime are the subjects of the next two chapters.

6. To Serve in the King's House: Work, Wages, and Manufactory Discipline in the Royal Tobacco Manufactories

IN A RECENT INTRODUCTION to a collection of essays on work and the meaning of work, Patrick Joyce argues that "ideologies of work are political as well as 'economic' . . . they are constructed in terms of the operations of law and the state as well as politics, rather than with reference to economic factors alone."[1] The argument is suggestive since "ideologies" about work which emerged out of Bourbon absolutism challenged, sometimes unintentionally, traditional values of authority, gender roles, and general behavior. A fundamental element of the *étatisme* of absolutist states of the eighteenth century was that, for the body politic to be strong, the individual needed to prosper as well. It was the eighteenth-century state that took charge of the organization of public health and sanitation, the establishment of hospitals and workhouses, schemes of public employment, and law and order. Like other absolutist monarchs, the Spanish Bourbons sought to clean up, control, and sculpt their citizens into useful, productive, and obedient servants. The tobacco manufactories provide something of a metaphor for such reform and the responses to them. The monopoly bureaucrats viewed them as institutions of order and prosperity. Certain sections of the population of Mexico saw the manufactories as symbols of the absence of good order, of the breakdown of traditional hierarchy, control, and stability, as symbols of a world which, if not quite upside down, was changing, and not necessarily for the better.[2]

The matter of who could work, and the legal ability to do so, lay at the heart of economic reforms which sought to pull down the barriers of guilds and which encouraged women to enter the workforce as "productive" members of a society.[3] The lifting of guild restrictions against women was part of a larger attack on the monopolistic guild system, which the Count of Campomanes argued was the main cause of the backwardness of Spanish industry in general.[4] With the exception of the glaring contradiction of the restrictions which the monopoly imposed on the manufacture of cigars and cigarettes, the tobacco manufactories manifested the Bourbon reformers' ideal vision of late colonial industry: unhindered access to employment, freedom from guild restrictions, appropriate work for women, and a salaried workforce. Although the general rationale behind the establishment of the manufactories was to provide employment for the urban poor, manufactory work was deemed to be particularly "appropriate" for women, especially since they played such an important role in the private trade. In effect, the reorganization of the tobacco trade provides a clear example of ways in which the discourse of the political economy of the Bourbons constructed gender in particular trades. Work in the manufactories was gradually organized according to "a scheme that employed masculine and feminine symbols to identify the positive and negative poles."[5]

The organization and management of the tobacco manufactories presented problems typical of many early industrial establishments. As economic historians have observed, "the concentration of large numbers of workers and subjecting them to discipline, regularity . . . was one of the most difficult problems encountered by early factory masters. Cheap labor was no advantage unless it could be effectively transplanted from the traditional to the modern sector."[6] The tobacco workers proved to be no exception in the difficulties they presented their managers. We will begin with a description of the recruitment and composition of the tobacco manufactory workforce and then consider the organization of work and wages. Finally, we will examine the content of and results of work discipline within the manufactories.

Unlike many other employers in Mexico, urban or rural, manufactory managers did not experience problems with labor shortages but with labor discipline. The manufactories' ability to attract labor was indisputable.[7] The estimated totals of manufactory workers in colonial Mexico for selected years between 1769 and 1809 are shown in table 20. The number of manufactory workers (including administrative personnel) increased from an estimated total of 12,013 in 1795 to 13,316 in 1809.

All of the tobacco manufactories were located in large towns or cities which, by the middle of the eighteenth century, had labor surpluses based on growing urban populations, a combination of natural demographic growth and in-migration from the surrounding provinces.[8] Urban poverty grew worse throughout the late eighteenth century, as the number of migrants from the provinces to the cities increased. Women in particular suffered from shortages of em-

Table 20. Distribution of Work Force of Mexico's Tobacco Manufactories, 1769–1809

Year	Mexico	Guada-lajara	Puebla	Queré-taro	Oaxaca	Orizaba	Guada-lupe	Totals
1769	400							
1770	900							
1771	5,600					639		
1772	7,400							
1793	7,161							
1794	8,133							
1795	7,074	1,550	1,027	1,397	610	355		12,013
1796	8,988	1,403			433			
1797	8,976			2,103				
1798*	5,522	1,356	919	1,478	493	369		10,137
1799					457	371	1,381	
1800							1,444	
1809	5,437	1,160	1,228	3,706	610	335	840	13,316

Source: AGN, Tabaco 495; AGN, Renta de Tabaco 119, AGN, Tabaco 241, AGN, Tabaco 149, AGI, Mexico 2302, AGN, Tabaco 482, AGI, Mexico 2277, AGI, Mexico 2292, AGI, Mexico 2296.

*The figures for 1798 are estimates. The original figures reported did not include the supervisory categories. We added in proxy supervisory figures taken from those reported for 1795. The figures may err on the high rather than the low side.

ployment. Widows or abandoned married women with children sought work in managing taverns, as domestic servants, or turned to prostitution.[9] Not surprisingly, in a world which offered few opportunities to women workers, the tobacco manufactories came to occupy an important role in their lives. Among the working poor, employment in a tobacco manufactory was one of the preferred occupations, especially when compared to domestic service or work in an *obraje* (textile manufactory). With a willingness to employ girls and women, and with little skill required, the manufactories could draw upon a significant population, large enough to allow the *dirección general* to reduce wages in the later part of the century. The task of rolling cigarettes was not perceived to be particularly difficult. As a consequence, the manufactories were inundated by requests for work. The manufactory administrator complained that twice and even four times as many people as were needed requested employment in the Mexico City manufactory.[10] As the manufactory administrators were to find out, however, there was a special skill in rolling cigars and cigarettes, and not everyone possessed it. The manufactories in Guadalajara and Oaxaca employed only women workers from the very beginning (with the exception of management and some supervisors); the others employed both men and women. In 1790 tobacco workers constituted approximately 12 percent and 26 percent, respectively, of the economically active populations of Mexico City and Querétaro.[11] Measured another way, of the most important industrial activities in late eighteenth-century Mexico City, the tobacco manufactory employed 55.1 percent of workers engaged in industrial work who received a money wage (a total of 12,697), followed by 380 textile workshops with 12.8 percent of such workers, and, in third place, food production with 9.3 percent.[12]

We have already argued that the large numbers of workers employed in the manufactories, particularly in Mexico City, reflected the coordination between the organization of internal markets by the monopoly administration and the level of production required to meet domestic demand, but who were the workers, and what was the composition of the manufactory workforce? Workers in the tobacco manufactories were drawn from a variety of social classes: former tobacco shop owners and their employees, semiskilled or unskilled men and women from the urban populations of the manufactory towns, and migrants; patronage positions were 'awarded' by the viceroy or *director general* to retired bureaucrats or their relatives and to other "deserving cases."

The result was a workforce differentiated according to gender, marital status, social status, race, and skill. The former tobacco shop owners and their families comprised, according to the *director general*, "a considerable number . . . (including children) who work in the *fábrica*."[13] The inspector-general reported that "entire families came from the nearby provinces of San Andrés Chalchicomula, Tepeaca, and Tehuacan" to work in the newly established manufactory in Orizaba.[14] The *padrón* of 1791 for Orizaba confirms the employment of families, with entries for male relatives such as two brothers, both cigar makers, and a clerk whose brother was listed as a packer, all employed in the same manufactory. In 1811 a sample of the tobacco workers in the Mexico City manufactory demonstrated that the majority of male workers were married, whereas the majority of women workers (72 percent) were either single or widowed, a figure which represents the growing concentration of impoverished women in the tobacco industry.[15]

The racial cartography of the tobacco workers suggests a predominance of Spanish, mainly creole and mestizo workers. Supervisory positions and positions as guards were dominated by penisulars and creoles.[16] In the Querétaro manufactory, leading administrative posts were occupied by peninsular Spaniards, while supervisory positions were dominated by creoles. Celia Wu found that, even among the cigarette rollers, creoles predominated "with some 60 percent of the total, the rest being mestizos and only a handful of mulattoes."[17] The Orizaba manufactory workforce had an even higher concentration of Spanish workers; of the 176 male tobacco manufactory workers identified in 1791, 90 percent (158) were Spanish, 8 percent (14) mestizo, and 2 percent (4) *castizo* (of Spanish and mestizo parentage). The cigar makers were predominately creoles.[18] In 1811, out of a sample of 1,753 cigarette rollers who worked in the Mexico City manufactory, 67 percent were Spanish, 16 percent were Indian, and 15 percent were *castas* (of mixed racial background).[19] General descriptions of the workers by manufactory bureaucrats rarely included racial characterizations. Rather, the workers were characterized in class terms, such as the ubiquitous "plebe" or *operarios* (workers). This imposed a homogeneity upon the workers which did not exist, a point to which we shall return in chapter 7.[20]

Contemporary observers believed that the manufactories acted as magnets for migrants from the surrounding countryside. José de Gálvez went so far as to claim that the Mexico City manufactory was responsible for the "notorious increment" in the population of the city because "it has attracted, is attracting, and will attract many poor families to this capital."[21] Recent studies suggest, however, that the Mexico City manufactory served its under- and unemployed residents rather than provincial migrants. An estimated 69 to 76 percent of the tobacco factory employees were from the capital, which leaves between 24 and 31 percent of manufactory workers as migrants.[22]

Contemporary assessments by monopoly bureaucrats of the numbers dependent upon work in the manufactories were based not simply upon those actually employed, but also on the family units they helped to support. The numbers calculated were arrived at by multiplying the number of workers by an estimated two dependents, which amounted to a minimum of 20,000.[23] Based on such calculations, and taking the estimated population of Mexico City for 1790 of 112,926, we see that almost one-fifth of the city's inhabitants depended, in some measure, upon manufactory work for survival.[24] With this in mind, the caution exercised over the years by the *dirección general* about reforms and the colonial government's desire to avoid social tensions and antagonisms is understandable.

Descriptions of the manufactories and the physical work space are rare, but the few which exist suggest that the workers endured hot, dusty, cramped conditions, breathing in the cloying air filled with tobacco dust. The first site of the tobacco manufactory in Mexico City could only accommodate 400 workers, closely packed together with little room to move. As Díaz de la Vega reported years later, "It was a shameful thing to see them, they had nowhere to eat."[25] First established in the Calle de la Cadena in several contiguous houses, as the manufactory work force expanded, operations were moved to the parish of Santa Catarina, where production began in January 1771. The new location offered greater space for the workshops, contained in three large buildings which allowed easy communication between them. Inside there were twenty-eight rooms with iron railings and windows, a well, and stables for the pack animals. Don Francisco Saavedra de Sangronis described the interior of the manufactory. "It is a kind of large compound divided by boards and rush mats into workshops for the various tasks. The divisions are compact but small. Five thousand men and two thousand women work in this factory daily."[26] Men entered the manufactory from the south, from a street called the Calle de la Fábrica de los Hombres; women entered from the north, from the Calle de la Fábrica de las Mugeres.

In 1793 the Mexico City administrator, Miguel Puchet, voiced concern about the extremely cramped conditions for the workers. There was often no room in the workrooms for some of the women cigarette makers, who took their *tareas* (piecework quotas of a specified number of cigarettes or cigars to be rolled each day) outside in the alleyways by the manufactory. Hardly conducive to conscientious work, such ad hoc measures also exposed them to colds and fevers, especially during the summer rains. The regional manufactories fared little better. At the beginning of the nineteenth century, Alexander von Humboldt visited the tobacco manufactory in Querétaro and commented that "the rooms are clean but poorly ventilated, very small and, as a result, very hot."[27]

The existence of an immensely unhealthy workplace is corroborated by the concern of the workers to organize a form of guaranteed medical aid and the high rates of sickness among them. Like most hot, confined spaces, the Mexico City manufactory was vulnerable to fires and acted as a conduit for contagious diseases. The workers suffered more than once from epidemics which ravaged Mexico City. In 1779 the administrator of the manufactory received orders not to admit any more workers until the worst effects of an epidemic subsided.[28] The great fever epidemic which swept through Mexico City in 1813 killed an estimated 801 workers.[29] Although fires broke out on several occasions, no major damage was done, or at least none was reported.

Cigarette and cigar makers suffered from the effects of inhalation of tobacco dust and contracted fatal diseases, most commonly tuberculosis.[30] Workers complained that no one could work for more than three-quarters of an hour without stopping and going outside to throw water on themselves to wash off tobacco dust. Some were also afflicted by a gradual weakening of the muscles and nerves of their hands until they could no longer control them.[31] The eventual result was an inability to complete their *tareas* and to support themselves.

The Concordia, the tobacco workers' mutual aid society, provided a much needed buffer against complete destitution, a risk faced by all workers. Table 21 gives an account of the money spent on medicines for sick or ailing Concordia members over a seven month period in 1782. Without comparable accounts for a variety of years, it is difficult to interpret the true significance of these figures. Taking them at face value, it is striking that almost one-third of the manufactory work force was (or claimed to be) sick enough to require medicine of some kind. This seems to be consistent with figures available for 1791–1793. As table 22 indicates, in 1791 1,349 workers were registered as 'cured'; in 1792 and 1793, 1,274 and 2,035 workers respectively were registered as "cured." The majority of Concordia benefits went to the sick, a massive 73 percent in 1792 and 1793 (see table 32). Table 22 also indicates the number of deaths and burials of workers from the Mexico City manufactory, roughly 170 per year, or 2 percent of the total manufactory work force. The death rates do not seem particularly high but in the absence of mortality rates for other occupations it is hard to interpret their real significance. The numbers registered as ill and in need of medical aid, however, suggest the insalubrious nature of work in the manufactories, exacerbated by poor diets and harsh living conditions.

The only improvement in the working conditions of the manufactories occurred when the state-financed manufactory in Mexico City was completed. On 20 May 1807, thirty years after its initial conception, the manufactory opened its doors to the tobacco workers. One advantage of the new manufactory was its design which allowed for better lighting, better ventilation, and more room for the workers, so that they would be less prone to inhalation of tobacco dust.[32] An estimated 5,200 cigarette rollers could work within its walls. The Patio de Mujeres (women's work area) contained eleven-

Table 21. *Number of Requests for Medicine by Sick Workers, Mexico City Manufactory, 1782*

	Requests	Peso Value
February	1,302	300
March	1,556	370
April	1,832	441
May	1,944	468
June	2,174	547
July	2,120	497
August	2,100	481

Source: AGN, Tabaco 500, report of Concordia *conciliarios*, f.18v.

Table 22. *Concordia Benefits Paid to Workers, Mexico City, 1791–1793*

Benefits Category	1791	1792	1793
Recorded deaths	175	161	169
Number of burials	175	159	169
Number of marriages	173	135	186
Number of sick aided		1,274	2,035
Number of cured	1,349		
Number of invalids		27	57
Number of prisoners		123	49

Source: AGI, Mexico 2313.

and-a-half rooms, 250 workers in each room. The monopoly saved an estimated 12,000 pesos a year in rent for warehouses and buildings serving as manufactories. Located in the Potrero de Atlampa, on the southwestern side of the city, an area previously designated for the Botanical Gardens, its opening was publicized in the *Gaceta de México.* Neoclassic in style, it was described as a "solid building of beautiful and elegant construction, of 200 square *varas,* with fountains for the greatest comfort and better service of the offices and employees."[33] Even so, the majority of those who had worked in the Mexico City manufactory since it first opened waited almost thirty-two years before benefiting from a more salubrious workplace. Unfortunately, even that lasted only a few years, before the Mexican Insurgency of 1810 disrupted production.

The concentration of vast numbers of workers in the manufactory permitted a division of labor according to occupation and wage. The work force was divided into eleven separate categories, which ranged from supervisory and administrative tasks to manual work dominated by the cigarette rollers. Administrative employees and supervisory employees were paid fixed annual or day salaries. The manual workers, for the most part, were paid according to piecework rates determined by their *tareas.*

Bureaucrats and the supervisory employees organized and managed the work force. The administrator of the Mexico City manufactory was a key figure, for the most part perceived of as the nemesis of the workers. Between 1769 and 1822 the Mexico City manufactory had four administrators, the two most important being Isidro Romaña, appointed in 1769, and Miguel Puchet, who was appointed in 1792 and occupied the position until his death in 1807. The administrator was required to live on the manufactory premises, consult with the *directores generales* on manufactory policy, and supervise all operations. The manufactory also had its own *contador.* Benito de Betosolo was appointed to the position in 1773 and held it until 1803. The *contador's* responsibilities included the receipt and delivery of raw materials and funds, payments of salaries, wages, and rents, and all corresponding accounts. He worked closely with the administrator, although able to consult directly with the *dirección general.* All decisions which affected manufactory policy and worker management were made by the manufactory administrator, in consultation with the *dirección general* and *fiscal* and, when necessary, with royal assessors and *oidores* of the Audiencia of Mexico City. The management structure of the regional manufactories was similar, although on a much smaller scale. Increasingly, formal work discipline affected the manufactory administration as much as it did the workers. By 1820 the manufactory administrative employees were required to be at work between 8 a.m. and 1 p.m. and between 3 p.m. and 5 p.m. To explain absences, their "time" sheets contained sections such as "illness," "legitimate," or "without cause or notice."[34]

There were three categories of work supervisors, the *maestros mayores* (chief supervisors), the *sobrestantes mayores* (head foremen/women), and the *maestros* and *maestras de mesa* (foremen/women). The *sobrestantes mayores* generally managed the daily work allocation. They drew up daily lists of workers, kept accounts of work completed, and calculated the wages to be paid. The *maes-tros* and *maestras de mesa* supervised the offices into which the *patios* of the Mexico City manufactory were divided. These were generally composed of teams of seventy or more workers. Each *ofi-cina* (workroom) consisted of one *maestro de mesa*, four *embol-vedores* (wrappers) and three *recontadores* (recounters). Based on production requirements, each workroom was responsible for a specific quantity of cigars or cigarettes on a daily basis and specialized in one class of cigar or cigarette only. It was the responsibility of the supervisory staff to ensure that cigars and cigarettes were well-made and correctly packed according to class and number per packet, not an easy task.

The administrative and managerial hierarchy was supplemented by guards, who kept order with backup from local city regiments.[35] Although a military presence became stronger by the end of the eighteenth century, the extent of the efficiency of the manufactory guards and supplemental troops is questionable, especially if the extremely low guard-worker ratio is taken into consideration.[36] By 1798 the average ratio of guards to male workers in the Mexico City manufactory was 1 : 100; for female workers, it was 1 : 145. In addition to the military, the Church also played an important mediating role between the manufactory workers and their employer during times of conflict, as we shall see in Chapter 7.

Whereas in the private tobacco industry workers were responsible for the manufacture of cigars and cigarettes from beginning to end, in the manufactories, at least for the cigarette rollers, sorting, shredding, rolling, weighing, counting, and packing became separate processes. Cigarette rollers found themselves responsible for a smaller range of tasks in the production process. The cigar makers, however, retained their responsibility for all aspects of cigar rolling until they delivered their day's output to their supervisors for clipping, counting, and packing.

The *tercios* (bales) of tobacco received from the *villas* were stored in the monopoly's warehouses in the manufactory and in cellars throughout Mexico City. Tobacco leaves selected for cigarettes were laid out, dried, and stored in sacks overnight. The *cernidores* (shredders) ground the tobacco into a powder (*cernido*, which was different from snuff) ready for cigarette manufacture. Simple hand-operated mills and sieves provided the basic tools for such an operation. Both the drying and grinding of tobacco were regarded as central to the productive process, as a good yield in quality and volume of ground tobacco meant less wastage. One pound of tobacco yielded approximately twelve ounces of tobacco powder, which raised the cost of an ounce of leaf from an average of 1.5 *granos* to 2 *granos*. The different grades of leaf were mixed only after being ground.

The cigarette rollers, called variously *torcedores* (rollers), *operarios* (workers), *cigarreros* (cigarette makers), or *fabricantes* (manufactory workers), formed, by far, the most numerous *cuerpo* or collective body of workers in the manufactories. The cigarette rollers arrived at the manufactory each morning, bringing paper prepared at home the previous evening. The rollers folded the paper and formed tubes (the process of *encanalado*) into which was placed the shredded tobacco. The number of cigarettes to be made from each sheet of paper depended on its class. One sheet of paper, for example, yielded 86 number 10 cigarettes or 124 more slender number 14 cigarettes. Supervisors informed the workers which *corte* (size of cut) they needed to use and stipulated the method of folding the paper. Although workers were ordered not to vary the method, they routinely ignored instructions which slowed them down and jeopardized their completion of a *tarea*. Too rapid and careless rolling often produced cigarettes which fell apart in the consumer's hands. Supervisors destroyed poorly made cigarettes or cigars, but the workers suffered the cost by having to pay for the paper used to replace their first attempts. It took about three to four weeks to train a competent cigarette maker or cigar roller.

On being admitted to the Mexico City manufactory, cigarette makers received a *boleta* (a "ticket" of sorts) which indicated their duties and wages. The new worker's name was added to the *lista* (combined manufactory register and worksheet). Workers were ordered to keep the *boleta* and to present it each day when they came to the manufactory. Provided the worker arrived before 8 a.m., he or she would receive a *tarea* and, with consistent satisfactory behavior and good work, there was no reason why he or she could not eventually be promoted to a better-paying position.[37]

Cigar manufacture was carried out by the *pureros* (cigar makers). The *maestros de puros* daily checked the *tercios* of leaf tobacco, noted their weight and cost, separated the leaves of adequate quality, and distributed them among the cigar makers. Tobacco leaves used for cigars were dampened prior to their use to restore their moisture content, making them easier to roll into cigars. Dry tobacco leaves slowed down the rolling process and reduced the cigar maker's income. Cigar making required training, knowledge, and ability, but individuals who rolled cigars quickly and deftly were born with the skill, they did not learn it.[38]

The finished cigars and cigarettes passed from the cigarette rollers and cigar makers to the *embolvedores* (wrappers) and then to the *recontadores* (recounters). The latter's duties consisted of the preparation of the *cajillas* or *papeles* (packets) in which the manufactured product was wrapped or boxed. The *recontadores* inspected the manufactory's products for defects and counted the correct number of cigarettes according to class to be placed in the packets. They also collected the baskets of cigars of each individual cigar maker, with the worker's *nombrete* (name or sign) attached to them. The *embolvedores* received and examined the cigars to verify that they were of a good standard, and destroyed those which were unacceptable. The cigars accepted were then sorted according to class and number corresponding to individual packets, wrapped, then returned to the cigar maker. As a final step in the process, the *maestros* noted the individual *tareas* or portions completed by each worker. After a series of accounting procedures, the packets of cigars passed to the *oficina de encajonado* (packing section) and were packed in large wooden crates by *encajonadores* (packers), ready for transport to the monopoly's *estanquillos*.

The manufactory workforce also included *carpinteros, gritonas, selladores* (carpenters, shouters, stampers), *obleros* (glue makers) and the corps of tobacco manufactory guards. The latter's main duty was to inspect every worker on their entry to and exit from the building. As workers entered and left the manufactories each day they were met by registry guards who examined them "from their ears to their feet". Drunks and those who threatened to disrupt the workers or an orderly work environment were prohibited from entry. The two meals of the day, breakfast and lunch, were served at the registry doors by relatives or *rancheros* (local food vendors). All food baskets were examined to prevent introduction of pulque or any kind of alcohol, and reexamined to prevent smuggling out of paper and tobacco. The Mexico City manufactory generally employed two head guards and forty male and female guards. A small group of eight to ten night watchmen (*guardas de pito*) remained in the manufactory after it closed each day until it reopened the following day. The Mexico City manufactory (and, in theory, all the others) was guarded every night of the year and on all fiesta days.

The manufactories reflected the structure of a large-scale concentration of labor with an elite core of supervisory staff on a fixed wage, who organized and directed a mass of semiskilled and unskilled workers on a piecewage. The internal hierarchy of the Mexico City and Orizaba manufactory labor force and its distribution according to occupation in 1794 is shown in table 23. Although a detailed breakdown is unavailable for the remaining manufactories,

Table 23.   *Breakdown of Manufactory Work Force by Occupation, Mexico City and Orizaba, 1795*

	% of Total Work Force	
Occupation	Mexico	Orizaba
Cigarreros	81	48
Pureros	6	36
Embolvedores	3	5
Recontadores	3	2
Embolvedores de Puros	0.5	
Cernidores	2	4
Gritonas, Selladores	2	2
Maestros & Maestras de Mesa	1	1
Sobrestantes	1	1
Guardas	1	
Administration	0.5	1

Source: Calculated from table 4, p. 242 in McWatters, "The Royal Tobacco Monopoly," and AGN, Tabaco 495, report of manufactory employees by *contador general* Francisco Maniau y Ortega, 20 July 1795; for Orizaba, AGN, Tabaco 495, report of Francisco Maniau y Ortega, *contador general,* 20 July 1795.

(Totals may not add up to 100 because of rounding)

by 1794 the total number of cigarette and cigar rollers in the Guadalajara, Oaxaca, Puebla, and Querétaro manufactories as a proportion of the total work force was estimated at between 87 and 94 percent, roughly the same proportion as Mexico and Orizaba.[39] Despite a division of labor, the cigarette and cigar rollers formed the overwhelming majority of manufactory workers; work in the state manufactories remained fundamentally manual.

Creating a regular work force, with its implied build-up of skill and dependability, proved difficult for the Bourbon managers. The supervisory workers, however, demonstrated a very low turnover within their ranks, which suggests that such positions were attractive and offered the best opportunities compared to other alternatives. Several case studies illustrate the longevity of employment and patterns of promotion of supervisory workers within the manufactories. In 1793 forty-one-year-old José Bocanegra y Cantabrana earned 600 pesos annually as a *maestro mayor.* A widower, he had worked for twenty-four years in the manufactory, beginning at the age of seventeen when it opened in 1770. He began as a *sobrestante,* a position which he occupied for nine and a half years. He was promoted to *sobrestante mayor segundo* (after seven and three-quarter years), then worked as a *sobrestante mayor primero* (after one and three-quarter years). Bocanegra received another promotion to *maestro mayor* in 1789, one of the highest supervisory positions. It had taken him twenty years to climb the promotional ladder. José Manuel Ruiz's career followed a similar pattern. Married, and forty-three years old, he earned 500 pesos yearly as a *sobrestante mayor*. He began in 1772, at the age of twenty-two, as a *guarda*, receiving promotions to *sobrestante, guarda mayor, sobrestante mayor segundo*, and, in 1788, *sobrestante mayor primero*. By 1793 Ruiz's service to the manufactory amounted to twenty-one years. A more varied case of upward promotion is the career of an *escribiente* (scribe) in the Mexico City manufactory. Mariano Hurtado de Mendoza began work in 1772 at the age of thirteen as a *recontador*. After five and a half years he worked as an *embolvedor*, and after seven and three-quarter years was promoted to *maestro*. After a short stint of only eight months he became a *guarda* for three years and, finally, in 1789, at the age of thirty-four, was appointed as an *escribiente*, with a daily salary of 11 reales.[40]

The promotional sequence and careers of women workers show similar patterns. Doña María Fuentes, a *maestra mayor*, entered the manufactory in 1771, worked as an *empapeladora, embolvedora, guarda*, and *sobrestanta* (paper sorter, wrapper, guard, and forewoman) until 1784, when she was promoted to *maestra mayor* (head forewoman). Doña Ignacia Arbiso, also a *maestra mayor*, went to work in the manufactory in 1771. She began as a *recontadora*, and then received promotions to *embolvedora, maestra*, and *sobrestanta*. In 1807, thirty-six years later, she was named *maestra mayor*. Doña Manuela Gamboa began work in 1781 as a cigarette roller, became a *recontadora*, and then was promoted to *embolvedora*. In 1800, after nineteen years, she was promoted to the position of *guarda*. All of these women died between 1814 and 1825, after a lifetime of work in the state tobacco manufactories.[41] Table 24 illustrates the longevity of employment of the female supervisory staff. Thirty-nine percent of the total female supervisory staff in 1812 started their employment in the Mexico City manufactory between 1771 and 1780 and possessed an average of thirty-seven years of service. If we expand the period of initial employment by another decade, fully 63 percent of the supervisory staff that started at the manufactory between 1771 and 1790 was still listed as working there by 1810.[42] Like the monopoly bureaucracy, the supervisory ranks in the manufactories were composed of "career" and professional tobacco workers, whose interests lay with the monopoly.

Table 24. Decade of Entry of Female Supervisory Staff into Mexico City Manufactory, 1771–1820

	1771–1780	1781–1790	1791–1800	1801–1810	1811–1820+	ND/A
	39% (93)	24% (56)	14% (32)	16% (37)	7% (16)	1% (2)
Total years of service as of 1812	(42–33)	(32–23)	(22–13)	(12–3)		

Total number = 236; (totals may not add up to 100 because of rounding)

Source: AGN, Fondo de Real Hacienda, Administración de la Real Renta del Tabaco, Contaduría, Caja 79, Libro que consta el tiempo y los destinos que han servido las guardas, sobrestantas, maestras, embolvedores y recontadores de esta Real Fabrica de Puros y Cigarros de México hasta fin de diciembre de 1812, ff. 4–215 v.

Such stability in the supervisory ranks, however, placed limits on the opportunities for promotion for workers from the lower ranks.

While we are confident in arguing that the supervisory staff demonstrated low rather than high turnover in their ranks, the evidence for the cigar and cigarette rollers is mixed. Monopoly reports suggest that there was a high turnover among the *cigarreros,* especially the men, a characteristic which was used as a justification for employing women only. The *director general* repeatedly complained about the male cigarette rollers and emphasized their shiftlessness, epitomized by their continuous migration and the abandonment "of their souls as well as their families so that (the women) find themselves without fathers, husbands, brothers, or sons."[43] The point remains, however, that since cigarettes and cigars continued to be made, the turnover may not have been as high as the periodic complaints suggest.

There are virtually no reports of any form of coerced labor (debt peonage), and certainly nothing similar to what Jean Stubbs found for the Cuban cigar makers, that is, the restrictions on their movements and the imposition of the *libreta* system. The 1851 *libreta* was a compulsory card which indicated the worker's name and the amount of debt owed to his employer. Until the debt was cleared, the worker (technically) could not leave the factory or be employed by any other manufacturer.[44] The only reference to the practice of debt peonage (not its extent or its importance) came from the intendant of Querétaro, the area where debt peonage was strongest in the textile industry. Domínguez reported in 1801 that the tobacco manufactory was successful in its attempts to end debt peonage, and that it had stopped giving wage advances in the 1790s. Although the manufactory administrator had feared that a labor shortage would result, Domínguez commented that the reverse had occurred, that no scarcities existed, and that he recommended that the practice of advances on wages and debt peonage be outlawed.[45]

Individual lives changed after the reorganization of the tobacco industry for those people who went to work in the manufactories, and scholars are correct to draw attention to the effects of the reorganization of the tobacco industry on the social, economic, and cultural relations of the workers. There is no question that the manufactories demanded a division of labor and created a new hierarchy with defined areas of activity, skill, and promotion. The sheer size of the workplace, compared to the small workshops or homes which typified private tobacco businesses, and the numbers of workers concentrated in one place must have demanded considerable psychological and physical readjustments but also provided new opportunities for collective action, the consequences of which will be discussed fully in Chapter 7. The possibility of owning a tobacco store or workshop vanished.[46] The most that remained was for an apprentice cigar or cigarette roller to work his or her way up through the ranks to the supervisory levels. We would speculate, however, that, although the work regime was modified, the organization of production in the manufactories remained fundamentally the same as in private to-bacco workshops but was practiced on a much larger scale. 'Same trade, different boss' gave something of the ethos of "business as usual" to the reorganization of the tobacco industry. Continuities with previous working arrangements which bridged the home and workplace made the impact of the manufactory regime less sharp. Perhaps the most significant bridge between work and home was the "putting out" practice of the manufactories. Every evening cigarette rollers received quantities of paper, based on their *tareas*, to prepare at home for the following day's work in the manufactory, prepara-tion which they often carried out with the aid of their families. In addition, the *dirección general* eventually established an *escuela de amigas* in the manufactory to take care of nursing babies and young children. The ability to bring children into the manufactory and to prepare part of the day's work at home, exploitative as it may be, per-mitted a flexible integration of manufactory and domestic work, and provided some continuity with past practice.

There is some evidence that the old *maestro*-apprentice relation-ship continued within the manufactory workshops. Initially, the ad-ministrator recruited six *cigarreros* renowned for the high quality of their products to begin production in the Mexico City manufactory. Appointed as *maestros*, each one was to manage their own *oficina* and be responsible for everything that occurred within them. Each of the six *maestros* headed their individual *cuadrillas* (crews), and their products were distinguished by individual seals indicating the *maestro*'s initials (a practice current among most guilds). The logic of this practice, according to the *dirección general*, was to permit consumers to complain directly to the *maestro* responsible for any defective products. To what extent this practice endured throughout the manufactories' development is unknown. Such continuity, how-ever, could not remove the reality that the workers' new *maestro* was, in fact, the king, a reality of which they were not unaware.

In the early years of manufactory employment, workers could ex-pect to earn as much in the manufactories as they had in private workshops and at home, and even possibly experienced a temporary increase in their wages. The *factor* in Puebla observed that, far from being opposed to the manufactories, many workers welcomed its establishment because they could earn more in the manufactory than from spinning cotton or even in the private tobacco shops, and because their income was more secure.[47] Once all private shops were abolished, however, wages were reduced for most workers, and some nonmonetary perks were gradually phased out.

The method of wage payment differed according to occupation within the manufactories. The administrative staff received yearly salaries, supervisory employees received fixed day rates (*jornal*), and others, predominately cigarette and cigar rollers, received piecework rates (*a destajo*). Table 25 summarizes the fixed wage and piecework rates of the Mexico City manufactory between 1769 and 1810, and table 26 shows the comparative wage levels for the six manufactories between 1790 and 1794. The rates suggest reasonable parity of remuneration for specific tasks within the manufactories, with the predictable exception of consistently higher payments made in Mexico City. Between 90 and 97 percent of the manufactory workforce was composed of pieceworkers.

Variation in income of the manufactory workers was wide. The money amount earned by a worker depended on a number of variables in addition to his or her job, such as whether they were quick at their tasks, whether other family members worked in the manufactory, and the wider domestic context of their lives. Supervisory workers earned the most lucrative wages, between 140 and 600 pesos annually (assuming a full working year of 280 days). The most fortuitous position was if several family members were employed together in the manufactory. Two cigarette rollers, for example, in a good year, could earn a combined income of between 140 and 280 pesos; two cigar rollers, a combined income of between 280 and 560 pesos; the combined earnings of a *maestro* married to a cigarette roller could total between 175 and 490 pesos. Placing relatives in the manufactory and pooling incomes were strategies favored by the workers, judging from their petitions to the administrator requesting jobs for their children and relatives. It is impossible to quantify the number falling into this category, but it does indicate the situation of a fortunate few who could make a good, if onerous, living in the tobacco manufactories. The opposite, of course, pertains to those workers with large families who were the only wage earners, or single and widowed individuals trying to scrape together a living on the base piecework rates. Incomes could drop dramatically to a low of 35 pesos.

Manufactory wages experienced different trends in the late eighteenth century, as shown in table 25. As the decades wore on, the

Table 25. Salaries and Wages of Employees of the Mexico City Manufactory, 1771–1801 (selected years)

	1771	1775	1779	1788	1794	1801
Salaries and Day Wages						
Administrador	1,400	2,000	2,000	2,000	2,000	2,000
Contador	800		1,500	1,500	1,500	1,500
Oficial Mayor	600		1,000	1,000	1,000	1,000
Oficial Segundo	450		700	800	800	800
Pagador	550		800	800	800	800
Pagador Segundo	400		700	700	600	600
Escribientes					11 rls	11 rls
Fiel de Almacenes	650		800	800	800	800
Maestro Mayor	500–550	500–700	400–600	600	500–600	600
Maestra Mayor			350–450	350–450	350–450	350–450
Maestros		5.5 rls			8 rls	
Maestras						
Maestras Segundas				350		
Maestra Mayor de Puros			400–500			
Sobrestante Mayor	450		450–500	450–500	450–500	500
Sobrestantes		6.5–8 rls	8 rls	9–11 rls	9–11 rls	
Sobrestantas		5–7 rls		9 rls		
Guarda Mayor		4.5–8 rls	7.5 rls	450	450	450
Guarda Vista		4.5–8 rls		450	450	
Guarda de Registro	400	4.5–8 rls	6.5–7.5 rls	9 rls	9 rls	
Guardas de Noche				5 rls	5 rls	
Guardas (male)		4.5–8 rls		9 rls		
Guardas (female)		6–7.5 rls		9 rls		
Guardas de Pito		4.5–8 rls		4 rls		

Pieceworkers

Pieceworkers				
Maestros de Mesa	7.5 rls	8 rls	8 rls	8 rls
Maestras de Mesa	6.5–7.5 rls		8 rls	8 rls
Embolvedores	3.25–5 rls	4–4.5 rls	4.5–5.25 rls	4.5–6.5 rls
Embolvedoras	2.5–4 rls			3.5–6.5 rls
Recontadores	2.5–3.5 rls	3.5–4.5 rls	3.5–3.75	3.5–5.75 rls
Recontadoras				
Cigarreros (male and female)	5–10 rls	4–9.25 rls		2–4 rls
Pureros (male and female)		9 gns–2 rls		4–8 rls
Cernidores	3–7 rls		3.5 rls	3.5–6 rls
Encajonadores	4–8 rls		4 rls	4 rls
Selladores	2.5–8 rls		2.5–7.5 rls	3.5 rls
Empapeladores				2 rls
Escogedores de Papel				4 rls
Mojadores				
Gritones	1.5–3 rls	2 rls	2–2.5 rls	2–2.5 rls
Gritonas	2 rls			2 rls
Cuidadora de Comunes			3.25 rls	3.25 rls
Obleros				5–6.5 rls
Recortadores de Oblea				3 rls
Carpintero				7 rls

Source: AGI, Mexico 2281, Relación de los empleados que havia en el año de 1775; AGN, Tabaco 241, report of Maniau y Ortega, 20 July, 1795; McWatters, table 7, p. 245; various miscellaneous reports from AGN, Tabaco, Renta de Tabaco.

Table 26. Salaries of Manufactory Employees of the Six State Tobacco Manufactories, 1790–1794

	Mexico	Guadalajara	Querétaro	Puebla	Oaxaca	Orizaba
Administrador	2,000 (1)	800 (1)	800 (1)	800 (1)	500 (1)	700 (1)
Contador	1,500 (1)					
Interventor		500 (1)	500 (1)	600 (1)	500 (1)	450 (1)
Oficial Mayor	1,000 (1)					
Oficial Segundo	800 (1)					
Escribientes	11 rls (4)					
Pagador	800 (1)			800 (1)		
Pagador Segundo	600 (1)					
Fiel de Almacén	800 (1)					
Maestros Mayores	600 (1)					
Maestras Mayores	450 (1)					
Maestras Segundas	350 (1)					
Maestros de Mesa	280 (17)			10 rls (1)		10 rls (1)
Maestras de Mesa	8 rls (35)			280 (3)		
Maestros		8 rls (1)	7–8 rls (6)	8 rls (6)	5 rls (1)	6 rls (2)
Maestras		7 rls (4)	7 rls (3)			
Sobrestantes Mayores	500 (2)		500 (1)			
Sobrestantes	9–11 rls (34)		7 rls (6)	8 rls (5)	8 rls (1)	350 (1)
Sobrestantas	9 rls (18)	7 rls (4)	7 rls (3)	7 rls (3)	4 rls (4)	
Guardas Mayores	450 (2)					

Guardas Vista	450 (1)			
Guardas de Registro	9 rls (23)	365 (8)	365 (3)	
Guardas (male)			280 (2)	
Guardas (female)	9 rls (20)	7–9 rls (6)	8 rls (5)	
Guardas de Pito	4 rls (10)	7–8 rls (9)	228 (1)	210 (1)
Guardas Veques (male)		5 rls (6)	4 rls (1)	
Guardas Veques (female)	3 rls (1)	1 rl (1)	2 rls (1)	
Gritones	2.25–2.5 rls (4)	1.5–3 rls (3)	2–2.5 rls (2)	4 rls (1)
Gritonas	2 rls (6)	1 rl (2)	2 rls (2)	
Portera			1.5 (2)	6 rls (1)
Encajonadores	3–7 rls (37)	3 rls (2)	6 rls (2)	8 rls (1)
Selladores	3–7.5 rls (20)	4 rls (1)	4 rls (4)	3 rls
Cernidores	3.5–6 rls (157)	5 rls (30)	4–5 rls (15)	210 (1)
Carpintero	7 rls (1)	3 rls (4)		
Escojedores de Papel	4 rls (20)		4 rls (12)	
Obleros	5–6.5 rls (9)	5 rls (3)		
Recortadores de Oblea		3 rls (5)		

Source: AGN, Tabaco 241, report of *contador general* Maniau y Ortega, 20 July 1795.

Note: The pieceworkers, the cigar and cigarette makers, *recontadores*, and *embolvedores*, were not listed individually. Their piecework rates were listed as 4–8 reales and 2–4 reales, respectively, in Mexico City, where the rates for *recontadores* and *embolvedores* were set at 3.5–6.25 reales.

Figures are in pesos except where indicated for daily wages in reales. The figures in parenthesis indicate the number employed in the individual positions.

administration reduced the entry wage of workers. Supervisory employees on fixed day wages experienced small upward adjustments.
Male workers at the supervisory levels tended to earn marginally
higher rates than women, but wages for both increased between
1775 and 1794: *maestras'* rates increased from between 5 and 7 reales to 9 reales while that of *maestros* increased from between 6.5
and 8 reales to between 9 and 11 reales. At the same time, it should
be emphasized that the work load was higher for women supervisors. In 1798 each *maestro mayor* and *maestro* was responsible for
25 workers (rollers through *embolvedores*). *Maestras mayores* and
maestras were responsible for 52 workers, virtually a double workload. Guards also experienced nominal wage increases between 1775
and 1794. The shifts in piecework rates were mixed. Cigarette
rollers' piecework rates declined from between 5 and 10 reales per
tarea to between 4 and 9.25 reales per *tarea* in 1779. In the 1790s
they declined further, by a massive 60 percent, to what became the
standard rate of between 2 and 4 reales per *tarea*. Cigar rollers' rates
experienced an opposite trend, a considerable increase from between
0.75 real and 2 reales in 1779 to between 4 and 8 reales by 1794. The
excess supply of labor for the manufactories meant that the *dirección general* was under no pressure to raise wages, quite the opposite. But the reduction in piecework rates for cigarette rollers resulted in problems of labor discipline and irregular attendance, a
point to which we shall return. The reductions are also related to a
wage differential based on gender and a steady divergence in craft
skills, as cigar and cigarette rolling became defined as male and female work respectively. What is not clear is the degree to which the
respective *tarea* rates changed over the decades. Table 27, however,
illustrates the *tarea* and piecework rates for 1779.

The *dirección general's* wage policy also sought to maintain the
tobacco workers' customary wages and 'perks', reproducing them
within the manufactories, only to phase them out gradually to reduce labor costs. Originally, the *boletos* given to new cigarette rollers stipulated that, apart from the piecework rate, a worker was also
to receive 1 1/2 reales on Saturdays for chocolate, on the condition
that he or she had worked a full week and completed three *cuadernos* (booklets of cigarette paper) each day. Five cigarettes were also
distributed to the workers for every *cuaderno* completed. In 1777
the *dirección general* ruled that the custom of paying a bonus for
chocolate be discontinued. A specified number of cigarettes or cigars
to be smoked while on the job remained as a nonmonetary input. In
1795 the *director general* reported that "almost all 12,000 workers
smoke while working . . . the majority smoke one packet of ciga-

**Table 27. *Tareas and Piecework Rates,*
*Mexico City, 1779***

Class	Packets/Day	Number	Daily Rate (reales)
Cigarettes			
10s	59	2,124	4
11s	49	2,352	4
12s	53	2,544	4.5
13s	60	2,880	7
14s	64	3,072	9.25
Cigars			
5s	21	108	0.75
7s	20	144	1
10s	21	216	1.66
14s	20	288	2

Source: AGN, Tabaco 65, Betasola to Díaz de la Vega, 20 February 1779.

rettes daily, others less, at half a packet daily."[48] In addition to changes in wage levels, workers' wages were subject to deductions or "fines," to cover the cost of wasted materials. Any paper damaged or cut incorrectly by workers was not replaced free but had to be purchased by them, a regulation designed to make them more "careful" in their work, and which cost them an average of 4 reales per capita per year.[49]

As employees of the colonial state, were the tobacco workers somehow privileged in comparison with other urban workers, part of an 'aristocracy of labor'? It would seem not. Men and women tobacco workers (with the exception of supervisory workers) earned wages comparable to, but certainly not higher than those of semiskilled and unskilled workers. We have yet to develop a good price and wage series for colonial Mexico, but a fragmentary profile of nominal wage rates for different occupations in the late eighteenth century indicates that the average salary for artisans ranged from 4 reales to 1 peso (8 reales), and, for nonskilled and semiskilled laborers, from 2 to 4 reales. For the majority of the manufactory workforce, earnings were no higher, but the relative security of the work and membership in the Concordia offered advantages which many workers would not have been eligible for in other trades, given their level of skill and background. For women in particular the manufactories offered a more lucrative position, especially since the most common female occupation of domestic servant paid only between

Table 28. Range of Annual Incomes of a Manufactory Worker Compared with Annual Subsistence Requirements for Families of One to Six Persons

Daily Wage (reales)	Annual Income (in pesos)						No. of Persons	Annual Subsistence Income (pesos)
	130 days	150 days	180 days	220 days	260 days	280 days		
1	16.25	18.75	22.5	27.5	32.5	35.0	1	34
2	32.5	37.5	45.0	55.0	65.0	70.0	2	68
3	48.75	56.25	67.5	82.5	97.5	105.0	3	102
4	65.0	75.0	90.0	110.0	130.0	140.0	4	136
5	81.25	93.75	112.5	137.5	162.5	175.0	5	170
6	97.5	112.5	135.0	165.0	195.0	210.0	6	204
7	113.75	131.25	157.5	192.5	227.5	245.0		
8	130.0	150.0	180.0	220.0	260.0	280.0		
9	146.25	168.75	202.5	247.5	292.5	315.0		
10	162.5	187.5	225.0	275.0	325.0	350.0		
11	178.75	206.25	247.5	302.5	357.5	385.0		

Source: Scardaville, p. 67; McWatters, tables 8 & 9, p. 247; author's calculations of range of incomes.

1 and 1 1/2 reales daily.[50] Most manufactory workers experienced wage decreases between 1770 and 1795, but thereafter the trend in manufactory wages was similar to a general trend in both rural and urban nominal wages, which remained stable during the eighteenth century.[51]

What do the manufactory wages tell us about the workers' standard of living and well being? To begin with, an assessment of what a money wage means in the context of a preindustrial economy is difficult. Lyman Johnson, among others, cautions that "the use of wage series to infer changes in the earnings of workers is dangerous at best," given the differences and distinctions which must be made between wages and income.[52] An additional problem involves the degree and constancy of continuous, regularly held, and remunerated employment. None of the usual assumptions surrounding wage labor and regular payment for such work hold for the eighteenth century. Calculations of subsistence wages for the working poor or the 'threshold of poverty' vary. Based on the cost of tortillas, *chiles*, frijoles, rent, clothing, and miscellaneous household items, Michael Scardaville estimated that the per capita subsistence income in Mexico City at the end of the eighteenth century totalled approximately 3/4 real daily or 34 pesos annually. An 'average' lower-class family in late colonial Mexico City of approximately four persons required an income of 136 pesos per year to survive. Scardaville calculated two series of projected incomes for individuals, one based on 'full' employment, that is, a worker employed six days a week for fifty-two weeks (unlikely), and one based on 'underemployment', assuming a three-day work week. His comparison between annual incomes and subsistence levels demonstrates the inadequacy of a wage income for most of the urban poor. Pressure to survive in Mexico City generally resulted in some, if not all, family members, including children, going to work, assuming they could find employment.[53]

Table 28 shows the possible range of incomes for manufactory workers according to different lengths of a working year, compared to Scardaville's calculation of required subsistence incomes (based on money only). A single wage earner in a family with four dependents, occupying a position in a manufactory at the lowest level of pay, as a cigarette roller on a piecerate of 2 reales, would not earn the estimated 136 pesos required for subsistence, but only half of that, 70 pesos. In order to earn above the subsistence rate, a worker would have to be employed for a full year, at the highest piecework rate of 4 reales. A major determinant of the level of a worker's wage was how often he or she worked, and, for pieceworkers, the ability to complete their daily *tareas*. Therefore, the regularity of work and the length of the working day and year must be considered.

Fluctuations in employment and irregular work patterns make it difficult to estimate an average working day, week, or year. Several examples demonstrate the variation in length and content of the working year in the Mexico City manufactory. A summary of the *tareas* worked in 1780 shows what is close to a 'modern' working year of 267 days, punctuated by religious holidays.[54] The months of January, April, July, October, and November were the most stable working months, in terms of full six-day weeks. December and January were the most erratic, due to Christmas celebrations. Calculations of the number of days worked by cigarette rollers, based on the number of packets of cigarettes manufactured each year, suggest fewer working days per year between 1779 and 1809, a minimum of 134 and a maximum of 230. Within a regular year, however, there were fluctuations in the *tareas* distributed to workers. The work sheets for 1780 show that the workers in the Patio de México worked at least fourteen days when the number of *tareas* worked was reduced by one-third to one-half. During the workweek of 17–22 January, the number of *tareas* worked in each of the workshops ranged between 73 and 80; on 20 January, they were reduced to between 26 and 40; by the following Monday, the range was back to between 70 and 80. From mid-October until the end of December 1780, the quantity of *tareas* distributed also showed a sustained reduction, with an average range of between 40 and 70.[55] In accordance with its paternalist stance, the monopoly reduced everyone's *tarea* proportionately, rather than give only a percentage of workers a full *tarea*. However, it still resulted in a reduced income for workers.

Another example of the fluctuations in the working week is taken from a weekly notation of the number of days worked by the *embolvedores de puros* (cigar wrappers) during the week of 5–10 March 1792. Of fifteen workers, six worked a full week (six days), Monday to Saturday, four worked five days, two, four days, one, three and one-half days, one, three days, and one, two days. It is not known whether the worker or the manufactory decided on the number of days worked.[56]

There is also mixed evidence about the length and content of the 'working day'. The manufactory regulations give the impression of an ordered and uniform workday, but practice suggests something rather different. Time was measured by nearby church bells, and the accompanying devotional exercises helped to pace the workday. The monopoly bureaucrats possessed a precise sense of time and the effort required for various tasks:

The clock of the Convent of Santo Domingo chimed 9 A.M. and the meals received by the workers stopped. A man sang the Ave María at the door of the *patio* . . . the *sobrestantes*, having settled the workers, began the *desoje* at 2 minutes after 9 A.M. and finished this task at 9 : 36 A.M., spending thirty-four minutes on this operation, which consists of unwrapping a bundle of tobacco and spreading its leaves in the sun . . . The tobacco is then left to dry. The workers go to their workrooms and others go to grind 15 *tercios* of *escamocha* . . . spending little more than fifteen minutes, since they began the task at 9 : 38 and finished at 9 : 53. This tobacco is for the cigarettes.[57]

For male supervisors the working day began at 7 A.M., for female supervisors at 7 : 30 A.M., and could finish any time between 5 P.M. and 8 P.M. Technically, the cigar and cigarette rollers of both sexes could be admitted to the manufactory from 7 A.M. until 8 : 30 A.M., after which time no worker was allowed to enter. Their day ended at 4 P.M. The working day could last ten to twelve hours for supervisory workers and six to eight hours for cigar and cigarette rollers. The workday, however, was not the same for all workers. A description by the manufactory administrator illustrates the point. "At 9 A.M. those who did not choose to work left after having collected their paper quotas for the next day; at noon, those workers who had completed their *tarea* or a part of it, or because they wished to leave, could do so; from 3 P.M. until 4 P.M. workers could leave as they finished their day's work."[58]

Pieceworkers, mainly cigarette and cigar rollers, measured a working day not by the hour but by the amount of cigars or cigarettes produced. Recent analyses of piecework demonstrate that, as a labor practice, it was, and is, double-edged. Richard Price has argued that while Marx saw piecework as the form of wage most suited to capitalism because it ensured a maximum intensity of labor, he did not foresee the ability of workers to manipulate piecework to their own needs. "The inherent ambiguity of piece-work—its potential for either subordination or resistance—was well expressed by Hugh Scanlon in 1967 when he remarked that although all the ills of engineering could be blamed on piece-work, engineers fight to retain it because 'you have the man on the floor determining how much effort he will give for a given amount of money.'"[59] It is also argued that piece wages probably provided a better incentive to efficient work than any control of supervisory personnel. This may have applied to the tobacco workers after the 1790s, but only by way of quantity rather than quality of the product.[60] Piecework offered advantages to both worker and monopoly, to the latter because it permitted adjustments in the level of production, to the former because the flexibility permitted the workers to manage their own time priorities, control their workday, and develop strategies to compensate for the ebbs and flows in manufactory work.

Time, defined by the length of the working day, only became an issue from the workers' perspective when their work quotas became increasingly difficult to complete.[61] In 1794 the *cuerpo de cigarreros* requested that their workday be extended by one hour. They explained in their petition that, although the workday ran from 7 A.M. until 4 P.M., one and a half hours were taken up in the settlement of workers, breakfast, and delivery and selection of tobacco leaf, which left seven and a half hours. For many of the cigarette rollers, especially those who had worked in the manufactory for more than twenty years, this was inadequate time to complete a *tarea* of 56 packets of well-made cigarettes. Some days the quality of paper was poor and the tobacco badly shredded, which slowed down their work. They complained about the administrator who imposed too strict a time limit, and argued that experience showed the quality of cigarettes to have been better under his predecessor who allowed them more time.[62] Consider the scale of work here in terms of cigarettes and cigars to be made per minute based on a seven- or eight-hour day:[63]

10s	2,124 = 4–5 cigarettes/minute		5s	108 = 1 cigar/4 minutes	
12s	2,544 = 5–6 cigarettes/minute		7s	144 = 1 cigar/3 minutes	
13s	2,880 = 6–7 cigarettes/minute		10s	216 = 1 cigar/2 minutes	
14s	3,072 = 6–7 cigarettes/minute		14s	288 = 1 cigar/1.5 minutes	

The *dirección general* eventually agreed to a thirty-minute extension until 4:30 P.M., but only for elderly, infirm, and new unskilled workers. The reason for not granting a full hour was the potential for fire hazards, especially during winter when candles were required to provide light for the workers.[64]

Spanish imperial policies affected the lives and income of workers who neither knew nor probably cared about Spain's pursuit of power in Europe. The dependence upon imports of paper from Spain, however, made the results of such high politics painfully tangible through reduced quotas, layoffs, and temporary closures of manufactories. Guadalajara, for example, was closed down for three weeks in May 1798 due to lack of paper supplies.[65] There were compensations for the workers, a result of paternalist policies, which eased the economic hardships but could not eliminate them. In 1818 the workers of the Guadalupe manufactory received loans to cover their daily needs when the manufactory closed down. When they returned to work, they requested that repayments of the loans be suspended because reduced work quotas were in effect due to lack of paper. Their request was approved.[66] Those were the fortunate ones. Others found different solutions to layoffs and short time. Anna María Villaverde, a twenty-two-year-old widow from Puebla, while laid off from the manufactory, resorted to prostitution to support her family. She earned an average of 3 1/2 pesos per day, whereas for her work as a cigarette roller she earned between 4 reales and 1 peso per day.[67] The point to consider here is that, even with a regular work regime (or as regular as could be expected in the eighteenth century) the fluctuations in *tareas*, combined with a decrease in wages for the majority of the workforce, created imperatives among the workers to find additional ways of earning a living, imperatives which conflicted with the manufactories' demands for a stable, regular work force.

Bourbon reform measures sought to increase the strength of the state and the prosperity of its subjects, to produce a "culture utilitaire et culture dirigée."[68] Throughout the eighteenth century, the colonial state was haunted by fears of political disorder and the degeneration and immorality of Mexico's lower classes. Both private and public life came under the scrutiny of the Bourbon reformers, and it seemed at times as though the colonial state waged its own internal war on the activities of the populace.[69] Drinking and gambling were regulated, the popular expression of religious practices was attacked, and the forces of law and order were expanded. Regulation of movement, of space, and of morals provided the backdrop to the social and political advantages the manufactories offered in addition to their profit potential. Manufactory discipline and social discipline were inseparable.[70]

The tobacco manufactories provided a miniature version of the Bourbon project to reform and control the colonial populace. Within this context the *dirección general* viewed the manufactories' role as a vehicle through which to create not just discipline and order, but also "the perfect school to instruct all who work there not only in their tasks but in all those qualities which make a civil man . . . because in the manufactory every person lives subject to the voice which commands."[71] In the minds of the bureaucrats, then, good workers and obedient servants of the state were synonymous. Manufactory regulations provided the basis for inculcating habits of regular, diligent work, sobriety, and obedience. In the long term, the transformation of the workers into good servants of the state remained unaccomplished from the administration's perspective.

Manufactory authority was presented in the guise of paternalism. The informal name given to the manufactory in Mexico City was the Casa del Rey (House of the King); in response, the workers used the term *El Rey Padre* (the Father-King) when referring to their "employer." The manufactory functioned as a microcosm of colonial Spanish hegemony, in which the ideals of political authority and religious orthodoxy were constantly promoted and upheld. Supervisors at all levels were instructed that the administrator as well as the *dirección general* would consider workers' petitions or grievances. Grievances were channeled from workers to supervisors, the administrator, the *dirección general*, and ultimately the viceroy and monarch. In so doing, guided by its "unwritten constitution," the colonial state encouraged negotiation and compromise and created a channel through which to absorb conflict.[72]

Two documents issued by the viceroy Croix formed the foundation of the manufactory regime. The first, the general *ordenanzas* for state tobacco manufactories, were published on 15 June 1770 and outlined the duties of manufactory employees from the administrator down to the cigarette rollers. The second consisted of the Reglamento de Penas, a set of regulations designed to develop an organized, productive work force. The manufactory regulations, posted in the manufactories and read out loud to a largely illiterate work force, emphasized obedience to the rules on a voluntary or involuntary basis. This is made abundantly clear in clause 8: "subordination to the management is to be observed religiously and should be enforced through reason and persuasion, but punishment of delinquents is not incompatible with fair treatment."[73]

Three broad groups of infractions which the administration sought to eliminate to improve organization and discipline may be identified as follows: (i) those which related to achieving a reliable, organized work environment by penalizing late arrival to work, failure to register with the manufactory guards, theft of monopoly goods, incorrect or poor folding of paper, and careless shredding or deliberate wastage of tobacco; (ii) those which mandated obedience and which regulated worker-supervisor relations penalizing disobedience and physical attacks on supervisory staff or on other workers; (iii) those which encouraged good morals and 'civil' behavior by punishing drunken or offensive behavior, gambling and card playing in the manufactory, commerce, gossip, and other 'scandalous' actions. All of these infractions carried gradations of punishment which ranged from a stint in the manufactory stocks, payment for materials wasted, or suspension from work, to permanent prohibition from employment in any of the state tobacco manufactories. Workers were also prohibited from carrying out reprisals against supervisors who punished them for infractions of manufactory rules. The final clause of the manufactory regulations stipulated that the manufacture of cigars and cigarettes should be done as well as possible without variation of any kind.[74] Such regulations remained in effect after the insurgency and provided a basis for those issued in new manufactories under the auspices of the monopoly in the 1840s.

Regulations extended into the realm of appearance and daily dress of the workers. They became the target of Revillagigedo the Younger's reformist zeal and absolutist penchant for uniforms. Horrified at the partially-clad working population of Mexico City (a moral rather than functional view—the manufactories were hot, stuffy places in which to work), he ordered all workers of the Mexico City manufactory and the food vendors who supplied the workers to wear clothing as itemized in a royal order. Anyone who did not conform risked refusal of entry to work until the requisite clothing was acquired. The cost of the clothing required (shirt, trousers, stockings, hat, shoes) totaled 23 pesos 4 1/2 reales, which amounted to almost one-third of a cigarette roller's average annual wage. The money to cover the cost of the clothing was deducted in small amounts over a period of four months, until the necessary amount had been saved, at which point the administrator handed the sum to the worker with express orders to purchase the clothing. Although workers were rarely quiet about objectionable orders, no instances of worker outrage occurred following the announcement of the order.[75] Indeed, the *directores generales* reported to the viceroy that "making the people of this type dress well, something that has never been done in New Spain, has produced a change in them, and now they are like new workers."[76] Whether the clothing regulation was maintained over the decades which followed is not known.

The ideal behavior of a productive work force, as epitomized in the manufactory regulations and their inherent values, often remained just that, an ideal, rather than an accomplished goal. In 1783 guards and *maestros* in Mexico City complained of the increasing insubordination of the workers and the difficulties encountered in the management of more than 5,000 individuals. They drew a very vivid picture of daily life in the manufactory which suggested violence of a more serious nature. "It is a rare day in which one or several of the workers do not leave (the manufactory) bleeding from blows or wounds which have been inflicted upon them by other workers."[77]

The manufactory administrator vehemently denied that such actions occurred or, if they did, that they certainly did not happen more than once or twice a month.[78] Requests from manufactory administrators for additional guards and troops to help control unruly worker behavior grew during the last decades of the eighteenth century. The administrator of the Querétaro manufactory asked for, and was granted, a troop to guard the treasury of the manufactory. The treasury itself was constructed of adobe, not very solid, and its contents were very vulnerable to theft, not just from local thieves or bandits, but also from the workers themselves who were, in the administrator's view, "riotous and rebellious."[79] Domestic scuffles abounded. Ana Rodríguez, a cigarette roller in the Mexico City manufactory, found herself indebted to her cousins for the cost of making some petticoats at the price of one peso each. The latter demanded full payment one Saturday, when wages were being settled and paid. Instead of settling her debt, Ana attacked her cousins and tried to hit them. After scuffles and complaints to the *maestra mayor,* Ana, in anger, threw the money at her 'creditors' and left, leaving five reales with the *maestra.*[80] It was the early 1790s before any serious attempts were made to enforce discipline, and then primarily due to the direction of one man, the Mexico City manufactory administrator, Miguel Puchet. Puchet epitomized the type of professional bureaucrat which the Spanish Bourbons desired, only to stifle their actions by expediency and conservatism.

The Mexico City manufactory became the main target of reorganization primarily because of its size and location at the very center of Mexico's largest and most powerful city and because of the strategic problems created by such a high number of workers for both social control and economic supervision.

Shortly after his appointment to administrator of the Mexico City manufactory in 1792, Puchet complained that discipline was lax and the quality of the product poor due to inadequate supervision. Puchet focused on two central problems, an excess of workers and a need to improve work discipline, specifically regarding regularity of attendance at the rolling tables. Puchet argued that the public in general, especially those seeking domestic servants, would benefit from the dismissal of surplus workers. He believed that such a scarcity existed "because all go to the manufactory to acquire more leisure because of the amount of time which they have free once they leave work."[81] Even workers who had "completed apprenticeships . . . abandon their trades to free themselves from the subjection they experience in their own trades and which they do not find in manufacturing."[82] Puchet suggested several ways to decrease the labor force: no one was to receive paper if their names did not appear on the manufactory register; the fifteen to twenty vacancies which occurred each month due to deaths and dismissals did not necessarily have to be filled; children should not be permitted to roll cigarettes when there were older workers who required complete *tareas*. In the women's workrooms, only the registered female workers should be permitted to roll cigarettes and not, as had developed, a bevy of relatives who came to work with the rollers on the pretext that they could not be left at home. Young men and women introduced as sons or daughters "who could not be left at home" were, in fact, unrelated to the women cigarette rollers. They had met the women workers on their way to the manufactory and offered them a small payment in return for the favor of being taken into the manufactory, where, after a while, they demanded "rights to which they have no claim."[83] Under no circumstances was employment to be given to cigarette rollers who came to the Mexico City manufactory looking for work after they had been dismissed from one of the other manufactories.[84]

A related problem concerned the number of children who "worked" in the manufactory. In 1793 Puchet estimated that there were four hundred children brought to the manufactory every day, who distracted their mothers' attention. Even the viceroy was alarmed at their presence and observed that "they play and chase around and generally interrupt production; they are left in a state of shameful liberty and idleness; some are as old as eight years and still do not know how to make the sign of the cross."[85] The result was the establishment of an *escuela de amigas*. All of the children, with the exception of those nursing, were to be placed in the care of one woman worker who was to be responsible for teaching them Christian doctrine and the saying of the Rosary. It was every mother's responsibility to produce one packet of cigarettes on behalf of the 'babysitter' so that she could be paid her usual wage.[86] But that was just a small part of Puchet's reorganization plan for the manufactory work force. The viceroy approved of Puchet's general policy of reducing the number of workers of the Mexico City manufactory on the condition that it be carried out prudently and slowly so as to avoid riots or conflicts.[87] Actually, it took conflict—a worker protest in 1794 and a plot to kill the administrator—before Puchet received any serious royal support for his policy to reduce the number of workers. In the meantime, the manufactory administrator faced an increasingly unwieldy work force.

Work discipline, the bête noire of all early manufacturing establishments, proved to be a major problem for the tobacco manufactory administrators and remained a problem throughout the period of Bourbon management. What becomes abundantly clear is that the workers retained some control over the disposal of their time, which enabled them to use their positions in the manufactories to their best advantage. This is a Mexican variant on a theme well rehearsed by economic and social historians of worker responses to time and work discipline. As Alf Lüdtke has argued, "It is clear that the introduction of factory regulations fixed neither the extent nor the content of work time . . . the workers . . . pursued a varying . . . struggle to control the expenditure of their labor power."[88]

In 1796 the manufactory administrator elaborated on the problems of enforcing regular work habits, "since the workers have always been able to come and go from their work as they please."[89] The problem was not that workers did not go to work each day, but that they often only worked for half a day and left at noon, having only completed a portion of their *tareas.* It was very rare for all *tareas* to be completed in a working day, and the *sobrestantes mayores* often returned paper to the stores unworked because workers left early, leaving their *tareas* unfinished. There were, the administrator concluded, "great difficulties in assigning a determined number of workers to each workroom, when it depends entirely on their will whether they come to work or not."[90] Puchet reported that approximately 4,900 *tareas* were distributed daily, based on the number of workers listed and the supervisors' estimation of who could manage only part of a *tarea.* Yet not more than a total of 3,600 were completed. For Puchet, the unfinished 1,300 were due to "the continuous and voluntary lack of attendance by workers on a regular basis."[91] Furthermore, not all workers listed were equally skillful at the worktable, and even less the workers admitted to replace absentee cigarette rollers. He complained bitterly about the continued absenteeism of his own work force as well as that of the Querétaro manufactory. In his view, workers, both men and women, often chose instead to attend bullfights and exhibited a marked predilection for the *toro* over the *tarea.*[92] We must also bear in mind that these are merely observations and tell us nothing about the frequency of worker absenteeism, which was undoubtedly less than bureaucratic reports would have us believe, as the petition from the *cuerpo de cigarreros* for a longer working day in 1794 discussed earlier suggests. A certain number of worker substitutes, who worked for half or a quarter of a *tarea,* were always employed, to act as replacements if workers did not show up or became ill. Listings of such substitutes indicate, however, that their numbers were neither extensive nor adequate to cover reported numbers of absentee workers.[93]

Drunkenness contributed to absenteeism. In the tobacco workers' equivalent of 'Blue Monday', some workers would arrive at the manufactory at 8 : 30 A.M. on Monday morning, collect their paper allocations for the next day's *tarea*, and leave.[94] According to the manufactory administrator, the number of workers engaging in this practice normally was about five hundred.[95] Another practice of the workers which illustrates their continued ability to manage their time in the workplace was known as *la voz fletes*. Veteran cigarette rollers and supervisors alike "sold" their *tarea* to their *fleteros* (generally children, apprentice workers, or relatives). While these substitutes (generally less skilled) filled their piecework quotas, the workers left the manufactory to tend to other needs, but returned in time to make the delivery of their *tareas* to their supervisors. The repeated prohibitions against the practice of *fleteros* are indicative of the popularity and persistence of the practice among the workers.[96]

Clearly the workers found ways in which to manipulate the work regime to their own needs. The *dirección general* could not enforce a fixed number of workers because of changes in the level of demand, which required flexibility in the numbers employed. In response to this, however, workers found that piecework enabled them to retain control over their time. According to a frustrated *director general*, "there are many days on which, due to work or business which they claim they have, they leave the manufactory . . . and stop their rolling even though they deprive themselves of income as a result of an incomplete *tarea*."[97] Uncertainty of work, inadequate wages, and a family economy which was not necessarily completely monetized shaped the workers' constructions of time and tasks so that "the emphasis is on uncertain outcomes. Timing becomes crucial in the experience of work . . . The points of intersection between an individual's or family's life-cycle with wider economic movements become vital in understanding how people experience work in a total sense."[98]

Puchet's policy to reduce the number of workers in the Mexico City manufactory gained additional support after the tobacco workers' Paper Riot in 1794. Shortly after its resolution, the *dirección general* received orders from Spain to reduce the high numbers of workers on the grounds that they constituted a potential threat to the political and social stability of the city. If any changes were to be made, now was the time to reorganize the manufactories and reduce the labor force of the Mexico City manufactory, with the support of the royal order of 1795. This is a classic example of political and economic considerations reinforcing one another, even though the reforms had different origins.[99] Puchet's program went ahead quite quickly. In 1797 reductions began in earnest. Positions which became vacant were not filled, penalties were instituted for worker absenteeism, criminal acts were prosecuted more vigorously and punished by suspension or dismissal. A further order of 17 February 1798 decreed that all recently hired workers, including *forasteros* (migrants), and those workers who possessed other skills were to be dismissed, so that they could be more useful to the 'republic'.[100] The workers who remained found themselves subjected to new conditions of work, such as the eight-day absence rule which stated that any worker absent for eight consecutive days or more without a legitimate excuse would not be permitted to work in the manufactory again. The regulation, however, enabled workers to miss work for one or several days within a given week (fondly described by economists as exercising a 'leisure preference') and return without penalty. Migrant workers whose families lived outside of Mexico City also were permitted time off to travel to see them. Provided they acquired the requisite permission to travel from the administrator, they would not lose their rights to Concordia benefits as a result of absences.[101] All of these new regulations were supported by new Concordia rules implemented in 1792, which increasingly tied access to benefits to regular work in the manufactories. The results of manufactory reorganization are shown in table 20, which indicates the shift in the concentration of tobacco workers away from Mexico City and into the provinces, notably Querétaro, which experienced the largest expansion. Between 1795 and 1809 the percentage of the total number of manufactory workers concentrated in the Mexico City manufactory declined from 59 to 41 percent, whereas in Querétaro the trend was reversed, with an increase from 12 to 28 percent of the total number of manufactory workers. By 1809 69 percent of the total work force was concentrated in these two manufactories as shown in table 29. The policy to reduce the Mexico City manufactory work force was successful. As of 6 September 1797 there were an estimated 8,976 workers of both sexes; almost one year later, by 31 October 1798, 5,007 remained employed in the manufactory, a reduction of 3,969. The *director general* reported that reductions in the work force had been carried out slowly, with skill and prudence, and without the slightest sign of trouble, despite bureaucratic fears of worker violence and protest.[102]

A renewed commitment to employing only women became evident, possibly reinforced by a royal decree of 1799 which stated that women and girls were permitted "to engage in all labors and manufactures compatible with their strength and the decorum of their sex, regardless of guild ordinances and governmental regulations to

Table 29. Percentage Distribution of Work Force among the Seven Tobacco Manufactories, 1795 and 1809

	1795		1809	
	No.	%	No.	%
Mexico	7,074	59	5,437	41
Guadalajara	1,550	13	1,160	9
Puebla	1,027	9	1,228	9
Querétaro	1,397	12	3,706	28
Oaxaca	610	5	610	5
Orizaba	355	3	335	3
Guadalupe	—	—	840	6

Source: See Table 20.

the contrary."[103] Assumptions about the perceived advantages of female workers were quite blatant, if not necessarily accurate: women were less prone to riot, easier to control if they did, and in general better at their craft than men. Puchet thought they provided a more moral, stable work force, since women workers "are more constant in the work and do not abandon it with the same ease as the men."[104] As early as 1798 (and probably before) women predominated as cigarette rollers. Out of a total of 5,007 workers in the Mexico City manufactory, 80 percent were cigarette rollers; 65 percent of these were women. The increasing predominance of women is represented in table 30. The total percentage of women employed in the manufactories increased from 54 percent to 72 percent in 1809. The increase in the number of female workers in the Mexico City manufactory is striking—from under one half to almost three-quarters of its total workforce. Only the Orizaba manufactory registered a contrary trend, as the percentage of male workers increased from 45 percent in 1795 to 58 percent in 1809 (possibly as a result of the emphasis on cigar rolling). Between 1795 and 1810 the manufactory administrator's attempts to reduce the number of workers in the Mexico City manufactory and to enforce the employment of women as cigarette rollers was successful. In the process, however, women tobacco workers not only bore the brunt of cigarette production, but did so under increasingly exploitative conditions, as piecework rates declined for a task which, over the decades, had become increasingly defined as female, while piecework rates for the male-dominated craft of cigar rolling increased.

The changes implemented to improve worker discipline may have

Table 30. *Percentage Distribution of Workers among Manufactories by Gender for 1795 and 1809*

	1795				1809			
	Female		Male		Female		Male	
	No.	%	No.	%	No.	%	No.	%
Mexico	3,055	43	4,019	57	3,883	71	1,554	29
Guadalajara	1,532	99	18	1	1,136	98	24	2
Puebla	510	50	517	50	744	61	484	39
Querétaro	605	43	792	57	2,574	69	1,132	31
Oaxaca	589	97	21	3	586	96	24	4
Orizaba	195	55	160	45	140	42	195	58
Guadalupe	—	—	—	—	492	59	348	41
Totals	6,486	54	5,527	46	9,555	72	3,761	28

Source: See Table 20.

had some effect on worker productivity. Although crude and subject to all kinds of caveats, a simple single factor productivity estimate suggests that output per worker increased over the years, possibly as a result of "learning by doing," but perhaps also reflecting intensification of labor:[105]

Year	Cigarette Packet Equivalents/Worker
1795	8,848
1798	7,157
1809	11,493

If the calculation is made based on the numbers of cigarettes or cigars (that is, the actual individual units, not packets), using an average number of cigarettes per packet according to the different classes, there is still an increase in the number of individual units. Even taking into consideration the different numbers of total workers in ratio to total production of packets of cigars and cigarettes, it seems that the post-1790 rationalization of the manufactories began to yield results by the first decade of the nineteenth century in terms of output per worker, but with a definite bias towards quantity and not quality. In 1817 the *director general* reported that the standard of manufactory cigars and cigarettes still left a great deal to be desired and resulted in constant losses to the monopoly as consumers sought out contraband products.[106] In the long run, however, the potential increases in output remained small and soon reached their limit.

In this chapter we have seen that free-wage labor brought workers to the manufactories but did not result in a disciplined, regular work force. Manufactory labor and the problems experienced by the manufactory administrators in disciplining their workers present us with a way to think about the wider context of urban life and work in late colonial Mexico. On the one hand, the tobacco workers of Mexico City reported that "the majority of our people are so poor that the day they do not work, they do not eat."[107] On the other hand, in his study on crime and the urban poor in Mexico City in the late eighteenth century, Michael Scardaville argued that, although numerous unskilled and semiskilled occupations were represented among those arrested, of all occupational groups, workers from the Mexico City tobacco manufactory committed the highest rate of crime.[108] More specifically, the tobacco manufactory workers were arrested for gambling twice as often as the group with the next highest arrest rate for gambling (weavers).[109] In the early nineteenth century, however, the tobacco workers do not feature so prominently among those occupational groups arrested in Mexico City.[110] Like the working poor in eighteenth-century Europe, urban workers, including the tobacco workers, were subject to a moralizing discourse concerned with "the morality of industriousness and the preoccupation with *luxe* and *débauche*."[111] As monopoly bureaucrats asked: "Who among them [the tobacco workers] ever considers tomorrow, today?"[112] The workers' behavior presents paradoxes with which social and economic historians of preindustrial society are familiar: the coexistence of poverty with "degenerate" activities such as gambling and drinking. Michael Sonenscher suggests that the paradoxes can be understood if it is recognized that survival—food, housing, and other consumption—was not predicated exclusively upon a money wage, and that the problem for urban workers was maintaining a continuity of income when there was no necessary continuity of work. "The imbrication of life and work, the varying imperatives of a substantial number of different time schedules, intersecting with one another and calling for an extended repertoire of modes of negotiation, co-operation or conflict, meant that work itself existed within a context which was not always and not exclusively defined in a monetary way."[113]

Discretionary movement in and out of the workplace made possible by piecework was undoubtedly a response to changing needs of household economies and individual workers alike. Despite the

regularity of manufactory work, declining wages and the potential
for layoffs only exacerbated uncertainty about daily survival and created imperatives which conflicted with those of the monopoly,
which demanded regular attendance and careful work habits. This
was the wider context in which attempts to enforce work discipline
and manufactory regulations took place, and which helped the tobacco workers modify the manufactory work regime to their own
needs.

In the long run, the monopoly's attempts to improve worker discipline and enforce regular attendance met with mixed results. The
combination of the reform of Concordia benefits, which became dependent on the length of time worked in the manufactories, and the
eight-day absence rule may have encouraged greater regularity of attendance by workers over the long term. Undoubtedly, however, the
economic imperatives experienced by the working poor in late colonial Mexico contributed as much to more regular and sustained attendance at the tobacco rolling tables as any gradual accommodation to manufactory regulations. At the beginning of the nineteenth
century, the viceroy summed up the manufactory workers of Mexico
City as "4,000 workers of both sexes, the majority of them ill-bred,
arrogant, restless, difficult to control, and discontented."[114] On balance, however, the state's fiscal gains from the tobacco manufactories were considerable, and production of cigars and cigarettes occurred without interruption between 1769 and 1810. The paternalist
ethos of the manufactory certainly did not prevent the *dirección
general* from implementing reforms which increased the profitability of the monopoly at the expense of the workers, nor from using
the power of the state (legal, religious, and, when necessary, although seldom, military,) to control the workers. The monopoly
proved to be at its least paternal in the gradual reduction of piecework rates paid to the cigarette rollers during the 1790s. Given the
inflationary pressures of the late eighteenth century, the tobacco
workers, in common with other workers and the rest of the colonial
population, suffered from the undermining of their money wages.[115]
The state gradually abolished many (not all) of the nonmonetary
"perks" and fined workers for paper spoiled due to lack of skill or
carelessness, the fine deducted from their weekly wages. In the process, the monopoly administration demonstrated the double-edged
nature of its paternalism, where "the affective and coercive are rarely
strangers."[116] After the 1790s efforts to improve worker discipline in
the Mexico City manufactory focused on the employment of women
and a reduction of the work force. As a result, cigarette rolling

became increasingly defined as women's work, while cigar rolling became increasingly dominated by men. Despite manufactory regulations and workroom discipline, the workers maintained a measure of autonomy in the arrangement of their working lives. But the imperatives of the manufactory administrators and the workers were not opposed in principle: one was dominated by the search for security, the other by regularity. While the two seem eminently compatible, the methods adopted to achieve the respective objectives were not. The workers' resentment of attempts to reform their lives was reflected in their grievances and other actions which conveyed an underlying concern with their ability to live their lives as they saw fit, and not according to the mandates of the colonial state or the demands of their jobs. The manufactory workrooms became transformed into battlegrounds for negotiated conflict between management and labor. Some battles were waged as continual, quiet, covert, individual acts; others were short-lived, collective, noisy remonstrations. It is to such battles and their significance for the tobacco workers that we now turn our attention.

7. Accommodation, Consensus, and Resistance: The Tobacco Manufactory Workers and the Colonial State, 1770–1810

IF THE OBJECT of the colonial state with regard to the tobacco workers, effectively its employees in the royal tobacco manufactories, was to contain social conflict, then, for the most part, it succeeded. The Mexico City tobacco manufactory, like many other early manufactories, was neither a "crucible of consciousness nor an epicenter of rebellion."[1] But, during the state-building process of the Bourbons and the monopolization of the tobacco trade, the workers proved themselves capable of defining and defending their interests and of shaping work in the manufactories to satisfy their own needs. Through an ongoing process of negotiation, they helped to shape the limitations of the Bourbon absolutist state and its powers as an employer. As we shall argue, however, there was something more at stake in the contention and conflict which developed between the monopoly and the tobacco workers than simply a question of wage levels or retention of customary practices. Manufactory regulations transcended the limits of the workplace and demanded reform of workers' morals and social mores, a reform which impinged upon the workers' wider culture and their private lives.[2] The workers' actions and grievances illustrate not only attempts to defend their material well-being, but also reflect a wider set of beliefs about the ways of the world and its order, beliefs which valued independence, upheld the moral obligations of the monarch, and which formed a critique of the excesses of Bourbon modernization. The discourse used by the workers to express such beliefs was shaped not by the vocabulary of Spanish laws per se, but by religion.[3] As such, the workers' defense of their interests provide us with an example of how popular religious beliefs shaped popular political action in the late eighteenth century.[4]

Recent trends in labor history have made historians question the wisdom of analyzing workers' actions within a teleological framework which judges those actions according to the degree to which politicization and class consciousness is or is not developed. Invariably, such interpretations with their normative hindsight assume that the workers remain passive agents who contribute to their own continued subordination and exploitation. In the case of the silver miners of Real del Monte, for example, Doris Ladd argues that their "victory" as a result of strike action created an obstacle to their own best interests, as "the flow of workers' class consciousness" was directed into "the mainstream of royal patronage."[5] Studies of the tobacco workers tend to assume the exploitative nature of their working conditions and, in the process, reduce the workers to objects rather than subjects.[6] Our approach to understanding the workers' actions and state-worker relations is very much influenced by the works of labor historians Michael Sonenscher and Richard Price, both of whom argue that scholars should avoid "the teleology of writing labor history as either conforming to or deviating from a certain trajectory."[7] This shifts one's perspective away from a normative, often ahistorical, argument, permits an assessment of the workers on their own terms, and takes into account their options and the constraints under which they operated.

We begin with the simple observation that monopoly-worker relations were characterized, for the most part, by a functioning consensus born of negotiation and compromise, rather than conflict. Why? Chapter 6 has already provided us with most of the reasons. The first relates to the opportunities for employment provided by the manufactories. There were few alternatives for work in the cities for semi-skilled and unskilled workers, particularly for women. The tobacco manufactories offered one of the best opportunities for survival in late-eighteenth-century Mexico. The abolition of the tobacco shops was a slow process which permitted the workers to adjust to such reorganization. Those individuals affected were assured of alternative employment in the manufactories. Second, the paternalist ethos of the manufactory was manifested in a number of ways. The monopoly presented itself as a paternal employer willing to assure workers of employment with similar rates of pay and "perks" such as were given them in the private workshops. The establishment of dispute procedures within the manufactories drew on long-established traditions of the Spanish state, institutionalized and channeled conflict, and dissipated worker conflict. Third, the wider imperial objectives of the colonial state favored social stability in its colonies resulting in decisions made in favor of worker demands which, in turn, perpetuated the legitimacy of the Bourbon polity. Fourth, the organization of work and wages contributed to divisions within the work force, which were reinforced by existing divisions based on status, gender, and ethnicity, and which prevented the formation of a broader class identity among the workers. The workers rarely engaged in collective protest—two walkouts and one strike in almost half a century. But perhaps the lack of collective protests indicates not their weakness or unsophistication, or "immaturity," but their ability to bring pressure to bear upon their employer, in this case, the colonial state, to satisfy their demands without having to resort to collective protest.[8] As a result, workers were incorporated as collaborators in the establishment of the manufactories and acquired a vested interest in the monopoly's existence, which was linked to their own.

What we have here, then, is a mutuality of interest, but a mutuality which was constantly challenged and renegotiated, with costs to both sides. As Richard Price argues, "men and women finding themselves in certain social relationships which involve authority and obedience are constantly struggling over the limits, the frontiers at which obedience begins and ends. It is in the continual search from both sides for a better bargain that the dynamic of the labor process in labor's history can be seen to lie."[9] The search for the "better bargain" brings us now to a consideration of the workers, their identities and associations, their interests, how they set about defending them, and with what success.

The transformation of the tobacco industry meant different things to different people. For some cigar and cigarette rollers who previously labored in a workshop under the authority of a *maestro cigarrero*, it simply meant a change of employer and location. For others, and we are thinking particularly of the single and widowed women, work in the manufactories may have resulted in new associations with other women workers and social identities. We have already argued that the transfer of the tobacco industry from private to public management incorporated change as well as continuity and transformation as well as modification of existing social relations. We must also consider the possibility that, while some workers viewed the monopolization of the tobacco trade as destructive of their livelihood and opportunities, others welcomed the opportunity to work in the manufactory, particularly in the light of so few alternatives for employment in the late eighteenth century.

Daily living, associations, and identities of the tobacco workers were rooted in and shaped by a variety of institutions and social relations which incorporated both work and home, the occupational *cuerpos* within the manufactory, the trade confraternity or mutual aid society, the Concordia, the family, and the neighborhood, church and tavern. Such associations enabled the workers to act collectively, yet also contributed to social cleavages among them.

Residential patterns suggest that many of the workers and their families lived concentrated together in barrios close to the manufactories. The neighborhood of Santa Ana in Querétaro was perceived to be inhabited by "low people [gente ruin] and workers of the Royal Tobacco Factory."[10] The parish of Santa Catarina y Mártir in Mexico City was a popular neighborhood for many of the workers and their families, who attended mass and were confessed in the local churches.[11] Single tobacco workers also lived in the same *casas de vecindad* (apartment houses) as tobacco workers with families.[12]

Another common social milieu for gatherings were the *pulquerías* (taverns). In the parish of Santa Catarina y Mártir, for example, there were four very popular ones, La Celaya, La Aguila, La Vizgaya, and Las Papas, frequented by the workers. This was much to the dismay of the ministers of the Real Tribunal de Cuentas, who observed that "it was not uncommon for almost fifteen hundred workers, most of them from the manufactory, to go to the *pulquerías* on their way home from the manufactory during the week."[13] Gambling was an equally popular pastime for the tobacco workers, as we saw in chapter 6. Cigarette rollers were arrested for gambling twice as often as the next most important group, the weavers.[14]

The workplace provided an opportunity for a variety of associations and interchange among workers. Inside the manufactories, daily interaction was fostered at the worktables, through membership in the different *cuerpos*, and, in the case of Mexico City, in the Concordia. There is no evidence that the tobacco workers were organized within a guild prior to the monopoly. The *"cuerpo"* of *cigarreros* which protested the establishment of the manufactories was probably constructed on an ad hoc basis specifically to make its opposition known. No other references were made to suggest the existence of such a body. One of the major changes in the workers' lives was the ability to form associations on a scale impossible in their previous situations which had dispersed them throughout Mexico City. If we refer back to Hirschman's model of "voice," discussed in chapter 3, what is interesting in the case of the tobacco workers is the creation of an opportunity, sanctioned by the colonial state, to find a new kind of "voice," or rather "voices," through the Concordia and the manufactory *cuerpos*. We will examine the formation and function of the workers' confraternity, the Concordia, and then consider the occupational *cuerpos*. It should be pointed out that the evidence presented for the Concordia all pertains to the Mexico City manufactory. While we suspect that the provincial manufactories possessed similar societies, we could find no documentary evidence of their existence.

The colonial state exhibited ambiguity towards corporate bodies in the late eighteenth century. On the one hand, it carried out an offensive against trade guilds and the corporate structure of the Church. On the other hand, it was instrumental in supporting the creation of new corporate entities, such as the military *fuero* and the mining guild, partly to create a sense of identification with and loyalty to the state. The tobacco workers proved to be beneficiaries of the latter practice. Indeed, it was the concentration of such large numbers of workers in one place which provided the imperative and conditions for the development of such corporate organization within the Mexico City manufactory. On their own initiative, the workers requested permission to organize a confraternity, the Concordia. The colonial state agreed to its establishment and approved its regulations. In so doing, it increased the dependence of workers upon the monopoly in order to benefit from their weekly monetary contributions, but, at the same time, the Concordia became the workers' symbol of independence and security.

Confraternities in general have received a great deal of attention from historians, especially concerning their economic, social, and political implications, and the values held by the members. As William Sewell puts it: "the moral community of the entire trade was not only an ideal; it was also a lived experience of daily life," and the mutual aid society served as "the moral and organizational centre of the trade, acting on behalf of all the workers, representing them in negotiations and leading them in struggles against the masters." [15] Many of the functions attributed to trade confraternities are not strictly applicable to the Concordia of the tobacco workers. The moral and social welfare dimensions are evoked in the Concordia clauses (including loyalty and obedience to the monarch) and in the very language used by the *concordantes* as *cuerpos* or bodies to convey a corporatist entity. But the Concordia became a focus of the workers' struggles, rather than a vehicle for them; that function devolved on the occupational *cuerpos*—the *embolvedores*, cigarette rollers, cigar makers, *cernidores*, and so forth.[16]

The idea and organization of the Concordia originated in direct response to workers' preoccupations about life in this world and the next. Its central function was to provide money to workers in time of need by building up a capital fund upon which workers could draw according to specified rules. Workers contributed 1/2 real on a weekly basis and, in so doing, acquired some protection against the vagaries of fate. In the workers' request for authorization and acceptance of the Concordia's constitution, they gave as part of its *raison d'être* to ensure that, when "God decides to take us from this life to the next, we have the necessary aid for the good of our souls, and that our bodies may be buried in church, and also for the support of those people who are closest to us, our wives and children, who are left destitute because of our death, or our mothers and fathers who can no longer look after themselves."[17] The workers encountered a strong ally in José de Gálvez, who applauded an institution which enabled the manufactory workers to "clothe the naked, aid the sick, and ensure decent burials for their members."[18]

The Concordia's general ordinances were drawn up in 1770 and approved by a royal order of 24 May 1771. Both male and female workers were eligible to join. By the end of 1771 the Concordia's membership totalled 5,600.[19] Tobacco workers who wished to become members of the Concordia were requested to contribute 1/2 real on a weekly basis. The Concordia's governing officials consisted of the manufactory administrator as director, two *maestros mayores* elected as *contador* and treasurer, and eleven *conciliarios* (representatives) chosen from the different manufactory *cuerpos*, including that of the cigarette rollers.

If a Concordia member requested aid, a notice was sent to the director. He, in turn, passed it on to the petitioner's workroom. The facts were verified for each individual case and, if all was in order, a cash amount was given to the applicant or taken to his or her sickbed or to prison. Although the contributions were standardized, there was a graduated scale of payments, according to the position of the worker. In case of sickness, for example, cigarette rollers, *recontadores*, and *embolvedores* were paid between 2 and 4 reales; supervisors, guards, and *sobrestantes* received between 1 and 2 pesos. The choice of whether to be cured in a hospital or at home when sick was left to the decision of the individual worker, although there were attempts on the part of the *dirección general* to make the workers go into one of the hospitals if they were ill. The cost of care in the various hospitals varied from 5 reales daily at San Andrés, 3 reales daily at San Juan de Dios and San Lazaro, to the cheapest rate, 1 real daily, at San Hipólito. A doctor was appointed at an annual salary of 250 pesos, paid for out of Concordia funds. Tobacco workers who received jail sentences were allocated the same amounts as the infirm. A form of pension existed for workers who completed at least ten years of service in the manufactory. Those who could no longer work at all were to receive 2 reales per day and a new shirt and trousers each year.[20] In the event of death, the deceased's next of kin received 30 pesos, which covered the cost of a decent burial, including the habit of San Francisco and twelve masses.[21]

If the Concordia's main function was to provide monetary benefits to support workers during illnesses and their relatives after their deaths, it also functioned as a source of credit from which workers could borrow money. Loans were made for a variety of reasons, the most common being marriages, baptisms, and coverage of fiesta days when the manufactory was closed. During Easter and other feast days, the Concordia paid out what the manufactory did not, in accordance with the usual wages. Such loans were repaid over a period of time at 2, 3, or 4 reales per week, although it is not clear whether interest was charged.[22]

At the center of the Concordia's establishment was the election and veneration of a patron saint. Originally, the Concordia members chose two patrons, San Isidro Labrador and the Virgin of Guadalupe.[23] San Isidro Labrador became the major patron saint, and an image of him was commissioned by the officials of the Concordia. On completion, it was placed by the workers in the church of Santiago Tlatelolco. Every May 15 his saint's day was celebrated with a mass and sermon and "all the solemnity and pomp possible."[24] The Virgin of Guadalupe, nevertheless, continued to play an important role in the lives of the workers, who often called upon her as their divine mediator and signed their petitions in "the name of the Virgin of Guadalupe."[25]

The supporters of the cult of Guadalupe, in turn, called upon the workers to provide economic aid to support the Virgin. The *cabildo* of the *villa* of Guadalupe sought contributions from the monopoly to support the choir and musicians at the shrine of Guadalupe. For a short period in 1795 the workers in Mexico City gave contributions "voluntarily and piously," with the wholehearted support of viceroy Branciforte, who was reportedly devoted to the Virgin. By staying at work after the completion of their own day's work, the workers rolled a small quantity of cigarettes, the value of which went to the *cabildo*. The task took about fifteen minutes and produced between 500 and 600 pesos monthly.[26] The Crown was not enthusiastic about this, observing that normally a worker desired nothing more than the arrival of the hour when he could rest and should not have to work overtime. Moreover, to make someone carry out a task without remuneration was excessive and burdensome, and such donations should not be made from the "sweat of the poor workers." Subsequently, the practice was prohibited.[27]

The Puebla tobacco workers, who described themselves as "im-

Table 31. *Concordia Income and Expenditure, 1770–1793*

Year	Income (pesos)	Expenditure (pesos)	Balance (pesos)
1770–1775	70,394	43,358	27,368
	(average of 11,732)	(average of 7,226)	(average of 4,561)
1781	8,650	4,323	4,326
1782	18,117	18,760	−643
1783	17,567	23,100	5,533
1784	19,324	23,951	−4,627
1785	21,195	21,900	−705
1786	23,273	25,997	−2,723
1787–1790	N/A		
1791	35,950	18,203	17,747
1792	44,241	26,214	19,461*
1793	42,346	34,858	9,026*

Source: AGI, Mexico 2313.

*The bookkeeping does not seem to have improved, since these balances are incorrect. For the figures on hand, they should balance out at 18,027 and 7,488 pesos, respectively.

passioned by and devoted to the Virgin," also wished to have an image which they could adore "in the most Christian way."[28] On learning what the Mexico City workers were doing, as a result of a letter from the Real Colegiata de Nuestra Señora de Guadalupe, they requested permission to make an extra packet of cigarettes per person per day, take a collection, and donate the value to complete the building of the Virgin's shrine. Once again, the initial request was granted, only to be repealed shortly thereafter.[29] The *cabildo* undoubtedly thought its prayers had been answered when the new small tobacco manufactory opened in 1799 in the *villa* of Guadalupe.[30]

Concordia funds were quite considerable, to the extent that investments were made in property, which included houses in the Calle Lagunilla and the Calle Berdeja, the rooms of which were rented out to workers. Table 31 shows the accounts of the Concordia between 1770 and 1793 and its deficits for 1782 to 1786.[31] The breakdown of the distribution of Concordia funds for 1770–1775 (aggregate figures) and 1791–1793 is shown in table 32. No records of the Concordia were found after 1793. Scattered references and records of a controversial case, which involved attempts by the colonial state between 1813 and 1814 to appropriate Concordia funds to help finance the royalist defense against the Mexican insurgents, indicate that it continued to operate throughout the first decades of the nineteenth century.[32]

Table 32. *Percentage Breakdown of Total Payments from Concordia Funds, 1770–1775 and 1791–1793 (in pesos)*

	1770–1775	1791	1792	1793
Aid to sick	12,633 (29%)*	5,371 (30%)**	19,002 (73%)	25,273 (73%)
Burials	22,567 (52%)	5,250 (29%)	4,789 (18%)	5,070 (15%)
Marriages		3,815 (21%)	1,620 (6%)	2,232 (6%)
Aid to prisoners			426 (2%)	202 (1%)
Payment for clothes	1,613 (4%)			
Salaries and miscellaneous	6,543 (15%)	3,767 (21%)	377 (1%)	2,081 (6%)

Source: Figures constructed from AGI, Mexico 2259, Papel instructivo del estado de la concordia . . . 1 January 1776; AGI, Mexico 2259, Papel instructivo del estado de la concordia establecida en la real fábrica de puros y cigarros de esta ciudad desde su erección hasta el día de su fecha, 1 January 1776; AGN, Tabaco 500, Conciliarios electos to Romaña, 23 August 1783; AGI, Mexico 2313, report of José de Alvarez, 22 January 1794.

*Includes payments to sick and prisoners combined.

**Represents payments made to cured sick only.

(Totals may not add up to 100 because of rounding)

It was not only the Concordia, however, which provided a focus of worker identity, but the individual *cuerpos*. The latter were organized around the different manufactory tasks described in Chapter 6, such as wrapping, shredding, rolling, stamping, and packing. It was the *cuerpos* which represented workers' grievances to the manufactory administration, not the Concordia. The existence of these two corporate entities, however, created tensions, as workers were brought together through membership in the Concordia, and divided again by the *cuerpos* according to their task-specific problems. The organization of labor in the manufactory, far from resulting in homogeneity of the work force, resulted in new identifications, boundaries, and vertical ties based on the occupational *cuerpos*. Even the largest group of workers, the cigarette rollers, were not leveled by the division of labor within the manufactory. The older cigarette rollers evaluated the meaning of their new positions, identity, and status. Possibly as a response to loss of control over who was hired and to the dilution of skills, they distinguished themselves as professional cigarette workers, *de la profesión* (by implication, skilled), as opposed to those workers who were employed in later years, literally "from the street," *de la calle* (by implication, unskilled). The distinction was pointed out on several occasions by workers who considered themselves *de la profesión* to justify complaints against reduced work quotas at a time when they perceived that workers classified by them as *de la calle* were still being hired.[33]

Descriptions of informal credit relations among the workers suggest relationships between workers which may have affected their responses to collective action and also suggest the survival of old master-apprentice relationships, cemented by monetary loans. The most generalized reference to loans and lending among workers was made by the manufactory administrator. He complained that many of the *sobrestantes*, who acted as small traders, "indulge in exorbitant usury that you could not find greater even among the Moors."[34]

The variety of associational forms reinforced divisions among the tobacco workers throughout the eighteenth and early nineteenth centuries. They maintained vertical as well as horizontal ties based on corporate divisions, and their loyalties were directed toward the king, their families, and their priests, not to one another in the sense of class identification. This was combined with the past experience of the workers and their conscious evaluation of it. As anthropologist William Roseberry has cautioned recently, "The past is constitutive of consciousness, but it is not as unambiguous as the models suggest." As a result, it may serve as "the basis for a critical response to the first emergence or introduction of capitalist social relations," but a response which is ambiguous and contradictory, accomodationist and defiant.[35] The objectives of the tobacco workers' actions were not to challenge the monopoly or the state, the source of their security, but to defend what they perceived to be their rights, which included a particular way of life which the colonial state had attempted to extinguish. It is in their strategies of protest that we see the coexistence of accommodation and defiance. We turn now to a closer examination of such strategies and their significance.

A review of worker petitions and actions reveals five broad areas in which the workers were brought into conflict with the monopoly: management of time and work discipline, which we have already discussed in the previous chapter; fraud and abuse of power by supervisory staff (including intimidation and physical abuse); wage levels; violation of customary practices (provision of nonmonetary "perks," access to raw materials); and hiring practices.

The Mexican tobacco workers' responses to their new work regime resemble those of many other workers in preindustrial and industrializing economies, who resist forms of policing which limit freedom of action. "Each of the steps taken by capital at one time or another to reduce the price of labor and increase its subordination encountered vigorous opposition. Wage contests, 'bargaining by riot,' strikes, and other collective actions, along with individual resistance . . . did not halt the development of capitalism, but they prevented employers from destroying every semblance of worker autonomy."[36]

If the practices of the workers reflected their beliefs about what was fair regarding the disposal of time and their use of it for their own, rather than the monopoly's, needs, the same could be said about their use of monopoly materials. As in many urban trades in Spanish America and Europe in the eighteenth century, "the relationship between work and wages was mediated by a variety of nonmonetary customs and rights."[37] By far the most widespread and controversial practice was embezzlement of cigars, cigarettes, paper, and tobacco. The sale of cigars and cigarettes formed part of the 'microeconomy' of the manufactories, which had two manifestations. Firstly, workers at all levels smuggled the products out and sold them on the streets. Secondly, supervisory workers sold the free cigarettes to which the workers were entitled, pocketing the money from these 'sales'.[38] Despite daily searches by manufactory guards, opportunities abounded for workers to take small quantities of tobacco and paper out of the manufactory. They sold these in the streets for whatever price people were willing to pay, often to acquire additional income to supplement the inadequate one gained from piecework. Once at the worktable, supervisors and workers alike could take advantage of the materials at their disposal. The greatest losses occurred due to the sanctioned manufactory practice of preparation of cigarette paper at home. Each evening supervisors distributed among the cigarette rollers their paper quotas for the next day, which they took home with them to cut and prepare. Access to paper had the same function for the tobacco workers as the *partido* (share of silver ore) for the miners in colonial Mexico, and certainly generated as much controversy when attempts were made to eliminate it.[39]

Puchet, the Mexico City manufactory administrator, described some of the workers as being defiantly overt in their actions. "When the workers go into the streets, with their books of paper, they begin to shout 'who will buy and who will sell.' Those who have already decided not to go to work the next day sell for 1 real paper which is valued at 1 1/2 reales per *mano*."[40] The quality of paper was much better than that found in local shops, where paper sold for at least 4 pesos, while that purchased from the cigarette rollers sold for 2 1/2 pesos. The buyers of such contraband paper were often those who preferred to 'roll their own', or reroll the ones purchased from the government tobacco shops.[41] When the cigarette roller returned to work, he was armed with cheap substitute paper bought or bartered from one of the stores close to the manufactory. For those supervisors who took their jobs seriously, this was not difficult to detect. From the perspective of the monopoly administrators, such practices amounted to theft and were punished as such. From the workers' perspective, it represented the protection of a source of income and may indicate the workers' expectations of retaining nonmonetary "perks" as part of their income and daily needs.[42]

Apart from shaping working conditions to their own needs, the most common method used by workers to defend their interests was that established by the state, the submission of petitions, a procedure which promoted negotiation and cooperation. Complaints came from both individuals and *cuerpos* and, more rarely, as a generalized response which cut across such *cuerpos*. We cannot illustrate each type of grievance, but the ones which follow exemplify the modus operandi of petition, negotiation, and resolution.

Within the workplace itself, apart from the reported fights and attacks among the workers themselves, accusations of maltreatment of pieceworkers by supervisory staff were not uncommon. In 1781 María Guadalupe, a Spanish worker recently dismissed from the Puebla manufactory, petitioned that she be reinstated in her position. According to her testimony, the *maestra* and administrator had refused to accept the cigarettes she made because of their poor quality. Shortly thereafter the administrator, *maestras*, *sobrestantas*, and *recontadoras* had attacked and hit her violently. María Guadalupe pointed out that she had been pregnant at the time and miscarried due to the punches she received. Her testimony revealed that such bad treatment was not unusual and that all workers were subject to similar treatment. In her opinion, "our king does not order that those who serve in the royal manufactory be ill-treated . . . for which I request it be ordered that the bosses of the manufactory not abuse the poor workers nor beat them."[43] Despite denials of María Guadalupe's accusations, the *director general* ruled that she be reemployed in the manufactory in Puebla.

In the same year, in the same manufactory, a series of complaints were brought against several manufactory *maestros* by the cigarette rollers for various fraudulent practices which affected the latter adversely. Such practices included the *maestros'* habit of distributing half a *tarea* to the regular workers while hiring their own workers to work at full *tareas* at lower wages, and appropriating the difference in wages themselves (a variation of the *fletero* practice). The *maestros* also stood accused of pocketing the weekly sums gathered from illegal sales of complementary cigarettes to workers.[44] The workers complained of being subject to "two years of tyranny," of being paid less for their *tareas* than stipulated in the regulations, and of being subject to the arbitrary behavior of the guards, who refused to place workers on the register if they took a dislike to any of them.[45] In their defense, the accused *maestros* asserted that, if one-half or one-third of a *tarea* was distributed, it was because the workers could only manage that amount of work.

After an investigation, the *director general* Hierro ordered the *factor* of Puebla to arrest the *maestro* Joaquín de Terán and place him in prison. The remaining six *maestros* and five *sobrestantes* involved were to be informed of the transgressions of which they had been accused and ordered to improve their behavior and to carry out their obligations honestly. If complaints were made against them in the future, they would be dismissed from their positions.[46] Terán was later absolved of the charges against him and reinstated in his position but warned to carry out his duties fairly and honestly and that, under no circumstances, were workers to receive any kind of gift or bribe.

Unfortunately, the example of a thorough investigation which demonstrated clearly to the supervisory staff that they were not above the rules of the manufactories failed to act as a deterrent to further fraud in the Puebla manufactory. In 1785 a new set of serious complaints were submitted anonymously by workers against the administrator, his *compadre*, a *maestro mayor*, and a *tercenista* for the "iniquities committed against the Real Hacienda and the poor."[47] The accusations included theft of packets of cigars, cigarettes, and supplies of paper, sale of the workers' allotment of cigarettes, and arbitrary treatment, such as refusing workers entry into the manufactory for an entire week if they failed to show up for work on Mondays. Further complaints concerned allegations that no work was distributed on Thursdays and Fridays and that workers were required to pay an annual 'fee' of 28 pesos to be admitted into the manufactory, when no such charge legally existed. An additional complaint addressed a recent regulation which forbade nursing mothers to bring their babies with them to work. As a result of the prohibition, the workers argued, many babies had perished. The appeal itself was directed to "your Excellency, so charitable and father of all the poor," along with a further request that any investigation be carried out in secret.[48] A postscript explained the lack of signatures. Should the administrator discover the identity of the petitioners, he would throw them out onto the streets, a common punishment for those who complained about the excesses of the manufactory bosses. The administrator often acquired "witnesses" through intimidation or collusion to support his testimony against his accusers before the *factor*. Consequently, the *factor* "will be deceived as usual."[49] The final outcome in this instance is unknown, but in 1786 complaints about the quality of the products from the Puebla manufactory abounded, which may indicate poor morale within the manufactory and worker response to a situation which the administration failed to improve.

Complaints against supervisors and administrators are not always easy to interpret. In the Puebla case discussed above, while many of the instances of fraud and maltreatment are indisputable, the decision not to admit workers if they observed 'Blue Monday' and the inability to provide work on Thursdays and Fridays may reflect distinctly different views concerning use of time, and what constituted acceptable work habits. Conflicting goals of labor and management over the quality of the product and acceptable work habits are illustrated in the following example.

In the Mexico City manufactory, *embolvedores* complained about their new *sobrestantes*, José Manuel Ruiz and Ildefonso de Ita, who recently transferred from management of cigarette production to cigar manufacture. The *embolvedores* complained of the "continuous disturbances and vexations which they experience at every step."[50] The problem centered on the number of cigars which the *sobrestantes* destroyed due to the poor quality of manufacture. Such action affected the workers adversely since the time spent working on the destroyed cigars was not remunerated. The workers believed that the *sobrestantes* made unfair judgments because they were inexperienced in rolling cigars, which was a skill very distinct from that of rolling cigarettes. They requested more moderate and judicious treatment and that future vacancies at the supervisory level be filled by promoting individuals from within their *cuerpo.*[51] The official response was not favorable to the *embolvedores'* petition, but the decision itself is not as important as the opposing perceptions demonstrated by the case and issues raised.[52]

The administrator made some astute observations about the case to the *director general.* The *sobrestantes'* only crime was the efficient management of their office and their attempts to ensure that the cigars which left the manufactory were well made and conformed to the required number, size, and weight. This meant that the *embolvedores* had to work harder for less money, since previously they had hurried to complete their *tareas,* thereby sacrificing the quality of the cigars. The *sobrestantes* refused to allow some of the *embolvedores* to go home at the normal time only when they failed to complete their work. The final decision of the *director general* required that the *sobrestantes* continue to do their best to assure a good product but be more prudent in their discipline and management. The *embolvedores* received a reprimand and were warned that if they failed to obey the *sobrestantes* they would be dismissed.[53]

Cases of unfair dismissal were often brought to the attention of the administrators and viceroy. Gertrudis Barrios Vitero and Ana Felipa Moreno were fired because of their participation in a *motín* (in this instance, a shouting match) and their refusal to pay their weekly contributions to the Concordia fund while its management was under investigation. Their dismissal left them as unemployed widows with large families and little income. An unusually rapid investigation revealed that the women had either misunderstood what was being asked of them and reacted accordingly or false information had been given in the first place. Subsequently, their petition to be rehired was granted.[54]

Wages and piecework rates created controversy. However, they did not predominate over other grievances, as they would among tobacco workers in the late nineteenth century. Requests for increased wages were often judged to be "impertinent, unfair, and ungrounded" and promptly dismissed.[55] The cases which follow illustrate the *di-*

rección general's tactics concerning workers' demands for increased wages and, at the same time, reveal the divisions and distinctions by *cuerpo* and within *cuerpos* in the manufactory workforce. They also illustrate that not all requests received positive responses from the monopoly administration, particularly those which concerned wage increases, nor did denials of requests result in knee-jerk protests.

In 1777 the *dirección general* reduced the wages of the cigarette makers of the Patio de México. The workers responded and hired a lawyer to protest the decision. Rafael de Molina, the lawyer in question, argued that the reductions violated the provisions of the *boleta* given to each cigarette maker prior to beginning work in the manufactory. Following little action on the part of the *dirección general,* a petition signed in the name of the *"comun de cigarreros"* arrived on the viceroy's desk. In the petition, the workers complained that many of the former tobacco shop owners had not yet received positions promised to them when the monopoly took over and were working for low wages. The decision to eliminate bonus payments for chocolate and the imposition of additional wrapping tasks created severe hardship among the workers. They protested, saying, "There is no law which says that a worker must work more to earn less." The *dirección general* remained unsympathetic, arguing that the changes were necessary to rationalize manufactory production and that a petition signed by only sixty-three individuals was insignificant.[56] No further action was taken by the workers.

Three years later, in 1780, the *selladores* petitioned for a wage increase to compensate for an increase in their work load. At the same time, thirty-three *maestros de mesa,* who earned 7 1/2 reales daily, requested a 1/2 real increase to make up a full peso.[57] The *selladores'* request was denied, but not that of the *maestros.* The latter's wage increase, nevertheless, was delayed for fear of the effect of the decision on the other workers. In February of the following year, the *fiscal* ordered that the increase be implemented immediately.[58] How the *selladores* reacted is not known.

A policy decision in 1797 to shift the *recontadores* and *embolvedores* in the *oficina de hombres* (men's workshops) from a fixed wage to piecework because of the 'advantages' it offered to both the monopoly and to the workers provoked petitions which demanded its revocation. The *embolvedor* held responsible for gathering signatures on the petition received for his trouble a two-month suspension from his job and a warning that he would be dismissed permanently if he continued with such "excesses."[59] No further action was taken by the *recontadores* or *embolvedores.*

After wages, promotions provoked considerable controversy and anxiety among workers, primarily as a result of what was an essentially static work pool at the supervisory level. At the same time, the inconsistent use of both rational and patrimonial criteria for appointments fostered resentment among the workers in much the same way as it did among the lower-rank bureaucrats. Doña Manuela Antonia Vera Villavicencia, a *recontadora* in the Oaxaca manufactory, applied to become a *guarda* or *sobrestanta* but was refused on the grounds that there were other workers with greater seniority who would be offended if she were given the promotion.[60] In 1819, however, the *maestras* of the Mexico City manufactory petitioned against "unfair" promotions of women less qualified than they to the positions of *guardas del registro*. The usual promotional sequence, a combination of seniority and merit, was *cigarrera, recontadora, embolvedora, maestra,* and then *sobrestanta* and *guarda*. A complicating element in this period was a viceregal order that war widows, generally Spanish women, were to be given preference for supervisory positions in the Mexico City manufactory. When implemented, it resulted in the placement of inexperienced Spanish women in the highest and best-paid supervisory positions, at the cost of experienced women workers. The administrator denied the validity of the *maestras'* complaints.[61]

A striking instance of worker resistance concerned the attempts to introduce various machines into the Mexico City manufactory discussed in Chapter 5. Such experiments, designed to perfect machines which would minimize wastage of raw materials, were frustrated due, in part, to sabotage by a group of workers. What is unclear, however, is the extent to which the 'saboteurs' were influenced by the administrator or had their own reasons to resist the machines. Accusations of sabotage surrounded the manufactory administrator, as investigators speculated that "it could be that the workers, to oblige Romaña as their immediate boss, or through capriciousness, without his orders, have worked with malicious intent. To this is attributed the placing of a small stone which damaged the machine so that it failed to produce the expected amount of tobacco."[62] Since the machines were never introduced and no more was heard about them, the case against the paleo-Luddites was not pursued.

The arbitration sought by workers encompassed antagonisms among the workers themselves and between workers and management. Occasionally, however, the workers sought aid from the monopoly administration to help solve their domestic problems, outside of the manufactory, which suggests that they took the idea of paternal obligation seriously. In 1800 several cigarette rollers complained of the excessive rents demanded of them in the *villa* of Guadalupe.[63] Prior to the opening of the manufactory, local residents were cautioned not to increase rents because of a sudden influx of people who came to work there. Rents averaged between 12 and 16 reales per month; after the opening of the manufactory, they jumped to 36 reales. The architect assigned to appraise the level of monthly rents suggested, in accordance with the state of the accommodation he examined, that a monthly rent of 30 reales was fair. The *fiscal* finally found in favor of the workers and decreed in 1805 that property owners must maintain their rents at the levels which existed prior to the establishment of the manufactory in the *villa*.[64]

Individual petitions, which reflected the workforce at its most atomized, also flowed into the administrator's office. Workers attending to their own needs and those of their families sought wage increases, promotions, pensions, retribution for abusive treatment at the hands of the supervisors, in short, improvement of their existing situation. In 1786 Juan José Ruiz, a worker in the Mexico City manufactory for twenty years, had suffered for two years from muscle spasms and could no longer work as a cigarette roller. Married, with two young sons, he had contributed 3 pesos annually to the Concordia funds and now requested that he be paid a pension. Although the final ruling on Ruiz's case could not be found, it is likely that his request would have been granted and a pension paid in accordance with Concordia rules.[65]

Workers' complaints often reflected antagonisms towards manufactory management. Specific individuals became the focus of aggression and represented the physical embodiment of workers' problems, perceived as "bad government." For the workers in the Mexico City manufactory, their nemesis proved to be the administrator. The general consensus among the tobacco workers was that the administrator was their "enemy" and they described him as a "despot" and "tyrant." For his part, the administrator complained of the toll that an excessively large manufactory workforce took on him with the daily flood of complaints and petitions. The workers' grievances concentrated on "maligning others of better merit or me . . . because I refuse to accede to their requests."[66]

The reactions of the colonial state to the workers' penchant for complaint bring to mind a point made by E. P. Thompson in his now much criticized, but still much quoted, article on the moral economy of the English crowd. Thompson argued that "this moral economy impinged very generally upon eighteenth century government and thought and did not only intrude at moments of disturbance."[67] Perhaps this is best illustrated in the Mexican case by the fact that the manufactory administrator's decisions were clearly guided by assessments of workers' reactions, usually negative, to changes in their daily routine. A clear example is to be found in the circumstances surrounding an investigation of Concordia funds in 1781. The beginning of the investigation coincided with Holy Week. The *dirección general* argued that although loans were normally advanced to the workers during the feast, with the investigation in process, no advances should be made. The administrator countered this suggestion. "Knowing the character and way of thinking of these people . . . we will have a riot aimed at the *dirección general* or the royal palace to request the loan."[68] For the administrator, the issue was not whether the action suggested was justified but how to avoid conflict. The loans were paid. Even with such preemptive actions, however, worker discontent could not always be bargained away.

State-worker relations, for the most part, reflect a continuity of Spanish imperial practice which encouraged negotiation and compromise, despite the centralizing and sometimes confrontational actions of the Bourbon state. That resolutions made by the monopoly were not always made in favor of the workers' petitions, and that the workers did not perpetually take to the streets suggests a general acceptance of the authority which made such decisions and its legitimate right to do so. There were limits to compromise, however, which resulted in collective protest by the tobacco workers. Worker dissatisfaction could escalate into walkouts and marches on the royal palace, work stoppages, shouting matches, and planned strikes (albeit in a primitive form), in other words, "bargaining by riot," a strategy which continued to be used by manufactory workers in the 1830s and 1840s. In the remainder of this chapter we will examine the most serious examples of state-worker conflict which demonstrate the causes and contingencies of such conflict. They serve to clarify further the nature of worker grievances, the responses of the state, and shed some light on the workers' perceptions of power, authority, and a moral order.

The first example of conflict is not actually concerned with strikes or street violence but with a protracted, successful legal battle of the tobacco workers against the *dirección general*'s attempts to abolish the Concordia. Although the final resolution in favor of the workers also worked to the advantage of the monopoly, the workers probably perceived the decision in their favor to be a result of a fair investigation, which only reaffirmed the paternalistic qualities of their employer.

Between 1770 and 1793 the Concordia's management became the

focus of suspicion, attack and investigation. Practically from its founding, an examination of the Concordia's account books from 1770 until 1783 revealed what was termed "an intolerable abuse and disorder in the management of the funds," disorder which included embezzlement by several members of the Concordia's council.[69] The immediate response of the *dirección general* and the manufactory administrator was to press for the Concordia's abolition. They argued that *concordantes* often failed to receive fair compensation in accordance with their contributions. They advised that the Concordia should be abolished, on the grounds that the majority of workers neither wanted nor benefitted from its operations, that all loans to workers should be called in, and that Concordia property (houses) should be sold.[70] The evidence suggests that behind allegations of such corporate mismanagement and abuse of the workers, lay the *dirección general*'s fear of the corporate qualities of the Concordia and the "representative voice so inclined to influence the very movements which one tries to avoid."[71] The workers, for once acting collectively as a *"cuerpo de varias clases"* (association of various classes), argued that they did not wish their Concordia abolished, only its "despotic management."[72] The determination of the workers to keep their Concordia is not difficult to understand. For many it was the only thing which stood between them and destitution. In a statement to the viceroy, despite threats from the administrator, the workers outlined the reforms necessary to eliminate past abuses: a new election of *conciliarios* to supervise the management, collection, disbursement, and investment of Concordia funds, and a reassertion of their "right" to elect officers. They requested that the chest which contained Concordia funds be moved out of the manufactory altogether and into the Hospital de San Juan de Dios and expressed their "right" to decide whether to remain at home when ill or to enter one of the hospitals.[73] Should their arguments be accepted, the workers' spokesmen argued, "with time and good government, we will have some of the most considerable funds in the city."[74]

The next decade witnessed an ongoing series of complaints, countercomplaints, and manipulative actions on the administrator's part to discredit the workers' actions. In retaliation, stubborn and persistent, the workers continued to petition the viceroy. With the aid and representation of José Toraia, the *procurador del número de la Real Audiencia* (solicitor), the workers explained the need for the Concordia and exposed the illegal practices of the administrator and his supporters.[75] The administrator's main ploy consisted of placing his own creatures from among the workers as the 'elected' *concil-*

iarios, who opposed the demands of the workers. A favorite tactic was intimidation of workers. When Marcelino Soto tried to collect signatures for a petition which outlined the workers' grievances, the administrator threatened him with imprisonment and the loss of his job if he continued with the petition.[76]

In 1791, ten years after the initial investigation began, Viceroy Revillagigedo decided against the abolition of the Concordia and ordered immediate implementation of revised Concordia regulations designed to prevent further abuses. Responsibility for their implementation was delegated to the *oidor* Don Ciriaco González Carbajal in his role as "protector" of the workers. The original governing regulations were finally amended and approved in 1792. While the colonial state may have taken its Christian and moral duties seriously to protect the poor and encourage them to better themselves, it did so with one eye on profit. The revisions represented a move by the *dirección general* to use the Concordia as a means to enforce what manufactory regulations had failed to achieve—regular attendance of workers.[77] The reforms made access to Concordia contributions increasingly dependent upon regularity of work in the manufactories. Death benefits were restricted to those who had worked in the manufactory for at least eight years, and all other benefits to a minimum of one year. Those workers who stopped working for at least a month, even though they had paid their weekly contributions, lost their benefits.[78] If they chose to return to the manufactory, "benefit" time had to built up from the time they reentered. Those workers who attended regularly year after year gained the security of access to loans, a daily income when sick, and assurance of a decent burial; those who did not found themselves excluded from Concordia benefits.[79] All of this was predicated on the assumption that efficient records would be maintained to prevent further abuse, fraud, and embezzlement. Significantly, clause 15 of the new regulations specified that "The original objective for which [the Concordia] was created must be observed in this manufactory, and that is to make sacrifices and place ourselves in the best service of the king."[80] The clause also stipulated that all supervisors were to remain vigilant and, at the slightest sign of disobedience or unruliness, the administrator was to be informed so that the perpetrators could be placed in the manufactory jail and await the viceroy's decision as to punishment.

Interpretations of the Concordia and the decision of the colonial state to permit its continuation vary. Some historians argue that it became the "tool" of the monopoly through which to dominate and control the workers.[81] We do not disagree that the Concordia was used to strengthen control over the workers' movements and to enforce regular attendance, but we would make two additional observations. The fact that there was no outcry against the revised Concordia regulations may reflect approval of them by many of the workers who worked regularly, expected to receive the benefits from their contributions, and, not surprisingly, wanted a more honest management of their funds. We would also argue that the Concordia possessed a wider symbolic importance for the workers, which transcended the issue of reformed regulations, and which countenanced their sense of independence. Suggestive here is their concern for the ability to control both institutional and personal space, as illustrated by two of the workers' demands already cited: removal of the Concordia treasury from the actual physical space of the manufactory to the Hospital de San Juan de Dios and the workers' insistence on their right to choose where to be ill.[82] The first was not implemented, but workers retained the right to choose whether to be cured in hospital or in their homes.

For the duration of Bourbon control of the tobacco manufactories, only three protests occurred, and only one of them required the presence of troops to restore order. A plan to burn part of the Mexico City manufactory and to kill the administrator was discovered and aborted in 1797. All of these events occurred in the Mexico City manufactory, although there is evidence that workers in the other manufactories were not passive. We will look briefly at the causes of the riots, their organization, and administrative response to them, and then draw some general conclusions about the 'politics' of riots.

The first outburst occurred on 6 September 1780, when two hundred workers from the Mexico City manufactory marched on the viceregal palace to protest an increased workload which did not, according to their understanding, incur increased wages. The workers received orders from the manufactory administration to produce an additional 250 cigarettes per day. Workers from the Puebla manufactory submitted petitions protesting the decision, while workers in Querétaro took to the streets and tried to prevent their fellow workers from entering the manufactory.[83] The second incident took place in Mexico City on 30 December 1782, when workers were ordered home due to a general inventory of manufactory stock (traditionally the last two days of December were reserved for this practice). Immediately following the announcement, "up went the cries and out they went to the palace . . . the mass entered without respect for the Guard, occupying the patios, stairs, and corridors. The extraordinary noise aroused the viceroy Mayorga who, on determining the cause with great prudence ordered the administrator to allow them to work. The workers were thus pacified and carried the order in triumph."[84]

In response to the workers' actions, a viceregal decree was posted on the entrance to the work *patios* and read out loud to the workers. The decree made very clear that monopoly authorities would not tolerate rioting and violent action. Any protesters would be dismissed immediately and their leaders apprehended, accused of sedition, and dismissed; if they could not be identified, all workers present in the area of shouting and commotion would be dismissed.[85]

The third protest, which we shall refer to as the Paper Riot, was clearly the most serious from both the monopoly's and the workers' perspectives. It also provides the clearest evidence of attempts to organize a strike. The origins of the controversial reform which culminated in the call for a strike are to be found in monopoly attempts to rationalize production and to reduce theft and waste of cigarette paper, as we saw in Chapter 6. Spain's wars and embargos interrupted shipments of paper, which called for economy of use and stockpiling. Paper shortages were made worse by 'appropriation' of paper by workers and wastage through careless rolling. The solution was to exercise greater control by making the cigarette rollers prepare their paper at work, as their first task each morning.

Following the posting of new orders in the Mexico City manufactory, which decreed that workers were no longer permitted to take paper home at night, petitions were submitted in the usual manner by cigarette rollers to protest the order. Denial of their request to suspend the reform provoked a hostile reaction. Posters were placed on the manufactory walls, some of which contained '*picardias*,' or malicious statements (unfortunately, their content was not revealed), appealing to their co-workers not to go to work the following day.[86] On Monday morning, 13 January 1794, an estimated crowd of 1,400 women and men workers (approximately one-quarter of the cigarette rollers) marched on the viceregal palace, shouting and demanding repeal of the order. Troops were ordered to dispel the crowds and make them return to work in the manufactory. Reportedly by 10:30 a.m. everyone had returned to work.[87] Once again, representatives in the "name of the workers" (both men and women) petitioned for the revocation of the order. They argued that the preparation of paper was simple but arduous and that a worker could not roll and twist in the same day without damaging his or her fingers and shoulders. Preparation at home with the help of family members took anywhere from one-half to two hours. The representatives conceded that theft and substitution of poor for high-quality monopoly paper occurred but argued that it actually was not a very advantageous practice because poor-quality paper could not be worked easily and quickly and jeopardized completion of a *tarea*.[88]

Assessments were made as to the long-term effects of the new work order on both workers and manufactory production. The manufactory administrator argued that, in the long term, the rate of production and the quality of products would decline. Preparation of paper at the beginning of each day placed an excessive burden on the workers. The workers, attempting to complete their *tareas* despite the extra work, would become exhausted and ill.[89] As a result of the investigation, the reform was quickly abolished. By 26 January 1794, two weeks after the riot, preparation of paper in workers' homes was practiced once again. To reassure the workers and as an act of mediation, Don Pedro Jacinto Valenzuela, the *alcalde del crimen*, went to the manufactory and announced to the assembled workers and supervisors the monopoly's intention to reestablish the old system. The workers' representatives responded by proclaiming their gratitude to the king, saying that "only with silence can we thank you. There is no other language more meaningful for a prince as perfect as your excellency."[90]

The *fiscal* was particularly concerned at the organization and scale of the riot, especially since the workers were not without a 'representative voice', yet had resorted to mob violence. He ordered that notices be placed throughout the manufactory, which made clear that in future any complaints or grievances must be made through the supervisors; if not, they would not be considered.[91] Don Pedro Jacinto Valenzuela received orders to investigate and discover those responsible for organizing the riot. Four men were implicated: José Baldemaría, a cigarette roller and author of the document which called on the workers to walk out and strike, and his cohorts José María Soria y Vélez, Paulino López, and Lino Córdoba. Baldemaría was prohibited from ever working in a tobacco manufactory again. López, Córdoba, and Soria y Vélez each received a four-month suspension from work.[92]

With the original method now reinstated, greater vigilance was required over the movement of stocks of paper to prevent the 'black market' trade practiced by the workers. The appropriation of paper has already been discussed. By all accounts, it continued even after the introduction of severe penalties and repeated orders against fraudulent use or theft of paper. In 1798 three workers were dismissed from the Mexico City manufactory for illegal trading in cigarette paper. The testimony of the accused revealed that a worker, Agustín Mondragón, met Marcos Gutiérrez, a *sellador*, in a wine tavern in the Calle de San Juan. The latter asked Mondragón if he wished to buy paper. After 15 May, along with Joaquín del Castillo, Mondragón purchased three, sometimes four, *cuadernos* on a daily basis for 1 real or 1/2 real. On discovery of such an arrangement, Gutiérrez was made to stand in the registry with the contraband paper hung around his neck. Mondragón was placed in the stocks. Eventually, all three were dismissed permanently from the manufactory.[93]

The resolutions of worker protest reveal the state's concessions to worker demands but also its actions designed to remove the possibility of such collective protest happening again. In the case of the Paper Riot, after a few months of the new system, with or without worker protest, the old method of paper preparation would undoubtedly have been reestablished to avoid a fall in cigarette production. However, the important considerations here are, first, that the resolution was ostensibly in the workers' favor, which affirmed the justice of the procedure of investigation and resolved the uncertainties created by the intended reforms, and, second, that the colonial state remained unwilling to undertake economic innovations at the price of social peace. After 1794 no further attempts were made by the Bourbon administrators to implement reforms in the organization of production in the manufactories. There was only one further instance of collective action on the part of the workers, uncharacteristically violent in its intention to burn some sheds in the manufactory and kill the manufactory administrator and anyone else who tried to stop them. The plan was discovered and aborted. The reason behind such violence was workers' perceptions that recently reduced *tareas* were unnecessary, especially as they believed there was plenty of paper in store in the manufactory. To make matters worse, there was a widespread rumor that new workers were being hired at the same time that *tareas* were being reduced. Selection of the administrator as target illustrates the common phenomenon of the "personalization" of workers' grievances.[94] As James Scott has suggested, "If personalization is partly a myth, then it is a powerful, politically enabling myth."[95] There were no reports of strikes or large-scale riots after the aborted effort of 1797. Petitions, negotiations, shouting matches, and walkouts continued apace as part of the daily negotiation between the workers and the monopoly.

The Paper Riot of 1794 confirmed the colonial state's worst fears and laid bare the contradictions of Bourbon state-building and the sometimes tenuous compatibility between social stability and economic prosperity. The ministers of the Real Tribunal and Audiencia de la Contaduría Mayor de Cuentas de México, in viewing the workers' 'record' of behavior up until 1796, argued that it was necessary to understand the reasons behind such 'commotions.' In general, they believed, the tobacco workers were happy with the little they earned and "their ideas and thoughts do not extend to sophisticated undertakings, nor to the interruption or disturbance of the rules of good order."[96] The motives for the three outbursts were simply to express dissatisfaction with rulings believed to be unfair and prejudicial to their work and incomes, although that certainly did not excuse the strategies adopted. None of the riots were directed at disturbing the peace of the neighborhood or at the well-being of the state. There was no evidence of any conspiracy to arouse the public or encourage violent sedition against the king or government. The ministers concluded that, with better management, the riots could have been avoided. To avoid repetition of such movements, the administrator needed to abolish any abuses and keep good order.[97] The ministers of the Real Tribunal de Cuentas denied that the workers constituted a political threat to Mexico City. "The majority of workers lack healthy principles and good education . . . although they work for a daily wage which provides their basic necessities, many prefer to indulge in vice, most commonly the drinking of pulque, *aguardiente*, or both, even when they cannot afford to. . . . At the same time, they are possessed of a timid and submissive spirit which makes them obedient and quick to carry out any orders, especially when aided by the troops, which they naturally respect."[98] Such soothing rhetoric, however, did not prevent a rapid move to rationalize and reduce the number of workers in the Mexico City manufactory in order to exert greater control. Not surprisingly, the decision to reorganize the manufactories and reduce the size of the one in Mexico City acquired greater urgency between 1794 and 1797. By 1798 the Mexico City manufactory labor force had been reduced by almost 2,000 workers, and bitter and protracted discussions as to whether the manufactories should or should not be abolished began. Another solution to social instability among the tobacco workers was to employ only women in the manufactories, particularly as cigarette rollers, a policy which was put into practice, as we saw in chapter 6.

The motivations of the workers, their actions, and testimonies illustrate their priorities and their capacity to act collectively, if not unanimously. Descriptions of the investigations into the 1794 and 1797 actions show how the workers were organized and supported by associations outside of, as well as inside, the manufactory, and demonstrate the strength of local intelligence networks. Workers repeatedly referred to conversations and petition gathering which took place in the barrios close to the manufactory, in the *pulquerías*, in the churches, and even in local hospitals, where it was an ailing worker who unwittingly revealed the protesters' plans.[99] Testimony from workers questioned after the Paper Riot demonstrated a mélange of strategies which ranged from the circulation of petitions to the more violent tactic of pelting with stones those who tried to enter the manufactory. There seemed to be a code of honor among most of the workers. When asked if they knew the names of the protest leaders, they either could not or would not reveal them. The supervisors responded in a different manner, apparently carrying out their mandate to protect the stability of the work force (and protecting their jobs) and admitted they would recognize the culprits.

But why did some workers believe themselves justified in their strike action against the monopoly? The participants and instigators of the strike, as far as we can ascertain, were all cigarette rollers, men and women, and made up one-quarter of the total number of cigarette workers. Other than these general characteristics, there is no information on the individual backgrounds of the participants, so we cannot know if they possessed other characteristics in common, for example, if they were recently employed, if they were migrants, and so on. We would speculate that they probably represented workers who were most recently employed and, therefore, earning the lowest piecework rates, and who worked only sporadically. But this is pure conjecture based on a suggestive theory of Jacques Rancière, who argues that "militant activity is perhaps inversely proportional to the organic cohesion of the trade, the strength of the organization, and the ideology of the group. . . . the highest level of militancy existed among the poor relations, those trades that were a crossroads or a catchall; . . . A strong militant identity among workers in a craft seems to imply a weak collective professional identity and vice versa."[100] Such a construction has an intuitive appeal and is possible given the variations within the manufactory work force, but, without a better sense of the strikers' general characteristics, it is impossible to make a compelling argument one way or the other. There is little doubt, however, that the protestors were provoked by a reform which threatened their livelihood and their standard of living and which would remove not only the flexibility of time which preparation of paper at home gave to them, but also access to a commodity which was used to supplement their income. It may even be that the Concordia reform, which demanded a certain commitment from the workers in terms of time spent in the manufactory in return for access to benefits, affected their perception of monopoly employment.

The testimonies also shed light on the 'spontaneity' of the riots, divisions among the workers, and responses from the public. As was the case with many other so-called 'spontaneous' riots, the workers planned, petitioned, and organized to present their grievances through legal channels. Workers' testimonies also provide evidence of a divided work force. It was the supervisors and guards who informed the administrator of the impending strike and protest after their accidental discovery of the plan, but not without weighing their options before they did so. That they harbored fears of being stoned by angry workers was quite evident, but they believed themselves independent enough to defy worker sanctions—an indication of freer association rather than of a tightly-knit community within the confines of the manufactory.[101] This also suggests that the reform did not affect them directly since they received fixed daily wages and that they preferred their jobs to protest. Outside of the Mexico City manufactory, the 'street' intelligence network was active, for conspirators and informants alike. Significantly, the reports provided by tavern owners and local artisans suggest at the very least suspicion and fear of the workers, confirming the fragmentation and divisions within Mexico's nascent working classes.[102]

What the workers' actions demonstrate above all is a form of plebian moral economy in action. The attempted prohibition against paper preparation at home provoked a response from the workers which highlighted two fears: a reduced capacity to complete daily work loads and loss of access to a commodity which assured them of a supplemental income. All of the workers' collective actions represented a hostile reaction in response to arbitrary action which permitted no time for adjustment and violated the sense of control and justice which the customary practice of petition permitted. The protests of the workers and the social and economic context within which they were played out resemble the situation of the journeymen of Nantes and Lyons in eighteenth-century France. "With the goal of mastership no longer a viable ideal . . . the frequent struggles between journeymen and masters over conditions of work and pay make sense both in the context of the working-man's declining economic situation and in terms of such workers' decisions to behave as if they had little or no hope of advancement in their trade guilds."[103]

The tobacco workers have left us precious little evidence to better understand their actions, beliefs, and aspirations, but perhaps enough to at least glimpse a part of their world. A final comment, then, and several speculations about the significance of the workers' actions and discourse.[104] The workers' strategies were eclectic and straddled the sacred and profane; they called on the Virgin of Guadalupe and on the monarch, but they also called on lawyers and upon one another and their families.[105] A similar eclecticism runs through their written expression, but the dominant pattern which emerges from the workers' discourse and which represents their vision of the world and its order is most closely linked with religious beliefs. The language of the workers is clearest in the documentation which the Paper Riot and Concordia investigation produced.

During the investigation of the Paper Riot of 1794, workers' testimony showed how the concept of being a "good Christian" could be interpreted as a legitimation of defiance as well as obedience. Miguel Landetegui, for example, a thirty-two-year-old creole and cigarette roller, described how, on the evening before the strike of 1794, he met José Espinosa in a church. Landetegui asked how it was possible for Espinosa to consider himself a good Christian if he would not make it clear to the administrator the damage which the new paper regulations would cause to the workers. On hearing Espinosa's response that a church was no place to discuss such matters, Landetegui responded that his concerns were indeed for "the greater honor and glory of God."[106]

During the protracted fight over the Concordia, the workers were careful in their petitions to profess loyalty to and trust in their king as "a Christian prince." At the same time, they compared themselves to the Children of Israel as seeking freedom from the "oppression" and "tyranny" of their own latter-day Egyptians, the manufactory administrator and his cronies.[107]

Such fragmentary evidence cannot be made to bear too heavy a burden, but we offer the following speculations about the tobacco workers' beliefs and ideas. Abuse of justice brought forth actions reminiscent of a moral economy at work, but construed through the idiom of popular religion. Relations of power and authority, of right and wrong, of obligation, were conceptualized through references to Christian behavior and based on biblical analogies which dealt with justice and power and its abuses. As Robin Briggs has argued in the case of early modern France, "Religion indeed provided the only fully developed set of concepts through which men could rethink their relationship to one another, to society and its institutions and to the physical world."[108] The workers' use of a religious idiom enabled them to articulate and defend the legitimacy of their demands while at the same time reaffirming their loyalty to their Christian king. When the workers protested, they sought to remind the monarch of his obligations, not to challenge him. Their perceptions of social relations and hierarchy were embedded in Christian teachings. At the apex of this elusive moral order of the workers was the king, who was to be obeyed, but who, in return, was to administer justice, a justice which incorporated the Old Testament meaning of judgment as being synonymous with good government. The workers appeared to place themselves in a reciprocal relationship with the king, and their petitions consistently reflect their perceptions of acceptable behavior by their supervisors and, by extension, their expectations of the government. Such expectations included certain "rights" which they claimed for themselves: the right to respect, the right not to be abused, the right to retain control over time and materials, in short, the right to justice.

Clearly, then, religion remained an effective force in the lives of the tobacco workers, as it did for the masses in general, and a force which the colonial state recognized.[109] Indeed, a major tactic of the state to pacify the workers was to request spiritual stormtroopers as well as military ones, particularly the Dominican fathers, "as they know this type of people and confess them."[110] What is not clear, however, is the degree to which the workers' actions were influenced by a wider conflict provoked by the Bourbon state's aggressive attacks on the Catholic Church, which reflected the moral dimensions of its absolutism. The antagonisms between church and state had social and cultural consequences. As David Brading has observed: "If the baroque culture of late Tridentine Catholicism succeeded in uniting both intellectual elite and the masses in common devotion and equal aesthetic delight, by contrast, its repudiation led to a growing division between educated opinion and popular religion."[111] Ultimately, what the terms of interaction between the colonial state and the tobacco workers may have signified was the growth of competing discourses which reflected different views about the meaning of life, religion, and society in general.[112]

It is also fair to say, however, that whatever the content of the workers' and the colonial state's ideas, or the symbols of such ideas, they were not fixed and unchanging, but rather part of a slow dialectic with the wider economy and society. We finish with a description of a ceremony which provides an example of the way in which such a dialectic may be shaped. The ceremony, intended to signify continuity of the old regime, not change, contained one traditional and one new symbol of authority, legitimacy, and order.

The Mexican Insurgency of 1810 disrupted the functioning of the manufactories. Production became erratic and a number of workers were laid off. How the tobacco workers responded to the insurgency is poorly documented; their response to a deceptive peace less so. On 6 June 1820, the tobacco workers employed in the manufactory of the Villa de Guadalupe gathered in the main patio facing a portrait of Ferdinand VII and, with their administrator and supervisors, swore fealty and allegiance to their king and protector and to the Constitution of Cádiz. Reportedly, the solemnity of the ceremony of allegiance at its conclusion provoked "applause and rejoicing" and cries of "Long live the constitution and the king" by the workers.[113] Despite the turmoil and insecurity caused by the insurgency, the colonial state continued to rehearse its rituals of authority and, this time, reminded the workers of their obligations of loyalty and obedience.[114] At the same time, the celebration made an association between the king and the constitution as a source of legitimacy and justice. Although this is a very thin thread to work with, the ceremony raises an interesting question about representation and perception of authority, justice, and legitimacy, and how they are, in turn, perceived, formulated, and, perhaps, reformulated by the masses. We know from Rodney Anderson's study of the Mexican workers that the Mexican Constitution of 1857 played an important role in their militant actions and the justification of labor's demands.[115] The challenge remains to further identify and explain how, in the early decades of the Mexican Republic, the role and attributes of the monarch were transferred to the constitution in the beliefs of the Mexican workers.

The tobacco workers' experience and strategies permit us to draw certain conclusions related to wider questions about work, workers, and popular political action in late colonial Mexico. If the reorganization of the tobacco trade accelerated proletarianization, it was on very uneven terms, both in a material and an ideological sense, and subject to forces which simultaneously encouraged and impeded the formation of a wider class consciousness. Historians who have argued that the reorganization of the private tobacco shops transformed the tobacco shop owners and their workers into a homogenous work force of wage earners, have overstated the case.[116] If anything, the workers' actions resemble what Alf Lüdtke, in his study of the nineteenth-century German factory workers, has identified as *Eigensinn*, a phenomenon whereby work experience and domestic situation promoted a sense of collective identity and, at the same time, a corresponding sense of individualism.[117] He raises doubts about the ability of work experience to serve as a guide to political action and suggests that the relationship is not necessarily a derivative one. This is a particularly welcome antidote to attempts to correlate political action with specific occupations. Traditionally, for example, tobacco workers have been associated with a high propensity for labor militancy, a predilection explained through the structure of the work process associated with making cigars and cigarettes. A case in point is provided by Louise Tilly's analysis of female tobacco workers in the French state tobacco factories, who called twenty-seven strikes during a period of thirty years, virtually one a year.[118] Recent case studies of tobacco workers, however, challenge any predictive model which could be applied to tobacco workers in large manufactories in general and call for a rethinking of such a characterization. Most of all, they point to the importance of examining the specific political, social, and economic context in which work in any occupation is carried out. Both Jean Stubbs and Patricia Cooper argue that opposing forces counteracted sustained collective action among cigar and cigarette makers in Cuba and the U.S.[119] Similar contradictory influences prevailed among the manufactory workers in colonial Mexico, particularly in Mexico City. It is clear that the composition of the workers endowed them with a rather protean quality based on the associations and divisions discussed in this chapter and the varying evaluations of the impact of the manufactory regime on their lives.

A second consideration here is that the tobacco workers' protests, their motivations, objectives, and strategies resemble generalized descriptions of protest in late colonial Mexico which may be summed up as being of the 'king and church' variety.[120] At the same time, they provide an example whereby more 'modern' forms of association (in the workers' case, large scale association within the manufactories, the *cuerpos* and the Concordia) cannot necessarily be assumed to have had more 'modern', objectives.[121] They defy simple categorization of 'traditional' and 'modern', 'preindustrial' and 'industrial', as did many urban rioters in eighteenth- and nineteenth-century Europe.[122]

What conclusions can we draw about state-worker relations in late Bourbon Mexico? The examples of state-worker conflict illustrate a paradox which confronted the colonial state and the monopoly management whereby associations created to maintain loyalty to and dependence upon the monopoly could be used to challenge the state's mandate. As a result, to renegotiate relations and continually reestablish peace, the colonial state acted in a concessive manner but attempted, at the same time, to turn such concessions to the monopoly's advantage. Both resulted in compromise solutions which, on the one hand, may have increased the state's control over the workers, but which, on the other hand, satisfied to some degree the demands made by the workers. Although the colonial state increased its control over workers' actions, they proved able to defend their interests, to negotiate for that 'better bargain' and, in the process, contributed to the limitation of both monopoly development and the powers of the colonial state. Nevertheless, the workers remained fragmented and retained an abiding faith in the king as a solution to, rather than as a part of, the problems they experienced. If we stand back from the workers' actions and look from a distance, their search for a 'better bargain' was not in vain, but they lived in a world in which they experienced "the ebb and flow of large oppressions, and small freedoms."[123] They possessed clear ideas of what constituted fair treatment and were quick to react if management violated the boundaries of such 'fairness'. They fought for a confraternity which in the absence of a decent life, assured them of a decent death, forged new associations with one another, and engaged in behavior which helped to shape the working day to their needs, behavior which sometimes brought them into open conflict with their employers and which would continue to do so long after the demise of the Bourbon State.

8. Postscript

THE TOBACCO MONOPOLY may have survived the Mexican insurgency of 1810 and the break from Spain, but it emerged bankrupt and in disarray. The monopoly, as it existed in Mexico between 1765 and 1856, fell into two distinct periods: one between 1765 and 1812, the last year in which the monopoly under Bourbon management financed itself and provided a surplus, and the other between 1813 and 1856. During the insurgency years between 1812 and 1821, the state expected the monopoly to continue to produce revenues, which were immediately extracted for support of the royalist forces. The systematic decapitalization of the monopoly plunged its operations into chaos; for the first time in fifty years, it could not finance itself. Such was the strategic value of the monopoly that, during the insurgency years, the state resorted to borrowing in order to continue to finance its operations so it could still be used as collateral to raise further loans effectively, borrowing money in order to be able to borrow more. The viceroy's requests for loans were met with demands for mortgages on all *alcabala* receipts of Mexico City, one half of which were pledged to obtain adequate capital to keep the monopoly, the gunpowder factory, and the royal mint in operation.[1] If the Bourbons believed the tobacco monopoly to be a fiscal golden goose, they managed to kill the creature with great alacrity.

The fact that the monopoly's operations were devastated by the insurgency is hardly surprising. What is, perhaps, more surprising is that tobacco continued to be produced under exceptionally adverse circumstances. The effect of the insurgency on tobacco production in the *villas* was disastrous. The estimated damage caused by the insurgency to the region amounted to at least half a million pesos, with 606 deaths during the eleven years of war in Orizaba.[2] Pleas for aid and protection by the planters' representative, Pablo de la Llave, at the Spanish Cortes were ignored.[3]

The depressing descriptions by the *director general* of the planters' situation were, for the most part, accurate. Credit and payment for crops were made in *libranzas* (bills of exchange) to be drawn against the monopoly treasury. To acquire cash, some planters exchanged their *libranzas* for goods, only to resell them for cash needed to cure their tobacco. Others found themselves at the mercy of merchants who cashed their *libranzas*, but at discount rates of 10 percent, 15 percent, or as high as 25 percent of the original value.[4] Desperate planters made futile journeys to Mexico City to plead their case personally with the *director general* and requested immediate credit to enable them to begin new production. All the *director general* could do was to "give them sufficient money to cover the cost of their return trip back to the *villas*."[5] No major credit advances were made to the planters of the *villas* after 1812. As the monopoly began to run up deficits and debts to planters and merchant speculators alike, the planters were exposed to decapitalization. Those who managed to continue to grow tobacco turned increasingly to contraband dealers.

The changes experienced by the manufactories are less clear. Shortages of paper, tobacco, and capital resulted in layoffs and closures. The Mexico City manufactory's operations, minimal as they may have been, were relocated to the Hospico de Pobres on a temporary basis in 1815, while armaments became the new product of the tobacco manufactory. It was the new republican government that decided to revive tobacco production in its old place in Atlampa, where employees continued to receive the same salary as under their Bourbon predecessors.[6] By 1825 a total of 705 male workers and 2,531 female workers were employed, a population which included workers absorbed in 1822 from the Guadalupe manufactory.[7] In 1828 the Bourbon tobacco manufactory of Mexico City was finally abolished and replaced the following year by the national manufactory of cigars and cigarettes.[8]

Throughout the insurgency period, the colonial state became more dependent upon private speculators. When, in 1816, the monopoly found itself virtually without funds and supplies of tobacco products, the decision was finally taken by the *dirección general* to negotiate a series of contracts with private citizens to raise capital as quickly as possible. In exchange for money and paper, portions of the remaining supplies of cigars and cigarettes were sold to civilians, generally merchants, who could sell the goods in areas where the monopoly could no longer operate safely. One of the most important contracts negotiated was with Juan Bautista Lobo in 1816. A merchant and member of the Consulado de Veracruz, Bautista Lobo paid 200,000 pesos to the monopoly, which was promptly dispatched to the *villas* to pay for tobacco. In addition, Bautista Lobo agreed to make monthly payments of 25,000 pesos: 15,000 pesos to be deposited in the monopoly's general treasury to finance the manufactories and transport; the remaining 10,000 pesos for use as an all-purpose general fund. Bautista Lobo was also obliged under the contract conditions to provide 50,000 reams of paper for the manufactories at a cost of 8 pesos per ream. All existing stocks of leaf in the *villas* were to be shipped to the general warehouses in Mexico City and Puebla. For his trouble, Bautista Lobo received supplies of cigars and cigarettes every month to be sold at the price he chose.[9]

In the first years after independence, the major concern of the Constituent Congress was how to finance the new state. It had few revenue sources left, especially with the devastation of the mining industry. The monopoly occupied a preeminent place in the reconstruction of public finances and the emerging relations between the national government and the states in early Republican Mexico, but its performance fell far short of expectations.

The initial consensus was in favor of abolishing the moribund monopoly, but contradictions abounded as contemporary economic thought grated against the needs of a struggling, embryonic, bankrupt Mexican state. The monopoly was denounced as contrary to the freedom and progress of man, morality, and the commercial interests of the Mexican people. The Mexican liberal José María Luis Mora gave no quarter when it came to a monopoly tainted by its Bourbon origins. "This monopoly was one of the most prejudicial to the public morale and to Mexican industry . . . it created a multitude of employees who through their swindles and immoral speculations . . . encouraged the most pernicious habits which have destroyed good faith."[10] Economically unacceptable, apparently in ruins, the monopoly was nonetheless retained, although its level of operations and restrictions was drastically cut. Monopoly regulation of the manufacture of cigars and cigarettes became an option for the individual Mexican states.[11] Farmers who wished to grow tobacco were required to apply to a local state representative of the monopoly (selected from the old Bourbon employees) and to stipulate the number of plants he wished to produce.

The congressional finance committee drafted laws which established the financial system of the central government and laid out the fiscal relations between the states and the government. In an initial annual budget, approximately 23 percent of government income was expected to come from tobacco revenues, matched in amount by import and export duties, *alcabalas*, and 30 percent from the states' contributions. According to an 1823 finance report, the government had lost almost 80 percent of the annual income from tobacco during and after the insurgency. Thereafter, the monopoly operations proved to be a source of disappointment. Tobacco revenues between 1825 and 1828 ranged from a low of 637,145 pesos to a high of 1,356,127 pesos.[12] Poor administration, contraband, and uncooperative states were repeatedly cited as reasons for the disappointing performance of the monopoly. The contribution of the monopoly to public revenues in the disastrous first decades of the Mexican Republic (until 1856, shortly after which the monopoly was completely abolished) never exceeded an estimated 9 percent and averaged 4 percent. Port taxes and foreign and domestic loans rapidly eclipsed tobacco revenues in total value.[13]

On 23 May 1829, organization and management of the tobacco monopoly was turned over to individual states which were to pay a production tax to the federal government, an order which left the states free to abolish the monopoly within their territorial jurisdiction if they so chose. By 1831, the *dirección general* had been abolished and replaced by the Compañía de la Renta del Tabaco, with five directors, three of whom were permanent and two temporary. The reorganization of administration made little difference. The appalling state of the Mexican treasury meant that it was in no position to manage an enterprise and the ailing monopoly fell prey to political groups in postindependence Mexico and joint-stock companies such as the Empresa del Tabaco, which gained exclusive rights to control the production, manufacture, and sale of tobacco.[14] Entrepreneurs who took over the monopoly's management were permitted to fix prices as they chose, which could be highly prejudicial to the planters. Such was the resentment from the planters that Rafael Argüelles, the grandson of Antonio Montes Argüelles, along with Lucas Alamán proposed that the Banco de Amortización should rent out monopoly rights for the departments of Mexico, Puebla, Oaxaca, and Veracruz to a company organized by them on behalf of the tobacco planters. The bank accepted Argüelles' proposal, but Argüelles and his supporters were outbid at a public auction for the rights of rental by a Mexico City lawyer, Manuel Castañeda Nájera. Castañeda secretly represented a company composed of important businessmen with interests in Mexico City, Guanajuato, and San Luis Potosí. After a number of protests by the planters, including a presentation of their grievances by Argüelles to the Mexican Supreme Court, the national government finally intervened. The settlement demanded that the *empresarios* in charge of the new company buy their tobacco exclusively from the Veracruz planters.[15] Contract conditions and prices nevertheless continued to be a source of conflict well into the 1850s, prior to the monopoly's abolition.[16]

The amount of attention directed toward the tobacco trade by the shrewdest entrepreneurs indicates "the unquestionable importance of the administration of the tobacco monopoly as one of the most productive activities of the epoch."[17] Indeed, the names of the outstanding nineteenth-century entrepreneurs dominate the negotiations for private control of the monopoly, names such as Manuel Escandón and Nicanor Béistegui. In 1849 the latter, with the aid of his father, became part of the management of the monopoly in Mexico City. His associates were Miguel Bringas, Manuel Escandón, and Manning and Mackintosh who, in 1848, negotiated a company contract with the government to manage the tobacco trade. In 1854 the government contracted the rental of the monopoly throughout the country, with the exception of Sinaloa, to the Compañía Arrendataria del Estanco del Tabaco. The company was formed by Manuel de Lizardi and Cayetano Rubio. Béistegui, Escandón, and Bringas became partners in the company. Short-lived, it was dissolved in 1859. Béistegui eventually sold all of his shares to Garruste, Labadie y Cía, who opened a major cigar factory in 1865. Ten years later, Ramón Balsa and his brother opened a cigar and cigarette factory in partnership in Veracruz, which eventually emerged as the most important and outstanding in the business. By the late 1890s the production of cigarettes in Mexico was dominated by three large companies, the Compañía Manufacturera El Buen Tono, La Cigarrera Mexicana, and La Tabacalera Mexicana, which, combined, controlled 62 percent of the domestic market. The remaining output was produced in hundreds of small shops distributed throughout Mexico.[18] The fate of the monopoly reflected the uncertainty of and shifts in the Mexican political economy of the nineteenth century. The monopoly was abolished in the spring of 1833, reestablished in 1847, and abolished again in 1856. It was finally resurrected in the twentieth century as Tabacalera Mexicana, established in 1972, to control the production of tobacco leaf for domestic and international companies.[19]

The financial needs of the colonial Spanish state determined the decision to establish the tobacco monopoly. In so doing, it created the largest single industry in Mexico, second only to silver mining. As a fiscal measure, the tobacco monopoly of colonial Mexico was a success and provides an example of the capacity of the colonial state to extract resources from its colonies. The state enterprise was capitalistic in its objectives to produce profits, and its manufactories depended on free wage labor. As a state enterprise, however, political and social objectives also influenced the monopoly's development. The state refused to risk changes which threatened to reduce the level of existing revenues, and sanctioned expedient policies to avoid disruptive political conflicts with planters or workers. The consequence for the monopoly was lack of investment and any innovations which could have improved its performance. Its management became increasingly characterized by conservatism rather than reform, which required investment and long-term planning.[20] In opting for safe monopoly profits, the enterprise was conducted along the lines of a 'satisficer' model as opposed to one in which the objective is to maximize profits. By the beginning of the nineteenth century, demand had outgrown the monopoly's productive capacities. The result was scarcity and contraband in tobacco. The monopoly's problems antedated the insurgency of 1810, which exacerbated, but did not create them.

One of the most difficult questions concerns the cost of the tobacco monopoly to the inhabitants and economy of colonial Mexico. This is related to a wider consideration of the general impact of government economic policies on the late-colonial economy. Theories of monopoly predict that it usually results in a net loss to society because it misallocates resources, charges excessive prices for its products, exploits its workers and suppliers, and creates impermanent employment. Monopoly sacrifices potential national income, because resources which cannot be used due to monopoly restrictions reduce the total income compared to what it would be in the absence of monopoly restrictions.[21] Assessments of the effects of tobacco monopolies on the economies of other Spanish American colonies, however, suggest that we cannot accept uncritically textbook theories about the consequences of monopoly. William McGreevy makes the orthodox argument that the tobacco monopoly in New Granada (Colombia), in combination with other Bourbon reforms, resulted in capital exports which reduced the potential capital stock in the country and hence the potential level of per capita income and consumption.[22] John Harrison views the results as somewhat more complex and argues that the export market in tobacco in Colombia developed under the guidance of the monopoly, rather than being stifled by it.[23] The cases of Venezuela and the Philippines suggest that the general population was deprived of a commercial activity, and the costs of monopoly were borne by suppliers and consumers through low purchase prices for tobacco and high prices for manufactured goods. At the same time, the studies of these countries' late-colonial economies suggest that the restrictive consequences of the monopoly's operations redirected resources, as opposed to leaving them idle. In Venezuela, monopoly revenues were employed in strengthening military defenses and the purchase of exportable agricultural commodities. Such expenditures provided substantial benefits to Venezuela, which offset, albeit not completely, the costs borne by suppliers and consumers and made them far less of a burden than the colonists were willing to concede.[24] In the case of the Philippines, the ban on tobacco production encouraged farmers no longer able to cultivate tobacco to produce other crops such as sugar and indigo, which became important export goods.[25]

In Mexico, the state reorganization of the monopoly went some way to creating a 'national' market in an economic context which was fundamentally composed of semiautarchic economic and cultural regions. It streamlined information about demand and coordinated production and distribution. There is even some suggestion that the manufactories resulted in increases in labor productivity. Exports of monopoly revenues in silver may have helped to keep inflation down. The major forward linkage per se was the manufacturing sector of the monopoly and the annual payments of 3,500,000 pesos distributed among administrators, bureaucrats, planters, and workers. Apart from the manufactories, however, there was no investment in New Spain's economy, but that had not been intended. At the same time, the monopoly possibly resulted in a contraction of the volume of trade. If we recall that the estimated value of the tobacco trade in 1746 was 12,348,000 pesos, the highest revenue earned under monopoly management in 1809 totalled 9,500,000 pesos, the rest of potential income probably lost to contraband. By placing the manufactories in a restricted number of towns, a widespread source of income among the rural poor, especially women and indigenous peoples, was eliminated. What remains difficult to evaluate, however, is the degree to which the resources released as a result of monopoly regulation found their way into other economic activities (legal and illegal) or remained idle. Even among those who worked for the monopoly, the benefits were uneven. Through its credit advances, the monopoly may have expanded the opportunities for small farmers and planters to produce tobacco on a larger scale and it certainly subsidized the intensification of tobacco production in the *villas*, but the major beneficiaries remained a small number of wealthy merchant-planters. No major transformation occurred in the relations of production, and, if the distribution of wealth was significantly altered, it leaned in the direction of the already prosperous or wealthy. The organization of tobacco production and the continuation of *avío* arrangements drained capital from the countryside and into the towns of Orizaba and Córdoba, and from there to the urban centers of Mexico, particularly Mexico City. Would both Mexico and the colonial state have been better off if the latter had simply imposed new taxes on the private tobacco industry? Again, it is difficult to say. Such speculation, however, depends upon one's assumptions about the role of the state in economic development and the conditions of colonial markets. In recent discussions of this question, we can discern two views of the role of the late-colonial state and economic development.[26] The first is that the Spanish state's regulatory and fiscal role misallocated resources which would not necessarily have been misallocated under free market conditions. The second is that we cannot assume that colonial Mexico possessed perfect market conditions, and that there were considerable market imperfections which misallocated resources independently of state regulation. It is also argued that Bourbon state intervention did not inevitably result in inefficient resource allocation, and that "resources redirected from agriculture into industry or mining experienced rising rather than falling productivity. Bourbon policies that promoted these shifts can hardly be thought of as inefficient particularly when the apparent level of unemployment in agriculture was high."[27] Like most economic activities in colonial Mexico, the monopoly was dependent on and ultimately restricted by its need for increased factors of supply necessary for growth, and it is unlikely that private tobacco production would have fared any differently. Either way, the preconditions for economic growth and transformation were not present. What the study of the monopoly also shows is how both market imperfections and Spanish colonialism reinforced one another to stifle its growth. In the end, however, it was the Mexican consumers and producers who paid the Bourbon piper in increased prices for monopoly products and low manufactory wages.

A study of the tobacco monopoly shows how a reorganization in taxation and state-building can affect social and economic interests, how it can consolidate them, eliminate them, or create new ones. The implementation of the monopoly affected the lives of thousands of people. Popular opposition and reaction ranged from contraband activities to petitions to be incorporated into the monopoly's operations, from hostility to tolerance and indifference. As Spain began to borrow increasing amounts of private capital to support government and defense costs, monopoly revenues acted as a source of capital and collateral, a de facto bank. Gradually, if begrudgingly, miners and merchants accepted its existence as a necessary tax, one which provided secure collateral for their seemingly never-ending loans to the colonial treasury. Indeed, the attraction of the monopoly as a tax already in place with a proven track record proved attractive to the Mexican liberals, despite their shibboleths which excoriated and condemned the monopoly.

The long-term impact of the monopoly on the social and economic makeup of the workers and planters was divergent. The political and economic objectives to displace the merchant-planters were unsuccessful, while the concentration of labor in the manufactories stimulated, unintentionally, popular political action among the workers. The actions taken by both of these groups, as they adjusted to their incorporation into monopoly operations, show us how they sought to satisfy their own needs based on a mutual interest in the monopoly's survival. It was the conditions under which work was carried out that were constantly renegotiated within the framework of monopoly operations, testimony to the continuity of a consensus state. The role of the state is clear in its attempts to create paternalist and co-optative relations with the tobacco workers and to provide institutions which channeled grievance and conflict. At the same time, the structure of the manufactories contributed to the capacity of the workers to resist unacceptable reforms through newly created corporate bodies. The manufactory workers carved out their own space, which enabled them to retain some autonomy over their lives and the content and pace of their work and to make their claim on the colonial state. Free wage labor was sufficient to bring workers to the manufactories, but the manufactory administrators could not transform the workers completely into a disciplined work force. The paradox of poverty and irregular work habits highlights the problem faced by employers in colonial Mexico but also by twentieth-century social historians. We have speculated in this study that the erratic attendance of workers at the tobacco manufactories suggests that survival was still not completely dependent upon a money wage. This must remain speculation until we have more microhistorical studies that document the daily lives of urban workers in late-eighteenth-century Mexico. Indeed, if this study has provided insights into the organization of the state tobacco manufactories, issues of work discipline, and the workers' responses, there are a number of questions which remain unanswered. Such questions range from how new social identities were formed in the tobacco manufactories among both men and women and how these represented their working identities, to how workers defined and formulated their positions in response to the wider political culture.

What also becomes evident is the way in which the Bourbon political economy helped to establish and consolidate sexual divisions of labor.[28] The colonial state may have expanded employment opportunities for women, but, through the recruitment of women as cigarette rollers and men as cigar makers, it helped to define the two occupations increasingly (although never exclusively) along gender lines. Cigarette rolling became associated with women's work and poorly remunerated. This occupational 'legacy' manifested itself, much to the detriment of women tobacco workers, when the manufacture of tobacco products was returned to the private sector between the 1830s and 1860s. By the 1880s three-quarters of Mexico's cigarette workers were women, the same proportion as at the end of the colonial period.[29] What began as a state reform, partly to help poor women in Mexico, unwittingly created the conditions for further deterioration of their position in the nineteenth century. Once the colonial state enterprise collapsed, divested of the protection of the corporate status which the state manufactory offered, the women workers emerged as even more fragmented, marginalized, and exploitable cheap labor for the private tobacco workshops. Their situation was only made worse by the general conditions for labor in nineteenth-century Mexico, as widespread unemployment of men marginalized women's bargaining position even further. If the reorganization of the colonial state and economy created the tobacco manufactories in 1765, the construction of the Mexican state and economy abolished them in 1856. What determined and shaped the capacity of the workers to continue to defend their interests in the next few decades and what role the Mexican state played in helping or hindering them constitute another chapter in the formation of the Mexican working class, one which has yet to be written.

In the case of the planters, monopoly policy and practice tended to strengthen the existing power structure and agrarian relations in the *villas*, despite attempts to change the financing of tobacco production. These relations persisted into the late nineteenth century. The incorporation of the *villas* into the tobacco monopoly's structure occurred at a time when tobacco as a commercial crop was becoming more important to their economies. As such, the monopoly accelerated a trend already in progress, but the sustained growth, experienced in particular by Orizaba, became increasingly dependent on a single crop. These constituted the costs and consequences of Spanish colonialism. The development of the tobacco economy, particularly in Orizaba, built on the existing planter elite and consolidated its power. While the smaller tobacco *rancheros* probably benefited in some measure from monopoly financing, the changing costs of production, which the monopoly's policy on purchase prices did little to help, began to undermine their capacity to withstand crises. The monopoly's ambitions , in turn, were undermined by the co-optation of wealthy planters and represented a return to traditional alliances between the colonial state and elites. Tobacco production under monopoly management was characterized by an increasing concentration of wealth and emphasis on the processing of tobacco by a few wealthy merchant-planters, who financed Indian *aviados* to produce the leaf. The survival of small properties, the *ranchos* and Indian villages, contributed to a limited supply of labor and kept wages high, which further reinforced the *avío* system in spite of monopoly credit.

The Bourbons may have disappeared, but the importance of tobacco to Veracruz did not, nor did the merchant-planters and their descendants. It was out of the colonial planter family networks that the alliances emerged between the military, the planters, and the *empresarios*, which coalesced around tobacco interests in the 1830s and 1840s. Such alliances were based as much on family networks as on economic and political interests. Negotiators with the national government included Rafael Argüelles, from the powerful Argüelles family. The sons and grandsons of the wealthy tobacco families of the 1790s—the Bringas, Argüelles, Garmendías, Mosqueras—could all be found in the political and economic intrigues which sought to control and protect the tobacco trade in the 1830s. In so doing they played a role similar to that of their fathers and grandfathers in relationship to the colonial state.

Appendix I

Total Revenues, Costs, and Profits of the Royal Tobacco Monopoly, 1765–1810 (in current pesos)

Year	Gross Revenues	Total Costs	Profits
1765/1766	1,417,846	1,178,748	239,097
1767	1,469,478	1,051,746	418,732
1768	1,532,294	724,912	807,381
1769	1,821,490	840,726	980,763
1770	2,027,958	1,211,865	816,093
1771	2,501,015	1,614,257	886,757
1772	2,859,268	1,899,680	959,538
1773	3,052,154	1,833,435	1,218,719
1774	3,192,111	1,950,572	1,241,538
1775	3,681,861	2,451,868	1,229,992
1776	3,845,742	2,330,951	1,514,790
1777	4,355,307	2,412,112	1,943,194
1778	5,094,362	2,661,211	2,433,151
1779	5,440,335	2,783,154	2,657,180
1780	5,668,107	2,682,891	2,985,216
1781	6,079,078	3,125,216	2,957,862
1782	6,389,522	3,148,593	3,240,929
1783	6,631,846	3,345,928	3,285,918
1784	6,705,496	3,347,651	3,357,844
1785	6,417,558	3,131,030	3,286,528
1786	5,824,996	2,733,252	3,091,643
1787	5,957,719	3,036,654	2,921,065
1788	6,243,182	3,336,941	2,906,240
1789	6,293,181	2,682,971	3,610,210
1790	6,235,314	2,337,349	3,397,965
1791	6,485,626	3,058,788	3,426,837
1792	6,705,635	2,991,003	3,714,631
1793	6,684,863	3,258,771	3,426,092
1794	6,526,351	3,417,539	3,108,812
1795	6,975,463	3,039,864	3,935,599
1796	7,336,539	3,400,312	3,936,227
1797	7,660,349	3,846,999	3,813,349
1798	8,251,574	3,711,778	4,539,796
1799	7,521,621	4,125,231	3,396,389
1800	7,433,159	4,020,558	3,412,600
1801	7,825,913	3,832,079	3,993,834

Appendix I (*continued*)

Year	Gross Revenues	Total Costs	Profits
1802	7,686,834	3,594,205	4,092,629
1803	7,747,528	4,196,914	3,550,614
1804	7,910,719	4,125,747	3,784,971
1805	8,599,623	4,325,279	4,274,344
1806	9,116,392	5,255,066	3,861,326
1807	9,417,204	6,287,423	3,129,781
1808	9,061,468	4,613,982	4,447,486
1809	9,558,697	5,978,747	3,579,950

Source: See Chapter 2, note 63.

Appendix II

Volume and Value of Tobacco Harvests Received by the Royal Monopoly from Orizaba and Cordoba, 1765–1807

| Year | Quantity (in pounds) | | | Value (in current pesos) | | Total Value (in current pesos) |
	Orizaba	Cordoba	Total	Orizaba	Cordoba	
1765	1,082,063	879,714	1,768,851	211,575	178,640	390,232
1766	794,293	483,367	1,277,691	208,334	144,271	352,606
1767	848,655	517,460	1,361,115	209,416	153,347	362,763
1768	662,854	535,528	1,198,382	135,718	130,960	266,678
1769	954,236	600,891	1,668,833	198,613	149,988	362,381
1770	935,627	466,573	1,402,573	175,389	101,952	277,341
1771			2,332,409	249,755	255,292	507,945
1772			2,543,926	322,823	293,994	616,784
1773			2,952,415	334,221	397,810	732,031
1774			2,952,458	289,328	397,981	686,815
1775	1,317,500 *	1,224,510 *	3,152,659	398,413	397,899	796,312
1776	1,317,616	1,224,398	2,535,282	318,057	312,776	630,834
1777			2,203,818	247,984	281,434	529,431
1778			2,363,272			631,099
1779	1,222,731	610,056	1,832,787	240,085	136,002	376,087
1780	1,166,411	671,200	1,837,611	213,734	144,326	358,050
1781				270,326	205,990	476,316
1782	2,053,940 *	1,967,070 *	4,021,010 *	424,713	398,750	823,463
1783	1,665,320 *	1,773,270 *	3,438,590 *	403,524	377,180	780,704
1784	1,633,360 *	1,755,250 *	3,386,910 *	396,472	386,951	783,423
1785	1,365,780 *	1,182,520 *	2,548,300 *	412,445	312,295	724,740
1786	1,443,810 *	1,005,890 *	2,153,965 *	352,200	228,770	580,970
1787	1,947,860 *	337,790 *	2,088,409	472,134	83,582	555,716
1788	3,088,050 *	834,530 *	3,552,348	656,833	100,220	757,053
1789	1,303,730 *	692,240 *	2,386,928	311,399	169,988	481,387
1790						
1791				408,535	500,895	909,430
1792				352,255	470,599	822,854
1793				423,925	591,891	1,015,816
1794						
1795				359,504	359,441	718,945
1796				541,152	356,195	897,347
1797				516,353	354,624	870,977

Appendix II (continued)

	Quantity (in pounds)			Value (in current pesos)		Total Value (in current pesos)
Year	Orizaba	Cordoba	Total	Orizaba	Cordoba	
1798	452,051	333,544	785,595			
1799	590,224	235,068	825,292			
1800	275,402	292,518	567,920			
1801	317,471	237,940	555,411			
1802	347,809	181,854	529,663			
1803	613,211	374,277	987,488			
1804	756,770*	405,801*	1,162,571*			
1805	944,661	369,819	1,314,480			
1806	998,131	389,885	1,378,016			
1807						

Source: Extracted from the *relaciones generales* for individual years located in the AGN, Ramo de Tabaco, Renta de Tabaco; in the AGI, Audiencia de México.

* These figures represent estimates of poundage calculated by multiplying the original quantities given in *tercios* by an average weight of 170 pounds per *tercio*.

Appendix III

Manufacture and Sales of Packets of Cigars and Cigarettes in Mexico, 1766–1809

	Cigars		Cigarettes	
Year	Manufactured	Sales	Manufactured	Sales
1766				
1767		633,861		1,462,480
1768		492,837		2,347,547
1769		592,935		3,373,719
1770	1,033,328	844,830	10,014,189	5,726,712
1771	2,388,517	1,624,109	29,745,865	17,740,712
1772	4,220,342	2,696,849	37,105,749	22,451,251
1773	5,399,622	3,485,702	23,878,048	27,871,436
1774	3,188,264	2,757,805	29,270,773	30,609,396
1775	2,833,897	3,224,372	48,739,144	41,266,127
1776		3,544,773		42,794,331
1777	3,492,814	4,495,725	50,520,163	53,905,315
1778	6,025,350	5,950,867	67,807,971	69,341,220
1779	8,007,165	6,322,795	77,888,792	74,730,532
1780	8,971,100	6,654,836	87,224,461	78,466,734
1781	7,986,408	8,174,939	104,351,998	83,380,016
1782	8,513,817	7,950,856	89,150,823	87,654,873
1783	9,496,131	8,091,265	91,735,455	91,027,902
1784	8,307,701	8,326,711	91,777,482	91,908,002
1785		7,849,427		88,002,137
1786		7,193,276		79,605,310
1787	7,223,930	7,129,027	92,086,999	81,901,463
1788	6,489,196		90,593,400	
1789	6,831,039		87,009,897	
1790	9,252,436		88,706,064	
1791	8,719,796		86,746,364	
1792	9,237,505	9,585,744	81,833,470	89,930,721
1793	11,007,595	9,939,056	84,846,221	89,437,612
1794	11,799,459		90,869,079	
1795	12,848,682		88,303,107	
1796	12,958,252	10,426,393	92,847,271	99,108,282
1797	10,249,608	10,353,013	96,323,594	104,423,327
1798	9,636,605	12,338,321	59,061,345	113,752,168
1799	14,289,851	21,355,046	76,884,959	87,548,816
1800	15,531,405	15,163,510	96,217,807	89,989,580

266   *Bureaucrats, Planters, and Workers*

Appendix III (*continued*)

	Cigars		Cigarettes	
Year	Manufactured	Sales	Manufactured	Sales
1801	16,116,159	15,168,921	99,250,374	97,976,248
1802	17,164,624	14,648,040	101,913,441	95,104,840
1803	15,236,785	15,023,004	102,892,288	97,428,579
1804	16,327,637	15,141,370	109,928,817	99,822,406
1805		16,551,456		111,381,283
1806		16,712,433		121,377,189
1807				
1808	17,989,225		128,312,895	
1809	16,085,927		130,532,955	

Source: Various *legajos* from the AGN, the AGI, and the Biblioteca Nacional, Mexico.

Notes

Abbreviations

AGI	Archivo General de Indias (Seville)
AGN	Archivo General de la Nación (Mexico City)
AHH	Archivo Histórico de Hacienda (Mexico City)
AMGH	Archivo Microfílmeco de Genealogía y Heráldica
ANO	Archivo Notarial de Orizaba
BN (Madrid)	Biblioteca Nacional (Madrid)
BN (Mexico)	Biblioteca Nacional (Mexico City)
BBL	Baker Business Library, Harvard University
BL	British Library (London)
BLAC	Benson Latin American Collection, University of Texas at Austin
HAHR	*Hispanic American Historical Review*
JLAS	*Journal of Latin American Studies*

Introduction

1. AGI, Mexico 2290, viceroy to Miguel Cayetano Soler, 26 June 1799.
2. See, for example, E. Arcila Farías, *Reformas económicas del siglo XVIII en Nueva España;* David A. Brading, *Miners and Merchants in Bourbon Mexico, 1763–1810;* Barbara Tenenbaum, *The Politics of Penury—Debts and Taxes in Mexico, 1821–1856;* Herbert S. Klein and Jacques Barbier, "Recent Trends in the Study of Colonial Public Finance," *Latin American Research Review* 23, no. 1 (1988); John J. Tepaske, "Economic Cycles in New Spain in the Eighteenth Century: The View from the Public Sector," in *Iberian Colonies, New World Societies—Essays in Memory of Charles Gibson,* ed. Richard L. Garner and William B. Taylor.

3. See H. I. Priestley, *José de Gálvez—Visitor General of New Spain, 1765–1771*, for an example of the former, and María Amparo Ros T, *La producción cigarrera a finales de la Colonia: La fábrica en México*, for an example of the latter. A wider study of the monopoly which focuses on the tobacco workers is the dissertation by David Lorne McWatters, "The Royal Tobacco Monopoly in Bourbon Mexico, 1764–1810."

4. Charles Tilly, *The Contentious French*, p. 83.

5. The literature is extensive, but for an introduction, see f.n. 8 of chap. 1.

6. William B. Taylor, "Between Global Process and Local Knowledge: An Inquiry into Early Latin American Social History, 1500–1900," in *Reliving the Past*, ed. O. Zunz, pp. 171–172; Eric Van Young, "The Raw and the Cooked: Elite and Popular Ideology in Mexico, 1800–1821," in *The Middle Period in Latin America—Values and Attitudes in the 17th–19th Centuries*, ed. Mark D. Szuchman. See also the views put forth by John H. Coatsworth in "The Limits of Colonial Absolutism: The State in Eighteenth-Century Mexico," in *Essays in the Political, Economic, and Social History of Colonial Latin America*, ed. Karen Spalding, p. 35.

7. Peter Evans et al., "Toward a More Adequate Understanding of the State," in *Bringing the State Back In*, pp. 350–351. See also Charles Bright and Susan Harding, "Processes of Statemaking and Popular Protest—An Introduction," in *Statemaking and Social Movements—Essays in History and Theory*, ed. Charles Bright and Susan Harding, pp. 3–5.

8. A. Lentin, *Enlightened Absolutism (1760–1790)—A Documentary Sourcebook*; H. M. Scott, ed., *Enlightened Absolutism—Reform and Reformers in Later Eighteenth-Century Europe*.

9. For a discussion on this point, see Van Young, "The Raw and the Cooked."

10. Stanley J. Stein, "Bureaucracy and Business in the Spanish Empire, 1759–1804: Failure of a Bourbon Reform in Mexico and Peru," *Hispanic American Historical Review*, 61, no. 1 (1981).

11. See, for example, Doris Ladd, *The Making of a Strike—Mexican Silver Workers' Struggles in Real Del Monte, 1766–1775*.

12. See Ros, *La producción cigarrera*, and "La real fábrica de tabaco ¿un embrión del capitalismo?" *Historias* 10 (July–September 1985); José González Sierra, *Monopolio del humo (elementos para la historia del tabaco en México y algunos conflictos de tabaqueros veracruzanos: 1915–1930)*. A less deterministic interpretation is provided by McWatters, "The Royal Tobacco Monopoly."

1. Monopoly, Tobacco, and Colonial Society

1. Lentin, *Enlightened Absolutism*, p. xiii.

2. Henry Kamen, *Spain, 1469–1714: A Society in Conflict*, p. 268.

3. See John Lynch, *Bourbon Spain, 1700–1808*.

4. For a summary of these thinkers and their policies, see Colin M. MacLachlan, *Spain's Empire in the New World—The Role of Ideas in Institu-*

tional and Social Change, chap. 4, and D. A. Brading, *The First America, The Spanish Monarchy, Creole Patriots and the Liberal State 1492–1867.*

5. Lynch, *Bourbon Spain*, p. 333.

6. MacLachlan, *Spain's Empire in the New World*, pp. 73–74.

7. José de Gálvez was eventually appointed as Minister of the Indies (1776–1787).

8. For background and interpretations of the Bourbon reforms in Spain, see Richard Herr, *The Eighteenth Century Revolution in Spain;* Lynch, *Bourbon Spain*. For the American reform efforts, see D. A. Brading, "Bourbon Spain and Its American Empire," in *The Cambridge History of Latin America*, ed. Leslie Bethell, vol. 1; Jaime Vicens Vives, ed., *Historia de España y América social y económica;* Lutgardo García-Fuentes, *El comercio español con América, 1650–1700;* Antonio García-Baquero González, *Cádiz y el Atlántico (1717–1778)*. For the reforms in Mexico, see Brading, *Miners and Merchants;* Hamnett, *Politics and Trade in Southern Mexico;* Burkholder and Chandler, *From Impotence to Authority;* Eduardo Arcila Farías, *Reformas económicas del siglo XVIII en Nueva España;* Nils Jacobsen and Hans-Jürgen Puhle, eds., *The Economies of Mexico and Peru During the Late Colonial Period, 1760–1810.*

9. Brading, "Bourbon Spain and Its American Empire," p. 405.

10. Tenenbaum, *The Politics of Penury*, p. 3.

11. For estimates of the growth and magnitude of government revenues in Mexico, see D. A. Brading, "Facts and Figments in Bourbon Mexico," *Bulletin of Latin American Research*, 4 (1985); Richard L. Garner, "Further Consideration of 'Facts and Figments in Bourbon Mexico,'" *Bulletin of Latin American Research*, 6, no. 1 (1987); Tepaske, "Economic Cycles in New Spain"; Richard J. Salvucci and Linda K. Salvucci, "Crecimiento y cambio en la productividad de México," *Revista Latinoamericana de Historia Económica y Social* 10 (1987): 67–89.

12. Gerónimo de Uztáriz, *The Theory and Practice of Commerce and Maritime Affairs*, p. 344. Jacques Necker, the French First Minister of Finance, in his *Treatise on the Administration of the Finances of France*, aptly described tobacco monopolies as "the most skillful fiscal inventions," an assessment which has remained valid into the twentieth century for many countries. Quoted in Jacob Price, *France and the Chesapeake—A History of the French Tobacco Monopoly, 1674–1791, and of its Relationship to the British and American Tobacco Trades*, p. 789.

13. For an introduction to the Mexican monopoly, see the description provided by Fabián de Fonseca and Carlos de Urrutia, *Libro de la razón general de la Real Hacienda en Nueva España por D. Fabián de Fonseca y D. Carlos de Urrutia, de orden del Virrey, Conde de Revillagigedo*, vol. VII, *Renta del Tabaco*. Although the author consulted the copy in the Biblioteca Nacional in Madrid (Mss 10.361), the *Historia general de Real Hacienda* is available in reprint editions, 6 vols., Mexico (1845–1853). Also useful are Herbert Ingram Priestley, *José de Gálvez—Visitor-General of New Spain, 1765–1771*, McWatters, "The Royal Tobacco Monopoly," and Arcila Farías,

Reformas Económicas, vol. 1, chap. 6, "El estanco del tabaco," pp. 113–138. For brief histories of tobacco monopolies in other Spanish colonies, see G. Céspedes del Castillo, "La renta del tabaco en el virreinato del Perú," *Revista Histórica* 21 (1954); Christine Hünefeldt, "Etapa final del monopolio en el virreinato del Perú: el tabaco de Chachapoyas," in *The Economies of Mexico and Peru*, ed. Nils Jacobsen et al.; A. Stapff, "La renta del tabaco en Chile de la época virreinal," *Anuario de Estudios Americanos* 18 (1961); John P. Harrison, "The Colombian Tobacco Industry from Government Monopoly to Free Trade, 1778–1876"; Jesús Antonio Bejarano and Orlando Pulido, *El tabaco en una economía regional: Ambalema, siglos XVIII y XIX*; Cam Harlan Wickham, "Venezuela's Royal Tobacco Monopoly, 1779–1810: An Economic Analysis"; Juan Carlos Arias Divito, "Dificultades para establecer la renta de tabaco en Paraguay," *Anuario de Estudios Americanos* 33 (1976), and "Auge y decadencia de la renta del tabaco en Buenos Aires," *Nuestra Historia* 22 (1978); Ed. C. de Jesus, *The Tobacco Monopoly in the Philippines—Bureaucratic Enterprise and Social Change, 1766–1880*; José Rivero Muñiz, *Tabaco: su historia en Cuba*; Fernando Ortiz, *Contrapunto cubano del tabaco y el azúcar*; Brian E. Coutts, "Boom and Bust: The Rise and Fall of the Tobacco Industry in Spanish Louisiana, 1770–1790," *The Americas* 42 no. 3 (January 1986). For the Portuguese version of monopolization of the tobacco trade, see Catherine Lugar, "The Portuguese Tobacco Trade and Tobacco Growers of Bahia in the Late Colonial Period," in *Essays Concerning the Socioeconomic History of Brazil and Portuguese India*, ed. Dauril Alden and Warren Dean.

14. M. Corina, *Trust in Tobacco: the Anglo-American Struggle for Power*, p. 45.

15. Priestley, *José de Gálvez*, p. 142.

16. AGN, Tabaco 390, Sánchez de Tagle to viceroy, 18 June 1743; AGN, Tabaco 390, project of Rodezno, 16 March 1746.

17. AGN, Tabaco 390, *fiscal* to viceroy, 17 July 1743; AGN, Tabaco 390, *fiscal* to Fuenclara, 27 April 1746.

18. John Lynch, *Bourbon Spain*, p. 162.

19. AGI, Mexico 2256, José Díaz de Lavendero to Enseñada, 1 October 1748. Lavendero occupied the position of Teniente Coronel, Capitán Comandante de la Compañía de Guardias de Corps de Caballería del Real Palacio de México.

20. AGI, Mexico 2256, José Díaz de Lavendero to Enseñada, 1 October 1748.

21. AGI, Mexico 2256, royal order of 27 June 1746.

22. AGN, Renta de Tabaco 40, report of Hierro, 27 April 1793.

23. Raymond de Roover, "Monopoly Theory Prior to Adam Smith," in *Business, Banking, and Economic Thought in Late Medieval and Early Modern Europe*, ed. Julius Kirshner, p. 303.

24. AGI, Mexico 2256, Cruillas to Esquilache, 1 December 1761.

25. McWatters, "The Royal Tobacco Monopoly," pp. 30–31.

26. For general interpretations of the role of tobacco in indigenous cultures, see Francis Robicsek, *The Smoking Gods—Tobacco in Maya Art*,

History, and Religion, and Johannes Wilbert, *Tobacco and Shamanism in South America.*

27. AGN, Tabaco 438, Bishop of Guadalajara to viceroy Croix, 4 November 1766.

28. AGN, Tabaco 241, reported by Díaz de la Vega, Manifiesto de las vicisitudes que ha tenido el sistema de la provision y abasto al Publico de vender el Tabaco, ya en rama, o ya en Puros y Cigarros, labrados en las Fabricas establecidas de cuenta del Rey, compreende desde el tiempo en que se mando estancar este fruto en este Reyno hasta el presente de la fecha. 10 July 1795 (hereafter cited as Manifiesto de las vicisitudes . . . Díaz de la Vega, 10 July 1795).

29. Brading, *Miners and Merchants,* pp. 124–128.

30. Stapff, "La renta del tabaco." Stapff argues that the trade operated out of Acapulco but was subject to restriction and contraction beginning in the 1630s when trade between Mexico and Peru was prohibited, long before the establishment of the monopoly.

31. AGI, Mexico 2256, José Díaz de Lavendero to Enseñada, 1 October 1748.

32. The *cigarros* or *papelillos* were a small cigar made of finely shredded tobacco rolled in an outer wrapper, not made of tobacco leaf, as with cigars, but generally of paper, maize leaf, or other material. They were much milder than cigars and smoked much more quickly. Robicsek argues that paper-wrapped cigarettes originated in the improvisational techniques of street beggars in Seville in the sixteenth century, who picked up discarded cigar butts, shredded them, and rolled them anew in scraps of paper. These "poor-man smokes" became known variously as *papeletes, papelillos, cigarros,* or *cigarillos.* See Robicsek, *The Smoking Gods,* p. 10.

33. AGN, Tabaco 241, Manifiesto de las vicisitudes . . . Díaz de la Vega, 10 July 1795).

34. Francisco Sedano, *Noticias de México,* vol. 1, pp. 79–80. Luis González Obregón refers to El Callejon de Tabaqueros in Mexico City but does not specify exactly where it was located. See his *Las calles de México,* p. 19.

35. Anonymous tract entitled *Defensa de las fabricas,* quoted in AGN, Tabaco 241, Notas remisivas . . ., Díaz de la Vega, 10 July 1795; AGI, Mexico 2284, Real Orden received by viceroy, January 1792.

36. AGI, Mexico 2275, Antonio del Frago to Arriaga, 12 February 1769.

37. AGN, Tabaco 241, Notas remisivas . . ., Díaz de la Vega, 10 July 1795.

38. AGN, Tabaco 89, *factor* of Guadalajara to *directores generales,* 28 February 1777.

39. AGN, Tabaco 89, *factor* of Valladolid to *directores generales,* 24 February 1777.

40. AGI, Mexico 1373, José Riva Agüero to *directores generales,* 1 December 1773, Testimonio . . . de lo operado sobre la extinción de cigarreros y establecimiento de estanquillos en esta ciudad de Méjico de cuenta de la Renta Real de Tabaco (hereafter refered to as Testimonio . . . sobre la extinción de cigarreros).

41. AGN, Tabaco 241, Notas remisivas . . ., Díaz de la Vega, 10 July 1795.

42. AGN, Tabaco 146, Razon de las cigarrerías y purerías que existen en esta capital de Mexico, segun la visita y reconocimiento que se practico en el mes de Agosto de 1770, Espinosa, 2 January 1772.

43. AGN, Tabaco 89, *factor* of Guadalajara to *directores generales*, 28 February 1777.

44. AGI, Mexico 1373, Riva Agüero to *directores generales*, 1 December 1773, Testimonio . . . sobre la extinción de cigarreros.

45. AGI, Mexico 241, Notas remisivas . . . Díaz de la Vega, 10 July 1795.

46. Ibid.

47. AGI, Mexico 1373, Riva Agüero to *directores generales*, Testimonio . . . sobre la extinción de cigarreros, 1 December 1773.

48. AGN, Tabaco 89, *factor* of Guadalajara to *directores generales*, 28 February 1777.

49. AGI, Mexico 2256, Calvo to viceroy, 22 October 1761; AGI, Mexico 2256, Espinosa to Esquilache, 2 March 1765; AGI, Mexico 2256, Armona to *junta de tabaco*, 6 September 1766; McWatters, "The Royal Tobacco Monopoly," p. 105.

50. AGN, Tabaco 495, *director general* to Branciforte, 28 August 1795.

51. AGN, Renta de Tabaco 47, royal order of 13 August 1764.

52. AGI, Mexico 2256, Espinosa to Esquilache, 27 August 1765.

53. AGI, Mexico 2256, Espinosa to Esquilache, 9 March 1765.

54. The *junta de tabaco* served as a bridge between the permanent administration and the top administrative body of the monopoly, the *dirección general*. Members were appointed on an ad hoc basis according to the problem at hand.

55. AGI, Mexico 2256, report of Cruillas, 16 September 1765; AGI, Mexico 2256, report of Espinosa, 20 September 1765.

56. AGI, Mexico 2256, report of Espinosa, 20 September 1765.

57. For contract arrangements in Yucatán, see AGI, Mexico 2263, Testimonio de la nueva contrata de tabaco celebrada para Yucatan por 4 años, 1788–91.

58. AGI, Mexico 2255, Espinosa to Arriaga, 24 January 1767.

59. AGI, Mexico 2256, Espinosa to Esquilache, 9 March 1765.

60. Priestley, *José de Gálvez*, 146.

61. AGI, Mexico 2256, Gálvez to Arriaga, 15 October 1765.

62. For an extended discussion of Gálvez' early and central role in the monopoly's establishment see Priestley, *José de Gálvez*, pp. 146–164.

63. AGI, Mexico 2256, Gálvez to Arriaga, 15 October 1765.

64. AGI, Mexico 2256, report of Francisco Fuentes y Sánchez, secretario de Camara del Virreinato y de la junta de tabaco, 22 September 1765; AGI, Mexico 2256, report of Borrachía, 24 December 1765.

65. Priestley, *José de Gálvez*, p. 147.

66. AGI, Mexico 2256, Gálvez to Arriaga, 15 October 1765.

67. AGI, Mexico 2256, Gálvez to Esquilache, 27 October 1765.

68. Ibid.

69. See Allan J. Kuethe, "The Development of the Cuban Military as a Sociopolitical Elite, 1763–83," *HAHR* 61, no. 4 (1981); and Allan J. Kuethe

and G. Douglas Inglis, "Absolutism and Enlightened Reform: Charles III, the Establishment of the Alcabala, and Commercial Reorganization in Cuba," *Past & Present* 109 (November 1985).

70. AGI, Mexico 2256, Gálvez to Arriaga, 22 December 1765.

71. AGI, Mexico 2256, Cossío to Gálvez, 23 November 1765.

72. AGI, Mexico 2256, Lardizábal to Gálvez, 23 November 1765.

73. AGI, Mexico 2256, Gálvez to Arriaga, 22 December 1765.

74. The *Cinco gremios mayores de Madrid*, or the Five Great Guilds of Madrid, were powerful commercial guilds which controlled the manufacture and sale of gold, silver, jewelry, silk, woolens, and spices, and in 1763 possessed the contract for the collection of the royal revenues of Madrid. AGI, Mexico 2275, report of Benito Linares, 18 December 1765. AGI, Mexico 2256, Gálvez to Esquilache, 23 December 1765.

75. AGI, Mexico 2256, Gálvez to Esquilache, 23 December 1765.

76. All were granted the rank of captain of the militias of Veracruz. See BN (Madrid) Mss 10.361, Fonseca and Urrutia, *Libro de la Real Hacienda*, vol. 7, f.18.

77. Linda K. Salvucci, "Costumbres viejas, 'hombres nuevos': José de Gálvez y la burocracia fiscal novohispana, 1754–1800." *Historia Mexicana* 33, no. 2 (October-December 1983).

78. AGI, Mexico 2256, Gálvez to Arriaga, 8 November 1765.

79. Ibid.

80. AGI, Mexico 2256, Espinosa to Arriaga, 12 November 1765.

81. AGI, Mexico 2256, Cruillas to Arriaga, 14 May 1766.

82. AGI, Mexico 2256, procurador general del ayuntamiento de la ciudad de Mexico to V.M., 26 October 1765.

83. Reported in AGN, Tabaco 241, Manifiesto de las vicisitudes . . . Díaz de la Vega to viceroy, 10 July 1795, 26–26v.

84. AGI, Mexico 2256, Armona to *junta de tabaco*, 6 September 1766.

85. AGI, Mexico 2257, Gálvez to viceroy, 26 April 1766.

86. AGI, Mexico 2256, Gálvez to Esquilache, 24 December 1765.

87. AGI, Mexico 2255, Títulos de empleos.

88. AGN, Tabaco 241, Manifiesto de las vicisitudes . . . Díaz de la Vega, 10 July 1795.

89. BN (Madrid), Mss 10.361, Fonseca and Urrutia, *Libro de la Real Hacienda*, vol. 7, f.56.

90. AGI, Mexico 2256, *fiscal* to viceroy, 6 December 1766.

91. Ibid.

92. See Brading, *Miners and Merchants*, p. 27.

93. AGI, Mexico 1373, Riva Agüero to *directores generales*, Testimonio . . . sobre la extinción de cigarreros, 1 December 1773.

94. AGN, Renta de Tabaco 47, Ordenanzas de la Real Renta de Tabaco, March 1768, reprinted in 1786.

95. Stanley Stein, "Bureaucracy and Business."

96. Ibid., p. 28.

97. For a lengthier critique of "Bureaucracy and Business," see Jacques A. Barbier and Mark A. Burkholder, "Critique of Stanley J. Stein's "Bureau-

cracy and Business in the Spanish Empire, 1759–1804: Failure of a Bourbon Reform in Mexico and Peru," *HAHR* 62, no. 3 (1982).

98. Kuethe and Inglis, "Absolutism and Enlightened Reform," p. 139.

99. Hamnett, *Politics and Trade*, pp. 25–26.

100. See Hamnett's discussion of this problem, *Politics and Trade*, pp. 32–35.

101. Hamnett, *Politics and Trade*, p. 33.

102. For a discussion of 'old' versus 'new' ideologies, see MacLachlan, *Spain's Empire in the New World*, chap. 5.

103. Ibid., p. 96.

104. Price, *France and the Chesapeake*, pp. 788–839.

105. AGI, Mexico 2256, report of Cruillas, 16 September 1765, and report of Espinosa, 20 September 1765.

106. AGN, Tabaco 241, Díaz de la Vega to Ex. Sr., 10 July 1795.

107. AGI, Mexico 2275, *factor* of Puebla to Gálvez, 10 December 1765; AGI, Mexico 2256, *factor* of Puebla to Gálvez, 13 December 1765.

108. Priestley, *José de Gálvez*, p. 158.

109. AGN, Tabaco 438, Bishop of Guadalajara to viceroy Croix, 4 November 1766; Reported in AGN, Tabaco 241, Manifiesto de las vicisitudes . . . Díaz de la Vega to viceroy, 10 July 1795, 26–26v.

110. Richard J. Salvucci, *Textiles And Capitalism in Mexico: An Economic History of the Obrajes, 1539–1840*, Chap. 4, "Nor More Servitude Than in Other Work," pp. 97–134.

111. Alexander von Humboldt, *Ensayo político sobre el reino de la Nueva España*, p. 297.

112. de Jesus, *The Tobacco Monopoly in the Philippines*; Wickham, "Venezuela's Royal Tobacco Monopoly."

113. AGI, Mexico 2258, Balthazar de Vidaurre, procurador del número de la Real Audiencia de la ciudad de México, 26 January 1773.

114. AGN, Tabaco 23, report of *contador general*, 22 June 1772, Resumen general del numero de cigarrerías que existen in este reyno de Nueva España; AGI, Mexico 2275, Razon de cigarrerías que existen en esta capital y provincias del reyno segun los avisos recividos por la dirección general, report by Antonio de Frago; AGN, Tabaco 241, Díaz de la Vega to viceroy, 28 August 1795; AGN, Tabaco 241, Notas remisivas . . . Díaz de la Vega, 10 July 1795; McWatters, "The Royal Tobacco Monopoly," p. 105.

115. AGI, Mexico 1373, José Riva Agüero to *directores generales*, 1 December 1773, Testimonio . . . sobre la extinción de cigarreros.

116. Ibid.

117. AGI, Mexico 2275, Frago to Arriaga, 12 February 1769.

118. Ibid.

119. Orders which reiterated the prohibitions against the small tobacco plots in Indian villages and towns were repeatedly sent to all *factores* of the monopoly. AGI, Mexico 2286, Díaz de la Vega to all *factores*, 20 August 1794.

120. AGI, 2278, Nota de las alcaldias mayores en cuyas jurisdicciones ha

acreditado la experiencia hay siembras fraudulentes de tabaco que causan grave daño, Hierro, Riva to José de Gálvez, 27 January 1778.

121. Eric Van Young, "Crime as Rebellion and Rebellion as Crime," in *The Other Rebellion: Popular Violence and Ideology in Mexico, 1810–1816.*

122. L. Kinnaird, "The Spanish Tobacco Monopoly in New Mexico, 1766–67," *New Mexico Historical Review*, 21 (1946): 328. For a general assessment of the role of tobacco among the mission Indians in Coahuila and Texas, especially the trading system of the Apaches, see AGI, Mexico 2284, report of *frey* Roque Jiménez, 19 June 1766, and report of viceroy Revillagigedo, 31 December 1792.

123. AGI, Mexico 2260, *comandante general de provincias internas* to Gálvez, 3 November 1778.

124. AGN, Tabaco 300, Angel de Antelo y Bermúdez to viceroy Mayorga, 26 April 1782; AGI, Mexico 2260, *comandante general de provincias internas* to Gálvez, 3 November 1778.

125. AGN, Tabaco 103, José Esteban to Ex. Sr., 1798.

126. *Gachupín* was a derogatory term for a Spaniard.

127. AGI, Mexico 2859, report of Agustín de Quiroga, 15 September 1791.

128. AGN, Tabaco 300, *alcalde mayor* to Ex. Sr., 14 November 1787.

129. *Pisiete*, the hispanicized spelling of the Nahuatl *piciétl* (tobacco), could mean tobacco plant, but it had a number of meanings which described variations in processing the tobacco leaf and in mixing it with other substances as a hallucinogenic or herbal remedy for sickness. See Robiscek, *The Smoking Gods*, pp. 37–38, 54.

130. AGN, Tabaco 523, viceregal order, 23 March 1804.

131. AGN, Tabaco 523, Dominga Sororio, Petra Velasco, María de Rojas to Ex. Sr., 1807.

132. AGI, Mexico 2859, report of intendant of Veracruz, 5 May 1791.

133. AGI, Mexico 2850, report of Francisco del Real, Orizaba, 15 November 1786.

134. AGI, Mexico 2294, Consejo de Indias, Sala la, intendant Manuel de Flon, 7 December 1796.

135. Ibid.

136. Ibid.

137. AGI, Mexico 2299, royal order of 20 July 1803.

2. Monopoly Bureaucrats and Monopoly Finances

1. See Linda Arnold, *Bureaucracy and Bureaucrats in Mexico City, 1742–1835*; Burkholder and Chandler, *From Impotence to Authority*; Susan Migden Socolow, *The Bureaucrats of Buenos Aires, 1769–1810: Amor al Real Servicio*; Brading, *Miners and Merchants*; Linda K. Salvucci, "Costumbres viejas, 'hombres nuevos.'"

2. Ordenanzas de la Real Renta del Tabaco para este reyno de Nueva España . . . de cuenta de S.M., 15 March 1768, AGN, Renta de Tabaco, 47.

3. A thorough account of the bureaucratic structure of the monopoly and the bureaucrats' duties is contained in BN (Madrid) Mss 10.361, Fonseca and Urrutia, *Libro de la Real Hacienda*, vol. 7. See also Joaquín Maniau Torquemada, *Compendio de la historia de la Real Hacienda escrita en el año de 1794.*

4. BN (Madrid), Mss 10.361, Fonseca and Urrutia, *Libro de la Real Hacienda*, vol. 7, f.44.

5. Surprisingly few records of these transactions showed up in archival collections.

6. BN (Madrid), Mss 10.361, Fonseca and Urrutia, *Libro de la Real Hacienda*, vol. 7, ff.54–56. See also AGN, Tabaco 303, Reglamento ó pauta que para la distribución de comison de tierra, de mar y mixtos, que se hicieren en las Indias ha formado con arreglo á reales determinaciones el contador general, 1787.

7. Priestley, *José de Gálvez*, pp. 153–154.

8. BN (Madrid) Mss 10.361, Fonseca and Urrutia, *Libro de la Real Hacienda*, vol. 7, f.54.

9. Joaquín Maniau Torquemada, *Compendio de la historia de Real Hacienda de Nueva España. Año de 1793*, f.165. It is substantially the same as the printed version dated 1794 and published in 1914 by Alberto M. Carreño (Mexico City, Imprenta de la Secretaría de Industria y Comercio).

10. AGI, Mexico 2260, Díaz de la Vega to Gálvez, 4 March 1778.

11. AGN, Tabaco 40, *hojas de servicio* for eleven administrations, 1765–1799; AGN, Fondo Real Hacienda, Tabaco Contaduría 93, *hojas de servicio*, 1798–1804. The information contained in the service records included name of employee, current position held, previous positions and duration, current salary, age, and civil status. Ethnic status and birthplace were very rarely indicated.

12. Brading, *Miners and Merchants*, p. 242.

13. AGN, Tabaco 40, Administrations of Mérida de Yucatán and Monterrey, 1765–1799, *hojas de servicio.*

14. AGI, Mexico 2288, *hojas de servicio.*

15. AGN, Tabaco 40, Administration of Valladolid, 1765–99, *hojas de servicio.*

16. AGN, Tabaco 40, Administration of Guadalajara, 1765–99, *hojas de servicio.*

17. AGN, Tabaco 40, calculated from the eleven administrations' records for the years 1765–1799.

18. AGN, Fondo Real Hacienda, Tabaco Contaduría 93, 1798–1804, *hojas de servicio.*

19. Arnold, *Bureaucracy and Bureaucrats*, p. 18.

20. The remaining 37 percent was divided between single men, who accounted for 26 percent, and widowers, who made up the final 11 percent.

21. AGI, Mexico 2289, *oficiales* of the *contaduría general* to Gardoqui, 27 March 1796.

22. AGI, Mexico 2289, *oficiales* of the *contaduría general* to viceroy, 27 March 1796.

23. Maniau y Ortega's sons were all born in Jalapa. See the entries in José Mariano Beristáin de Sousa, *Biblioteca hispanoamericana septentrional*, vol. 3. See also Arnold, *Bureaucracy and Bureaucrats*, p. 110.

24. Christina Renate Borchart de Moreno, *Los mercaderes y el capitalismo en la ciudad de México: 1759–1778*, p. 83.

25. S. Migden Socolow, *The Bureaucrats of Buenos Aires, 1769–1810: Amor al Real Servicio*, p. 243.

26. Linda K. Salvucci, "Costumbres viejas, 'hombres nuevos.'"

27. Migden Socolow, *The Bureaucrats of Buenos Aires*, quoted in fn. 12, p. 307.

28. AGI, Mexico 2256, Espinosa to Esquilache, 27 August 1765; Priestley, *José de Gálvez*, p. 143.

29. For individual listings and examples of such thefts and losses, see AGN, Tabaco 446, the general statements of each administration for the years 1767–1795. Legitimate losses were subsidized by the monopoly. The administrations of Orizaba and Córdoba consistently ran at a loss due to the high cost of the *resguardo* in proportion to local sales, but were covered out of general monopoly administrative funds.

30. BN (Madrid), Mss 10.361; Fonseca and Urrutia, *Libro de la Real Hacienda*, vol. 7, f.77. The tobacco planters and their workers are not included in this figure, so the number actually dependent upon the monopoly is much higher.

31. AGI, Mexico 2289, Azanza to Francisco Saavedra, 31 October 1798.

32. AGN, Tabaco 40, Administrations of Guadalajara and Mérida de Yucatán, 1765–99, *hojas de servicio*.

33. BN (Madrid) Mss 10.361, Fonseca and Urrutia, *Libro de la Real Hacienda*, vol. 7, ff.67–77; AGN, Factorias, 3, Nomina de los sueldos devengados en el mes de la fecha por los individuos empleados en el Resguardo de esta factoría, Juan de Arias, Agustín de Quiroga, 1794; AGN, Tabaco 113, Nomina de los sueldos . . . 1805.

34. Migden Socolow, *The Bureaucrats of Buenos Aires*, pp. 164–172. For a comparative perspective, see Migden Socolow's discussion of tobacco bureaucrats' salaries in Buenos Aires between 1778 and 1809. The *director general* of the monopoly in Buenos Aires could expect to earn half of what his counterpart would be paid in Mexico City.

35. AGI, Mexico 2264, Aranjuez, 3 May 1788.

36. AGI, Mexico 2282, Conde de Revillagigedo, 19 December 1789.

37. Brading, *Miners and Merchants*, p. 242.

38. AGI, Mexico 2288, Pedro Aparici, 29 April 1797.

39. AGI, Mexico 2280, governor José de Carrion to viceroy, 31 March 1779.

40. Lucas Alamán, *Historia de México*, vol. 1. Document no. 14, Extracto de la sentencia pronunciada por el consejo de Indias contra el virrey D. José de Iturrigaray, en la causa de su residencia, en la parte relativa á las sumas que debía pagar á la real hacienda, 366.

41. See Migden Socolow's discussion of this same point in *The Bureaucrats of Buenos Aires*, p. 247.

42. BN (Mexico) Mss 1332, report of *contador general*, 23 May 1775.

43. AGI, Mexico 2295, report of Hierro, 24 September 1792, Estado de las cuentas que hay sin fenecer en la contaduría general.

44. AGN, Tabaco 416, Joaquín Maniau to *director general*, 30 September 1807.

45. AGN, Tabaco 416, Díaz de la Vega to viceroy Iturrigaray, 16 October 1807.

46. AGN, Renta de Tabaco 35, Estado que manifiesta por factorias los resguardos que mantiene la Renta de Tabaco de este Reyno de Nueva España y sueldos que se les pagan por la misma Renta, 5 October 1782.

47. Compiled from AGN, Renta de Tabaco 1, Lista de los Guardas de que se componen los Resguardos de las Villas contratadas . . . Díaz de la Vega, 21 January 1789; AGN, Renta de Tabaco 35, Estado que manifiesta por factorias los resguardos que mantiene la Renta del Tabaco de este Reyno de Nueva España y sueldos que se les pagan por la misma Renta, 5 October 1782; AGN, Renta de Tabaco 30, Juan de Arias, Placido Henestrosa, 5 April 1794; AGN, Factorias, 3, Nomina de los sueldos devengados en el mes de la fecha por los individuos empleados en el Resguardo de esta factoría, Juan de Arias, Agustín de Quiroga, 1794; AGN, Tabaco 113, Nomina de los sueldos . . . 1805.

48. AGN, Renta de Tabaco 1, Francisco del Real to *directores generales*, 23 April 1788; AGN, Renta de Tabaco 1, *fiscal*, 22 March 1789.

49. AGI, Mexico 2306, report of *dirección general*, 26 November 1799.

50. AGI, Mexico 2289, *oficiales* of the *contaduría general* of the tobacco monopoly to Gardoqui, 26 April 1796; Ibid., 27 March 1796.

51. AGI, Mexico 2230, *hojas de servicio, contador general*, 1816.

52. Working on the assumption that all inhabitants smoked, Pelleramo calculated an average expenditure of one real daily per family, or 46 pesos yearly (an unrealistic estimate). Using Villaseñor's population figures for 1746 (thus underestimating his population base), he compared the actual income against the potential maximum for the three leading administrations, with the following results:

	Families	Actual Income (pesos)	Potential	Losses
Mexico	241,991	1,593,781	11,040,839	9,447,058
Valladolid	68,740	1,315,656	3,136,262	1,820,606
Guadalajara	23,907	1,097,660	1,090,660	

AGI, Mexico 2310, 2311, Testimonio del expediente instruido á instancia de don José Pelleramo, administrador general del Tabaco, sobre perjuicios que sufre la Renta de este Ramo, 1796.

53. AGI, Mexico 2302, report of López, 10 November 1817.

54. Arnold, *Bureaucracy and Bureaucrats*, pp. 21–23.

55. After Gálvez' death in 1787, the old ministry of the Indies was separated into two departments responsible for war and the exchequer, each subject to a different head. By 1790 responsibility for colonial administration was distributed among the Spanish monarchy's five permanent ministries of War, the Navy, the Exchequer, Justice, and State. Only the Council of the Indies, charged with judicial review, fiscal audit, and political consultation, remained solely concerned with the Americas. For the reorganization following Gálvez's demise and during the rule of Charles IV, see Jacques Barbier, "The Culmination of the Bourbon Reforms"; Allan J. Kuethe, "Towards a Periodization of the Reforms of Charles III," in *Iberian Colonies, New World Societies: Essays in Memory of Charles Gibson*, ed. R. L. Garner and W. B. Taylor; Brading, *Miners and Merchants*, pp. 56–81; see also Arnold, *Bureaucracy and Bureaucrats*, pp. 28–47.

56. Arnold, *Bureaucracy and Bureaucrats*, pp. 89–90.

57. Brading, *Miners and Merchants*, p. 63.

58. Brading, *Miners and Merchants*, p. 65. For a general assessment of the intendancy system, see Lillian Estelle Fisher, *The Intendant System in Spanish America*, and Luis Navarro García, *Intendencias de Indias*. For an administrative account of the conflicts and confusion caused by the implementation of the intendancy system for the tobacco monopoly in general, see John Lynch, *Spanish Colonial Administration, 1782–1810*; for the Río de la Plata case, see Juan Carlos Arias Divito, "La Real Ordenanza de Intendentes y la renta de tabaco," *Revista de historia del derecho* 2 (1983).

59. Barbier, "The Culmination of the Bourbon Reforms," p. 65.

60. Brading, *Miners and Merchants*, part 1, "The Revolution in Government"; Arnold, *Bureaucracy and Bureaucrats*, p. 128.

61. Salvucci, "Costumbres viejas, 'hombres nuevos.'" Salvucci examines the case of the appointment of Francisco de Astigarreta, the newly-arrived, unconnected, peninsular superintendent of the Mexico City *alcabala* district in 1795, who received unsolicited offers from five of the capital's most prominent merchants to stand bonds for him.

62. Migden Socolow, *The Bureaucrats of Buenos Aires*, p. 259.

63. Sources for monopoly revenues are as follows: for the years 1766–1790, AGN, Tabaco 241, Estado de los Productos totales Gastos y liqdo. de la Renta del Tabaco en los 27 años de su Estanco hta. el año de 1793; BN (Madrid), Mss 10.361, Fonseca and Urrutia, *Libro de la Real Hacienda*, vii, f.78; for 1792, 1793, and 1796–1806, extracted from the *relaciones generales*, AGN, Tabaco as follows: 1792, vol. 289, 1793, vols. 152 and 289, 1796, vol. 223, 1797, vol. 120, 1798, vol. 38, 1800, vol. 54, 1801–1803, vol. 96, 1804–1805, vol. 331, 1806, vol. 96. All remaining years were extracted from Tabla 1, Tabla que demuestra las ventas, los gastos y las utilidades sobre el tabaco, November 1843, R. C. Wyllie, "México. Noticia sobre su hacienda publica baja el gobierno español y despues de la Independencia," in *Documentos para el estudio de la industrialización en México, 1837–1845*, ed. G. B. Robinson, pp. 348–349. The *relaciones generales* were the annual monopoly accounts, which itemized annual gross revenues and total costs and

profits for the viceroyalty of Mexico. They are broken down into several sections and organized by region according to the monopoly's administrative divisions. The total revenues itemized in the annual accounts represent revenues from annual sales of tobacco products. Annual carry-overs of working capital for the individual administrations were minimal. Not all of the *relaciones* for each fiscal year of the period studied could be located. During the final writing of this work, several large *cajas* were found in the AGN, Indiferente General (unclassified), relating to the monopoly, which contained summary account books from regional administrations and which incorporated local *estanquillo* accounts. It was too late to integrate the data, but for any historian who wishes to follow up the development of the monopoly from a regional perspective, these *cajas* are a good place to start. We have chosen to leave the monopoly revenues in current pesos and not to deflate them, as we have yet to develop an acceptable price index by which to do so. Given that a good proportion of silver from tobacco sales was exported to Spain, however, it makes little sense to deflate it by a Mexican price index, even if we had one. For a discussion of the problem, see Arij Ouweneel and Catrien C. J. H. Bijleveld, "The Economic Cycle in Bourbon Central Mexico: A Critique of the *Recaudación del diezmo líquido en pesos*," *HAHR* 69, no. 3 (1989), and commentary by D. A. Brading in the same issue. Readers should be aware, however, that some authors choose to work with certain indices. For example, see John Coatsworth, "The Limits of Colonial Absolutism," and John T. Tepaske, "Economic Cycles in New Spain," p. 127.

64. Garner cautions his readers, correctly, that the data for the second half of the eighteenth century are the most controversial because of changes in treasury operations and that the effect of such changes on the economy have yet to be clarified. See Garner, "Further Considerations of 'Facts and Figments in Bourbon Mexico'," pp. 59–60.

65. Alexander von Humboldt, *Ensayo político sobre el reino de la Nueva España*, p. 550.

66. Mexico's administration incorporated Querétaro, and Valladolid incorporated Guanajuato, San Luis Potosí, and Zamora. Guanajuato eventually acquired its own provincial monopoly treasury. Guadalajara incorporated Bolaños, Tepic, and Zacatecas, while Durango encompassed Sombrerete, Parral, and Saltillo. Puebla's administrative jurisdiction included Jalapa until 1787 when it was shifted to the administration of Veracruz.

67. The full costs of the manufactory are not known, but by the time the decision was made to complete the building, half a million pesos had been already spent.

68. Alamán, *Historia de México*, vol. 1, p. 67.

69. See for example, Herbert Klein, "La economía de la Nueva España, 1680–1809: Un análisis a partir de las Cajas Reales," *Historia Mexicana* 34, no. 136 (1985).

70. McWatters, "The Royal Tobacco Monopoly," table 26, p. 277.

71. Priestley, *José de Gálvez*, pp. 387–388.

72. Jacques A. Barbier and Herbert S. Klein, "Revolutionary Wars and

Public Finances: the Madrid Treasury, 1784–1807," *Journal of Economic History*, 41, no. 2 (1981). See also Javier Cuenca Esteban, "Statistics of Spain's Colonial Trade, 1792–1820: Consular Duties, Cargo Inventories, and Balances of Trade," *HAHR* 61, no. 3 (1981): 328–330.

73. John Fisher, *Commercial Relations Between Spain and Spanish America in the Era of Free Trade, 1778–1796*, pp. 70–71, appendix C, table C2, p. 115. Figures were converted into pesos by a ratio of 20 reales de vellón to 1 peso fuerte. See Fisher, fn. 1, p. 43. Fisher cautions that the figure for tobacco imports is almost certainly an understatement, since it was not until 1786 that customs officials began systematically to record the value of tobacco imports rather than simply to note the consignment weights.

74. AGN, Tabaco 446, report of *contador general*, 31 July 1797.

75. See Javier Cuenca Esteban, "Of Nimble Arrows and Faulty Bows: A Call for Rigor," *HAHR* 64, no. 2 (1984) 303.

76. While the amounts listed provide an idea of the relative magnitude of the sums involved, the percentages are all based on reported annual incomes as opposed to cumulative account totals, which would have been different as moneys loaned to the Real Hacienda were (on occasion) paid back, shifted among different *cajas*, and entered into the monopoly credit account, thus augmenting the annual total income from monopoly sales.

77. Tenenbaum, *The Politics of Penury*, p. 1.

78. Ibid.

79. AGN, Tabaco 446, report of Maniau y Ortega, 1797; AGN, Tabaco 452, report of Maniau y Ortega, 30 April 1794.

80. AGN, Tabaco 392, royal order 8 July 1787.

81. AGI, Mexico 2290, report of Maniau y Ortega, 11 June 1799; AGI, Mexico 2293, report of Maniau y Ortega, 21 May 1802.

82. AGI, Mexico 2291, Díaz de la Vega to Azanza, 27 May 1799.

83. BN (Mexico) Mss 1332. Estado que manifiesta los reditos que ha satisfecho la Thesoreria general de la Real Renta de Tabaco de este Reyno de Nueva España el año de 1783 por los capitales impuestos en el al cinco por ciento sobre la Real Hacienda en las Caxas Reales de esta Ciudad los quales se redimieron el mismo año, 3 March 1783, ff.332–332. In the 1793 and 1794 accounts, private lenders included the Conde de Cortina (40,000 pesos), Conde de la Contramira (50,000 pesos), Francisco Ignacio de Iraeta (40,000 pesos), Antonio Bassoco (40,000 pesos), the Cabildo Eclesiástico de Santa Iglesia (60,000 pesos), the Caja del Juzgado General de Bienes de Difuntos (167,000 pesos), Angel Puyado (50,000 pesos), Gabriel Gutiérrez de Terán (25,000 pesos), for a total of 472,000 pesos or almost half a million pesos. AGI, Mexico 2286, report of Maniau y Ortega, 27 December 1794.

84. AGI, Mexico 2292, report of Maniau y Ortega, 28 December 1799.

85. See Appendices 2 and 3 in Jan Bazant, *Historia de la deuda exterior de México (1823–1946)*.

86. Tomás Murphy, Francisco Ignacio de Iraeta, and Isidro Ignacio de Icaza were the only three wholesale merchants who supported the implementation of free trade to Mexico in the late 1780s. The rest of the *Consulado* members bitterly denounced such a policy at precisely the same

time that they denounced the harmful effects of the tobacco monopoly. See John E. Kicza, "Mexican Merchants and Their Links to Spain, 1750–1850." For a discussion of Murphy's speculative activities with the tobacco trade and his dealings with the Empresa de Tabaco in postindependence Mexico, see David W. Walker, "Business as Usual: The Empresa del Tabaco in Mexico, 1837–44," *HAHR* 4, no. 64 (1984) 698.

3. Tobacco and Paper

1. AGI, Mexico 2255, Espinosa to Arriaga, 24 January 1767; AGN, Renta de Tabaco 8, viceroy to *directores generales*, 15 May 1770.

2. Albert O. Hirschman, *Essays in Trespassing—Economics to Politics and Beyond; Exit, Voice, and Loyalty: Responses to Decline in Firms, Organizations, and States.*

3. Hirschman, *Essays*, p. 237.

4. AGN, Renta de Tabaco 8, contract negotiations, Testimonio de contrata de las villas de Córdoba y Orizaba para las cosechas de tabacos de los años de 1765, 1766, y 1767, 21 February 1765. Lieutenant Miguel de Leiba Esparragoza, captain Félix de Gandara of Córdoba, and the *regidores* Juan Antonio de Cora and Manuel Montes Argüelles of Orizaba were duly "elected" by the tobacco growers to represent their interests.

5. AGN, Renta de Tabaco, *factor* of Orizaba Mendiola, Instrucción . . .; AGN, Tabaco 266, representatives, *directores generales*, and viceroy, 15 September 1767. Each planter was required to draw up a *relación jurada* (sworn statement) of the number of grades each of his *tercios* contained. At the expense of the planters, the *tercios* were delivered to monopoly warehouses in the *villas*. The inspector-general and his aides placed the *tercios* on wide tables, where they were opened, separated, and examined leaf by leaf to determine if their owners had classified them correctly. The value of the crop changed according to any alterations made by the inspector-general due to incorrect grading or damaged or putrified leaves. The local monopoly accountant noted the final grades, weight, and value of each crop.

6. AGN, Renta de Tabaco 48, report of *factor* of Orizaba, Mendiola, 5 January 1778.

7. See the discussion by Brian Hamnett, "Obstáculos a la política agraria del despotismo ilustrado," *Historia Mexicana* 20 (1971) 72–73.

8. AGI, Mexico 2256, Espinosa to viceroy, 18 December 1764.

9. AGI, Mexico 2256, Espinosa to representatives, contract negotiations, 30 January 1765.

10. AGI, Mexico 2256, Calvo to viceroy, 4 February 1765; AGI, Mexico 2256, Calvo to viceroy, 10 February 1765.

11. AGI, Mexico 2256, Calvo to viceroy and *junta de tabaco*, 2 January 1765; AGI, Mexico 2256, Calvo to viceroy, 10 February 1765; AGN, Renta de Tabaco 2, viceroy to *directores generales*, 8 August 1767.

12. See McWatters, "The Royal Tobacco Monopoly," p. 63.

13. AGN, Tabaco 266, contract negotiations, representatives, *directores generales* to viceroy, 15 September 1767. A salient characteristic of raw to-

bacco leaf is its propensity for loss of substance and quality during drying and wastage during transportation and storage.

14. Reassessments of crop value could reduce a planter's income quite considerably, and, since tobacco deliveries were never regraded upwards, accusations of deliberate and unfair regrading practices became another point of contention. Between 1765 and 1780 the lowest number regraded amounted to 14 percent in 1767, while the maximum was 64 percent in 1768, with an average of 30 percent for the whole period. AGN, Tabaco 389, report of Mendiola, *factor* of Orizaba, on the number of harvests regraded by the inspector-general Francisco del Real, 9 November 1782.

15. AGN, Tabaco 89, *fiscal* to viceroy, 20 November 1776.

16. AGI, Mexico 2277, directors of Real Compañía de Caracas to Arriaga, 21 January 1771.

17. For a detailed discussion of the problems, see McWatters, "The Royal Tobacco Monopoly," pp. 81–88.

18. AGN, Tabaco 29, *bando* of viceroy Bucareli, 1 October 1777.

19. AGN, Tabaco 266, Testimonio de la ratificación del convenio y contrata incierto . . . para los años de 1768 y 1769. AGN, Tabaco 467, testimony of the representatives from the *villas*, 30 October 1771; AGN, Tabaco 89, Diego Antonio Blanco to viceroy Bucareli, 7 August 1776; ANO, 1786, exp. 14–9–F, representatives' account, 15 April 1786.

20. AGN, Tabaco 89; most of these issues are dealt with in the Expediente formado á consequencia de representación de Don Diego Antonio Blanco sobre varios puntos del gobierno y manejo del común de cosecheros de tabaco de la villa de Córdoba.

21. AGN, Tabaco 29, *directores generales* to viceroy Bucareli, 14 August 1777.

22. Ibid.

23. Ibid.

24. AGN, Renta de Tabaco 2, viceroy to *ayuntamiento* of Córdoba, 18 March 1778.

25. AGN, Renta de Tabaco 2, inspector-general to *directores generales*, 25 March 1778.

26. AGN, Tabaco 26, planters of Córdoba to viceroy, no date.

27. AGN, Tabaco 30, *director general* to viceroy, 5 September 1781.

28. AGN, Renta de Tabaco 44, inspector-general to *directores generales*, 4 March 1778.

29. AGN, Tabaco 30, *director general* Hierro to *director general* of *alcabalas*, 20 February 1779.

30. Calculated from planter contracts contained in various *ramos* from AGN, Tabaco, Renta de Tabaco; AGI, Audiencia de México; ANO, notarial records.

31. AGN, Renta de Tabaco 2, inspector-general to *director general* Hierro, 7 January 1779.

32. AGN, Renta de Tabaco 2, inspector-general to *director general* Hierro, 31 March 1779.

33. AGN, Renta de Tabaco 2, *director general* Hierro to viceroy Mayorga, 18 December 1779.

34. AGN, Tabaco 35, viceroy Mayorga to Silvestre Díaz de la Vega, *contador general*, 17 October 1781.

35. AGN, Tabaco 30, report of *factor* of Córdoba, Juan de Arias, 4 July 1781; AGN, Tabaco 474, report of Silvestre Díaz de la Vega, *contador general*, 27 November 1781, Razon de los cosecheros de la villa de Córdoba.

36. AGN, Tabaco 276, Alejandro Fernández to viceroy, undated, Expediente sobre quejas de los cosecheros de las villas contra Francisco del Real.

37. AGN, Renta de Tabaco 18, parish priest of Córdoba to Bishop of Puebla, 4 August 1778.

38. AGN, Tabaco 352, parish priest of Izhuatlan to Viceroy Mayorga, 30 May 1780.

39. AGN, Renta de Tabaco 18, report of *fiscal*, 20 June 1780.

40. AGN, Tabaco 352, Juan José Sanz to viceroy, 12 June 1780; ANO, 1785A, exp. 8–14–F.

41. AGN, Tabaco 29, Antonio Hernández Navarro to viceroy, 15 October 1782.

42. The Montañes merchant, Pedro Antonio de Cossío, partly as a result of providing much-needed capital to help establish monopoly operations, was appointed as *administrador general* of the newly formed *aduanas* (customs) section (1767–1769, 1770–1779). Parallel to his rise in the 1770s was that of his brother, Joaquín, who received an appointment as administrator of *aduanas* in Puebla. Two brothers were placed in the two most strategic customs offices in Mexico for internal and external commerce, Puebla and Veracruz. After his appointment as *superintendente general de Real Hacienda*, in charge of the viceregal treasury, between 1779 and 1783, Cossío soon fell foul of Gálvez and subsequently fell from political grace. See Brading, *Miners and Merchants*, pp. 63, 112. For additional background on Pedro Antonio de Cossío, see Javier Ortiz de la Tabla y Ducasse, "Comercio y comerciantes Montañeses en Veracruz, 1785–1804," in *Santander y el nuevo mundo*, pp. 311–326; José Joaquín Real Díaz and Antonia M. Heredia Herrera, "Martin de Mayorga," in *Virreyes de Nueva España (1779–1787)*.

43. AGI, Mexico 2309, report of viceroy, 16 June 1781.

44. Quoted in Vicente Rodríguez García, *El fiscal de real hacienda en Nueva España (Don Ramón de Posada y Soto, 1781–1793)*, p. 110.

45. See Real Díaz and Heredia Herrera, "Martin de Mayorga," chap. 2, on Don Pedro Antonio de Cossío.

46. Quoted in Brading, *Miners and Merchants*, p. 63.

47. AGN, Renta de Tabaco 26, inspector-general to *directores generales*, 5 July 1786.

48. AGN, Renta de Tabaco 26, Argüelles to inspector-general, 12 July 1786.

49. AGN, Tabaco 501, inspector-general to *directores generales*, 16 April 1788.

50. AGN, Tabaco 501, *directores generales* Hierro and Riva Agüero to viceroy Flores, 20 May 1788.

51. AGN, Tabaco 501, *alcalde mayor* to *director general*, 27 May 1788.

52. AGN, Renta de Tabaco 48, *cabildo* of Córdoba to viceroy Revillagigedo, 29 September 1789.

53. Hirschman, *Essays in Trespassing*, p. 241.

54. AGN, Renta de Tabaco 1, Estado que demuestra los tabacos remitidos de la Nueva Orleans desde el año de 1778 a que se verifico el primer envio hasta fin del 1788.

55. Coutts, "Boom and Bust," p. 3.

56. By 1800, most planters had shifted to cotton production in response to the machinations of the Bourbon tobacco portfolio. Coutts, "Boom and Bust," p. 307.

57. AGN, Tabaco 241, Díaz de la Vega to Branciforte, 28 August 1795. For his lengthy treatise, see BN (Mexico), Mss 1337, Discurso sobre la decadencia de la agricultura en el reyno de Nueva España . . . 24 July 1788. Díaz de la Vega was not the only tobacco official with an interest in economic development. The administrator of tobacco in Cochabamba, Upper Peru (Bolivia), Don José Gómez Merino, held strong views about the economic reform and development of Cochabamba, which included state promotion of viticulture, olive tree cultivation, and the production of hemp and flax. See Brooke Larson, *Colonialism and Agrarian Transformation in Bolivia— Cochabamba, 1550–1900*, pp. 242–243.

58. For the key text to Bourbon thought on agriculture and landownership, see Gaspar Melchor de Jovellanos, *Informe . . . de ley agraria*.

59. AGI, Mexico 2298, José Francisco Rodriguez, Manuel Montes Argüelles to Ex. Sr., 4 September 1809.

60. AGN, Renta de Tabaco 9, Díaz de la Vega to viceroy, 8 August 1797.

61. The distinctions were as follows:

	Enteros	Rotos
1st grade	3 reales	2 7/8 reales
2nd grade	2 reales	1 7/8 reales
3rd grade	1 real	1 real

62. AGN, Tabaco 501, *bando* of viceroy Revillagigedo, 3 February 1790.

63. AGN, Tabaco 453, *directores generales* to *factor* of Córdoba, 1 April 1789.

64. AGN, Renta de Tabaco 9, *director general* Hierro to *factor* of Córdoba, 23 January 1793.

65. Tabaco 448, *director general* to viceroy, 13 May 1794. For a twentieth-century version of this and Tabamex's contract practices, see Norma Aida Giarracca de Teubal, "La subordinación del campesinado a los complejos agroindustriales. El tabaco en Mexico." See also Jesús Jáuregui et al, *Tabamex—un caso de integración vertical de la agricultura*.

66. AGI, Mexico 2259, Mendiola to *director general*, 19 January 1791.

67. AGN, Tabaco 453, Díaz de la Vega to viceroy, 26 February 1799.

68. AGN, Renta de Tabaco 9, *director general* to *factores* of the *villas*, 23 May 1795.

69. Lugar, "The Portuguese Tobacco Trade," p. 57. It is quite a striking comparison between the management styles of two government enterprises using the same crop. The registration lists in the Brazilian case contained information not just on the planter and his ethnic background, but also on the quality of soil and type of fertilization used. In the case of colonial Mexico, such information was not collected on an individual basis, and discussions of the soil and its relative fertility appear only in general reports and assessments of the regions of Orizaba and Córdoba by monopoly inspectors and *factores*.

70. AGN, Renta de Tabaco 88, report of Alejandro de Castro, 20 May 1801.

71. AGN, Renta de Tabaco 88, *fiscal* to viceroy, 31 July 1802.

72. AGN, Renta de Tabaco 88, petition of planters of Córdoba and Orizaba, José María Ortuño por los comunes de cosecheros de las villas de Orizaba y Córdoba y anexas de Zongolica y Huatusco, n.d. The statement bears a striking resemblance to complaints made by the cacao planters of Venezuela against the price policy of the Real Compañía Guipuzcoana, Spain's first monopoly company. The cacao planters attempted to resolve their differences by rebellion in 1749, and it was through a combination of force and reform that the rebellion was ended. See Robert J. Ferry, "The Price of Cacao, its Export, and Rebellion in Eighteenth-Century Caracas—Boom, Bust, and the Basque Monopoly," in *Essays on the Price History of Eighteenth-Century Latin America*, ed. Lyman L. Johnson and Enrique Tandeter.

73. AGN, Renta de Tabaco 88, José María Ortuño por los comunes de cosecheros de las villas de Cordoba y Orizaba y anexas de Zongolica y Huatusco, n.d.

74. Ibid.

75. AGN, Renta de Tabaco 88; Mendiola, *factor* of Orizaba, Rafael García to *director general*, 16 November 1803; Robles, *factor* of Córdoba, Marcos José de Hería to *director general*, 7 December 1803.

76. AGN, Tabaco 350, report of *factor* of Orizaba, 25 January 1804; AGN, Renta de Tabaco 88, *director general* to viceroy, 13 April 1804.

77. AGN, Tabaco 350, *director general* to viceroy, 25 April 1804.

78. AGN, Tabaco 350, inspector of tobacco for Córdoba to *factor* of Córdoba, 14 April 1804.

79. AGN, Renta de Tabaco 88, Real Tribunal de Cuentas to *fiscal*, 18 May 1804.

80. AGN, Tabaco 350, Mendiola, *factor* of Orizaba to planters of the *villas*, 13 June 1804.

81. AGN, Tabaco 231, Rafael García to Mendiola, 21 July 1804; AGN, Tabaco 350, *director general* to viceroy, 25 October 1804.

82. AGN, Renta de Tabaco 88, report of *contador general*, 17 April 1806.

83. AGn, Tabaco 420, *director general* to viceroy, 26 January 1809.

84. AGN, Renta de Tabaco 88, viceroy to *director general*, 14 May 1806.

85. AGI, Mexico 2296, report of viceroy, 26 September 1806; AGI, Mex-

ico 2296, viceregal decree, 19 February 1807. Like their counterparts in Mexico, the tobacco planters of Chiclayo in Peru refused in 1801 to meet their quotas and deliver their crops to the monopoly warehouses. They justified their boycott by the rising cost of transport and handling and succeeded in gaining price increases for their tobacco. See the discussion in Susan E. Ramírez Horton, *Provincial Patriarchs—Land Tenure and the Economics of Power in Colonial Peru*, p. 255–257.

86. AGN, Tabaco 350, Díaz de la Vega to viceroy, 5 July 1804.

87. AGN, Tabaco 231, *factor* of Orizaba to *director general*, 18 August 1804.

88. The Consolidación law ordered and forced sale of clerical properties and repayment and consolidation of clerical debts. The law affected the most important social groups in Mexico, who, in the absence of formal banks, routinely borrowed capital from the funds of the clerical corporations. See Asunción Lavrin, "The Execution of the Law of Consolidación in New Spain: Economic Aims and Results," *HAHR* 53, no. 1 (February 1973). For a wider discussion of the Consolidación as part of Spain's attempts to raise revenues, see Richard Herr, *Rural Change and Royal Finances in Spain at the End of the Old Regime*, chapters three, four, and five.

89. AGN, Tabaco 498, *contador general* to *director general*, 6 May 1808.

90. For the insurgents' activities around Orizaba and Córdoba, see Brian R. Hamnett, *Roots of Insurgency*, pp. 165–167.

91. Arcila Farías, *Reformas económicas*.

92. AGI, Mexico 2259, Bucareli to Gálvez, 27 July 1777. In Europe in the seventeenth and eighteenth centuries, Italy and Germany were the leading paper makers and exporters. See Hermann Kellenbenz, "The Organization of Industrial Production," in *The Cambridge Economic History of Europe*, vol. 5, ed. E. E. Rich and C. H. Wilson, p. 535. Very little has been written on the paper trade in Spanish America in general and in Mexico in particular. For a general overview of the latter, see Hans Lenz and Federico Gómez de Orozco, *La industria papelera en México*. For the early problems which beset investment in Mexico and the establishment of a paper industry in Mexico after independence, see Robert A. Potash, *Mexican Government and Industrial Development in the Early Republic: The Banco de Avío*, pp. 22–23.

93. BN (Madrid) Mss 10.361, Fonseca and Urrutia, *Libro de la Real Hacienda*, vol. 7, f. 63.

94. AGI, Mexico 2259, report of *directores generales* Hierro and Riva, 14 April 1777.

95. AGN, Tabaco 506, Miguel de Vallejo, administrator of *aduanas*, Cádiz, to viceroy Mayorga, 1 February 1782.

96. AGN, Tabaco 241, Díaz de la Vega to viceroy, 10 July 1795. For a general description of the paper industry in Valencia, see Vicent Ribes, *Los valencianos y América—el comercio valenciano con Indias en el siglo XVIII*, chap. 4.

97. AGI, Mexico 2263, Manuel Centurion to Ex. Sr., 14 March 1786 (Málaga); AGI, Mexico 2280, Juan Murphy, Jaime Setta, 11 September 1787 (Má-

laga); AGN, Tabaco 392, Pedro Porro to Manuel de Aldama, company agent, 8 January 1788 (Veracruz); AGI, Mexico 2281, Juan Murphy, 12 July 1788 (Málaga).

98. AGI, Mexico 2259, report of Hierro, de la Riva, 10 October 1776; AGN, Tabaco 241, report of *contador general,* 7 October 1795; AGI, Mexico 2268, Maniau Torquemada and Tomás Murphy to *director general,* 11 January 1799; AGI, Mexico 2268, report of Maniau Torquemada, 21 May 1800; AGN, Tabaco 96, report of Mexico City manufactory accountant, 11 February 1807; AGI, Mexico 2269, report of *contador general,* 11 December 1809.

99. AGI, Mexico 2268, viceroy Marquina, 11 June 1800.

100. AGI, Mexico 2267, Antonio Bassoco to viceroy Branciforte, 4 June 1797.

101. AGI, Mexico 2267, Acuerdo de la Junta Superior de Real Hacienda, 9 August 1797.

102. AGI, Mexico 2268, Maniau Torquemada, Tomás Murphy to *director general,* 11 January 1799.

103. Javier Ortiz de la Tabla, *Comercio exterior de Veracruz, 1778–1821—crisis de dependencia,* pp. 332–334. Tomás Murphy was the brother-in-law of viceroy Azanza and acquired his rights to trade from Azanza in 1798–1800. He also acquired licenses to import goods into Mexico from North America. See also Stanley J. Stein, "Caribbean Counterpoint," p. 34.

104. AGI, Mexico 2268, viceroy Marquina to Cayetano Soler, 27 December 1800.

105. AGI, Mexico 2268, Manuel de Quevedo, 6 April 1803.

106. AGI, Mexico 2268, *contador general,* Razón del papel que ha comprado la Renta á los comerciantes de Veracruz y de esta capital . . . , 21 May 1800.

107. Officials were ordered to investigate if there were, or had been, any paper mills which could be renovated and used to supply paper for the tobacco manufactories. The investigation revealed that a paper mill operated in Puebla in 1741 but only lasted for three years, and, in any case, witnesses described the paper produced as being of extremely bad quality, only good enough for wrapping food. AGI, 2267, *director general* to *factor* and accountant of Puebla, 13 July 1797; ibid., Francisco Antonio de Zamacona, Juan Maniau Torquemada to *director general,* 17 July 1797. Humboldt reported that there were no paper factories in New Spain. *Ensayo Político,* p. 453.

108. AGI, Mexico 2269, report of *contador general,* Estado del papel existente en los almacenes de la Renta de Tabaco de Nueva España, 11 December 1809. Humboldt reported prices per ream of white paper as follows:

1802   3 pesos
1803   3.5 pesos
1804   3.5 pesos
1805   9 pesos
1806   8 pesos

The figures for 1803 and 1804 reflect the resumption of normal shipments from Spain, only to be superceded by scarcities thereafter. See Humboldt, *Ensayo Político,* p. 609. Between 1802 and 1812 paper of all qualities and for a variety of uses, not just for the manufactories, constituted the second-most important export from Spain imported into Veracruz—15.08 percent of total exports, second only to textiles, which occupied the lion's share of 48.7 percent. See Ortiz de la Tabla, *Comercio exterior de Veracruz*, p. 233.

109. AGI, Mexico 2269, Salvador Fernando y Quintana, representative of the *fabricantes* to Cayetano Soler, 6 August 1803; José Gisbert y Domenech to Cayetano Soler, 28 August 1803.

110. Ibid.

111. AGI, Mexico 2269, representatives to secretario del Despacho de Marina, 24 May 1819.

4. Merchants, Rancheros, and Peasants

1. See Brading, *Miners and Merchants*, 28–29.

2. Daniel D. Arreola, "Nineteenth-Century Townscapes of Eastern Mexico," *The Geographical Review* 72, no. 1 (January 1982): 2–19; Lemoine Villicaña, "Documentos y mapas para la geografía histórica de Orizaba, 1690–1800," *Boletín del Archivo General de la Nación* 3 (1962): 491.

3. See Juan Carlos Garavaglia and Juan Carlos Grosso, "De Veracruz a Durango: un análisis regional de la Nueva España borbónica," *Siglo XIX* 11, no. 4 (July–December 1987): 9–52. The *diezmos* are somewhat problematical as an indicator, however. The series published by A. Medina Rubio in *La Iglesia y la producción agrícola en Puebla, 1540–1795* does indeed indicate an upswing which correlates with the introduction of monopoly production. But if we calculate the value of the *diezmo* deducted by the monopoly at 8 percent, the monopoly deductions (in money) for some years exceed the total value of *diezmo* collections reported for the *villas* by Medina Rubio.

4. Garavaglia and Grosso, "De Veracruz a Durango," p. 23.

5. Even if the annual carryovers are deducted from the listed *alcabala* figures, and the net *alcabala* income is used as a base figure, then the percentage contribution of tobacco increases. Data taken from AGN, Indiferente General, Alcabalas (in process of classification). The amounts of *gross alcabalas* collected may be found in Garavaglia and Grosso, *Las alcabalas Novohispanas (1776–1821)*, pp. 229–236.

6. AGN, Padrones 19, Relación de los pueblos, haciendas y ranchos de la jurisdicción de Orizaba, Padrón General de familias españolas, castizas y mestizas, 1791 (hereafter referred to as Padrón General de Orizaba, 1791).

7. ANO, 1804, exp. 1–10–F, Mendiola, 19 May 1804.

8. BL Add. Mss 17557, Descripción de Veracruz . . . por Dn. José de Quiroga . . . 1779. (See note 33 below.)

9. Cathy Duke, "The Family in Eighteenth Century Plantation Society in Mexico,"in *Comparative Perspectives on Slavery in New World Plantation Societies*, ed. V. Rubin and A. Tuden, p. 227.

10. See Adriana Naveda Chávez-Hita, *Esclavos negros en las haciendas azucareras de Córdoba, Veracruz, 1690–1830*. For assessments of the general development of sugar in the Veracruz region, see Patrick J. Carroll,

Blacks and Society in Colonial Veracruz. For an account of the first sugar enterprises in Orizaba, see Patricia Seed, "A Mexican Noble Family, the Counts of the Valle de Orizaba."

11. ANO, 1809, exp. 15–65–F.

12. AGN, Inquisición 937, Orizaba, Alcaldía Mayor, cabacera de curato y vicaria foranea del Obispado de la Puebla de Los Angeles, Orizaba, June 7 1754, ff.244–246v.

13. AGN, Padrones 19, Padrón General de Orizaba, 1791.

14. ANO, 1804, exp. 1–10–F, Mendiola, 19 May 1804.

15. AGN, Inquisición 937, Córdoba, Alcaldía Mayor, cabacera de curato y vicaria foranea del Obispado de la Puebla de Los Angeles, Córdoba, June 7 1754, ff.256–258v. By 1840, the population of the districts of Orizaba and Córdoba, was, respectively, 55,443 and 38,334. See Sergio Florescano Mayet, "Las divisiones políticas del Estado de Veracruz, 1824–1917," *Dualismo* 6, no. 1 (1977): 70. Also Vicente Segura, *Apuntes para la estadística del departamento de Orizaba,* 1831.

16. Eric Van Young, *Hacienda and Market in Eighteenth-Century Mexico, The Rural Economy of the Guadalajara Region, 1675–1820,* p. 35.

17. Calculated from Navarro y Noriega's population estimates of the intendancy of Veracruz: 19,379 Spanish, 28,432 Castas, and 137,774 Indians, out of a total population of 185,935. Quoted in Manuel Trens, *La Historia de Veracruz,* p. 593.

18. Peter Gerhard, *A Guide to the Historical Geography of New Spain,* for the jurisdiction of Orizaba, p. 206, and for the jurisdiction of Córdoba, p. 84.

19. William B. Taylor, *Landlord and Peasant in Colonial Oaxaca,* pp. 200–201. Eugene Wiemers argues that, although considerable renovation of abandoned sugar haciendas occurred by the beginning of the nineteenth century, smaller properties continued to play an important role. Eugene L. Wiemers, Jr., "Agriculture and Credit in Nineteenth Century Mexico: Orizaba and Córdoba, 1822–1871," *HAHR* 65, no. 3 (1985).

20. Chávez-Hita, *Esclavos Negros,* table 8, p. 86; AGN, Tabaco 307, report of Rafael García, 6 April 1805; Segura, *Apuntes,* pp. 63–79; BL Add.Mss 17557, Descripción de Veracruz . . . : por Dn. José de Quiroga . . . 1779. BL Add.Mss 17580, Villa y subdelegación de Córdoba de la Intendencia de la Nueva Veracruz. Estado de su población en 4 de noviembre de 1793 por Joaquín Pablo Gómez y Aza (hereafter cited as Villa y subdelegación de Córdoba . . . por Joaquín Pablo Gómez y Aza). ANO, various *expedientes.* In 1810, Navarro y Noriega listed a total of 60 haciendas and 157 *ranchos* for the entire intendancy. See Trens, *La historia de Veracruz,* pp. 416, 593. Van Young argues that the grain-producing haciendas on the outskirts of Guadalajara ranged between 4,000 and 5,000 acres in size, and it was not unusual for the local mixed-farming *ranchos* to be of a similar size. No hacienda, however, was as small as some of the two to five acre parcels rented out on the city *ejidos* or the numerous *ranchos* in the under-1,000 acre range. See Van Young, *Hacienda and Market,* pp. 109–111.

21. When the monopoly took over several tobacco *ranchos,* reports sub-

mitted by the local monopoly inspectors indicated the amount of tobacco which could be sown on the *ranchos*. Based on the quantities cited, the properties had to be at least between 200 and 1,200 acres. This represents a minimum size since it is unlikely that all of the land would be under tillage; reserve lands, grazing, and scrublands would add on several acres. AGN, Tabaco 307, report of Rafael García, 6 April 1805.

22. AGN, Padrones 19, Padrón General de Orizaba, 1791.

23. BL Add.Mss 17580, Villa y subdelegación de Córdoba . . . por Joaquín Pablo Gómez y Aza.

24. AGN, Tabaco 455, Matrícula General de cosecheros de la jurisdicción de Orizaba . . . verificado en el de 1770 con arreglo á los ordenes de la Dirección General de 26 abril 1769; ANO, 1810, exp. 8, 9, Registro de las escrituras de suplementos que da la renta del tabaco á los cosecheros de tabaco de Orizaba. (Hereafter referred to as *Registro de suplementos*). The ranges are derived from the owners' appraisals of their *ranchos* which appear in the declarations of the *Registros de suplementos*.

25. ANO, 1798–1800, exp. 20. *Registro de suplementos.*

26. Trens comments that at the beginning of the eighteenth century, landowners began their "usurpations" of land, most notably the Marqués de Sierra Nevada and the Conde del Valle de Orizaba. The Conde owned haciendas in Tecamaluca, Coatlapan, Rincón Grande, Xalapilla, Espinal Cabrera, San Lucas, Piletas, Encinal, Jazmin, Santiago, Pala, Ojo Zarco, and Ocotopec, all within the jurisdiction of Orizaba. The Marqués also possessed properties in Ocotopec, Tesmalaca, Infiernillo, Escamela, and Espinal. See Trens, *La Historia de Veracruz,* pp. 418–419. The Marqués del Valle de la Colina also owned the Hacienda de Sumidero. See ANO, 1756, exp. 14–13–F, f.37; ANO, 1772, exp. 11–15–F.

27. AGN, Padrones 19, Padrón General de Orizaba, 1791.

28. For the variations in *rancheros'* commercial operations, see D. A. Brading, *Haciendas and Ranchos in the Mexican Bajío, León, 1700–1860,* p. 151; Richard B. Lindley, *Haciendas and Economic Development— Guadalajara, Mexico at Independence,* p. 30.

29. AGN, Renta de Tabaco 88, Robles, *factor* of Córdoba to *director general,* 9 September 1801, and, *director general* to viceroy, 2 June 1804.

30. ANO, 1802, exp. 13–24–F, 13 September 1802, Eusebio Lucas Jiménez for the deceased governor of the Cabildo de San Miguel de Orizaba; ANO, 1805 exp. 6–19–F, 3 December 1805, Governor Francisco Gordiano Palafox; ANO, 1806 exp. 26–33–F, 24 December 1806, Governor Lorenzo José Vidal.

31. AGN, Tabaco 29, Expediente sobre resistencia que hacen el Governador y República de Naturales de Ixhuatlan á no querer admitir en arrendamiento varios pedazos de tierra que les propuso Dn. Francisco del Real para siembras de tabaco, 1778; AGN, Tabaco 474, Expediente sobre arrendamiento de tierras para cultivo de tabaco á los Indios de Ixhuatlan, y de lo que estos deven á la Renta de aquel fruto, January 1782.

32. Arróniz, *Ensayo de una historia de Orizaba* p. 282

33. BL Add.Mss 17557, Descripción de Veracruz y su provincia sobre la

cultura y preparaciones del tabaco en Córdoba y Orizaba por Dn. José de Quiroga, factor de tabacos en aquella capital en 1779, in *Noticias de América*, II (hereafter cited as Descripción de Veracruz . . . por Dn. José de Quiroga . . . 1779).

34. AGN, Tabaco 38, Rafael García to *director general*, 15 March 1795; AGN, Renta de Tabaco 38, Rafael García to *director general*, 25 March 1795. As a category of rural labor, the *pegujaleros* were not unique to central Veracruz. Enrique Florescano, in his classic work on maize prices and agricultural crises, provides a general definition for the term *pegujal* as the minimum parcel of land which supplied the annual needs of a family. See Enrique Florescano, *Precios del maíz y crisis agrícolas en México*, p. 145. Discussions of *pegujaleros* may also be found in Cheryl English Martin, "Haciendas and Villages in Late Colonial Morelos," *HAHR* 62, no. 3 (1982), and Claude Morin, *Michoacán en la Nueva España del siglo XVIII*.

35. The advancement of *avíos* was a common business practice in colonial Mexico. For its use in agriculture, see Van Young, *Hacienda and Market*, p. 111; for the production of cochineal, Hamnett, *Politics and Trade*, and in the silver mining industry, Brading, *Miners and Merchants*.

36. ANO, 1785–1810, *Registros de suplementos* for selected years.

37. AGN, Tabaco 32, contracts, 1778; ANO, 1807, exp. 9, contracts, 1807.

38. AGN, Renta de Tabaco 44, contratas, 1779.

39. ANO, 1810–1811, exp. 8, *Registro de suplementos*.

40. The estimated acreages are calculated on the basis of the average number of pounds produced per acre. They represent only a general estimate to gauge the magnitude of change and pressures on the land, and do not take into account changes in yields per acre as the eighteenth century wore on.

41. For an analysis of rural rebellion, see John Tutino, *From Insurrection to Revolution in Mexico—Social Bases of Agrarian Violence, 1750–1940*.

42. ANO, 1808 exp. 2–10–F, 21 May 1808.

43. Robert W. Patch, "Agrarian Change in Eighteenth-Century Yucatán," *HAHR* 65, no. 1 (1985): 36–38.

44. AGN, Renta de Tabaco 44, deputies of Córdoba and Orizaba to viceroy, 26 May 1767.

45. AGI, Mexico 1406, Mendiola's report, 5 January 1781.

46. AGN, Renta de Tabaco 88, Mendiola to *director general*, 16 November 1803.

47. ANO, 1778 exp. 8–12–F; ANO, 1785 exp. 17–28–F.

48. ANO, 1785B exp. 5–4–F; ANO, 1806 exp. 11–41–F, Junta Superior de Propios, 6 March 1807.

49. ANO, 1798 exp. 10–42–F, *fiscal*, 30 November 1798.

50. For an introduction to tobacco and its production, see B. C. Akehurst, *Tobacco*. Also for comparative purposes, see Paul G. E. Clemens, *The Atlantic Economy and Colonial Maryland's Eastern Shore: From Tobacco to Grain*; E. S. Morgan, *American Slavery, American Freedom*; G. A. Stiverson, *Poverty in a Land of Plenty—Tenancy in Eighteenth-Century Mary-*

land; W. Tatham, *An Historical and Practical Essay on the Culture and Commerce of Tobacco;* V. J. Wyckoff, *Tobacco Regulation in Colonial Maryland.* In Maryland, in colonial North America, tobacco fields usually lay fallow for about twenty years before they could be replanted with tobacco.

51. AGN, Renta de Tabaco 44, report of Mendiola, Pliego que ministra varios noticias reflexiones y prevenciones sobre las contratas de tabaco celebradas en este reyno de Nueva España por la Real Hacienda con los labradores de tabaco de las villas de Córdoba y Orizaba desde el año de 1765 hasta 1778. For a comparative situation in the production of coffee in nineteenth-century Costa Rica, see Ciro F. S. Cardoso, "The formation of the coffee estate in nineteenth-century Costa Rica," in *Land and Labour in Latin America,* ed. K. Duncan and I. Rutledge.

52. BL Add.Mss 17557, Descripción de Veracruz . . . por Don José de Quiroga . . . 1779.

53. AGN, Tabaco 405, Diligencias practicadas para que los cosecheros de esta villa firman la contrata que hicieron con el difunto Francisco del Real, Orizaba 1789.

54. AGI, Mexico 1406, report of Mendiola, *factor* of Orizaba, 5 January 1780; AGN, Tabaco 231, Rafael García to Mendiola, 15 February 1805.

55. AGN, Tabaco 231, Rafael García to Mendiola, 15 February 1805.

56. AGN, Tabaco 498, *contador general* to *director general,* 6 May 1808.

57. For a discussion of a "tobacco mentality," see T. H. Breen, *Tobacco Culture—The Mentality of the Great Tidewater Planters on the Eve of Revolution.*

58. The planting of seedbeds began in June or July. By mid- to late August sowing began, followed by removal from the nursery beds to the previously prepared hills. Plants were spaced at 2/3 *vara* (22 inches), since room was required for the eight or nine leaves which grew, on average, on each plant. Continuous topping and suckering were crucial if a high-grade crop was to result. Workers were needed to cover the crop five or six times each week to break the suckers off. Normally suckering was performed by experienced cutters who used a long, hardened thumbnail as their 'knife'. The actual cutting of leaves also demanded experienced cutters who could judge their maturity. Following the harvest, leaves were bundled, strung, and hung up to dry in tobacco sheds. Taking them down (*descolgar*) required, if possible, a rainy day so that the humidity helped to moisten the leaves, rendering them more pliable; dry, brittle leaves cracked easily, diminishing their value.

59. See Lugar, "The Portuguese Tobacco Trade," p. 35. Her calculations of worker output and yields confirm "the limited returns to scale in tobacco cultivation, the feature which attracted small farmers to it in times when slave labor was scarce." See also Joan Thirsk, "New crops and their Diffusion: Tobacco-growing in Seventeenth-century England," in *Rural Change and Urban Growth 1500–1800. Essays in English Regional History in Honour of W. G. Hoskins,* ed. C. W. Chalklin and M. A. Havinden, pp. 76–103.

60. ANO, 1765 exp. 5–8–F, petition of Cora and Argüelles, 23 February 1765. AGN, Tabaco 307, Rafael García to Mendiola, *factor* of Orizaba, 6 April 1805.

61. The inspector-general reported that "the tobacco fields are worked predominately by Indian work crews (*manos de quadrillas de Indios*)." AGN, Tabaco 428, Real to *directores generales*, 4 March 1786.

62. AGN, Renta de Tabaco 46, report of the inspector-general, 26 August 1774.

63. AGN, Renta de Tabaco 38, Rafael García to *directores generales*, 25 March 1795.

64. AGN, Padrones 19, Padrón General de Orizaba, 1791.

65. Ibid.

66. Ibid.

67. Ibid.

68. AGN, Renta de Tabaco 44, report of Antonio de Sobrevilla, 25 April 1781.

69. The average labor requirement for the cultivation of tobacco was one man per 10,000 plants (which required two acres of land). AGN, Renta de Tabaco 44, Francisco Antonio de la Llave to *directores generales*, 17 January 1774.

70. Compiled and calculated from AGN, Renta de Tabaco 44, deputies of the *villas* to viceroy, 26 May 1767; AGI, Mexico 1406, report of *factor* of Orizaba, Mendiola, 5 January 1780; AGN, Renta de Tabaco 44, inspector-general to *contador general* Silvestre Díaz de la Vega, 1 May 1781; AGN Renta de Tabaco 44, José Antonio de Arsú y Arcaya, *alcalde mayor* of Orizaba to viceroy, 9 April 1781; AGN Renta de Tabaco 44, report of Antonio de Sobrevilla, 25 April 1781.

71. See the discussion by Van Young, "The Rich Get Richer and the Poor Get Skewed: Real Wages and Popular Living Standards in Late Colonial Mexico."

72. AGN, Renta de Tabaco 26, inspector-general to *directores generales*, 4 March 1786.

73. Alan Knight, "Mexican Peonage: What Was it and Why Was It?" *JLAS* 18, part 1 (May 1986): 62. Also see Arnold J. Bauer, "Rural workers in Spanish America: problems of Peonage and Oppression," *HAHR* 59, no. 1 (1979). For sharecropping, see Stinchcombe's schema and view of economic efficiency of selfemployment over hired labor in "Agricultural Enterprises and Rural Class Relations," *The American Journal of Sociology*, 67 (1961): 165–176. See Evsey D. Domar, "The Causes of Slavery or Serfdom: A Hypothesis," *Journal of Economic History* 30 (1970): 18–32; Daniel Chirot, "The Growth of Market and Service Labour Systems in Agriculture," *Journal of Social History* 8 (1974–1975): 67–80.

74. AGN, Renta de Tabaco 18, *factor* of Orizaba Mendiola to viceroy Mayorga, 20 July 1781; AGN, Tabaco 474, *director general* Philipe de Hierro to viceroy Mayorga, 13 December 1781; AGN, Renta de Tabaco 18, *factor* of Orizaba Mendiola to *directores generales*, 27 January 1790.

75. ANO, 1808, exp. 13, 20, registro de suplementos.

76. ANO, 1782–1801, exp. 10–259–F.

77. AGI, Mexico 2309, Marcos González, Pedro Miranda de Zevallos to inspector-general, 2 February 1787.

78. AHH, 632–17, *directores generales* to viceroy, 10 May 1781.

79. Although the *repartimiento de indios* was officially abolished in Mexico in 1633, it continued to survive in various forms in various regions. For a comparative perspective, see Van Young, *Hacienda and Market*, pp. 242–245.

80. AGN, Renta de Tabaco 2, inspector-general to *directores generales*, 1 April 1778. AGN, Renta de Tabaco 18, *factor* of Orizaba Mendiola to *directores generales*, 3 February 1790.

81. AGN, Tabaco 352, Indian governors to *directores generales*, 7 June 1780.

82. AGN, Tabaco 307, viceroy to Real Tribunal de Cuentas, 5 May 1805.

83. AGN, Tabaco 307, inspector of tobacco Rafael García to *factor* of Orizaba, 6 April 1805; AGN, Tabaco 350, *director general* to viceroy, 22 August 1805.

84. AGN, Tabaco 350, inspector of tobacco Marcos José de Hería to *factor* of Córdoba, 14 April 1804.

85. Calculated from contract for 1789, AGN, Renta de Tabaco 18, *directores generales*, 20 May 1789. Matrícula que contiene las siembras de tabaco contratadas por los cosecheros de Orizaba y Zongolica, 1788 para el de 1789 (hereafter cited as Matrícula . . . 1788 para el de 1789).

86. AGI, Mexico 2275, Frago to Arriaga, 12 February 1769.

87. ANO, 1785A, exp. 11–121–F, f.27.

88. ANO, 1785A, exp. 11–121–F.

89. AGN, Tabaco 88, Mendiola to *director general*, 16 November 1803.

90. ANO, 1772, exp. 13–23–F, ff. 1–15.

91. AGN, Tabaco 501, planters of Orizaba and Córdoba to viceroy, 30 January 1788.

92. AGN, Renta de Tabaco 18, *directores generales*, 20 May 1789, Matrícula . . . 1788 para el de 1789.

93. AGN, Renta de Tabaco 18, *directores generales*, 20 May 1789, Matrícula . . . 1788 para el de 1789.

94. Ibid.

95. ANO, 1802, exp. 7, *Registro de suplementos*; ANO, 1804–1805, exp. 29, *Registro de suplementos*. In 1804 the remaining 200,000 *matas* were grown on Puy y Ochoa's *rancho* in Tlalpilla.

96. AGI, Mexico 2275, Frago to Arriaga, 12 February 1769.

97. ANO, 1794–1799, exp. 11, *Registro de suplementos*.

98. In 1804, for example, the harvest of Don Miguel de Pozo failed to cover the credit advanced by the monopoly, leaving a debt of 441 pesos. The *factor* Mendiola stipulated that the monopoly must be reimbursed first in preference to all other creditors of the planter, and it was. ANO, 1804 exp. 14–34–F. For other examples, see ANO, 1804 exp. 27–53–F.

99. ANO, 1806 exp. 22–115–F.

100. ANO, 1757, exp. 8–6–F.

101. ANO, 1803 exp. 14–19–F.

102. ANO, 1805 exp. 14–F.

103. ANO, 1786 exp. 2–10–F. For additional cases see ANO, 1819 exp. 6–11–F.

104. Bauer, "Rural Workers in Spanish America," p. 51.

105. Wiemers, "Agriculture and Credit," p. 535.

106. Such arrangements have many analogues in agrarian societies throughout the world and in different time periods. For an informative, if impassioned, analysis of the exploitation of Chinese peasants in the tobacco fields, see Chen Han-Seng, *Industrial Capital and Chinese Peasants—A Study of the Livelihood of Chinese Tobacco Cultivators*. For similar agrarian relations based on coffee economies, see Cardoso, "The Formation of the Coffee Estate in Nineteenth-Century Costa Rica"; Laird W. Bergad, *Coffee and the Growth of Agrarian Capitalism in Nineteenth-Century Puerto Rico*; William Roseberry, *Coffee and Capitalism in the Venezuelan Andes*.

107. Van Young, *Hacienda and Market*, p. 224. For a discussion of calculations of profit and rates of profit, see Samuel Amaral, "Rural Production and Labour in Late Colonial Buenos Aires," *JLAS*, 19, part 2 (November 1987). For assessment and discussion of rates of profit in colonial Mexico, see Brading, *Haciendas and Ranchos*, pp. 95–114; "Hacienda Profits and Tenant Farming," pp. 16, 29; Van Young, *Hacienda and Market*, pp. 224–235.

108. Calculated as the percentage of total expenditure represented by the difference between income and expenditure.

109. AGN, Administración General del Tabaco, Caja 128, *contador general, factor* of Córdoba, Libro mayor de caudales de la factoría de Córdoba, 28 March 1774; AGN, Tabaco 35, *director general* to viceroy, 28 June 1780.

110. AGN, Administración General del Tabaco, Caja 125, Data general de caudales de la factura de la real renta del tabaco de Orizaba . . . 1792.

111. ANO, 1804 exp. 26–41–F.

112. AGN, Renta de Tabaco 44, report of Mendiola, Pliego que ministra varios noticias reflexiones y prevenciones sobre las contratas de tabaco celebradas en este reyno de Nueva España por la Real Hacienda con los labradores de tabaco de las villas de Cordoba y Orizaba desde el año de 1765 hasta 1778.

113. The assessment of the planters is based on an analysis of 276 planter production profiles reconstructed from the *Registros de suplementos* located in the ANO, which contain the planter's name, where he or she produced tobacco, the quantity of tobacco to be produced, the amount of credit, securities put up, and names of *fiadores*. Additional information on planters who did not receive monopoly credit was found in the monopoly contracts, which listed the names of each planter, contract license number, and quantity to be produced. This was found in the AGN, Tabaco and Renta de Tabaco, various *legajos*, and AGI, Audiencia de Mexico, various *legajos*. The parish records of Orizaba were also used to supplement the data base on the planters.

114. AGN, Tabaco 38, Rafael García to *director general*, 15 March 1795; AGN, Renta de Tabaco 38, Rafael García to *director general*, 25 March 1795.

115. ANO, various *expedientes;* AGN, Padrones 19, Padrón General de Orizaba, 1791.

116. ANO, 1777, exp. 8–8–F; ANO, 1777, exp. 11–5–F; ANO, 1782, exp. 7–40–F.

117. AGN, Padrones 19, Padrón General de Orizaba, 1791.

118. Lemoine Villicaña, "Documentos y mapas para la geografía histórica de Orizaba (1690–1800)," doc. 6, Méritos de la villa de Orizaba para ser la sede del nuevo obispado que se proyecta crear, pp. 523–527.

119. AGN, Padrones 19, Padrón General de Orizaba, 1791.

120. Christon Archer, *The Army in Bourbon Mexico, 1760–1810,* pp. 153–154.

121. Duke, "The Family in Eighteenth-Century Plantation Society," p. 232.

122. AGN, Tabaco 501, Testimonio sobre el embargo intentado contra el cosechero de tabaco Antonio Montes Argüelles, 20 September 1786.

123. ANO, 1772, exp. 7–234–F.

124. ANO, 1787, exp. 4–77–F.

125. J. M. Tornel y Mendívil, "Fastos militares de iniquidad, barbario y despotismo del gobierno español ejecutados en las villas de Orizaba y Córdoba, hasta que se consumo la primera por los tratados de Córdoba en la guerra de once años por causa de la independencia y libertad de la nación Mexicana . . ." in *México por dentro y fuera bajo el gobierno de los virreyes* . . . ed. Hipólito Villaroel, pp. 2–3.

126. ANO, 1784, exp. 5–26–F; ANO, 1796, exp. 8–4–F; ANO, 1805, exp. 5–4–F, Francisco Puy y Ochoa, 7 December 1805.

127. See Van Young, *Hacienda and Market,* p. 173; Brading, *Miners and Merchants;* Lindley, *Haciendas and Economic Development.*

128. Van Young, *Hacienda and Market,* pp. 174–175.

129. Lindley, *Haciendas and Economic Development,* p. 19.

5. Organization, Production, and Policies

1. Jon S. Cohen, "Managers and Machinery: An Analysis of the Rise of Factory Production," *Australian Economic Papers* 20, no. 36 (June 1981): 25.

2. BN (Madrid) Mss 10.361, Fonseca and Urrutia, *Libro de la Real Hacienda,* vol. 7, f.58.

3. Joel Roberts Poinsett, *Notes on Mexico Made in the Autumn of 1822,* p. 65.

4. AGI, Mexico 2275, Frago to Arriaga, 12 February 1769; AGN, Tabaco 356, Díaz de la Vega, 31 August 1780.

5. D. C. Coleman, *Revisions in Mercantilism,* pp. 14–17.

6. See, for example, the discussion of autarchic regional economies by Van Young, in *Hacienda and Market.*

7. AGN, Tabaco 495, report of *contador general* Maniau y Ortega, 20 July 1795.

8. Originally it was argued that the monopoly gave twelve *cigarros* more

for one-half real than had the *cigarreros* before free trade was abolished, although there existed general confusion as to the actual numbers involved. There was agreement, however, that the number of *cigarros* per packet ought not be limited to a specific number but should be always proportional to the price of leaf and according to regional varieties and tastes. AGN, Tabaco 241, Manifiesto de las vicisitudes . . . Díaz de la Vega, 10 July 1795.

9. AGN, Tabaco 241, Manifiesto de las vicisitudes . . . Díaz de la Vega, 10 July 1795.

10. AGN, Renta de Tabaco 67, *factor* to *director general* Hierro, 9 January 1792.

11. BN (Madrid) Mss 10.361, Fonseca and Urrutia, *Libro de la Real Hacienda*, vol. 7, Tarifa de 1778, 1 January, f.140.

12. AGN, Tabaco 89, Riva to *directores generales*, 14 December 1774.

13. Ibid.

14. AGI, 2281, Relación No. 1 de los empleados que había en el año de 1775, Díaz de la Vega, 20 September 1788.

15. McWatters, "The Royal Tobacco Monopoly," p. 115.

16. BN (Madrid) MS 10.361, Fonseca and Urrutia, Libro del Real Hacienda, vol. 7, Tarifa de 1778, 1 January, ff.61–76.

17. AGI, Mexico 2270, Hierro to viceroy, 1 December 1776: Plan de sueldos . . . de los estanqueros, 1 January 1777.

18. AGN, Renta de Tabaco 68, Razón del premio que actualmente gozan los 58 estanquillos que propone el administrador del casco Don Raymundo Gómez, 17 August 1781.

19. McWatters, "The Royal Tobacco Monopoly," p. 124.

20. AGN, Tabaco 196, report of administrator on *estanquillos*, Mexico City, 5 November 1813.

21. AGN, Tabaco 89, *factor* to *directores generales*, 28 February 1777; AGN, Tabaco 196, report of administrator on *estanquillos*, Mexico City, 5 November 1813.

22. AGN, Tabaco 371, report of manufactory administrator Betosolo, 7 July 1795. For petitions from people who requested a position in an *estanquillo* or complained against "unfair" placement, see the cases discussed in AGI, Mexico 2292, María Loreto Lastra to viceroy, 26 March 1800; AGI, Mexico 2298, Doña Luisa Villavicencio to viceroy, 8 September 1810; AGI, Mexico 2300, José de Tejada to secretario del Estado y del Despacho de Hacienda, 10 September 1811; AGN, Tabaco 504, petition of María Josefa Aguilar, 15 October 1816; petition of Eusebio Pérez de Cosío, 15 January 1811; AGN, Tabaco 103, petition of José de Arce, undated.

23. According to Ramón María Serrera, transport costs within a radius of 60 to 100 leagues of Mexico City in 1792 amounted to 4 reales per *arroba*, quoted in Salvucci, *Textiles*, p. 145.

24. AGN, Tabaco 149, *contador general* to *director general*, 2 January 1799.

25. AGI, Mexico 2280, report of Francisco Machado, 24 January 1784. Also see AGI, Mexico 2260, Hierro, Riva to Gálvez, 26 June 1778; AGI, Mex-

ico 1403, Testimonio de consultas de la dirección general á el Exmo. Sr. Virrey y Ordenes de S.E. relativas á la escasez de tabacos de rama y sobre la falta y embargos de mulas, 1783.

26. AGN, Tabaco 344, Díaz de la Vega to viceroy, 9 February 1802.

27. AGI, Mexico 2289, report of Miguel Valero, 9 September 1793.

28. Calculated from various *legajos* from the AGN, AGI, and the Biblioteca Nacional, Mexico.

29. For a discussion of inventory investment, see *Introducing Economics*, ed. B. J. McCormick et al., pp. 585–587.

30. Sources for unit costs are as follows: 1776, AGI, Mexico 2259, report of Hierro, de la Riva, 10 October 1776; 1779, AGN, Renta de Tabaco 71, reports of Orizaba manufactory accountant, 1779; 1780, 1781, 1782, BN Mss 1332, manufactory accounts, f.265–265v, f.267–267v, and f.283v–284, respectively; 1806, AGN, Tabaco 96, manufactory account, 11 February 1807. The method used to calculate average total unit costs per cigarette-packet equivalent is as follows: based on monopoly figures, an average quantity for the amount of tobacco per packet of cigarettes was used to convert packets of cigars and leaf tobacco into packets of cigarette equivalents. The average amount used was 0.5 ounces per cigarette packet. An average quantity of 0.7 ounces per packet of cigars was used as a multiplier of packets of cigars manufactured. The resulting figure was divided by 0.5 ounces to convert to packets of cigarettes; pounds of leaf tobacco sold each year were incorporated since their acquisition and transport were obviously incorporated into costs of production to a greater magnitude than for snuff. The pounds of tobacco were simply converted into ounces and then into notional packets of cigarettes. Snuff was excluded on the basis of its marginal nature, comprising 0.5 percent of sales. Fixed costs were classified as administration and rents; variable costs as costs of tobacco, paper, transport, shipping, and manufacture. To calculate average unit costs, we used the following simple method: total fixed costs plus total variable costs equals total costs, divided by quantity produced (cigarette-packet equivalents) equals average fixed costs, plus average variable costs equals average unit costs. The same method was used to calculate unit costs of just cigars and cigarettes. The findings are not significantly different after 1780, and the trend line slopes very slightly downward. However, they register a starting cost of almost 5 *granos*. Once increased production of cigarettes and cigars was established after the abolition of private shops, the costs ranged between 2.19 and 3.54 *granos*, yielding between 3.81 and 2.46 *granos* on each packet, and the trend line slopes upward. For an introduction to economies of scale, see G. R. Hawke, *Economics for Historians*, pp. 55–56.

31. Barry Supple, "The Nature of Enterprise," in *The Cambridge Economic History of Europe*, vol. 5, ed. E. E. Rich and C. H. Wilson, p. 402.

32. John J. Tepaske, "Economic Cycles in New Spain," p. 127. See also Richard J. Salvucci and Linda K. Salvucci, "Crecimiento y cambio en la productividad de México," *Revista Latinoamericana de Historia Económica y Social* 10 (1987): 67–89, for an overview of the sectoral development

of the colonial Mexican economy; Van Young, "The Rich get Richer"; Richard L. Garner, "Price Trends in Eighteenth Century Mexico," *HAHR* 65, no. 2 (1985).

33. Ouweneel and Bijleveld, "The Economic Cycle in Bourbon Central Mexico," p. 520.

34. D. A. Brading, "Comments on 'The Economic Cycle in Bourbon Central Mexico: A Critique of the *Recaudación del diezmo líquido en pesos*,' by Ouweneel and Bijleveld," *HAHR*, 69, no. 3 (1989): 537.

35. John J. Tepaske and Herbert S. Klein, *Ingresos y egresos de la Real Hacienda en México;* also, for the records of the central treasury of Mexico City, see John J. Tepaske, *La Real Hacienda de Nueva España: La Real Caja de México (1576–1816).*

36. José Jesús Hernández Palomo, *La renta del pulque en Nueva España, 1663–1810.*

37. Robert C. Nash, "The English and Scottish Tobacco Trades in the Seventeenth and Eighteenth Centuries: Legal and Illegal Trade," *The Economic History Review*, 35, no. 3 (August 1982): 368. Jacob Price, in his study of the French tobacco monopoly, also observed that: "Tobacco was peculiar among commodities in the eighteenth century in that while it could be produced in quantity in temperate zones for little more than a penny per pound demand for it appeared relatively inelastic up to a retail price of about 4 shillings or 4 livre tournois per pound." *France and the Chesapeake*, vol. 2, p. 840. For an econometric analysis of tobacco consumption and elasticity of demand, see Roger P. Congard, *Etude économétrique de la demande de tabac.*

38. Ouweneel and Bijleveld, "The Economic Cycle in Bourbon Central Mexico."

39. Joel Mokyr, "Is There Still Life in the Pessimist Case? Consumption during the Industrial Revolution, 1790–1850," *The Journal of Economic History*, 58, no. 1 (March 1988): 75–76.

40. Nash, "The English and Scottish Tobacco Trades in the Seventeenth and Eighteenth Centuries," pp. 356–357.

41. For an introduction to the current state of research, see Lyman L. Johnson and Enrique Tandeter, *Essays on the Price History of Eighteenth-Century Latin America.*

42. A. Moreno Toscano, "Los trabajadores y el proyecto de industrialización, 1810–1867," in *La clase obrera en la historia de México—I. De la colonia al imperio*, ed. Enrique Florescano, pp. 315–316.

43. For an introduction to the issues, see Cohen, "Managers and Machinery"; S. A. Marglin, "What Do Bosses Do?" in *The Division of Labour: the Labour Process and Class Struggle in Modern Capitalism*, ed. André Gorz, 1978; Joel Mokyr, ed., *The Economics of the Industrial Revolution;* D. Landes, *The Unbound Prometheus.*

44. Salvucci, *Textiles*, chap. 2.

45. Joan Wallach Scott, *The Glassworkers of Carmaux*, p. 19; see also Myron Gutmann, *Towards the Modern Economy—Early Industry in Europe, 1500–1800.*

46. María Amparo Ros, "La real fábrica de tabaco," pp. 51–64.

47. Salvucci, *Textiles*, pp. 174–175.

48. For the full figures, see Table 19, Susan Deans, "The Gentle and Easy Tax—The Bourbons and the Royal Tobacco Monopoly of New Spain, 1765–1821."

49. AGN, Tabaco 495, Estado que manifiesta las libras de tabaco en rama: resmas del papel, y caudal efectivo que se han invertido en las manufacturas de puros y cigarros, y utilidad que han producido en la real fabrica de esta capital desde su erección que principio en junio de 1769 hasta fin de diciembre de 1794. Francisco Maniau y Ortega, 3 August 1795, f.28–28v.

50. Ros is mistaken when she argues that tobacco was "delivered" to the manufactories at the same price at which it was sold to the public. See Ros, *La producción cigarrera*, p. 21, and "La real fábrica de tabaco," pp. 51–64. The value of the tobacco used by the monopoly accountants is a notional value. For a discussion of this, see AGN, Tabaco 241, Manifiesto de las vicisitudes . . . Díaz de la Vega, 10 July 1795.

51. AGN, Tabaco 241, Manifiesto de las vicisitudes . . . Díaz de la Vega, 10 July 1795.

52. Ibid.

53. Ibid.

54. AGI, Mexico 2278, Díaz de la Vega to Viceroy Mayorga, 12 June 1781.

55. Ibid.

56. AGN, Renta de Tabaco 67, administrator to *directores generales*, 12 June 1786.

57. AGI, Mexico 2261, *fiel* of Tetecala to administrator, 16 April 1779.

58. AGI, Mexico 2261, Francisco de Aragon to administrator-general, 10 January 1780.

59. AGI, Mexico 2261, Francisco de la Cruz to José Peña, 17 January 1781. This *legajo* contains a further 124 letters and reports, all indicating consumer dissatisfaction.

60. AGI, Mexico 2261, *contador general* Diaz de la Vega to Gálvez, 28 May 1782. AGI, Mexico 2278, reports of *contador general*, 14 June 1781 and 17 October 1782, f.172v–173r.

61. José Antonio de Alzate y Ramírez is described by D. A. Brading as a "Mexican savant" engaged in a variety of activities, both scientific and literary. See Brading, *Miners and Merchants*, p. 142, and MacLachlan, *Spain's Empire in the New World*, pp. 81–82.

62. AGI, Mexico 2314, la Real Audiencia to viceroy, 25 February 1785. AGN, Tabaco 303, Testimonio de lo practicado desde el recivo de la real orden de 24 de mayo de 1785 sobre la utilidad de la maquina de don Alonso González para cenir el tabaco de la fabrica de cigarros; AGI, Mexico 2314, Hierro to viceroy, 30 July 1791.

63. Ibid.

64. The only other example of attempts to introduce machines occurred in 1777 when experiments were conducted with a paper-cutting machine in the Orizaba manufactory. Nothing came of the experiments. AGN, Tabaco 521, Romaña, Betosolo to *director general*, 3 July 1781.

65. AGN, Renta de Tabaco 67, Isidro Romaña to *directores generales,* 19 June 1786.

66. Ibid.

67. AGN, Renta de Tabaco 67, report of *directores generales,* 5 August 1786.

68. See Jacques A. Barbier, "The Culmination of the Bourbon Reforms, 1787–1792," *HAHR* 57 (1977): 67. The French tobacco monopoly was subject to the same scrutiny, indecision, and ambivalence. It was temporarily abolished, but reestablished by Napoleon in 1810. It was the lack of fiscal alternatives as opposed to any penetrating defense of monopoly which influenced such a decision. See Price's discussion, *France and the Chesapeake,* vol. 2, pp. 788–839.

69. AGN, Tabaco 495, report of *contador general,* 29 September 1795.

70. AGN, Tabaco 495, *director general* to viceroy Branciforte, 28 August 1795.

71. AGN, Tabaco 241, *contador general* to *director general,* 8 October 1795.

72. AGN, Tabaco 241, report of the ministers of the Tesorería General de Ejército y Real Hacienda, 23 November 1795.

73. AGN, Tabaco 241, report of the Real Tribunal de Cuentas de la Contaduría Mayor de México y Audiencia to viceroy, 9 March 1796.

74. AGN, Tabaco 241, *fiscal de* Real Hacienda to viceroy, 6 June 1797.

75. Ibid.

76. Ibid.

77. AGN, Tabaco 344, Díaz de la Vega to Berenguer de Marquina, 9 February 1802.

78. AGN, Tabaco 344, report of *fiscal* Borbon, 18 April 1803.

79. AGN, Tabaco 344, Díaz de la Vega to viceroy, 12 July 1802; AGN, Tabaco 344, Díaz de la Vega to viceroy, 20 August 1802.

80. AGN, Tabaco 344, Feliciano de Sander to *director general,* 29 December 1801.

81. AGN, Tabaco 149, viceroy to *director general,* 21 September 1797.

82. AGN, Tabaco 241, *director general* to viceroy, 31 March 1799.

83. Ibid.

84. AGN, Tabaco 344, Puchet to *director general,* 4 January 1802.

85. AGN, Tabaco 149, *contador general* to *director general,* 14 May 1804.

86. AGN, Tabaco 524, Díaz de la Vega to viceroy, 21 September 1803; AGI, Mexico 2255, Informe sobre concesión a la Renta de Tabaco de varios auxilios que pidió su don Silvestre Díaz de la Vega para la prosperidad de aquella y otros puntos incidentes promovidos por el mismo director.

87. AGI, Mexico 2292, Díaz de la Vega to Ministro de Estado y del Despacho Universal de Hacienda de Indias, 29 July 1799.

88. AGI, Mexico 2870, Testimonio seguido sobre causa de extermino de tavacos en la jurisdicción de Papantla por el Cabo de la Ronda de Tesuitlan D. Agustin Galcia . . . 1802.

89. McWatters, "The Royal Tobacco Monopoly," p. 207.

90. Ravi Ramamurti, *State Owned Enterprises in High Technology Industries*, pp. 281–282.

6. To Serve in the King's House

1. Patrick Joyce, "The historical meanings of work: An introduction," in *The Historical Meanings of Work*, ed. Patrick Joyce, p. 19.
2. For a critique of the tobacco manufactories and their 'immorality', see AGN, Tabaco 476, Proyecto de Antonio de San José Muro, 1797. For background on Muro, see J. S. Fox, 'Antonio de San José Muro, political economist of New Spain', *HAHR*, 21 (1941), 410–416. See also the critique by the Consulado de México contained in Renta de Tabaco, 49, Manifiesto que se hace en defensa de las Fabricas de cuenta de S.M. . . . contra el equivocada concepto del Real Tribunal del Consulado de Mexico [1797?] (cited hereafter as Manifiesto que se hace en defensa de las Fabricas). Also see the discussion by Joan W. Scott of hostility to manufactories in France, "'L'ouvrière! Mot impie, sordide . . .': Women workers in the discourse of French political economy, 1840–1860," in *The Historical Meanings of Work*, ed. Patrick Joyce, p. 131.
3. Sylvia M. Arrom, *The Women of Mexico City, 1790–1857*, pp. 26–27.
4. Arrom, *The Women of Mexico City*, p. 27.
5. Joan Wallach Scott, *Gender and the Politics of History*, p. 75.
6. Mokyr, "The Industrial Revolution," p. 30. See also Cohen, "Managers and Machinery," p. 37. Cohen argues that "It was at least in part because of the problems associated with managing workers (the riskiness of the undertaking) that so many early factory masters proceeded with such caution."
7. By way of comparison, one of the most successful tobacco manufactories, in Tonneins on the Garonne, employed approximately 1,400 to 1,500 workers in 1789; Le Havre employed between 400 and 500 workers in 1788. See Price, *France and the Chesapeake*, vol. 2, p. 415. The elegant baroque tobacco manufactory of Seville employed approximately 2,000 workers. Women were not permitted entry until 1812. See José M. Rodríguez Gordillo, "El personal obrero en la Real Fábrica de Tabaco," *Sevilla y el Tabaco*, pp. 68–75. Madrid's tobacco factory employed over 800 workers, declining to 600 by 1822. See J. Pérez Vidal, *España en la historia del tabaco*, p. 241. Comparisons with other tobacco manufactories in Spanish America are made difficult by the fact that very few of the other colonies sustained a manufacturing element within their operations—quite the opposite in fact. The doomed manufactories of Trujillo and Lima in Peru had a combined labor force of 663 workers. Guillermo Céspedes del Castillo, "La renta del tabaco en el virreinato del Peru," *Revista Histórica* 9 (1960): 19. The closest parallel within the Spanish Empire was the tobacco manufactory opened in Manila in the Philippines in 1782, which, by 1783, employed more than 1,000 workers. Governor Bosco petitioned Viceroy Gálvez in 1784 for permission to build a new manufactory which would house between 5,000 and 6,000 workers. See Ed. C. de Jesus, *The Tobacco Monopoly in the Philippines—Bureaucratic Enterprise and Social Change, 1766–1880*, p. 39.

8. For discussions on migration in the late eighteenth and early nineteenth century, see Scardaville, "Crime and the Urban Poor—Mexico City in the Late Colonial Period," pp. 53–63; also Van Young, "The Rich Get Richer," and "Islands in the Storm"; Moreno Toscano and Aguirre Anaya, "Migrations to Mexico City."

9. Scardaville, "Crime and the Urban Poor," pp. 173–175. For an account of women in colonial Mexico City, see Arrom, *The Women of Mexico City.*

10. Don Francisco Saavedra de Sangronis, *Journal of Don Francisco Saavedra de Sangronis during the commission which he had in his charge from 25 June 1780 until the 20th of the same month of 1783,* ed. Francisco Morales Padrón, journal entry for 29 November 1781, p. 259.

11. Ros, "La real fábrica de puros y cigarros," p. 48. Ros uses a figure of 60,999 for a total working-age population for Mexico City, and 11,400 for Querétaro.

12. See Tables 2 and 3 on pp. 14–15 in Jorge González Angulo Aguirre, *Artesanado y ciudad a finales del siglo xviii.*

13. AGI, Mexico 2264, Díaz de la Vega to Ex. Sr, 22 January 1798.

14. AGI, Mexico 2277, Francisco del Real to José de Gálvez, 23 December 1771.

15. Brun's analysis is based on a sample of 1,753 cigarrette rollers taken from the 1811 census. Gabriel Brun Martínez, "La organización del trabajo y la estructura de la unidad domestica de los zapateros y cigarreros de la ciudad de México en 1811," in *Organización de la producción y relaciones de trabajo en el siglo XIX en México,* p. 147.

16. Ros, "La real fábrica de puros y cigarros," pp. 52–55. Ros' analysis of the *padrón* made in 1800 of Indians in the Mexico City tobacco manufactory indicates that of 7,074 manufactory workers only 525 (7.4 percent) were Indian tributaries. She calculated that they constituted 7 percent of the total number of pieceworkers, equivalent to 88 percent of all Indian workers. No Indians were found in the ranks of the administrative personnel.

17. Celia Wu, "The Population of the City in Querétaro in 1791," *Journal of Latin American Studies* 16 (1984): 298.

18. Calculated from AGN, Padrones 19, Padrón General de Orizaba, 1791.

19. Brun Martínez, "La organización del trabajo," p. 147.

20. As late as 1819 the *maestras* of the small manufactory of Guadalupe complained to the viceroy about an order which stipulated that under no circumstances were female factory workers of 'inferior class' (class and race here are conflated, but race was still the issue in the complaint) to be promoted to higher positions. The outcome of the incident is not known, but the case is illustrative in itself. AGN, Tabaco 167, *maestras mayores* to viceroy, 5 November 1819.

21. Scardaville, "Crime and the Urban Poor," p. 52.

22. Gabriel Brun Martínez, "La organización del trabajo," p. 147.

23. AGN, Tabaco 241, Díaz de la Vega to viceroy, 10 July 1795. The *director general* used a calculation of 6,400 workers, with two family members

for each worker. His total came to 22,200 people but 6,400 × 3 = 19,200. The estimated size of a family household seems to err on the low side. See Sherburne F. Cook and Woodrow Borah, *Essays in Population History: Mexico and the Caribbean*, vol. 1, chap. 3.

24. The population totals for Mexico City are taken from Florescano, *Precios del maíz*, p. 171.

25. AGN, Tabaco 241, report of Díaz de la Vega, 10 July 1795.

26. Don Francisco Saavedra de Sangronis, *Journal*, entry for 29 November 1781, p. 259.

27. Von Humboldt, *Ensayo Político*, p. 453.

28. AGN, Tabaco 241, report of Díaz de la Vega, 10 July 1795.

29. AGN, Tabaco 489, juez protector de la Real Concordia to viceroy, 6 July 1814.

30. One description of a Cuban tobacco factory vividly conjures up the conditions endured by the workers: "Physically the cigar and cigarette makers are a sorry lot. The continual odor of tobacco, their constant labor with bodies bent over tables, calling into play no muscle, no exertion . . . excepting the exercise of their fingers—this cannot fail to have its effect." Cited in Stuart Bruce Kaufman, *Challenge and Change: The History of the Tobacco Workers International Union*, pp. 3–4.

31. Rule discusses craft palsies whereby symptoms were aggravated by the necessity of performing a customary act which involved a repeated muscular action in a particular position. "The repeated coordination of movement breaks down and spasm, tremor, pain, weakness, and loss of control occurs in the muscles concerned. Work becomes less careful and the finer kinds soon pass beyond the capabilities of the sufferer. Task efficiency declines and reduces the earning power of the worker." See John Rule, *The Experience of Labour in Eighteenth-Century English Industry*, p. 82. More specifically, Patricia Cooper refers to "'cigar makers' neurosis,' a muscular dysfunction which reduced a worker's speed and sometimes resulted in a total inability to work. Probably caused by repetitive work and the cigar makers' cramped and stationary position, it included shoulder, arm, and head pain and, in the worst cases, the cigar maker lost some muscle control in one of his hands." Patricia Cooper, *Once a Cigar Maker—Men, Women, and Work Culture in American Cigar Factories, 1900–1919*, p. 101.

32. There existed a contradiction between the physical conditions which benefited the workers and those which benefited stored tobacco. The latter required a humid atmosphere to conserve moisture in the leaves and prevent premature drying out and brittleness (which also made it very difficult to work with), while workers needed plenty of ventilation to reduce the concentration of tobacco dust in the air.

33. Sonia Lombardo de Ruiz, *La Ciudadela: Ideología y estilo en la arquitectura del siglo xiii*, p. 54.

34. AGN, Fondo de Real Hacienda, Administración de la Real Renta de Tabaco, Contaduría, Caja 94, manufactory report, 31 January 1820.

35. Three of the most important military patrols consisted of the Regimiento Urbano del Comercio, the Escuadrón de Caballería Urbana, and the

Regimiento de Infantería de Nueva España. The viceroy Revillagigedo, apparently fearful of the presence of so large a concentration of workers, began construction on a group of military barracks "as an additional security measure." Scardaville, "Crime and the Urban Poor," p. 61.

36. AGN, Tabaco 371, Puchet to *director general*, 12 November 1792.

37. AGN, Tabaco 89, manufactory administrator, n.d.

38. Cooper, *Once a Cigar Maker*, p. 63.

39. AGN, Tabaco 241, report of *contador general*, 20 July, 1795; AGN, Fondo Real Hacienda, Administración de Tabaco-Contaduría 101, Lista de los Maestros y Maestras de Mesa . . . y otros individuos, Real Fabrica de Querétaro, 1792.

40. Individual cases reported in AGN, Tabaco 452.

41. AGN, Fondo de Real Hacienda, Administración de la Real Renta de Tabaco, Contaduría, Caja 79, Libro que consta el tiempo y los destinos que han servido las guardas, sobrestantas, maestras, embolvedores y recontadores de esta Real Fabrica de Puros y Cigarros de Mexico hasta fin de diciembre de 1812, fols. 4–215v.

42. Ibid.

43. AGI, Mexico 2264, Díaz de la Vega to Ex. Sr., 22 January 1789.

44. Jean Stubbs, *Tobacco on the Periphery—A Case Study in Cuban Labour History, 1860–1958*, p. 73.

45. John S. Leiby, *Colonial Bureaucrats and the Mexican Economy*, pp. 67–69.

46. A useful introduction to the sociological and economic effects and consequences of large-scale industrial organization is Robert Max Johnson, *The Formation of Craft Labor Markets*.

47. AGI, Mexico 2275, Manuel de Aldama to José de Gálvez, 10 December 1765.

48. AGN, Tabaco 241, Díaz de la Vega to Branciforte, 28 August 1795.

49. AGN, Tabaco, AGI, Audiencia de Mexico, Estados Generales for the years 1774–1776, 1792–1800.

50. Van Young, "The Rich Get Richer," Appendix B; Gabriel Haslip-Viera, "The Underclass," in *Cities and Society in Colonial Latin America*, ed. Louisa Schell Hoberman and Susan Migden Socolow, Table 10.4, p. 295; Salvucci, *Textiles*, pp. 98–100.

51. Van Young, "The Rich Get Richer," p. 21 and pp. 32–42. Also see the discussion by Richard L. Garner, "Prices and Wages in Eighteenth-Century Mexico," in *Essays on the Price History of Eighteenth-Century Latin America*, ed. Johnson et al, pp. 73–108.

52. Lyman Johnson, "Wages, Prices, and the Organization of Work in Late Colonial Buenos Aires," unpublished paper, p. 6.

53. See Scardaville, "Crime and the Urban Poor," p. 67; Haslip-Viera calculated an annual subsistence income for a family of 3.8 persons of between 129 and 262 pesos; see "The Underclass," p. 294.

54. AGN, Tabaco 356, Razon de las tareas . . ., *contador general*, 23 July 1781.

55. Ibid.

56. AGN, Tabaco 515, Betosolo to *director general*, 16 March 1792.

57. AGI, Mexico 2285, *fiscal de lo civil y de real hacienda* to viceroy, 13 January 1794.

58. AGN, Tabaco 376, report of *director general*, 17 February 1794.

59. Richard Price, "The labour process and labour history," *Social History* 8, no. 1 (January 1983): 63. Note also Rule's observation, that "a man could control his own pace when working in his cottage is evident, but the pattern was also characteristic of the small workshops, where men paid by the piece came and went with an irregularity which did not pose too many problems for employers with little investment in fixed capital." Rule, *The Experience of Labour*, pp. 52–55.

60. Mokyr, "The Industrial Revolution," pp. 27–30.

61. Rule, in his study of English workers, discusses the complaints made by weavers over the length of the factory day, the problem being that they could never work the hours they could at home "nor make the best of their time—they were restricted by the number of hours imposed upon them by the Masters." See Rule, *The Experience of Labour*, pp. 57–61.

62. AGN, Tabaco 376, *director general*, 17 February 1794.

63. From a comparative perspective cigarette makers in New York City in 1885 averaged 2,000 cigarettes per day; only the very fast and experienced ones completed up to 3,500 per day. Cigar makers could expect to roll between 200 and 400 cigars per day, and 150 for more difficult styles. See Stuart Bruce Kaufman, *Challenge and Change*, p. 3, and Cooper, *Once a Cigar Maker*, pp. 62–63. The impact of cigarette rolling machines becomes evident in terms of daily output. The Bonsack cigarette machine, one of the first to be introduced into cigarette factories, rolled between 750 and 1,000 cigarettes per minute. Modern cigarette machines produce 2,500 cigarettes per minute. See Stubbs, *Tobacco on the Periphery*, pp. 3–6. Although hand-rolled cigars have retained a loyal international market, even cigar production has succumbed to machine production.

64. AGN, Tabaco 376, *director general*, 17 February 1794.

65. AGN, Tabaco 241, report of administrator of the Guadalajara manufactory, 1798.

66. AGN, Tabaco 177, *fiscal*, 3 March 1818.

67. Scardaville, "Crime and the Urban Poor," pp. 178–180.

68. Lynch, *Bourbon Spain*, p. 261.

69. See Juan Pedro Viqueira Albán, *¿Relajados o reprimidos? Diversiones públicas y vida social en la ciudad de México durante el Siglo de las Luces;* Haslip-Viera, "The Underclass"; Michael Scardaville, "Alcohol Abuse and Tavern Reform in Late Colonial Mexico," *HAHR* 60, no. 4 (November 1980); D. A. Brading, "Tridentine Catholicism and Enlightened Despotism in Bourbon Mexico," *Journal of Latin American Studies* 15 (1983): 1–22.

70. Richard Price, *Labour in British Society—An Interpretive History*, p. 39.

71. AGN, Renta de Tabaco 49, Manifiesto que se hace en defensa de las Fabricas.

72. John Leddy Phelan, "Authority and Flexibility in the Spanish Impe-

rial Bureaucracy," *Administrative Science Quarterly* 5, no.1 (June 1960).

73. AGN, Tabaco 146, Ordenanzas de la Real Fabrica de Puros y Cigarros, 15 June 1770; AGN, Renta de Tabaco 67, Prevenciones de la dirección general, que deben observarse exactamente en la fabrica de puros y cigarros de esta capital . . . March 20 1792, clause 8. The literature on early factory organization demonstrates striking similarities in terms of structures and the content of rules imposed on workers. See Reinhard Bendix, *Work and Authority in Industry—Ideologies of Management in the Course of Industrialization.*

74. AGN, Renta de Tabaco 67, Prevenciones de la dirección general, que deben observarse exactamente en la fabrica de puros y cigarros de esta capital . . . March 20 1792, clause 14.

75. BN, Mexico, Mss 1338, "Para vestir a la plebe de la ciudad de Mexico, 1790–1792," ff.15–43.

76. Norman F. Martin, "La desnudez en la Nueva España." *Anuario de Estudios Americanos*, 29 (1972): 15.

77. AGN, Tabaco 512, guards and *maestros* to *director general*, 17 June 1783.

78. AGN, Tabaco 512, administrator to *fiscal*, 3 July 1783.

79. AGN, Tabaco 411, administrator to *director general*, 8 September 1780.

80. AGN, Tabaco 500, Romaña to Gálvez, 1771. Apparently, Ana did not return to the manufactory to claim her five reales or her job.

81. AGN, Tabaco 482, Puchet to Díaz de la Vega, 12 August 1794.

82. Ibid.

83. AGN, Renta de Tabaco 67, Puchet to *director general*, 5 January 1793.

84. Ibid.

85. AGI, Mexico 2287, Branciforte to Gardoqui, 28 June 1796.

86. Ibid. The *contador general*, in response to the order for all manufactories to establish *escuelas de amigas*, reported that workers in the provincial manufactories did not take their children to work with them, rendering the *escuelas* unnecessary.

87. AGN, Renta de Tabaco 67, *director general* to Puchet, 14 March 1793.

88. Alf Lüdtke, "The Historiography of Everyday Life: The Personal and the Political," in *Culture, Ideology and Politics*, ed. R. Samuel and G. Stedman-Jones, p. 44; E. P. Thompson, "Time, Work Discipline and Industrial Capitalism," *Past & Present* 38 (1967). Also see Steven L. Kaplan and Cynthia J. Koepp, *Work in France—Representations, Meaning, Organization, and Practice.* For a compelling analysis of resistance, its process and manifestations, see James C. Scott's works, *Weapons of the Weak—Everyday Forms of Peasant Resistance* and *Domination and the Arts of Resistance—Hidden Transcripts.*

89. AGN, Tabaco 358, Puchet to *director general*, 9 February 1797.

90. AGN, Tabaco 371, Puchet to *director general*, 30 April 1796.

91. Ibid.

92. AGN, Tabaco 358, Puchet to *director general,* 9 February 1797. The U.S. cigar workers' equivalent diversion was baseball. See Cooper, *Once a Cigar Maker.*

93. In 1794, 45 *supernumerios* or substitute workers were listed out of a total of 8,133 workers (including children). For the implications of contemporary use of substitute workers in modern factories, see Albert K. Rice, *Productivity and Social Organization—The Ahmedabad Experiment,* p. 79.

94. For a general treatment of drinking and drunkenness in Mexico, see William B. Taylor, *Drinking, Homicide, and Rebellion in Colonial Mexican Villages.*

95. AGN, Tabaco 358, Puchet to *director general,* 9 February 1797.

96. AGN, Renta de Tabaco 67, *dirección general* to Romaña, Betosolo, 2 September 1791. See also AGN, Renta de Tabaco 67, Prevenciones de la dirección general, que deben observarse exactamente en la fabrica de puros y cigarros de esta capital . . . March 20 1792.

97. AGN, Tabaco 371, Díaz de la Vega to Branciforte, 14 October 1797.

98. Richard Whipp, "'A Time to Every Purpose': An Essay on Time and Work," in *The Historical Meanings of Work,* ed. Patrick Joyce, p. 222.

99. AGN, Tabaco 149, Royal Order of 8 January 1795. No definition of "excessive" appears. Jacques Barbier argues that by 1795 problems had reached "crisis proportions," as insurrectionary publications circulated in various cities and towns, including Mexico City, Caracas, and Quito. See Barbier, "The Culmination of the Bourbon Reforms," p. 67. The manufactory workers' riot simply provided further evidence of colonial disorder and added momentum to reforms which sought to restrict large gatherings of people in one place, in an attempt to prevent further insubordination and outbursts.

100. AGN, Tabaco 358, Puchet to *director general,* 6 September 1797.

101. AGN, Tabaco 500, Testimonio de los Autos formados sobre extinctión de la Concordia.

102. AGN, Tabaco 241, Díaz de la Vega to viceroy, 31 March 1799.

103. Arrom, *The Women of Mexico City,* p. 27.

104. AGN, Tabaco 482, Puchet to Díaz de la Vega, 12 August 1794.

105. As Stephen Marglin has argued, "the discipline and supervision afforded by the manufactory had nothing to do with efficiency, at least as this term is used by economists. Disciplining the workforce meant a larger output in return for a greater input of labour, not more output for the same input." Stephen Marglin, "What Do Bosses Do? The Origins and Function of Hierarchy in Capitalist Production," in *The Division of Labour: The Labour Process and Class-Struggle in Modern Capitalism,* ed. André Gorz, p. 36.

106. AGI, Mexico 2302, report of López, 10 November 1817.

107. AGN, Tabaco 500, *procurador del numero* of the Real Audiencia to Ex. Sr., 1 February 1781.

108. Scardaville, "Crime and the Urban Poor," p. 61.

109. Scardaville, "Crime and the Urban Poor," p. 93.

110. See Teresa Lozan Armendares' discussion, *La criminalidad en la ciudad de México 1800–1821*. The discrepancy, of course, may be a function of the samples selected by Scardaville and Lozan Armendares.

111. Michael Sonenscher, "Work and Wages in Paris in the Eighteenth Century," in *Manufacture in Town and Country before the Factory*, ed. Maxine Berg, Pat Hudson, and Michael Sonenscher, p. 171. Also see Louis Chevalier, *Laboring Classes and Dangerous Classes in Paris during the First Half of the Nineteenth Century*, and William H. Sewell, *Work and Revolution in France—The Language of Labor from the Old Regime to 1848*.

112. McWatters, "The Royal Tobacco Monopoly," p. 160.

113. Sonenscher, "Work and Wages in Paris," p. 148.

114. AGI, Mexico 2294, viceroy Marquina to Crown, 26 February 1802.

115. See the arguments of Van Young, "The Rich Get Richer"; Garner, "Price Trends"; Tepaske, "Economic Cycles in New Spain"; Florescano, *Los precios del maíz*; Haslip-Viera, "The Underclass."

116. Patrick Joyce, *Work, Society and Politics: The Culture of the Factory in Later Victorian England*, p. 95.

7. Accommodation, Consensus, and Resistance

1. Michelle Perrot, "On the Formation of the French Working Class" in *Working Class Formation*, ed. Ira Katznelson and Aristide Zolberg, p. 89.

2. As has been argued for economic reforms which affected the journeymen in eighteenth- and nineteenth-century Europe, "reform . . . promulgated by . . . the authorities, was directed not only against a specific form of economy but also against a specific form of popular culture." Hans-Ulrich Thamer, "Journeyman Culture and Enlightened Public Opinion," in *Understanding Popular Culture—Europe from the Middle Ages to the Nineteenth Century*, ed. Steven L. Kaplan, p. 227.

3. Raul Carranca y Trujillo argues that guild regulations constituted regular legislation for labor but that the *Recopilación de las Leyes de los Reynos de las Indias* could be considered a legitimate labor code and that the *Leyes* made up a body of law in many respects without equal for their time. See "Las ordenanzas de gremios de Nueva España," *Crisol*. Ladd elaborates on Carranca's argument and concludes that "there were libraries full of labor legislation in Madrid and Mexico City." She refers to the "time-honored formula to oblige the Crown to intervene on the workers' behalf." Doris M. Ladd, *The Making of a Strike*, p. 122.

4. See Marc Venard, "Popular religion in the eighteenth century," in *Church and Society in Catholic Europe of the Eighteenth Century*, ed. William J. Callahan and David Higgs, pp. 138–154; also Robin Briggs, *Communities of Belief—Cultural and Social Tension in Early Modern France*. When we use the term "popular," it is not in the sense of crude schematic distinctions between "popular" and "elite" culture. Rather we agree with recent assessments which suggest that common material (beliefs, codes and

activities) is used in different and distinctive ways. Roger Chartier argues that it is "no longer tenable to try to establish strict correspondences between cultural cleavages and social hierarchies creating simplistic relationships between particular cultural objects and specific social groups. On the contrary, it is necessary to recognize the fluid circulation and shared practices that cross social boundaries." See Roger Chartier, "Texts, Printing, Readings," in *The New Cultural History*, ed. Lynn Hunt, pp. 169–171.

5. Ladd, *The Making of a Strike*, p. 122.

6. See Ros' argument in *La producción cigarrera*, pp. 44–46.

7. Price, *Labour in British Society*, pp. 7–12. See also Sonenscher, *Work and Wages*. For the Latin American case specifically, see Emilia Viotti da Costa, "Experience versus Structure: New Tendencies in the History of Labor and the Working Class in Latin America—What Do We Gain? What Do We Lose?" *International Labor and Working-Class History* 36 (Fall 1989).

8. Sonenscher, *Work and Wages*, p. 367.

9. Richard Price, "The labour process and labour history," *Social History* 8, no.1 (January 1983): 62.

10. Ruth Behar, "Sex and Sin, Witchcraft and the Devil in Late Colonial Mexico," *American Ethnologist* 14, no.1 (1987): 49. See also Celia Wu's discussion of residential patterns of the tobacco workers in "The Population of the City in Querétaro in 1791," *Journal of Latin American Studies* 16 (1984): 277–307.

11. Ros, *La producción cigarrera*, pp. 70–75.

12. Brun Martínez, "La organización del trabajo," p. 153.

13. AGN, Tabaco 241, Real Tribunal y Audiencia de la Contaduría Mayor de Cuentas de México, 9 March 1796. See Scardaville, "Crime and the Urban Poor," especially his argument that "the drinking house functioned as a reassuring institution in a society kept in a constant state of flux. With accelerating corn price, periodic epidemics, and job insecurity, the tavern was a pillar of strength in a time of uncertainty," p. 218. For comparative discussions on the role of drinking and taverns, see Thomas Brennan, *Public Drinking and Popular Culture in Eighteenth-Century Paris*, and Daniel Roche, *The People of Paris—An Essay in Popular Culture in the 18th Century*.

14. Scardaville, "Crime and the Urban Poor," p. 93.

15. Sewell, *Work and Revolution in France*, pp. 58, 165.

16. For the functions and social and political significance of trade confraternities, see Sewell, *Work and Revolution in France*, Chap. 2, pp. 16–39.

17. AGI, Mexico 2259, La concordia de fabricantes de puros y cigarros del reyno pide la confirmación de sus constituciones, 28 August 1776.

18. AGN, Renta de Tabaco 49, Manifiesto que se hace en defensa de las Fabricas. . . .

19. AGN, Renta de Tabaco 49, Manifiesto que se hace en defensa de las Fabricas. . . .

20. AGN, Renta de Tabaco 49, Manifiesto que se hace en defensa de las Fabricas. . . .

21. Sewell argues that the concern with a decent burial was understandable "in a society that viewed life on earth as a trial, a pilgrimage, and a preparation for life eternal . . . Nothing could state more eloquently either the corporation's concern for the whole person or the permanence of the members' commitment to the trade and to one another than the centrality of funerals in the corporation's ceremonial life." Sewell, *Work and Revolution in France*, p. 36.

22. AGI, Mexico 2259, La concordia de fabricantes . . ., 28 August 1776.

23. AGI, Mexico 2259, maestros de la mesa and junta de Concordia, 15 January 1776.

24. AGI, Mexico 2313, Testimonio del Quaderno que contiene la Real Orden sobre el Establecimiento y Arreglo de la Concordia de la Fabrica de puros y cigarros.

25. AGN, Tabacco 393, los operarios y operarias de oficinas de puros de la Real Fabrica to administrator, 29 February 1820. For a general discussion of the role of the Virgin of Guadalupe in late colonial Mexico, see William B. Taylor, "The Virgin of Guadalupe in New Spain: An Inquiry into the Social History of Marian Devotion," *American Ethnologist* 14, no. 1 (February 1987).

26. AGN, Tabaco 241, Díaz de la Vega, 10 July 1795.

27. AGI, Mexico 2290, San Lorenzo, 15 November 1798.

28. AGN, Tabaco 533, Los operarios de ambos sexos to viceroy, 1796.

29. Ibid.

30. Delfina E. López Sarrelangue, *Una villa mexicana en el siglo XVIII*.

31. For the 1790s, income and expenditure incorporated the following items: Income: weekly collection of 1/2 real; collection from the deceased and their debts; interest on property valued at 7,000 pesos; repayments of marriage loans. Expenditure: Costs of collection, property, marriages, cured sick, and burials; loans for marriages and loans over Easter and Christmas; salaries for employees; general costs and extraordinary costs.

32. AGN, Tabaco 489, Rafael Lardizábal, *juez protector de la Real Concordia* to viceroy Calleja, 6 July 1814.

33. This distinction was made clear during an investigation into the reasons why some workers had planned to burn tobacco sheds in the manufactory in 1797. AGN Tabaco 358, *contador general* to *director general*, 11 September 1797.

34. AGN, Tabaco 500, Romaña to Gálvez, 1771.

35. William Roseberry, *Anthropologies and Histories—Essays in Culture, History and Political Economy*, pp. 222–223.

36. See Catharina Lis and Hugo Soly, "Policing the Early Modern Proletariat, 1450–1850," in *Proletarianization and Family History*, ed. David Levine, p. 212.

37. Sonenscher, "Work and Wages in Paris," p. 147.

38. AGN, Renta de Tabaco 67, *director general* to Romaña, Betosolo, 2 September 1791.

39. See Ladd, *The Making of a Strike.*

40. AGN, Tabaco 376, Puchet to *director general*, 2 December 1793.

41. There was nothing peculiar about this practice. Accounts of tobacco industries in other countries refer to rerolling by consumers before the introduction of cigarette rolling machines, which ensured uniformity in size, content, and quality of cigarettes.

42. In the case of the development of English capitalism, John Rule argues that the " 'criminal' activity among workers in the early factories occurred during the transformation of the wage from a form in which monetary payment constituted a part (although a substantial one) of the wage to one based exclusively on a monetary payment." See Rule, *The Experience of Labour*, p. 125.

43. AGN, Tabaco 521, *director general* to administrator, 17 March 1781.

44. AGN, Tabaco 506, Expediente sobre quejas de los operarios de la fabrica de cigarros de Puebla contra los maestros y sobrestantes de ella, July 1782.

45. AGN, Tabaco 506, Francisco Antonio de Zamacona, *factor* and administrator of the Puebla Manufactory (no date).

46. AGN, Tabaco 506, *director general* Hierro, assessor Castañeda, 22 December 1781.

47. AGN, Renta de Tabaco 67, anonymous letter, 1 January 1785.

48. Ibid.

49. Ibid.

50. AGN, Tabaco 515, eleven signatures and "those who cannot sign their names" to viceroy, March 1792.

51. Ibid.

52. AGN, Tabaco 515, Benito Betosolo to *director general*, 16 March 1792. The administrator pointed out a few anomalies with the *embolvedores'* petition. Several *embolvedores* included under the category of those who could not write he knew to be literate, and therefore drew the conclusion that they did not wish to be party to such "false" accusations. Conversely, Mariano Díaz's signature appeared on the petition, yet the administrator claimed he could not write.

53. AGN, Tabaco 515, *director general* Hierro to viceroy Revillagigedo, 13 April 1792; AGN, Tabaco 515, *fiscal* Posada, April 27, 1792.

54. AGN, Tabaco 515, Ciriaco González Carbajal to viceroy, 29 February 1792; AGN, Tabaco 515, viceroy Revillagigedo, 2 March 1792. As is evident in these citations, the workers' petition was dated 29 February 1792, and the order to rehire them was dated 2 March 1792. The usual case was that many monopoly employees at all levels often found themselves in limbo due to bureaucratic procrastination or sheer overwork before their cases were dealt with, often a case of years rather than months.

55. AGN, Tabaco 371, report of *contador general*, 27 October 1796, on a request submitted by the *maestros de mesa* of the Mexico City manufactory regarding an increase from 85 to 125 in the number of *tareas* to be manufactured daily. The increase resulted in a larger number of workers to supervise, which meant more work for the *maestros* with no increase in their wages.

56. This incident is discussed in full in McWatters, "The Royal Tobacco Monopoly," pp. 156–158.

57. AGN, Tabaco 521, *director general* to viceroy, 23 December 1780.

58. AGN, Tabaco 521, *fiscal*, 27 February 1781.

59. AGN, Tabaco 281, *fiscal*, 13 February 1797.

60. AGN, Tabaco 281, Puchet to *director general*, 26 July 1797. Vera Villavicencia used her husband's ten-year service as a *guarda mayor de noche* and *guarda de registro* as vicarious experience and as part of her 'qualifications' and need for the position, although to no avail.

61. AGN, Tabaco 316, report of administrator, 17 June 1819.

62. AGI, Mexico 2314, Real Audiencia to viceroy Gálvez, 25 February 1785.

63. AGN, Fondo Real Hacienda Caja 121, Los operarios de la Fabrica de Cigarros de la Villa de Nuestra Señora de Guadalupe sobre exceso en los arrendamientos de casas, 1800, ff.1–15v.

64. AGN, Fondo Real Hacienda Caja 121, *fiscal* Borbon to viceroy, 7 November 1805.

65. AGN, Tabaco 103, Ruíz to Ex. Sr., no date or place, 1786.

66. AGN, Tabaco 482, Puchet to *director general*, 12 August 1794.

67. E. P. Thompson, "The Moral Economy of the English Crowd in the Eighteenth Century," *Past and Present* 50 (February 1971): 79.

68. AGI, Mexico 2313, Romaña, Pérez de Acali to *director general*, 9 April 1781.

69. AGI, Mexico 2313, report of Romaña, Pérez de Acali, 4 May 1781.

70. AGN, Tabaco 500, *fiscal*, 30 April 1781. The *dirección general* argued in favor of abolishing the Concordia on repeated occasions, 3 and 6 April 1781, and 13 February 1783. See AGN Tabaco 500, report of Bataller, assessor-general, 24 July 1781.

71. AGI, Mexico 2264, *director general* to viceroy, 1797. For full details see AGN, Tabaco 500, Testimonio de los Autos formados sobre extinción de la Concordia.

72. AGN, Tabaco 500, *Testimonio . . .*

73. Ibid.

74. AGN, Tabaco 500, procurador del numero de esta Real Audiencia por todo el cuerpo de operarios . . . to Ex. Sr., 1 February 1781.

75. AGN, Tabaco 500, procurador del numero de esta Real Audiencia por todo el cuerpo de operarios . . . to Ex. Sr., 1 February 1781. See also AGN Tabaco 500, operarios to Ex. Sr., 11 February 1782, AGN, Tabaco 500, report of Bataller, assessor-general, 20 June 1783, AGN, Tabaco 500, gremio de operarios to Ex. Sr., no date.

76. AGN, Tabaco 500, gremio de operarios to Ex. Sr., no date.

77. The elected *conciliaros* were to be composed of four cigarette rollers, two *maestros,* two *sobrestantes,* two *guardas,* one *embolvedor,* one *recontador,* one *encajonador,* one cigar roller, and one *cernidor.* The administrator, however, continued as director and possessed a casting vote, although the Concordia representatives recognized only the viceroy as their immediate head and judge.

78. The presence of *forasteros* in the manufactory work force was acknowledged and given consideration. Workers whose families lived outside of Mexico City were permitted time off to travel to see them. Provided they acquired the requisite permission to travel from the administrator, they would not lose their benefits on their return. AGN, Tabaco 500, Testimonio de los Autos. . . .

79. AGI, Mexico 2313, viceroy Revillagigedo to Conde de Lerena, 27 July 1791.

80. AGN, Tabaco 500, Testimonio de los Autos formados sobre extinción de la Concordia.

81. Ros views the Concordia as a response to the need to defend the family economy in the wake of the impact of the manufactory upon the workers. In the process, it became an organ of control of the manufactory administration and never for the purpose of the defense of labor, salaries, or even to improve the conditions of work. Ros, *La producción cigarrera*, pp. 82–83. For an interpretation of the Concordia as the state's exploitative mechanism for ensuring the reproduction of the manufactory's labor force, see González Sierra, *Monopolio del humo*, pp. 60–61. Yves Aguila sees the Concordia as a stepping stone to the formation of a trade union. See Yves Aguila, "Albores de la seguridad social en México, 1770: La Concordia de la Manufactura de Tabacos," *Jahrbuch Für Geschichte* 24 (1987): 351–352.

82. For a discussion of the idea of space "as a strategic element in games of power, as a stake in social struggles," see Michelle Perrot "On the Formation of the French Working Class," pp. 83–84.

83. AGN, Renta de Tabaco 2, viceroy to *director general*, 6 September 1780.

84. AGN, Tabaco 241, Díaz de la Vega to viceroy, 10 July 1795.

85. AGN, Renta de Tabaco 67, report of administrator Romaña, 26 January 1792.

86. AGI, Mexico 2285, testimony of Espinosa, before Valenzuela, José Mariano Benítez, notary, 1794.

87. AGI, Mexico 2285, viceroy Revillagigedo to Gardoqui, 3 February 1794.

88. AGN, Tabaco 376, Andrés Fuentes, José Maria Soria, José Rodrigo Roson, operarios to Viceroy Revillagigedo; AGN, Tabaco 376, Hierro to Revillagigedo, 16 January 1794.

89. AGN, Tabaco 376, Puchet to *director general*, 17 January 1794.

90. AGN, Tabaco 376, workers' representatives to *director general*. Also see letter from *director general* to viceroy Revillagigedo, 29 January 1794.

91. AGI, 2285, report of *fiscal*, 19 March 1794.

92. AGI, Mexico 2285, *alcalde del crimen* Valenzuela, 19 March 1794.

93. AGN, Tabaco 281, assessor, *contador general*, 26 June 1797.

94. AGN, Tabaco 358, José Luis Rodríguez to Puchet, September 8 1797. AGN, Tabaco 358, *contador general* to *director general*, 11 September 1797, Puchet's report, 14 September 1797, *contador general* to *director general*, AGN, Tabaco 358, Cosme de Mier y Trespalacios to viceroy, 11 September 1797, 21 September 1797, and 18 September 1797.

95. See James Scott's discussion of the process of personalization, whereby economic rationality becomes equated with malevolence in the workers' perceptions. *Weapons of the Weak*, p. 347.

96. AGN, Tabaco 241, Report of Real Tribunal y Audiencia de la Contaduría Mayor de Cuentas de México, 9 March 1796.

97. Ibid.

98. Ibid.

99. AGI, Mexico 2285, testimony of a guard before the *alcalde crimen* and notary, 1794. He testified that a worker stood outside the manufactory and asked other workers as they left work to donate 1/2 real or whatever they could afford to put together a petition to request withdrawal of the order over paper.

100. Jacques Rancière, "The Myth of the Artisan: Critical Reflections on a Category of Social History." In *Work in France—Representations, Meaning, Organization, and Practice*, ed. Steven L. Kaplan et al., p. 321.

101. Craig Calhoun suggests that what is important "about a sense of belonging" is not someone's "identification of membership in a bounded collectivity, but the modification of his consideration of alternative courses of action on the basis of the communal relations to which he belongs. If he takes certain concrete relations for granted as immutable, then this consciousness does act to limit the range of options he considers, and to constrain his action in favour of the community." See Craig Calhoun, "Community: Toward a Variable Conceptualization for Comparative Research," in *History and Class—Essential Readings in Theory and Interpretation*, ed. R. S. Neale, p. 90. For an analysis of worker response to the workplace and social change and the use of "occupational community," see David F. Crew, *Town in the Ruhr*, chap. 5, "The Foundations of Worker Protest: Miners and Metalworkers," pp. 159–194.

102. See Moreno Toscano, "Los trabajadores."

103. Cynthia M. Truant, "Independent and Insolent: Journeymen and Their 'Rites' in the Old Regime Workplace," in *Work in France*, ed. Kaplan and Koepp, p. 138.

104. For the problematics of constructing belief systems or "mentalities," particularly when religion is involved, see Jacques Le Goff "Mentalities: A History of Ambiguities," and Alphonse Dupront, "Religion and Religious Anthropology," in *Constructing the Past—Essays in Historical Methodology*, ed. Jacques Le Goff and Pierre Nora.

105. See AGN, Tabaco 393, los operarios y operarias de oficinas de puros de la Real Fabrica to administrator, 29 February 1820. See William B. Taylor, "The Virgin of Guadalupe in New Spain," and his essay "Between Global Process and Local Knowledge," pp. 158–162. An instructive reading on the interaction between faith, assumptions, and action is John Henry Newman, *Essay in Aid of a Grammar of Assent*.

106. AGI, Mexico 2285, *fiscal* to viceroy, 13 January 1794.

107. AGN, Tabaco 500, *gremio de operarios* to Ex. Sr., (no date).

108. Robin Briggs, *Communities of Belief—Cultural and Social Tension in Early Modern France*, pp. 381–382.

109. Brading argues that there was "little decline in popular religion in late eighteenth-century Mexico: the long-term process of secularisation and erosion of faith which had undermined the position of the Church in Europe was barely noticeable in Mexico other than at the level of recruitment for the mendicant orders." p. 22. See Brading, "Tridentine Catholicism."

110. AGN, Tabaco 358, Cosme de Mier y Trespalacios to viceroy, 11 September 1797.

111. Brading, "Tridentine Catholicism," p. 20. See also his discussion of church-state relations in late colonial Mexico in *The First America*, chapts. 21 and 22.

112. See Georges Duby, "Ideologies in social history." For discussions of the problem in early modern Europe, see Briggs, *Communities of Belief*, and Venard, "Popular Religion in the Eighteenth Century."

113. AGN, Fondo Real Hacienda, Caja 94, Acta de juramento que de la Constitución Política de la Monarquia Española sancionada por las Cortes generales y extraordinarios en el año de 1812 hicieron en 6 de junio de 1820 los empleados en la fabrica de cigarros de la Villa Nuestra Señora de Guadalupe.

114. For a discussion of the significance of ceremonies, see Elizabeth Hammerton and David Cannadine, "Conflict and Consensus on a Ceremonial Occasion: The Diamond Jubilee in Cambridge in 1897," *The Historical Journal* 24, no. 1 (1981): 111–146. The authors argue that ceremonial occasions cannot be assumed to represent consensus on the part of the participants in a Durkheimian sense. Rather, what they may celebrate is the resolution of particular conflicts or provide reassurance during times of instability, uncertainty, and adjustment to changing circumstances. Also see Robert Wuthnow, *Meaning and Moral Order—Explorations in Cultural Analysis*, and David I. Kertzer, *Ritual, Politics, and Power.*

115. Rodney D. Anderson, *Outcasts in Their Own Land—Mexican Industrial Workers, 1906–1911.*

116. Ros, *La producción cigarrera*, p. 44.

117. Alf Lüdtke, "Cash, Coffee-Breaks, Horseplay: Eigensinn and Politics Among Factory Workers in Germany circa 1900," in *Confrontation, Class Consciousness, and the Labor Process—Studies in Proletarian Class Formation*, ed. Michael Hannagan and Charles Stephenson, pp. 65–96.

118. Tilly concluded that "The particularities of their work situation accounted for the assertiveness of these women in defining and acting in their interests . . ." and that the "organization and scale of the industry promoted association by grouping many women together and possibly even by segregating women in certain positions." See Louise A. Tilly, "Paths of Proletarianization: Organization of Production, Sexual Division of Labor, and Women's Collective Action," *Signs* 7, no. 2 (Winter 1981): 414.

119. See Cooper, *Once a Cigar Maker*, p. 324; Stubbs, *Tobacco on the Periphery*, pp. 77–88.

120. For an overview of indigenous rebellion in colonial Mexico, see Taylor, *Drinking, Homicide and Rebellion*; Friedrich Katz, "Rural Uprisings in Preconquest and Colonial Mexico," in *Riot, Rebellion, and Revolution—*

Rural Social Conflict in Mexico, ed. Friedrich Katz; Anthony F. McFarlane, "Civil Disorders and Popular Protests in Late Colonial New Granada," *Hispanic American Historical Review* 64, no. 1 (February 1984); for a detailed analysis of a mineworkers' strike, see Ladd, *The Making of a Strike*. For a comparative analysis of the popular response to the 'big' movements of history, the development of capitalism and the state, see Tilly, *The Contentious French*.

121. Charles Tilly, "Collective Violence in European Perspective," in *The History of Violence in America: Historical and Comparative Perspectives*, eds. Hugh D. Graham and Ted R. Gurr.

122. Robert J. Holton, "The Crowd in History: Some Problems of Theory and Method," *Social History* 3, no. 2 (May 1978). One example of an argument based on polarities of traditional and modern forms of protest may be found in Silvia M. Arrom, "Popular Politics in Mexico City: The Parián Riot, 1828," *HAHR* 68, no. 2 (1988): 267.

123. Christine Stansell, *City of Women—Sex and Class in New York, 1789–1860*, p. 221.

8. Postscript

1. Tenenbaum, *The Politics of Penury*, p. 11. AGI, Mexico 2266, viceroy to *director general* Francisco José Bernal, 16 January 1817; AGI, Mexico 2302, 16 April 1818; AGI, Mexico 3202, Crown to viceroy, 22 April 1818; AGN, Fondo de Real Hacienda, Caja 121, report of ministers of tesorería general de ejército y Real Hacienda, 13 May 1819.

2. J. D. Isassi, *Memorias de lo acontecido en Córdoba en tiempo de la revolución para la historia de la independencia mejicana*, p. 49; José María Tornel y Mendívil, "Fastos Militares . . . ," pp. 2–3.

3. Herrera Moreno, *El cantón de Córdoba*, p. 241. See also AGN, Tabaco 444, *factor* of Córdoba to *director general*, 17 April 1818; Tornel y Mendívil, "Fastos Militares . . . ," p. 8. For an account of the insurgency in general, and from a regional perspective, see Hamnett, *Roots of Insurgency*.

4. AGN, Tabaco 424, *director general* to viceroy, 6 December 1811.

5. AGN, Tabaco 424, *director general* to viceroy, 6 December 1811.

6. BN (Mexico), Caja Fuerte, Guía de hacienda de la república mexicana. Parte legislativa. Esteva, secretaría de ministerio de hacienda, Mexico, 30 April 1825, pp. 118–119.

7. BN (Mexico), Caja Fuerte, Guía de hacienda de la república mexicana. Parte legislativa. Esteva, secretaría de ministerio de hacienda, Mexico, 30 April 1825, pp. 116–119.

8. BN (Mexico), Caja Fuerte, Guía de hacienda de la república mexicana. Parte legislativa. Esteva, secretaría de ministerio de hacienda, Mexico, 30 April 1825, pp. 91–119.

9. AGN, Tabaco 424, *director general* to viceroy, 27 September 1817.

10. Quoted in Trens, *La historia de Veracruz*, p. 534.

11. BN (Mexico), Caja Fuerte, Guía de hacienda de la república mexicana. Parte legislativa. Esteva, secretaría de ministerio de hacienda, 30 April 1825, pp. 215–226.

12. Iyo Kunimoto, "The Formation of the Early Mexican Federal System: An examination of the Financial Framework," *Annals of Chuo University*, Tokyo, 1 (March 1980):15–30; Baker Business Library, M–1, Mss relating to the tobacco monopoly and industry, 1821–1850.

13. Tenenbaum, *The Politics of Penury.*

14. Walker, "Business as Usual."

15. Ibid., pp. 678–680. The new company became known as the Compañía Empresaria de los Seis Departamentos. In addition to the original four departments, Michoacán and Guanajuato were soon added.

16. BL, Informe de la Dirección General del tabaco sobre la queja elevada al supremo gobierno por la diputación de cosecheros de Orizaba acerca de la siembra que pretendía hacer aquel distrito en el año corriente. Mexico, 1851.

17. Rosa María Meyer, "Los Béistegui, especuladores y mineros, 1830–1869," in *Formación y desarrollo de la burguesía en México*, ed. Ciro F. S. Cardoso, p. 131.

18. Stephen H. Haber, *Industry and Underdevelopment—The Industrialization of Mexico, 1890–1940,* pp. 48–51.

19. See Jesús Jáuregui, Murilo Huschick, Hilario Itriago, and Ana Isabel García Torres, *Tabamex—un caso de integración vertical de la agricultura,* and Norma Aida Giarracca de Teubal, "La subordinación del campesinado a los complejos agroindustriales. El Tabaco en Mexico."

20. For a discussion of the Spanish state's conservatism in fiscal policy in general, see Jacques A. Barbier and Herbert S. Klein, "Revolutionary Wars and Public Finances: The Madrid Treasury, 1784–1807," *Journal of Economic History* 41, no. 2 (June 1981): 331–334.

21. For a discussion of the pros and cons of monopoly, see Fritz Machlup, *The Political Economy of Monopoly—Business, Labor and Government Policies,* pp. 73–75. Also see Arnold C. Harberger, "Monopoly and Resource Allocation," *American Economic Review* 44, no. 2 (May 1964).

22. William P. McGreevy, *An Economic History of Colombia, 1845–1930,* p. 29.

23. Using the examples of Ecuador, Venezuela, and Mexico, Harrison argues, "When the growth of the tobacco industry is examined, the evidence is overwhelming that not only the areas of production but also the European markets were developed under the guidance of the state-managed tobacco monopoly and were only later turned over to private individuals for exploitation." Harrison, "The Evolution of the Colombian Tobacco Trade," pp. 163–164.

24. Wickham, "Venezuela's Royal Tobacco Monopoly," pp. 167–169.

25. de Jesus, *The Tobacco Monopoly in the Philippines,* pp. 197–203.

26. For divergent views of the roles of the state in the economy of eighteenth-century Mexico, see Coatsworth, "The Limits of Colonial Absolutism: The State in Eighteenth Century Mexico," pp. 25–51, and Salvucci

and Salvucci, "Crecimiento y cambio en la productividad de México,"
pp. 67–89.

27. Salvucci and Salvucci, "Crecimiento y cambio en la productividad de
México," p. 72.

28. Joan Wallach Scott, *Gender and the Politics of History*, p. 163.

29. Anderson, *Outcasts in Their Own Land*, pp. 224–225.

Glossary

abasto de carnes: monopoly of meat supply in a city or town

abogado: lawyer, attorney

adelea: loose cigarettes as change in a transaction

administrador: administrator

administrador general: chief official of a local branch of the Tobacco Monopoly

aduana: customs agency

agraciados: individuals who received special favors in return for services rendered to the King

aguardiente: liquor

alcabala: sales or excise tax

alcalde del crimen: junior judge in *audiencia*

alcalde mayor: district magistrate

alcalde ordinario: municipal magistrate

almacenes generales: general warehouses used for storing tobacco and paper

arbitristas: Spanish economists and writers who formulated reforms designed to improve Spain's economy

arrendatarios: renters

arrieros: muleteers

arroba: unit of weight equal to twenty-five pounds

asesor: legal advisor to a government agency

asoleo: process of drying tobacco before grinding

Audiencia: high court of justice

aviador: financial backer

avíos: supplies of goods and cash advanced on credit by *aviador*

ayuntamiento: town council

bando: proclamation

boleta: type of "ticket" or work pass that indicated the duties and wages of individual workers in the royal tobacco manufactories

cabildo: town council

caja matríz: central treasury

caja real: provincial treasury

cajero: apprentice merchant

cajones: large packing crates or chests for packets and cartons of cigars and cigarettes

casas de vecindad: colonial apartment house; multiple family dwelling

castas: castes, racial mixtures

castizos: offspring of mestizo-white parents

cernido: ground or shredded tobacco for cigarettes

cernidores: tobacco leaf grinders

cigarrera: female cigarette roller

cigarrería: privately owned tobacco shop

cigarrero: male cigarette roller

cigarro: cigarette

Cinco gremios mayores de Madrid: Five Great Guilds of Madrid, which controlled the manufacture and sale of gold, silver, jewelry, silk, linens, woolens, and spices

clientela: patron-client relationship in which patrons or powerful individuals provide protection and favors to their less powerful clients in return for receiving services, obedience, and loyalty

cofradía: lay confraternity or religious brotherhood

comiso: confiscation of contraband

compañía de gremios de paños de Madrid: Woolen Manufacturers' Guilds of Madrid

Concordia: tobacco workers' confraternity or mutual aid society

Consolidación de Vales Reales: the attempt by the crown to appropriate the funds of pious foundations and chantries. The law of 1804 required church and associated organizations to consolidate their capital by paying it into a royal office in exchange for an annuity of 3 percent guaranteed by royal tax revenues.

consulado: merchant guild

contador: accountant

contador general: chief accountant of the Tobacco Monopoly

contador interventor: auditor

contador mayor: senior accounts clerk

contaduría: accounts section of a government agency

contaduría general: general comptroller of the Tobacco Monopoly

cosechero: tobacco planter or grower

creole, criollo: a Spaniard born in America

cuaderno: booklet of cigarette paper

cuadrillas: here, work crews in the tobacco manufactories

cuerpo: body or association

cuerpo de cosecheros: association of tobacco planters

decano: senior *oidor* of the *audiencia*

(a) destajo: piecework

dirección general: central office of the Tobacco Monopoly responsible for management of the agency's offices and operations throughout the viceroyalty

director general: director-general of the Tobacco Monopoly

embolvedores: wrappers

encajonadores: packers

encanalado: process of folding paper into tubes ready for cigarette rolling

enteros: whole, unbroken tobacco leaves

escribano: notary

escribiente: scribe

escuela de amigas: here, a type of nursery school for tobacco workers' children located in the Mexico City tobacco manufactory

estado general: statement of annual accounts of the Tobacco Monopoly

estanco, estanquillo: shop licensed by the Tobacco Monopoly to sell its products

estanquero, estanquera: licensed tobacconist

factor: manager of a *factoría*

factoría: Tobacco Monopoly administrative district

feria de Jalapa: trade fair located in Jalapa

fiador: bondsman

fianza: bond

fiel: administrator of a *fielato*

fiel de la tercena: tobacco warehouse manager

fielato: administrative district within a *factoría*

fiscal de lo civil: prosecuting attorney in civil cases

fiscal de real hacienda: Crown attorney

flotistas: import merchants

forasteros: migrants

fuero: legal privileges granted to certain groups, usually such corporations as the church and the military

gachupín: derogatory term for Peninsular Spaniards

gañán: peon

gente de razón: well-born people of Spanish descent, lit. "people of reason," usually applied to non-Indians

grano: monetary unit worth one-twelfth of a *real*

granza: cuttings and waste tobacco

gremio de tabaqueros: here, association of tobacco planters

gritones: callers or shouters employed in the tobacco manufactories, who shout out meal times and deliver messages *guardas:* guards in the tobacco manufactories

guardas mayores: head guards of the tobacco manufactories

guías: here, licenses granted to muleteers by the Tobacco Monopoly to transport tobacco and tobacco products

hacendado: owner of a *hacienda*

hacienda: large landed estate

hojas de servicio: service records of employment

instrucciones: official guidelines

intendente: intendant, chief administrator of a large district or intendancy

interino: interim position

interventor: supervisor

(al) jornal: fixed daily wage

junta: a committee or government board

Junta de Ministros: a special interministerial committee, the purpose of which was to propose policies designed to increase revenues from the Spanish American colonies

junta de real hacienda: chief financial committee of viceroyalty

junta de tabaco: committee to oversee the establishment of the Tobacco Monopoly and thereafter set up on an ad hoc basis to advise the *dirección general* on special problems

junta superior de real hacienda: superior board of the royal exchequer; special committee for fiscal affairs

justicias ordinarios: magistrates

la voz fletes: practice whereby veteran cigarette rollers and supervisors "sold" their *tarea* to children or apprentice workers or relatives. While their substitutes (generally less skilled) carried out their piecework quotas, the workers left the manufactory, allegedly to work at another job, but returned in time to make the delivery of their *tareas* to their supervisors. They paid their substitutes a nominal amount and pocketed the remainder of the day's earnings.

libranza: promissory note, bill of exchange

libreta: system in use in the tobacco factories in Cuba in the nineteenth century, the *libreta* was a compulsory card that indicated the worker's name and the amount of debt owed to her or his employer. Until the debt was cleared, the worker (technically) could not leave the factory or be employed by any other manufacturer.

macuchi: a variety of tobacco that grows wild

maestros, maestras de mesa: table foremen and forewomen

maestros, maestras mayores: chief supervisors in the tobacco manufactories

manojo: small bundle of leaf tobacco

masa remisible: government revenues from the tobacco, quicksilver, and playing-card monopolies, which, technically, were shipped directly to Spain

mata: tobacco seedling, plant

mayordomo: steward

molino: mill

motín: riot, public disturbance

nuevas labores de cigarros: experimental methods to produce cigarettes and cigars, usually designed to reduce costs of production

obraje: workshop or factory, usually for textiles

oficial: clerk in the Tobacco Monopoly bureaucracy or in a government agency

oficial de contaduría: clerk in the accounts section of the Tobacco Monopoly or in a government agency

oficial de libros: bookkeeper

oficial mayor: chief clerk

oficial pagador: cashier

oficinas: workrooms within the tobacco manufactories

oidor: judge in *audiencia*

operario: tobacco manufactory worker, usually a cigarette or cigar roller *ordenanzas:* ordinances

orden general: general regulation

padrón: census

palmeta: flat stick used to smooth the outer wrapping of cigarettes

palos y granza de tabaco: cuttings and waste tobacco

patio: work area in the tobacco manufactories

patio de mujeres: women's work area in the tobacco manufactories

pegujaleros: subsistence peasant farmers

peninsular: a Spaniard born in Spain

peso: silver coin worth 8 *reales de plata*

picardías: malicious, offensive comments

pisiete: concoction made of tobacco scraps and lime; when chewed it produced juices that acted as a stimulant

polvo: finely powdered tobacco

principales: here, wealthiest and most important members of a community

procurador: solicitor

propietario: owner

protomedicato: the Board of King's Physicians

pulpería: general store

pulque: alcoholic drink made from the juice of the maguey plant

pulquería: tavern, bar

purera: female cigar roller

purería: cigar shop, workshop

purero: male cigar roller

puro: cigar

rama: leaf tobacco

ranchito: very small farm or settlement

rancho: small estate, small village of farmers

rapé: snuff

real: coin; if of silver, worth one-eighth of a *peso*

reales cajas: Royal Accounts Office

real hacienda: Royal Treasury

Real Renta de Tabacos: Royal Tobacco Monopoly

recontadores: recounters

regidor: town councillor

reglamento: rules that govern agency conduct

relación jurada: sworn testimony, oath

repartimiento de indios, repartimiento de labor: system of Indian draft labor

repartos: forced distribution and sale of goods to Indian communities

resguardo: police arm of the Tobacco Monopoly charged with policing the countryside to prevent contraband production of tobacco

rotos: broken or damaged tobacco leaves

sartas: bundles of tobacco leaves

selladores: stampers

sobrestantes, sobrestantas: foremen and forewomen in the tobacco manufactories

sobrestantes, sobrestantas mayores: chief supervisors in the tobacco manufactories

súchil: bonus payment to encourage adequate recruitment of Indian labor required for work in the tobacco fields

superintendente subdelegado de real hacienda: superintendent of the exchequer

supernumerario: individual who occupies a temporary or unauthorized extra position in a government agency or in the tobacco manufactories

suplementos: supplementary credit provided by the Tobacco Monopoly to tobacco planters

tabaco de polvo. See polvo

tarea: full day's work, work quota

teniente: lieutenant, assistant

teniente general: lieutenant general

tercenas: warehouses

tercenistas: warehouse managers

tercio: bundle of tobacco leaves, usually 170 pounds in weight

tesorería: treasury section of a government agency

tesorero: treasurer

tierra adentro: generally refers to the area that extends from the Bajío north to the Provincias Internas, which included Sinaloa, Sonora, the Californias, Nueva Vizcaya, Coahuila, Texas, and Nuevo México

tlacos: copper coins or shop tokens

torcedor: cigarette roller

trapiche: sugar mill

Tribunal de Cuentas: Court of Audit; chief auditing agency

vara: unit of measure, about 33 inches

vecino: citizen of a municipality

villa: town

visitador: Tobacco Monopoly inspector

Select Bibliography

Manuscripts

Great Britain

British Library
Additional Mss. vols. 17557, 17578, 17580, 17656.b, 21537.
Egerton Mss. vol. 374.

Mexico

Archivo General de la Nación
Diezmos, vol. 17.
Indiferente General, Alcabalas, Tabaco (documents in process of classification).
Inquisición, vol. 937.
Padrones, vol. 19.
Renta de Tabaco, vols. 1, 2, 6, 7, 8, 9, 12, 18, 26, 30, 31, 35, 37, 40, 44, 46, 47, 48, 49, 53, 67, 68, 69, 70, 71, 73, 88.
Tabaco, vols. 19, 21, 23, 26, 28, 29, 30, 31, 35, 38, 40, 53, 54, 65, 73, 77, 89, 96, 103, 113, 120, 130, 141, 146, 149, 151, 152, 155, 160, 167, 177, 178, 196, 222, 223, 231, 241, 266, 276, 280, 281, 289, 300, 303, 307, 316, 331, 344, 350, 352, 356, 358, 363, 371, 376, 389, 390, 392, 393, 405, 411, 412, 416, 420, 428, 438, 446, 448, 452, 453, 455, 459, 460, 466, 467, 471, 474, 476, 482, 483, 489, 495, 498, 500, 501, 504, 506, 509, 512, 515, 521, 523, 524, 526, 533.
Fondo de Real Hacienda
Administración de Tabaco-Contaduría, cajas 93–93, 101, 121, 125, 128.
Archivo Histórico de Hacienda
Legajos 488-2, 632-17, 936-40, 991-2.
Archivo Microfílmeco de Genealogía y Heráldica
Matrimonios—Españoles, Parroquia de San Miguel, Orizaba, 1777–1794, 30061, roll no. 2562.
Biblioteca Nacional (Mexico)
Mss. vols. 1332, 1337, 1338, 1589.

Archivo Notarial de Orizaba, expedientes 1736, exp. 10-F-9; 1756, exp. 21-2-F; 1757, exp. 9-F-101; 1761, exp. 1-19-F; 1765, exp. 5-8-F; 1772, exp. 4-11-F; 1777, exp. 8-8-F; 1778, exp. 8-12-F; 1782, exp. 7-40-F; 1782–1801, exp. 10-259-F; 1784, exp. 5-26-F; 1785A, exp. 8-14-F; 1785A, exp. 11-121-F; 1785B, exp. 5-4-F; 1786, exp. 2-10-F; 1786, exp. 14-9-F; 1787, exp. 4-77-F; 1789, exp. 1-8-F; 1794–1799, exp. 11; 1796, exp 8-F; 1798, exp. 10-42-F; 1798–1800, exp. 20; 1800–1801, exp. 19; 1802, exp. 7; 1802–1803, exp. 7; 1803, exp. 9-7-F; 1804, exp. 14-34-F; 1804–1805, exp. 29; 1805, exp. 14-F; 1806, exp. 11-41-F; 1808, exp. 2-10-F; 1809, exp. 14-53-F; 1810, exp. 8, 9; 1810–1811, exp. 8; 1819, exp. 6-11-F; 1826, exp. 4-73-F; 1831–1832, exp. 6-24-F.

Spain

Biblioteca Nacional (Madrid)
    Mss. 10.361—Libro de la razón general de la Real Hacienda en Nueva España formado por D. Fabián de Fonseca y D. Carlos de Urrutia, de orden del Virrey, Conde de Revillagigedo. Vol. VII—Renta del Tabaco.
Archivo General de Indias
    Audiencia de Mexico, legajos 1373, 1403, 1406, 2230, 2255–2270, 2274–2278, 2280–2282, 2284–2302, 2306, 2309–2311, 2313–2314, 2850, 2870, 3202.

United States

Baker Business Library, Harvard University
    M-1, Mss relating to the tobacco monopoly and industry, 1821–1850.
Benson Latin American Collection, University of Texas at Austin
    Mss. by Joaquin Maniau Torquemada, *Compendio de la historia de Real Hacienda de Nueva España. Año de 1793.* Genero García Collection.

Printed Documents and Contemporary Works

Alamán, Lucas. *Historia de México.* 5 vols. Mexico City: Editorial Jus, 1942.
Beristáin de Sousa, José Mariano. *Biblioteca hispanoamericana septentrional.* 3d ed. 5 vols. Mexico City: Ediciones Fuente Cultural, 1947.
Calendario manual y guía de forasteros en México. For the following years: 1766–1770, 1772–1775, 1778–1779, 1782–1785, 1787–1788, 1793–1801, 1803–1822, 1825. Mexico City: Zúñiga y Ontiveros.
Campillo y Cosío, José del. *Nuevo sistema de gobierno económico para América.* Madrid: Imprenta de B. Cano, 1789.
Canga Argüelles, José. *Diccionario de hacienda, con aplicación á España.* Madrid: Imprenta de M. Calero y Portacarro, 1833–1834.
Carroll, Patrick J. *Blacks in Colonial Veracruz: Race, Ethnicity, and Regional Development.* Austin: University of Texas Press, 1991.

de la Porte, Joseph. *Veracruz y Oaxaca en 1798 por d. P. E.* Translated by d. Pedro Estaba. Mexico City: Vargas Rea, 1946.

Dictamen sobre la renta del tabaco que ha presentado al soberano congreso: La comisión especial encargada de hacer el análisis de la memoria del ministro de hacienda linda en la sesión de 12 de noviembre. Mexico City, 1823.

El Conde de Rida. *Instrucción general del cultivo de los tabacos.* Havana, 1764.

Guía de hacienda de la replicana Mexicana. Secretaría de ministerio de hacienda, Mexico City, 30 April 1825, in *Calendario manual, 1825.* Mexico City: Zúñiga y Ontiveros, 1825.

Informe de la dirección general del tabaco sobre la queja elevada al supremo gobierno por la diputación de cosecheros de Orizaba acerca de la siembra que pretendía hacer aquel distrito en el año corriente. Mexico City, 1851. [LAS 512/3 - B.L.]

Isassi, José Domingo. *Memorias de lo acontecido en Córdoba en tiempo de la revolución, para la historia de la independencia Mejicana.* Jalapa: Imprenta del Gobierno, 1827.

Memoria de la comisión de hacienda sobre la renta [de tabaco]. Mexico City, 1822.

Mora, José María Luis. *México y sus revoluciones.* Edited by Agustín Yáñez. 3 vols. Mexico City: Editorial Porrúa, 1950.

Poinsett, Joel Roberts. *Notes on Mexico—Made in the Autumn of 1822.* New York: Praeger, 1969.

Rodríguez y Valero, José Antonio. *Cartilla histórica y sagrada de Córdoba.* Mexico City: Imprenta de la Bibliotheca Mexicana, 1759.

Segura, Vicente. *Apuntes para la estadística del departamento de Orizava, formados por su gefe cuidadano Vicente Segura. . . . en el año de 1826.* Jalapa: Oficina del Gobierno, 1831.

Tatham, William. *An Historical and Practical Essay on the Culture and Commerce of Tobacco.* London: Vernor and Hood, 1800.

Tornel y Mendívil, José María. "Fastos militares de iniquidad, barbarie y despotismo del gobierno español ejecutados en las villas de Orizaba y Córdoba en la guerra de once años por causa de la independencia y libertad de la nación Mexicana . . ." In *Mexico por dentro y fuera bajo el gobierno de los virreyes . . .*, edited by Hipólito Villaroel. Mexico City: Imprenta de A. Valdés, 1831.

Ustáriz, Gerónimo de. *The Theory and Practice of Commerce and Maritime Affairs.* Translated by John Kippax. London: [printed for John and James Rivington . . . and John Crofts], 1751.

von Humboldt, Alexander. *Ensayo político sobre el reino de la Nueva España.* 2d ed. Mexico City: Editorial Porrúa, 1973.

Villaroel, Hipólito. *México por dentro y fuera bajo el gobierno de los virreyes . . .* Mexico City: Imprenta de A. Valdés, 1831.

Printed Secondary Works

Books

Akehurst, C. *Tobacco.* London: Longman, 1968.

Altman, Ida B., and James Lockhart, eds. *Provinces of Early Mexico: Variants of Spanish American Regional Evolution.* Los Angeles: UCLA Latin American Center Publications, University of California, 1976.

Anderson, Perry. *Lineages of the Absolutist State.* London: Routledge Chapman & Hall, 1974.

Anderson, Rodney D. *Outcasts in Their Own Land: Mexican Industrial Workers, 1906–1911.* DeKalb: Northern Illinois Press, 1976.

Anna, Timothy E. *The Fall of the Royal Government in Mexico City.* Lincoln: University of Nebraska Press, 1978.

Archer, C. I. *The Army in Bourbon Mexico, 1760–1810.* Albuquerque: University of New Mexico Press, 1977.

Arcila Farías, Eduardo. *Reformas económicas del siglo XVIII en Nueva España.* 2 vols. Mexico City: SepSetentas, 1974.

Arents, George. *Tobacco, Its History: Illustrated by the Books, Manuscripts, and Engravings in the Library of George Arents, Jr., Together with an Introductory Essay, a Glossary, and Bibliographic Notes by Jerome E. Brooks.* 5 vols. New York: Rosenbach Company, 1937–1952.

Arnold, Linda. *Bureaucracy and Bureaucrats in Mexico City, 1742–1835.* Tucson: University of Arizona Press, 1988.

Arrom, Silvia M. *The Women of Mexico City, 1790–1857.* Stanford: Stanford University Press, 1985.

Arróniz, Joaquín. *Ensayo de una historia de Orizaba.* Mexico City: Editorial Citlaltépetl, 1980.

Bauer, Arnold. *Chilean Rural Society, from the Spanish Conquest to 1930.* Cambridge: Cambridge University Press, 1975.

Bazant, Jan. *Alienation of Church Wealth in Mexico.* Cambridge: Cambridge University Press, 1971.

Bejarano, Jesús Antonio, and Orlando Pulido. *El tabaco en una economía regional: Ambalema, siglos XVIII y XIX.* Bogotá: Universidad Nacional de Colombia, 1986.

Bendix, Reinhard. *Work and Authority in Industry—Ideologies of Management in the Course of Industrialization.* New York: John Wiley and Sons, 1956.

Berg, Maxine, Pat Hudson, and Michael Sonenscher, eds. *Manufacture in Town and Country before the Factory.* Cambridge: Cambridge University Press, 1983.

Bergad, Laird W. *Coffee and the Growth of Agrarian Capitalism in Nineteenth Century Puerto Rico.* Princeton: Princeton University Press, 1983.

Bobb, B. *The Viceregency of Antonio María Bucareli in New Spain, 1771–1779.* Austin: University of Texas Press, 1962.

Borchart de Moreno, Christina R. *Los mercaderes y el capitalismo en la ciudad de México: 1759–1778*. Mexico City: Fonda de Cultura Económica, 1984.

Brading, D. A. *The First America: The Spanish Monarchy, Creole Patriots and the Liberal State 1492–1867*. Cambridge: Cambridge University Press, 1991.

———. *Haciendas and Ranchos in the Mexican Bajío, León 1700–1860*. Cambridge: Cambridge University Press, 1978.

———. *Miners and Merchants in Bourbon Mexico, 1763–1810*. Cambridge: Cambridge University Press, 1971.

———. *The Origins of Mexican Nationalism*. Cambridge: Centre of Latin American Studies, Cambridge University Press, 1986.

———. *Prophecy and Myth in Mexican History*. Cambridge: Centre of Latin American Studies, Cambridge University Press, 1984.

Breen, T. H. *Tobacco Culture: The Mentality of the Great Tidewater Planters on the Eve of Revolution*. Princeton: Princeton University Press, 1985.

Brennan, Thomas. *Public Drinking and Popular Culture in Eighteenth Century Paris*. Princeton: Princeton University Press, 1988.

Burkholder, Mark A., and David S. Chandler. *From Impotence to Authority—the Spanish Crown and the American Audiencias, 1687–1808*. Columbia: University of Missouri Press, 1977.

Calderón Quijano, José Antonio. *Los virreyes de Nueva España en el reinado de Carlos III*. 2 vols. Seville: Escuela de Estudios Hispano-Americanos, 1967–1968.

Calero, Carlos. *Orizaba*. Mexico City: Editorial Citlaltépetl, 1970.

Callinicos, Alex. *Making History: Agency, Structure, and Change in Social Theory*. Ithaca, N.Y.: Cornell University Press, 1988.

Cardosa, Ciro F. S., ed. *Formación y desarrollo de la burguesía en México, siglo XIX*. Mexico City: Siglo XXI, 1978.

Carranca y Trujillo, Raul. *Las ordenanzas de gremios de Nueva España*. Mexico City: Crisol, 1932.

Chandler, Alfred D. *The Visible Hand: The Managerial Revolution in American Business*. Cambridge, Mass: Harvard University Press, 1977.

Chávez-Hita, Adriana Naveda. *Esclavos negros en las haciendas azucareras de Córdoba, Veracruz, 1690–1830*. Jalapa: Centro de Investigaciones Históricas, Universidad Veracruzana, 1987.

Chávez Orozco, Luis, ed. *Agricultura e industria textil de Veracruz: Siglo XIX*. Jalapa: Universidad Veracruzana, 1965.

———. *Historia y leyendas de las calles de México*. Vol. 1. Mexico City: El Libro Español, 1944.

Chayanov, A. V. *The Theory of Peasant Economy*. Edited by Daniel Thorner, Basile Kerblay, R. E. F. Smith, and R. D. Irwin. 1966.

Chevalier, Louis. *Laboring Classes and Dangerous Classes in Paris during the First Half of the Nineteenth Century*. Translated by Frank Jellinek. Princeton: Princeton University Press, 1981.

Cole, C. W. *Colbert and a Century of French Mercantilism*. 2 vols. New York: Columbia University Press, 1939.

Coleman, D. C., ed. *Revisions in Mercantilism*. London: Methuen & Co., 1969.

Congard, Roger-Paul. *Etude économétrique de la demande de tabac*. Paris: Armand Colin, 1955.

Cook, Sherburne F., and Woodrow Borah. *Essays in Population History: Mexico and the Caribbean*. 3 vols. Berkeley: University of California Press, 1974–1980.

Cooper, Patricia A. *Once a Cigar Maker: Men, Women, and Work Culture in American Cigar Factories, 1900–1919*. Chicago: University of Illinois Press, 1987.

Corina, M. *Trust in Tobacco: The Anglo-American Struggle for Power*. London: M. Joseph, 1975.

Crew, David F. *Town in the Ruhr*. New York: Columbia University Press, 1979.

Davis, Ralph. *The Rise of the Atlantic Economies*. London: Weidenfeld and Nicolson, 1973.

de Jesus, Ed. C. *The Tobacco Monopoly in the Philippines: Bureaucratic Enterprise and Social Change, 1766–1880*. Quezon City: Ateneo de Manila University Press, 1980.

de la Tabla y Ducasse, Javier Ortiz. *Comercio exterior de Veracruz, 1778–1821—crisis de dependencia*. Seville: Escuela de Estudios Hispano-Americanos, 1978.

Devine, T. M. *The Tobacco Lords: A Study of the Tobacco Merchants of Glasgow and Their Trading Activities, 1740–90*. Edinburgh: Donald, 1975.

De Vries, Jan. *The Economy of Europe in an Age of Crisis, 1600–1750*. Cambridge: Cambridge University Press, 1976.

Duncan, K., and Ian Rutledge, eds. *Land and Labor in Latin America: Essays on the Development of Agrarian Capitalism in the Nineteenth and Twentieth Centuries*. Cambridge: Cambridge University Press, 1977.

Evans, Peter B., Dietrich Rueschemeyer, and Theda Skocpol. *Bringing the State Back In*. Cambridge: Cambridge University Press, 1985.

Fallas, M. A. *La factoría de tabacos de Costa Rica*. San José: Editorial Costa Rica, 1972.

Fisher, John. *Commercial Relations between Spain and Spanish America in the Era of Free Trade, 1778–1796*. Liverpool: Center for Latin American Studies, 1985.

Fisher, Lillian E. *The Intendant System in Spanish America*. Berkeley: University of California Press, 1929.

Florescano, Enrique, ed. *Ensayos sobre el desarrollo económico de México y América Latina, 1500–1975*. Mexico City: Fondo de Cultura Económica, 1979.

———. *La clase obrera en la historia de México: De la colonia al imperio*. Vol. 1. Mexico City: Siglo XXI, 1980.

———. *Origen y desarrollo de los problemas agrarios de México, 1500–1821*. Mexico City: Ediciones Era, 1976.

————. *Precios del maíz y crisis agrícolas en México, 1708–1810.* Mexico City: Ediciones Era, 1969.

Florescano, Enrique, and Isabel Gil. *Descripciones económicas generales de Nueva España, 1784–1817.* Mexico City: SEP-INAH, 1973.

Florescano, Enrique, and Isabel Gil Sánchez. *Descripciones económicas regionales de Nueva España, provincias del Centro: Suedeste y Sur, 1766–1877.* Mexico City: SEP-INAH, 1976.

Florescano Mayet, Sergio. *El camino México-Veracruz en la época colonial.* Jalapa: Centro de Investigaciones Históricas, Universidad Veracruzana, 1987.

Garavaglia, Juan Carlos, and Juan Carlos Grosso. *Las alcabalas Novohispanas (1776–1821).* Mexico City: Archivo General de la Nación, 1987.

García-Fuentes, Lutgardo. *El comercio español con América, 1650–1700.* Seville: Diputación Provincial-EEHA, 1980.

Garner, Richard L., and William B. Taylor, eds. *Iberian Colonies and New World Societies: Essays in Memory of Charles Gibson.* State College, Pa.: Privately published, 1986.

Gerhard, Peter. *A Guide to the Historical Geography of New Spain.* Cambridge: Cambridge University Press, 1972.

González, Antonio García-Baquero. *Cádiz y el Atlántico (1717–1778).* 2 vols. Seville: Diputación de Cádiz-EEHA, 1976.

González Angulo Aguirre, Jorge. *Artesanado y ciudad a finales del siglo XVIII.* Mexico City: Fondo de Cultura Económica, 1983.

González Obregón, Luis. *Las calles de México.* Mexico City: Imprenta Manuel León Sánchez, 1944.

González Sierra, José. *Monopolio del humo (elementos para la historia del tabaco en México y algunos conflictos de tabaqueros veracruzanos: 1915–1930).* Jalapa: Centro de Investigaciones Históricas, Universidad Veracruzana, 1987.

Gutmann, Myron. *Toward the Modern Economy: Early Industry in Europe, 1500–1800.* New York: Alfred A. Knopf, 1988.

Haber, Stephen H. *Industry and Underdevelopment: The Industrialization of Mexico, 1890–1940.* Stanford: Stanford University Press, 1989.

Hamnett, Brian. *Politics and Trade in Southern Mexico.* Cambridge: Cambridge University Press, 1971.

————. *Roots of Insurgency: Mexican Regions, 1750–1824.* Cambridge: Cambridge University Press, 1986.

Hanagan, Michael P. *Nascent Proletarians: Class Formation in Post-Revolutionary France.* Oxford: Basil Blackwell, 1989.

Han-Seng, Chen. *Industrial Capital and Chinese Peasants: A Study of the Livelihood of Chinese Tobacco Cultivators.* Shanghai: Kelly and Walsh, 1939.

Harrison, Mark. *Crowds and History: Mass Phenomena in English Towns, 1790–1835.* Cambridge: Cambridge University Press, 1988.

Hawke, Gary R. *Economics for Historians.* Cambridge: Cambridge University Press, 1980.

Hernández Palomo, José Jesús. *La renta del pulque en Nueva España, 1663–1810.* Seville: Escuela de Estudios Hispano-Americanos, 1979.

Herr, Richard. *The Eighteenth Century Revolution in Spain.* Princeton: Princeton University Press, 1958.

———. *Rural Change and Royal Finances in Spain at the End of the Old Regime.* Berkeley: University of California Press, 1989.

Herrera Moreno, Enrique. *El cantón de Córdoba.* 2 vols. Tacubaya, Mexico: Editorial Citlaltépetl, 1959.

Hirschman, Albert O. *Essays in Trespassing: Economics to Politics and Beyond.* Cambridge: Cambridge University Press, 1981.

———. *Exit, Voice, and Loyalty: Responses to Decline in Firms, Organizations, and States.* Cambridge, Mass: Harvard University Press, 1970.

Holmes, Douglas R. *Cultural Disenchantments: Worker Peasantries in Northeast Italy.* Princeton: Princeton University Press, 1989.

Jacobsen, Nils, and Hans-Jürgen Puhle, eds. *The Economies of Mexico and Peru during the Late Colonial Period, 1760–1810.* Berlin: Colloquium Verlag, 1986.

Jáuregui, Jesús, Murilo Huschick, Hilario Itriago, and Ana Isabel García Torres. *Tabamex: Un caso de integración vertical de la agricultura.* Mexico City: Editorial Nueva Imagen, 1980.

Johnson, Lyman L., and Enrique Tandeter. *Essays on the Price History of Eighteenth-Century Latin America.* Albuquerque: University of New Mexico Press, 1990.

Johnson, Robert Max. *The Formation of Craft Labor Markets.* New York: Academic Press, 1984.

Joyce, Patrick. *Work, Society, and Politics: The Culture of the Factory in Later Victorian England.* New Brunswick, N.J.: Rutgers University Press, 1980.

Kamen, Henry. *Spain, 1469–1714: A Society in Conflict.* London: Longman, 1983.

Kaplan, Steven L., and Cynthia J. Koepp, eds. *Work in France: Representations, Meaning, Organization, and Practice.* Ithaca, N.Y.: Cornell University Press, 1986.

Kaufman, Stuart B. *Challenge and Change: The History of the Tobacco Workers International Union.* Champaign: University of Illinois Press, 1987.

Kertzer, David I. *Ritual, Politics, and Power.* New Haven: Yale University Press, 1988.

Ladd, Doris M. *The Making of a Strike: Mexican Silver Workers' Struggles in Real Del Monte, 1766–1775.* Lincoln: University of Nebraska Press, 1988.

———. *The Mexican Nobility at Independence, 1780–1826.* Austin: University of Texas Press, 1976.

Lafaye, Jacques. *Quetzalcóatl and Guadalupe: The Formation of Mexican National Consciousness, 1531–1813.* Chicago: University of Chicago Press, 1976.

La Force, James C., Jr. *The Development of the Spanish Textile Industry, 1750–1800*. Berkeley: University of California Press, 1965.

Landes, David. *The Unbound Prometheus*. Cambridge: Cambridge University Press, 1969.

Larson, Brooke. *Colonialism and Agrarian Transformation in Bolivia: Cochabamba, 1550–1900*. Princeton: Princeton University Press, 1988.

Leiby, John S. *Colonial Bureaucrats and the Mexican Economy*. New York: Peter Lang, 1986.

Lentin, A. *Enlightened Absolutism (1760–1790): A Documentary Sourcebook*. Newcastle-upon-Tyne: Avero Publications, 1985.

Lenz, Hans, and Federico Gómez de Orozco. *La industria papelera en México*. Mexico City: Editorial Cultura, 1940.

Lindley, Richard B. *Haciendas and Economic Development: Guadalajara, Mexico, at Independence*. Austin: University of Texas Press, 1983.

Lombardo de Ruiz, Sonia. *La ciudadela: Ideología y estilo en la arquitectura del siglo xviii*. Mexico City: UNAM, 1980.

López Sarrelangue, Delfina E. *Una villa mexicana en el siglo XVIII*. Mexico City: UNAM, 1957.

Lozan Armendares, Teresa. *La criminalidad en la ciudad de México, 1800–1821*. Mexico City: UNAM, 1987.

Ludlow, Leonor, and Carlos Marichal, eds. *Banca y poder en México (1800–1925)*. Mexico City: Editorial Grijalbo, 1986.

Lynch, John. *Bourbon Spain, 1700–1808*. Oxford: Basil Blackwell, 1989.

———. *Spanish Colonial Administration, 1782–1810: The Intendant System in the Viceroyalty of the Río de la Plata*. London: Athlone Press, 1958.

McCormick, B. J., P. D. Kitchin, G. P. Marshall, A. A. Sampson, and R. Sedgwick. *Introducing Economics*. 2d ed. London: Penguin Books, 1978.

McGreevy, William P. *An Economic History of Colombia, 1845–1930*. Cambridge: Cambridge University Press, 1971.

Machlup, Fritz. *The Political Economy of Monopoly: Business, Labor, and Government Policies*. Baltimore: Johns Hopkins University Press, 1952.

Maclachlan, Colin M. *Spain's Empire in the New World: The Role of Ideas in Institutional and Social Change*. Berkeley: University of California Press, 1988.

Medina Rubio, Aristides. *La iglesia y la producción agrícola en Puebla, 1540–1795*. Mexico City: Centro de Estudios Históricos, El Colegio de México, 1983.

Meek, W. T. *The Exchange Media of Colonial Mexico*. New York: King's Crown Press, 1948.

Migden Socolow, Susan. *The Bureaucrats of Buenos Aires, 1769–1810: Amor al Real Servicio*. Durham, N.C.: Duke University Press, 1987.

Mokyr, Joel, ed. *The Economics of the Industrial Revolution*. Totowa, N.J.: Rowman & Allanheld, 1985.

Moore, Barrington. *Injustice: The Social Bases of Obedience and Revolt*. White Plains, N.Y.: M. E. Sharpe, 1978.

Moreno Toscano, Alejandro. *Ciudad de México, ensayo de construcción de una historia.* Mexico City: INAH, Colección Científica 61, 1978.

Morgan, Edmund S. *American Slavery, American Freedom.* New York: Norton, 1976.

Morin, Claude. *Michoacán en la Nueva España del siglo XVIII: Crecimiento y desigualdad en una economía colonial.* Mexico City: Fondo de Cultura Económica, 1979.

Navarro García, Luis. *Intendencias en Indias.* Seville: Escuela de Estudios Hispano-Americanos, 1959.

Newman, John Henry. *Essay in Aid of a Grammar of Assent.* Notre Dame: University of Notre Dame Press, 1979 [1870].

Nieto, Vicente. *Padrón de Jalapa.* Mexico City: Editorial Citlaltépetl, 1971.

Ortiz, Fernando. *Contrapunteo cubano del tabaco y el azúcar.* Barcelona: Editorial Ariel, 1973.

Ots Capdequí, José María. *El estado español en las Indias.* Mexico City: Fondo de Cultura Económica, 1941.

Parry, John H. *The Spanish Theory of Empire.* Cambridge: Cambridge University Press, 1940.

Pasquel, Leonardo. *La ciudad de Veracruz.* Mexico City: Editorial Citlaltépetl, 1958.

Payno, Manuel. *Los bandidos de Río Frío.* Mexico City: Editorial Porrúa, 1959.

Pérez Vidal, José. *España en la historia del tabaco.* Madrid: Centro de Etnología Peninsular, 1959.

Phelan, John Leddy. *The People and the King: The Comunero Revolution in Colombia, 1781.* Madison: University of Wisconsin Press, 1978.

Potash, Robert A. *Mexican Government and Industrial Development in the Early Republic: The Banco de Avío.* Amherst: University of Massachusetts Press, 1983.

Poulantzas, N. *Political Power and Social Classes.* Translated by Timothy O'Hagan. London: Routledge Chapman and Hall, 1987.

Price, Jacob M. *France and the Chesapeake: A History of the French Tobacco Monopoly, 1674–1791, and of Its Relationship to the British and American Tobacco Trades.* 2 vols. Ann Arbor: University of Michigan Press, 1973.

Price, Richard. *Labour in British Society: An Interpretative History.* London: Croom Helm, 1986.

Priestley, Herbert I. *José de Gálvez: Visitor-General of New Spain, 1765–1771.* Berkeley: University of California Publications in History, vol. V, 1916. Reprinted Philadelphia: Porcupine Press, 1980.

Ragland, R. L., and J. A. Flippo. *How Tobacco Is Raised and Prepared for Market.* Richmond, Va., 1873.

Ramamurti, Ravi. *State Owned Enterprises in High Technology Industries.* New York: Praeger, 1987.

Ramírez, Susan E. *Provincial Patriarchs: Land Tenure and the Economics of Power in Colonial Peru.* Albuquerque: University of New Mexico Press, 1986.

Ribes Iborra, Vicent. *Los valencianos y América: El comercio valenciano con Indias en el siglo XVIII.* Valencia: História i Societat/2, Diputació Provincial de Valéncia, 1985.

Rice, Albert K. *Productivity and Social Organization: The Ahmedabad Experiment.* London: Tavistock Publications, 1958.

Rich, E. E., and C. H. Wilson, eds. *The Cambridge Economic History of Europe.* Vol 5. Cambridge: Cambridge University Press, 1977.

Rivera Cambas, Manuel. *Historia antigua y moderna de Jalapa y de las revoluciones del estado de Veracruz.* 17 vols. Tacubaya, Mexico: Editorial Citlaltépetl, 1959.

Rivero Muñiz, José. *Tabaco, su historia en Cuba.* 2 vols. Havana: Instituto de Historia, Comisión Nacional de la Academia de Ciencias de la República de Cuba, 1964–1965.

Robert, J. C. *The Tobacco Kingdom: Plantation, Market, and Factory in Virginia and North Carolina, 1800–1860.* Durham, N.C.: Duke University Press, 1938.

Robicsek, Francis. *The Smoking Gods: Tobacco in Maya Art, History, and Religion.* Norman: University of Oklahoma Press, 1979.

Robinson, G. B. *Documentos para el estudio de la industrialización en México, 1837–1845.* Mexico City: Secretaria de Hacienda y Crédito Público, 1977.

Roche, Daniel. *The People of Paris: An Essay in Popular Culture in the 18th Century.* Leamington Spa: Berg, 1987.

Rodríguez García, Vicente. *El fiscal de real hacienda en Nueva España (Don Ramón de Posada y Soto, 1781–1793).* Oviedo: Universidad de Oviedo, 1985.

Ros, María Amparo. *La producción cigarrera a finales de la colonia: La fábrica en México.* Mexico City: Cuaderno de Trabajo 44, Instituto Nacional de Antropología e Historia, 1984.

Roseberry, William. *Anthropologies and Histories: Essays in Culture, History, and Political Economy.* New Brunswick, N.J.: Rutgers University Press, 1989.

———. *Coffee and Capitalism in the Venezuelan Andes.* Austin: University of Texas Press, 1983.

Rubin, V., and A. Tuden, eds. *Comparative Perspectives on Slavery in New World Plantation Societies.* Annals of the New York Academy of Sciences, vol. 292. New York: New York Academy of Sciences, 1977.

Rule, John. *The Experience of Labour in Eighteenth Century English Industry.* New York: St. Martin, 1981.

Saavedra de Sangronis, Don Francisco. *Journal of Don Francisco Saavedra de Sangronis during the commission which he had in his charge from 25 June 1780 until the 20th of the same month of 1783.* Edited by Francisco Morales Padrón. Translated by Aileen Moore Topping. Gainesville: University of Florida Press, 1989.

Salvucci, Richard J. *Textiles and Capitalism in Mexico: An Economic History of the Obrajes, 1539–1840.* Princeton: Princeton University Press, 1987.

Schwartz, Stuart B. *Sugar Plantations in the Formation of Brazilian Society, Bahia, 1550–1835*. Cambridge: Cambridge University Press, 1985.

Scott, H. M., ed. *Enlightened Absolutism: Reform and Reformers in Later Eighteenth-Century Europe*. Ann Arbor: University of Michigan Press, 1990.

Scott, James C. *Domination and the Arts of Resistance: Hidden Transcripts*. New Haven: Yale University Press, 1990.

———. *The Moral Economy of the Peasant*. New Haven: Yale University Press, 1976.

———. *Weapons of the Weak: Everyday Forms of Peasant Resistance*. New Haven: Yale University Press, 1985.

Scott, Joan Wallach. *Gender and the Politics of History*. New York: Columbia University Press, 1988.

———. *The Glassworkers of Carmaux*. Cambridge, Mass.: Harvard University Press, 1974.

Sedano, Francisco. *Noticias de México*. Vol. 1. Mexico City: Colección Metropolitana, n.d.

Sewell, William H. *Work and Revolution in France*. Cambridge: Cambridge University Press, 1980.

Shafer, R. J. *The Economic Societies in the Spanish World, 1763–1821*. Syracuse, N.Y.: Syracuse University Press, 1958.

Sierra, Catalina. *El nacimiento de México*. Mexico City: UNAM, 1960.

Sierra, Luis F. *El tabaco en la economía colombiana del siglo XIX*. Bogotá: Dirección de Divulgación Cultural, Universidad Nacional de Colombia, 1971.

Slicher Van Bath, B. J. *The Agrarian History of Western Europe, A.D. 500–1850*. Translated by Olive Ordich. London: Edward Arnold, 1963.

Sonenscher, Michael. *Work & Wages: Natural Law, Politics, and the Eighteenth Century French Trades*. Cambridge: Cambridge University Press, 1989.

Spalding, Karen, ed. *Essays in the Political, Economic, and Social History of Colonial Latin America*. Newark: University of Delaware, Latin American Studies Program, 1982.

Stansell, Christine. *City of Women: Sex and Class in New York, 1789–1860*. New York: Alfred A. Knopf, 1986.

Stiverson, G. A. *Poverty in a Land of Plenty: Tenancy in Eighteenth Century Maryland*. Baltimore: Johns Hopkins University Press, 1978.

Stubbs, Jean. *Tobacco on the Periphery: A Case Study in Cuban Labour History, 1860–1958*. Cambridge: Cambridge University Press, 1985.

Szuchman, Mark D., ed. *The Middle Period in Latin America: Values and Attitudes in the 17th–19th Centuries*. Boulder and London: Lynne Reiner Publishers, 1989.

Taylor, William B. *Drinking, Homicide, and Rebellion in Colonial Mexican Villages*. Stanford: Stanford University Press, 1979.

———. *Landlord and Peasant in Colonial Oaxaca*. Stanford: Stanford University Press, 1972.

Tenenbaum, Barbara. *The Politics of Penury: Debts and Taxes in Mexico, 1821–1856*. Albuquerque: University of New Mexico Press, 1986.
Tepaske, John J. *La real hacienda de Nueva España: La real caja de México, 1576–1816*. Mexico City: INAH, Colección Científica 41, 1976.
Thompson, Guy P. *Puebla de los Angeles: Industry and Society in a Mexican City, 1700–1850*. Boulder: Westview Press, 1989.
Tilly, Charles. *The Contentious French*. Cambridge, Mass.: Harvard University Press, 1986.
———, ed. *The Formation of National States in Western Europe*. Princeton: Princeton University Press, 1975.
Trens, Manuel B. *Historia de Veracruz*. 6 vols. Jalapa: Jalapa-Enríquez, 1947.
Tutino, John. *From Insurrection to Revolution in Mexico*. Princeton: Princeton University Press, 1986.
Van Young, Eric. *Hacienda and Market in Eighteenth Century Mexico: The Rural Economy of the Guadalajara Region, 1675–1820*. Berkeley: University of California Press, 1981.
Velasco Ceballos, Rómulo. *La administración de D. Frey Antonio María de Bucareli y Ursúa*. 2 vols. Publicaciones del Archivo General de la Nación, 29. Mexico City: Secretaría de Gobernación, 1936.
Vicens Vives, Jaime, ed. *Historia social y económica de España y América*. 5 vols. 2d ed. Barcelona: Editorial Vicens-Vives, 1971.
Viqueira Albán, Juan Pedro. *¿Relajados o reprimidos? Diversiones públicas y vida social en la ciudad de México durante el Siglo de las Luces*. Mexico City: Fondo de Cultura Económica, 1987.
Von Thünen, Johann Heinrich. *The Isolated State*. Translated by Carla M. Wartenberg. Edited with an introduction by Peter Hall. Oxford, New York: Pergammon Press, 1966.
Wilbert, Johannes. *Tobacco and Shamanism in South America*. New Haven: Yale University Press, 1987.
Wuthnow, Robert. *Meaning and Moral Order: Explorations in Cultural Analysis*. Berkeley: University of California Press, 1987.
Wyckoff, V. J. *Tobacco Regulation in Colonial Maryland*. Baltimore: Johns Hopkins University Press, 1936.
Yeomans, K. A. *Statistics for the Social Scientist*. 2 vols. Harmondsworth: Penguin Books, 1979.

Articles and Unpublished Papers

Aguila, Yves. "Albores de la seguridad social en México, 1770: La Concordia de la Manufactura de Tabacos." *Jahrbuch Für Geschichte* 24 (1987): 335–352.
Amaral, Samuel. "Public Expenditure Financing in the Colonial Treasury: An Analysis of the Real Caja de Buenos Aires Accounts, 1789–91." *HAHR* 64, no. 2 (May 1984): 287–295.
———. "Rural Production and Labour in Late Colonial Buenos Aires." *JLAS* 19 (November 1987): 235–278.

Anderson, Rodney D. "Race and Social Stratification: A Comparison of Working-Class Spaniards, Indians, and Castas in Guadalajara, Mexico in 1821." *HAHR* 68 (1988): 209–243.

Arcila Farías, Eduardo. "La administración de la renta del tabaco en Venezuela." *Anuario de estudios americanos* 31 (1974): 55–77.

Arias Divito, Juan Carlos. "Auge y decadencia de la renta del tabaco en Buenos Aires." *Nuestra Historia* 22 (1978): 195–201.

———. "Dificultades para establecer la renta de tabaco en Paraguay." *Anuario de Estudios Americanos* 33 (1976): 1–17.

———. "La Real Ordenanza de Intendentes y la renta de tabaco." *Revista de historia del derecho* 2 (1983): 341–376.

Arreola, Daniel D. "Nineteenth-Century Townscapes of Eastern Mexico." *Geographical Review* 72, no. 1 (January 1982): 2–19.

Arrom, Silvia M. "Popular Politics in Mexico City: The Parián Riot, 1828." *HAHR* 68, no. 2 (1988): 245–268.

Barbier, Jacques A. "The Culmination of the Bourbon Reforms, 1787–1792." *HAHR* 57 (1977): 51–68.

Barbier, Jacques A., and Herbert S. Klein. "Revolutionary Wars and Public Finances: The Madrid Treasury, 1784–1807." *Journal of Economic History* 41, no. 2 (1981): 315–339.

Barbier, Jacques A., and Mark A. Burkholder. Critique of Stanley J. Stein's "Bureaucracy and Business in the Spanish Empire, 1759–1804: Failure of a Bourbon Reform in Mexico and Peru." *HAHR* 62, no. 3 (1982): 460–468.

Bauer, Arnold J. "Rural workers in Spanish America: Problems of Peonage and Oppression." *HAHR* 59, no. 1 (1979): 34–63.

Behar, Ruth. "Sex and Sin, Witchcraft, and the Devil in Late-Colonial Mexico." *American Ethnologist* 14, no. 1 (February, 1987): 34–54.

Bierck, H. A. "Tobacco Marketing in Venezuela, 1798–1799: An Aspect of Spanish Mercantilistic Revisionism." *Business History Review* 39 (1965): 489–502.

Brading, D. A. "Bourbon Spain and Its American Empire." In *The Cambridge History of Latin America*, vol. 1, edited by Leslie Bethell. Cambridge: Cambridge University Press, 1984.

———. Comments on "The Economic Cycle in Bourbon Central Mexico: A Critique of the *Recaudación del diezmo líquido en pesos*," by Ouweneel and Bijleveld. *HAHR* 69, no. 3 (1989): 531–538.

———. "El mercantilismo ibérico y el crecimiento económico en la América Latina del siglo XVIII." In *Ensayos sobre el desarrollo económico de México y América Latina (1500–1975)*, edited by E. Florescano. Mexico City: Fondo de Cultura Económica, 1979.

———. "Facts and Figments in Bourbon Mexico." *Bulletin of Latin American Research* 4, no. 1 (1985): 61–64.

———. "Government and Elite in Late Colonial Mexico." *HAHR* 53 (1973): 389–414.

——— "Hacienda Profits and Tenant Farming in the Mexican Bajío, 1700–1860." In *Land and Labour in Latin America: Essays on the De-*

velopment of Agrarian Capitalism in the Nineteenth and Twentieth Centuries, edited by K. Duncan and I. Rutledge. Cambridge: Cambridge University Press, 1977.

———. "Tridentine Catholicism and Enlightened Despotism in Bourbon Mexico." *JLAS* 15 (1983): 1– 22.

Brenner, R. "Agrarian Class Structure, Economic Development in Pre-Industrial Europe." *Past and Present* 70 (1976): 30–75.

Bright, Charles, and Susan Harding. "Processes of Statemaking and Popular Protest: An Introduction." In *Statemaking and Social Movements: Essays in History and Theory*, edited by Charles Bright and Susan Harding. Ann Arbor: University of Michigan Press, 1984.

Broeze, F. J. A. "The New Economic History, the Navigation Acts, and the Continental Tobacco Market, 1770–1790." *Economic History Review* 26 (1973): 668–678.

Brun Martínez, Gabriel. "La organización del trabajo y la estructura de la unidad doméstica de los zapateros y cigarreros de la ciudad de México en 1811." In *Organización de la producción y relaciones de trabajo en el siglo XIX en México*. Cuaderno de Trabajo 29. Mexico City: Instituto Nacional de Antropología e Historia, 1978.

Calhoun, Craig. "Community: Toward a Variable Conceptualization for Comparative Research." In *History and Class: Essential Readings in Theory and Interpretation*, edited by R. S. Neale. Oxford: Basil Blackwell, 1984.

Cardoso, Ciro F. S. "The Formation of the Coffee Estate in Nineteenth-Century Costa Rica." In *Land and Labour in Latin America*, edited by K. Duncan and I. Rutledge. Cambridge: Cambridge University Press, 1977.

Carroll, Patrick J. "Estudio sociodemográfico de personas de sangre negra en Jalapa, 1791." *Historia Mexicana* 23 (1973): 111–125.

Céspedes del Castillo, Guillermo. "La renta de tabacos en el virreinato del Perú." *Revista Histórica* 21 (1954): 138–163.

Chaunu, Pierre. "Veracruz en la segunda mitad del siglo XVI y primera del XVII." *Historia Mexicana* 9 (1960): 521–557.

Chartier, Roger. "Texts, Printing, Readings." In *The New Cultural History*, edited by Lynn Hunt. Berkeley: University of California Press, 1989.

Chirot, Daniel. "The Growth of Market and Service Labour Systems in Agriculture." *Journal of Social History* 8 (1974–1975): 67–80.

Coatsworth, John J. "The Limits of Colonial Absolutism: The State in Eighteenth Century Mexico." In *Essays in the Political, Economic, and Social History of Colonial Latin America*, edited by K. Spalding. Newark: Latin American Studies Program, University of Delaware, 1982.

Cohen, Jon S. "Managers and Machinery: An Analysis of the Rise of Factory Production." *Australian Economic Papers* 20, no. 36 (June 1981): 24–41.

Coutts, Brian E. "Boom and Bust: The Rise and Fall of the Tobacco Industry in Spanish Louisiana, 1770–1790" *The Americas* 62 (January 1986): 289–309.

Cuello Martinell, M. A. "La renta de los naipes en Nueva España." *Anuario de Estudios Americanos* 22 (1965): 231–335.

Cuenca Esteban, Javier. "Of Nimble Arrows and Faulty Bows: A Call for Rigor." *HAHR* 64, no. 2 (1984): 297–303.

——. "Statistics of Spain's Colonial Trade, 1792–1820: Consular Duties, Cargo Inventories, and Balances of Trade." *HAHR* 61, no. 3 (1981): 381–428.

de la Tabla y Ducasse, Javier Ortiz. "Comercio y comerciantes Montañeses en Veracruz (1785–1804)." In *Santander y el Nuevo Mundo*. Santander: Centro de Estudios Montañeses, 1977.

de Roover, Raymond. "Monopoly Theory Prior to Adam Smith: A Revision." In *Business Banking and Economic Thought in Late Medieval and Early Modern Europe*, edited by Julius Kirshner. Chicago: University of Chicago Press, 1974.

Domar, Evsey D. "The Causes of Slavery or Serfdom: A Hypothesis." *Journal of Economic History* 30 (1970): 18–32.

Duby, Georges. "Ideologies in social history." In *Constructing the Past: Essays in Historical Methodology*, edited by Jacques Le Goff and Pierre Nora. Cambridge: Cambridge University Press, 1985.

Duke, C. "The Family in Eighteenth Century Plantation Society in Mexico." In *Comparative Perspectives on Slavery in New World Plantation Societies*, edited by V. Rubin and A. Tuden. Annals of the New York Academy of Sciences, vol. 292. New York: New York Academy of Sciences, 1977.

Dupront, Alfonse. "Religion and Religious Anthropology." In *Constructing the Past: Essays in Historical Methodology*, edited by Jacques Le Goff and Pierre Nora. Cambridge: Cambridge University Press, 1985.

Ekelund, Robert B., Jr., and Robert D. Tollison. "Economic Regulation in Mercantile England: Heckscher Revisited." *Economic Inquiry* 18, no. 4 (1980): 567–599.

English Martin, Cheryl. "Haciendas and Villages in Late Colonial Morelos." *HAHR* 62, no. 3 (1982): 407–427.

Ferry, Robert J. "The Price of Cacao, Its Export, and Rebellion in Eighteenth-Century Caracas: Boom, Bust, and the Basque Monopoly." In *Essays on the Price History of Eighteenth Century Latin America*, edited by Lyman L. Johnson and Enrique Tandeter. Albuquerque: University of New Mexico Press, 1990.

Fisher, John. "Soldiers, Society, and Politics in Spanish America, 1750–1821." *Latin American Research Review* 17 (1982): 217–222.

Florescano, Enrique. "El problema agrario en los últimos años del virreinato." *Historia Mexicana* 20, no. 4 (1971): 477–510.

Florescano Mayet, Sergio. "Las divisiones políticas del Estado de Veracruz, 1824–1917." *Dualismo* 6, no. 1 (1977): 39–110.

Fox, J. S. "Antonio de San José Muro: Political Economist of New Spain." *HAHR* 21 (1941): 410–416.

Garavaglia, Juan Carlos, and Juan Carlos Grosso. "De Veracruz a Durango:

Un análisis de la Nueva España borbónica." *Siglo XIX* 11, no. 4 (July–December 1987): 9–52.

Garner, Richard L. "Further Considerations of 'Facts and Figments in Bourbon Mexico.'" *Bulletin of Latin American Research* 6, no. 1 (1987): 55–63.

———. "Prices and Wages in Eighteenth-Century Mexico." In *Essays on the Price History of Eighteenth-Century Latin America,* edited by Lyman L. Johnson and Enrique Tandeter. Albuquerque: University of New Mexico Press, 1990.

———. "Price Trends in Eighteenth-Century Mexico." *HAHR* 65, no. 2 (1985): 279–325.

González, Angulo J., and R. Zarauz Sandoval. "Los trabajadores industriales de Nueva España, 1750–1810." In *La clase obrera en la historia de México: De la colonia al imperio,* vol. 1, edited by E. Florescano. Mexico City: Siglo XXI, 1980.

Gray, L. D. "The Market Surplus Problems of Colonial Tobacco." *Agricultural History* 2 (1928): 1–34.

Gray, Stanley, and Vertrees J. Wyckoff. "The International Tobacco Trade in the Seventeenth Century." *Southern Economic Journal* 7 (1940): 18–25.

Hammerton, Elizabeth, and David Cannadine. "Conflict and Consensus on a Ceremonial Occasion: The Diamond Jubilee in Cambridge in 1897." *Historical Journal* 24, no. 1 (1981): 111–146.

Hamnett, Brian. "The Mexican Bureaucracy of the Bourbon Reforms, 1700–1770: A Study in the Limitations of Absolutism." Institute of Latin American Studies *Occasional Papers* (Glasgow) 26 (1979).

———. "Obstáculos a la política agraria del despotismo ilustrado." *Historia Mexicana* 20 (1970): 55–75.

Harberger, Arnold C. "Monopoly and Resource Allocation." *American Economic Review* 44, no. 2 (May 1964): 77–87.

Harrison, John. "The Evolution of the Colombian Tobacco Trade to 1875." *HAHR* 32 (1952): 163–174.

Haslip-Viera, Gabriel. "The Underclass." In *Cities and Society in Colonial Latin America,* edited by Louisa Schell Hoberman and Susan Migden Socolow. Albuquerque: University of New Mexico Press, 1986.

Holton, Robert J. "The Crowd in History: Some Problems of Theory and Method." *Social History* 3, no. 2 (May 1978): 219–233.

Hünefeldt, Christine. "Etapa final del monopolio en el virreinato del Perú: El tabaco de Chachapoyas." In *The Economies of Mexico and Peru during the Late Colonial Period, 1760–1810,* edited by Nils Jacobsen and Hans-Jürgen Puhle. Berlin: Colloquium Verlag, 1986.

Johnson, Lyman L. "The Entrepreneurial Reorganization of an Artisan Trade: The Bakers of Buenos Aires." *The Americas* 37, no. 2 (1980): 139–160.

———. "The Silversmiths of Colonial Buenos Aires: A Case Study in the Failure of Corporate Social Organization." *JLAS* 8 (November 1976): 181–213.

————. "Wages, Prices, and the Organization of Work in Late Colonial Buenos Aires." Unpublished paper.

Joyce, Patrick. "The Historical Meanings of Work: An Introduction." In *The Historical Meanings of Work*. Cambridge: Cambridge University Press, 1987.

Juárez Martínez, A. "Las ferias de Jalapa, 1720–78." *Primer Anuario* (1977): 17–44.

Katz, Friedrick. "Rural Uprisings in Preconquest and Colonial Mexico." In *Riot, Rebellion, and Revolution: Rural Social Conflict in Mexico*, edited by Friedrick Katz. Princeton: Princeton University Press, 1988.

Kellenbenz, Hermann. "The Organization of Industrial Production." In *The Cambridge Economic History of Europe*, vol. 5, edited by E. E. Rich and C. H. Wilson. Cambridge: Cambridge University Press, 1977.

Kicza, John E. "Mexican Merchants and Their Links to Spain, 1750–1850." Unpublished paper, presented at Congress of Americanistas, Amsterdam, 1988.

Kinnaird, L. "The Spanish Tobacco Monopoly in New Mexico, 1766–67." *New Mexico Historical Review* 21 (1946): 328–339.

Klein, Herbert S. "La economía de la Nueva España, 1680–1809: Un análisis a partir de las Cajas Reales." *Historia Mexicana* 34 (1985): 561–609.

————. "Structure and Profitability of Royal Finance in the Viceroyalty of the Rio Plata in 1790." *HAHR* 53 (1973): 440–469.

Klein, Herbert S., and Jacques A. Barbier. "Recent Trends in the Study of Colonial Public Finance." *Latin American Research Review* 23, no. 1 (1988): 35–62.

Knight, Alan. "Mexican Peonage: What Was It and Why Was It?" *JLAS* 18 (May 1986): 41–74.

Kriedte, Peter. "Proto-industrialization between Industrialization and Deindustrialization." In *Industrialization before Industrialization*, edited by Peter Kriedte, Hans Medick, and Jürgen Schlumblom. Translated by Beate Schempp. Cambridge: Cambridge University Press, 1981.

Kuethe, Allan. "Towards a Periodization of the Reforms of Charles III." In *Iberian Colonies, New World Societies: Essays in Memory of Charles Gibson*, edited by R. L. Garner and W. B. Taylor. State College, Pa.: Privately published, 1986.

————. "The Development of the Cuban Military as a Sociopolitical Elite, 1763–83." *HAHR* 61, no. 4 (1981): 695–704.

Kuethe, Allan J., and G. Douglas Inglis. "Absolutism and Enlightened Reform: Charles III, the Establishment of the Alcabala, and Commercial Reorganization in Cuba." *Past & Present* 109 (November 1985): 118–143.

Kunimoto, Iyo. "The Formation of the Early Mexican Federal System: An Examination of the Financial Framework." *Annals of Chuo University* (Tokyo) 1 (March 1980): 15–30.

Land, A. C. "The Tobacco Staple and the Planter's Problems, Technology, Labour, Crops." *Agricultural History* 44 (1969): 69–81.

Lavrin, Asunción. "The Execution of the Law of Consolidación in New Spain: Economic Aims and Results." *HAHR* 53, no. 1 (February 1973): 27–49.

———. "Mundos en contraste: Cofradías rurales y urbanas en México a fines del siglo XVIII." In *La iglesia en la economía de América Latina siglos XVI al XIX*, edited by A. J. Bauer. Mexico City: INAH, 1986.

Le Goff, Jacques. "Mentalities: A History of Ambiguities." In *Constructing the Past: Essays in Historical Methodology*, edited by Jacques Le Goff and Pierre Nora. Cambridge: Cambridge University Press, 1985.

Lemoine Villicaña, E. "Documentos y mapas para la geografía histórica de Orizaba (1690–1800)." *Boletín del Archivo General de la Nación* 3 (1962): 461–527.

Lis, Catherina, and Hugo Soly. "Policing the Early Modern Proletariat, 1450–1850." In *Proletarianization and Family History*, edited by David Levine. Orlando: Academic Press, 1984.

Lüdtke, Alf. "Cash, Coffee-Breaks, Horseplay: Eigensinn and Politics among Factory Workers in Germany circa 1900." In *Confrontation, Class Consciousness, and the Labor Process: Studies in Proletarian Class Formation*, edited by Michael Hanagan and Charles Stephenson. Westport, Conn.: Greenwood Press, 1986.

———. "The Historiography of Everyday Life: The Personal and the Political." In *Culture, Ideology, and Politics*, edited by Rafael Samuel and Gareth Stedman-Jones. London: Routledge & Kegan Paul, 1982.

Lugar, Catherine. "The Portuguese Tobacco Trade and Tobacco Growers of Bahia in the Late Colonial Period." In *Essays Concerning the Socioeconomic History of Brazil and Portuguese India*, edited by Dauril Alden and Warren Dean. Gainesville: University Presses of Florida, 1977.

McFarlane, Anthony F. "Civil Disorders and Popular Protests in Late Colonial New Granada." *HAHR* 64, no. 1 (February 1984): 17–54.

Marglin, Stephen. "What Do Bosses Do? The Origins and Function of Hierarchy in Capitalist Production." In *The Division of Labour: The Labour Process and Class Struggle in Modern Capitalism*, edited by André Gorz. Hassocks: Harvester Press, 1976.

Martin, Norman F. "La desnudez en la Nueva España." *Anuario de Estudios Americanos* 29 (1972): 261–294.

Meyer, Rosa María. "Los Béistegui, especuladores y mineros, 1830–1869." In *Formación y desarrollo de la burguesía en México, siglo XIX*, edited by Ciro F. S. Cardoso. Mexico City: Siglo XXI, 1978.

Mokyr, Joel. "The Industrial Revolution and the New Economic History." In *The Economics of the Industrial Revolution*, edited by Joel Mokyr. Totowa, N.J.: Roman & Allanheld, 1985.

———. "Is There Still Life in the Pessimist Case? Consumption during the Industrial Revolution, 1790–1850." *Journal of Economic History* 58, no. 1 (March 1988): 69–72.

Moreno Toscano, Alejandra. "Los trabajadores y el proyecto de industrialización, 1810–1867." In *La clase obrera en la historia de México: De la colonia al imperio,* vol. 1, edited by Enrique Florescano. Mexico City: Siglo XXI, 1980.

Moreno Toscano, Alejandra, and Carlos Aguirre Anaya. "Migrations to Mexico City in the Nineteenth Century: Research Approaches." *Journal of Interamerican Studies and World Affairs* 17, no. 1 (February 1975): 27–42.

Nash, Robert C. "The English and Scottish Tobacco Trades in the Seventeenth and Eighteenth Centuries: Legal and Illegal Trade." *Economic History Review* 35, no. 3 (August 1982): 354–372.

Ouweneel, Arij, and Catrien C. J. Bijleveld. "The Economic Cycle in Bourbon Central Mexico: A Critique of the *Recaudación de diezmo líquido en pesos.*" *HAHR* 69, no. 3 (August 1989): 479–530.

Patch, Robert W. "Agrarian Change in Eighteenth-Century Yucatán." *HAHR* 65, no. 1 (February 1985): 21–49.

Perrot, Michelle. "On the Formation of the French Working Class." In *Working Class Formation,* edited by Ira Katznelson and Aristide Zolberg. Princeton: Princeton University Press, 1986.

Phelan, John Leddy. "Authority and Flexibility in the Spanish Imperial Bureaucracy." *Administrative Science Quarterly* 5, no. 1 (June 1980): 47–65.

Price, Richard. "The Labour Process and Labour History." *Social History* 8, no. 1 (January 1983): 57–75.

Rancière, Jacques. "The Myth of the Artisan: Critical Reflections on a Category of Social History." In *Work in France: Representations, Meaning, Organization, and Practice,* edited by Steven L. Kaplan and Cynthia J. Koepp. Ithaca, N.Y.: Cornell University Press, 1986.

Real Díaz, José Joaquín, and Antonia M. Heredia Herrera. "Martin de Mayorga." In *Los virreyes de Nueva España en el reinado de Carlos III,* vol. 2, edited by José Antonio Calderón Quijano. Seville: Escuela de Estudios Hispano-Americanos, 1967–1968.

Rees, P. "Origins of Colonial Transportation in Mexico." *Geographical Review* 65 (1975): 323–334.

Rodríguez Gordillo, José Manuel. "El personal obrero en la Real Fábrica de Tabaco." In *Sevilla y el Tabaco.* Seville: Imprenta Alvarez, S.L., 1984.

Ros, María Amparo. "La real fábrica de puros y cigarros: Organización del trabajo y estructura urbana." In *Ciudad de México, ensayo de construcción de una historia,* edited by Alejandra Moreno Toscano. Colección Científica 61. Mexico City: INAH, 1978.

———. "La real fábrica de tabaco: ¿un embrión del capitalismo?" *Historias* 10 (July–September 1985): 51–64.

Salvucci, Linda K. " 'Costumbres viejas, Hombres nuevos' ": José de Gálvez y la burocracia fiscal novo-hispana (1754–1800)." *Historia Mexicana* 33, no. 2 (1983): 224–264.

Salvucci, Richard J., and Linda K. Salvucci. "Crecimiento y cambio en la productividad de México." *HISLA—Revista Latinoamericana de Historia Económica y Social* 10 (1987): 67–89.

Scardaville, Michael C. "Alcohol Abuse and Tavern Reform in Late Colonial Mexico." *HAHR* 60, no. 4 (November 1980): 643–671.

Schlumblom, J. "Excursus: The Political and Institutional Framework of Proto-Industrialization." In *Industrialization before Industrialization,* edited by Peter Kriedte, Hans Medick, Jürgen Schlumblom. Translated by Beate Schempp. Cambridge: Cambridge University Press, 1981.

———. "Relations in Production—Productive Forces—Crises in Proto-Industrialization." In *Industrialization before Industrialization,* edited by Peter Kriedte, Hans Medick, Jürgen Schlumblom. Translated by Beate Schempp. Cambridge: Cambridge University Press, 1981.

Schwartz, Stuart B. "Colonial Brazil: The Role of the State in a Slave Social Formation." In *Essays in the Political, Economic, and Social History of Colonial Latin America,* edited by Karen Spalding. Newark: University of Delaware, Latin American Studies Program, 1982.

Sonenscher, Michael. "Work and Wages in Paris in the Eighteenth Century." In *Manufacture in Town and Country before the Factory,* edited by Maxine Berg, Pat Hudson, and Michael Sonenscher. Cambridge: Cambridge University Press, 1983.

Spalding, Karen. "Introduction." In *Essays in the Political, Economic and Social History of Colonial Latin America,* edited by Karen Spalding. Newark, Delaware: University of Delaware, Latin American Studies Program, 1982.

Stapff, A. "La renta del tabaco en el Chile de la época virreinal." *Anuario de Estudios Americanos* 18 (1961): 1–63.

Stein, Stanley J. "Bureaucracy and Business in the Spanish Empire, 1759–1804: Failure of a Bourbon Reform in Mexico and Peru." *HAHR* 61, no. 1 (1981): 2–28.

———. "Caribbean Counterpoint: Veracruz vs. Havana: War and Neutral Trade, 1797–1799." In *Géographie du capital marchand aux Amériques, 1760–1860,* edited by Jeanne Chase. Paris: Centre d'études nordaméricaines, 1987.

Stinchcombe, Arthur. "Agricultural Enterprises and Rural Class Relations." *American Journal of Sociology* 67 (1961): 165–176.

Supple, Barry. "The Nature of Enterprise." In *The Cambridge Economic History of Europe,* vol. 5, edited by E. E. Rich and C. H. Wilson. Cambridge: Cambridge University Press, 1977.

Taylor, William B. "Between Global Process and Local Knowledge: An Inquiry into Early Latin American Social History, 1500–1900." In *Reliving the Past: The Worlds of Social History,* edited by O. Zunz. Chapel Hill: University of North Carolina Press, 1985.

———. "The Virgin of Guadalupe in New Spain: An Inquiry into the Social History of Marian Devotion." *American Ethnologist* 14, no. 1 (February 1987): 9–33.

Tepaske, John J. "Economic Cycles in New Spain in the Eighteenth Century: The View from the Public Sector." In *Iberian Colonies, New World Societies: Essays in Memory of Charles Gibson,* edited by

Richard L. Garner and William B. Taylor. State College, Pa: Privately published, 1986.

——. "The Financial Disintegration of the Royal Government of Mexico during the Epoch of Independence." In *The Independence of Mexico and the Creation of the New Nation*, edited by Jaime E. Rodríguez O. Los Angeles: UCLA Latin American Center Publications, 1989.

Thamer, Hans-Ulrich. "Journeyman Culture and Enlightened Public Opinion." In *Understanding Popular Culture: Europe from the Middle Ages to the Nineteenth Century*, edited by Steven L. Kaplan. New York: Mouton, 1984.

Thirsk, Joan. "New Crops and Their Diffusion: Tobacco-Growing in Seventeenth-Century England." In *Rural Change and Urban Growth 1500–1800: Essays in English Regional History in Honor of W. G. Hoskins*, edited by C. W. Chalklin and M. A. Havinden. London: Longman, 1974.

Thompson, Edward P. "Eighteenth-Century English Society: Class Struggle without Class?" *Social History* 3, no. 2 (May 1978): 133–165.

——. "The Moral Economy of the English Crowd in the Eighteenth Century." *Past and Present* 50 (February 1971): 76–136.

——. "Time, Work Discipline, and Industrial Capitalism." *Past & Present* 38 (1967): 56–97.

Tilly, Charles. "Collective Violence in European Perspective." In *The History of Violence in America: Historical and Comparative Perspectives*, edited by Hugh D. Graham and Ted R. Gurr. New York: Praeger, 1969.

Tilly, Louise A. "Paths of Proletarianization: Organization of Production, Sexual Division of Labor, and Women's Collective Action." *Signs* 7, no. 2 (Winter 1981): 400–417.

Truant, Cynthia M. "Independent and Insolent: Journeymen and Their 'Rites' in the Old Regime Workplace." In *Work in France: Representations, Meaning, Organization, and Practice*, edited by Steven L. Kaplan and Cynthia J. Koepp. Ithaca, N.Y.: Cornell University Press, 1986.

Tutino, John. "Family Economies in Agrarian Mexico, 1750–1910." *Journal of Family History* 10, no. 3 (1985): 258–271.

——. "Hacienda Social Relations in Mexico: The Chalco Region in the Era of Independence." *HAHR* 55 (1975): 496–528.

Van Young, Eric. "The Age of Paradox: Mexican Agriculture at the End of the Colonial Period, 1750–1810." In *The Economies of Mexico and Peru during the Late Colonial Period, 1760–1810*, edited by Nils Jacobsen and Hans-Jürgen Puhle. Berlin: Colloquium Verlag, 1986.

——. "Crime as Rebellion and Rebellion as Crime." In *The Other Rebellion: Popular Violence and Ideology in Mexico, 1810–1816*, by Eric Van Young. Forthcoming.

——. "Islands in the Storm: Quiet Cities and Violent Countrysides in the Mexican Independence Era." *Past & Present* 118 (February 1988): 130–155.

——. "Mexican Rural History since Chevalier: The Historiography of the

Colonial Hacienda." *Latin American Research Review* 18 (1983): 5–61.

———. "The Raw and the Cooked: Elite and Popular Ideology in Mexico, 1800–1821." In *The Middle Period in Latin America: Values and Attitudes in the 17th–19th Centuries,* edited by Mark D. Szuchman. Boulder and London: Lynne Reiner Publishers, 1989.

———. "The Rich Get Richer and the Poor Get Skewed: Real Wages and Popular Living Standards in Late Colonial Mexico." Unpublished paper, presented at the All-University of California Group in Economic History, 1987.

———. "Urban Market and Hinterland: Guadalajara and Its Region in the Eighteenth Century." *HAHR* 59 (1979): 593–635.

Venard, Marc. "Popular Religion in the Eighteenth Century." In *Church and Society in Catholic Europe of the Eighteenth Century,* edited by William J. Callahan and David Higgs. Cambridge: Cambridge University Press, 1979.

Viotti da Costa, Emilia. "Experience versus Structure: New Tendencies in the History of Labor and the Working Class in Latin America—What Do We Gain? What Do We Lose?" *International Labor and Working-Class History* 36 (1989): 3–24.

Walker, David W. "Business as Usual: The Empresa del Tabaco in Mexico, 1837–44." *HAHR* 64, no. 4 (1984): 675–705.

Whipp, Richard. "'A Time to Every Purpose': An Essay on Time and Work." In *The Historical Meanings of Work,* edited by Patrick Joyce. Cambridge: Cambridge University Press, 1987.

White, L. A. "Punche: Tobacco in New Mexican History." *New Mexico Historical Review* 18 (1943): 386–393.

Wiemers, Eugene L., Jr. "Agriculture and Credit in Nineteenth Century Mexico: Orizaba and Córdoba, 1822–1871." *HAHR* 65, no. 3 (1985): 519–546.

Wu, Celia. "The Population of the City of Querétaro in 1791." *JLAS* 16 (1984): 277–307.

Dissertations and Theses

Deans, Susan. "The Gentle and Easy Tax: The Bourbons and the Royal Tobacco Monopoly of New Spain, 1765–1821." Ph.D. dissertation, Cambridge University, 1984.

Flory, R. J. D. "Bahian Society in the Mid-Colonial Period: The Sugar Planters, Tobacco Growers, Merchants, and Artisans of Salvador and the Recôncavo, 1680–1725." Ph.D. dissertation, University of Texas at Austin, 1978.

Giarracca de Teubal, Norma Aida. "La subordinación del campesinado a los complejos agroindustriales: El tabaco en México." Master's thesis, Universidad Nacional Autónoma de México, 1983.

Harrison, John P. "The Colombian Tobacco Industry from Government Monopoly to Free Trade, 1778–1876." Ph.D. dissertation, University of California, Berkeley, 1952.

McWatters, David Lorne. "The Royal Tobacco Monopoly in Bourbon Mexico, 1764–1810." Ph.D. dissertation, University of Florida, 1979.

Scardaville, Michael C. "Crime and the Urban Poor: Mexico City in the Late Colonial Period." Ph.D. dissertation, University of Florida, 1977.

Seed, Patricia. "A Mexican Noble Family, the Counts of the Valle de Orizaba." Master's thesis, University of Texas at Austin, 1976.

Tutino, John. "The Hacienda in Mexico Society: Elites and Peasants, 1750–1810." Ph.D. dissertation, University of Texas at Austin, 1976.

Wickham, Cam H. "Venezuela's Royal Tobacco Monopoly, 1779–1810: An Economic Analysis." Ph.D. dissertation, University of Oregon, 1975.

Index

Printed and bound by CPI Group (UK) Ltd, Croydon, CR0 4YY

16/04/2025

14658534-0002